NUMBERS DON'T LIE

NUMBERS DON'T LIE

New Adventures in Counting and
What Counts in Basketball Analytics

Yago Colás

UNIVERSITY OF NEBRASKA PRESS   LINCOLN

Library of Congress Cataloging-in-Publication Data
Names: Colás, Santiago, 1965– author.
Title: Numbers don't lie: new adventures in counting
and what counts in basketball analytics / Yago Colás.
Description: Lincoln: University of Nebraska Press,
[2020] | Includes bibliographical references and index.
Identifiers: LCCN 2020007544
ISBN 9781496216144 (hardback)
ISBN 9781496223449 (epub)
ISBN 9781496223456 (mobi)
ISBN 9781496223463 (pdf)
Subjects: LCSH: Basketball—Statistics. | Basketball—
Statistical methods. | Basketball—History.
Classification: LCC GV885.55 .C62
2020 | DDC 796.323—dc23
LC record available at https://lccn.loc.gov/2020007544

Set in Arno and Meta by Laura Buis.
Designed by N. Putens.

For Claire, with gratitude and love

[The universe] . . . is written in mathematical language.
—GALILEO GALILEI, *The Assayer*

And David's heart smote him after that he had numbered the people. And David said unto the Lord, I have sinned greatly in that I have done: and now, I beseech thee, O Lord, take away the iniquity of thy servant; for I have done very foolishly.
—2 SAMUEL 24:10

CONTENTS

PART 1. COUNTING

ILLUSTRATIONS

TABLES

PREFACE

#1. Measuring Me

I stood in my socks in our unfinished basement. My body tingled with anticipation, but from my heels to my head I tried to make it as straight and flat and still as the poured concrete it was pressed against. I looked straight ahead, as level as possible. My father held a metal ruler flat against the top of my head, its sharp edge pressed perpendicular to the wall.

"*Ahora, ¡quédate quieto!*" he commanded.

I froze. Not just my bones and muscles and face, but all the way to my cells and the blood in my beating heart, I froze. Absolute zero. It was important to keep perfectly still or everything would be inaccurate and ruined.

My father ran the freshly sharpened point of a pencil along the edge of the ruler against the wall, making a clean, straight line. I could hear the even, steady scratch of the lead. I didn't need to be told to step out from under the ruler and get out of the way.

With one hand my father held the flat metal tab at the end of his heavy-duty tape measure against the floor where my heels had been a moment before. Pushing its right angle securely into the corner, he jammed it still more firmly, just for good measure. "*Pon tu dedo aquí, y mantenlo fijo.*" Nervously, I obeyed, getting down on the cool floor and putting my finger against the tab, careful not to let it move. I felt him push his own finger against mine, as if to nail it to the precise spot. Then, one end anchored, he slowly raised himself up, unspooling the tape measure up the wall toward the freshly drawn black line.

Watching silently I saw the numbers appear from inside the metal housing, first inches, then the larger, bold "1" in red: the first foot; 2, the second foot. The inches rolled by and I counted them rapidly in my mind—32, 33, 34, 35, 36—then the big red "3": the third foot. But I *already* knew I was more than three feet tall. I couldn't even remember ever being less than three feet tall: 37, 38, 39.

And besides, I was good at math. I knew there were twelve inches in a foot, and so I knew that the key number was 47; that after 47 the next inch would be 48 and 48 was four feet: my goal.

As my father's hand climbed steadily up the wall toward the pencil mark, I observed more closely as the inches crept upward into the mid-forties. It slowed down, I could see the tall half-inch—and even the shorter quarter-inch—hash marks march by: 45, 46, 46½. It slowed to a crawl: 47, 47¼, 47½. Almost there: 47¾.

Focused intently on the parade of numbers, I'd lost track of where the mark on the wall was in relation to the moving metal housing. I was surprised when my gaze came to an abrupt halt. The tape measure had stopped. The numbers held still, the red number "4" remained inside the housing, waiting stubbornly.

I had failed to become four feet tall.

Desire and shame, science and imagination, and pragmatic determination collided to form in me a kind of primordial soup. Its first issue was my daily practice—resolved upon then and there—of dangling from the pull-up bar in the laundry room doorframe for as long as I could stand.

It was the closest I could get, I guess, to racking myself.

But it would not be enough.

ACKNOWLEDGMENTS

This book may be the most peculiar thing I have written, or at least published. Completing it has certainly been the most peculiar experience I've had as a writer. For, in the midst of doing so, I have undergone a still-unfinished odyssey of seismic changes to my professional and personal life. As a result, my debts here extend not only to those who have directly impacted the manuscript with their insightful and constructive feedback but also to those who have been carrying me through my cataclysm with emotional and material support.

I thank students, first of all, at the University of Michigan and at Oberlin College, particularly those who knew enough to be interested in this topic before I did, and whose insistence on the importance of analytics helped prime my own interest.

Over the years that I have been working on this project, I have been fortunate to be able to present—with funding from the University of Michigan and Oberlin College—my research to scholars from a variety of disciplines. Mary McDonald, Murray Phillips, Matthew Klugman, Noah Cohan, Johnny Smith, Jennifer Stirling, Andrew Edgar, David Andrews, Shannon Jetty, Cheryl Cooky, Richard Shusterman, Kia Hook, Falk Heinrich, and Else-Marie Bukdahl all provided important constructive criticisms and encouragement.

I began this project with an unresolved antagonism toward basketball analytics. Luckily some of the interlocutors I found in that world were patient enough to abide my petulant objections and (since those objections were often rooted in ignorance) generous enough with their own knowledge to help me understand their work. Through their contributions, I learned not only about the topic of this book but also about my resistance to it and, therefore, about myself. In particular, Seth Partnow, Mara Averick, Ian Levy, Todd Whitehead, and Dean Oliver were always ready to offer an informed, balanced response to both my knee-jerk outrage and my uncomprehending questions. Fergus Connolly likewise offered vital support at a crucial moment.

Rob Taylor, my editor at the University of Nebraska Press, who has assembled one of publishing's most vital and varied sports lists during his tenure there, fulfilled a fantasy of mine—to be published by the same press as James Naismith—by taking the project on and unflappably steering me (and my drama) through to the end. His assistant, Courtney Ochsner, and project editor, Elizabeth Zaleski, likewise patiently guided me through the many steps involved in turning a bunch of manuscript pages into the book in front of you, as did, of course, the many individuals working behind the scenes at the University of Nebraska Press. Amanda Jackson's sensitive and thorough copyediting sharpened and clarified my voice.

My colleagues Tim Elgren, Silke Weineck, and Stefan Szymanski provided me with friendship and the sort of enthusiastic conversation about my work that kept it alive, not least by each of them bringing to those conversations their own, very different and far more substantial stocks of expertise and interest.

Kevin Blackistone understood and named the vital germ of this project—the relationship between my father and his numbers and me and my basketball—before I did. Had he not said so, and had it not been he who said so, I doubt I'd have had the courage to carry it through.

My friends Lucia Trimbur, Tim McCrory, Jimmy King, and Grant Farred, and my siblings, Antonio and Juan Colás and Maria Trainor, did not directly impact the manuscript, but that might only be because they were too busy fielding my endless phone calls and talking me through some of the worst moments of my life. Without them I'd almost certainly have given up, not only on this book but on many other things as well. Similarly, Diane Welch, Rowan O'Riley, and Bill Kaiser, in extraordinary acts of generosity, opened their homes to me when I did not have one and created an atmosphere in which I could write. My son Owen and his partner Trudie both fielded my endless phone calls *and* opened their home to me.

My parents were dead before I really began work on this book. But their influence on it will be evident throughout. In some ways this book is as much a reckoning with the fact of their deaths as it is a reckoning with the history of counting in basketball. The astronomer Natalie Batalha says that at the nexus of art and science is wonder. It is an over-simplification, to be sure, to reduce my father to "science" and my mother to "art"—if only because she was more mystic than artist, though she was passionately interested in art, especially literature. Indeed, both my mother and father were much more than those blocky categories can capture. I appreciate that with her pithy phrase Batalha invites us to tie together two areas of human endeavor that are often set at odds with each other, and to tie both of them to something that we can all experience in daily life, even if we are neither artists nor scientists. But maybe, like my mother and father, art and science are already more than just art and science. Maybe they are always their nexus: wonder. Maybe that's Batalha's point. I don't know. I do know that this book has been fueled more by wonder than anything I have ever published, and I believe that whatever is worthwhile in it stems from a curious, wondering disposition that I'm certain was instilled in me by mother and father, each in their own utterly unique way, as well as through the interplay, both intensely loving and intensely contentious, between them.

My last and deepest debt is to Claire Solomon. Her contributions to this work go far beyond suggesting or commenting on ideas, though her own boundless curiosity often yielded avenues of exploration that I'd not have come across otherwise, connections I'd not have made on my own. They go beyond feedback on drafts of the manuscript—though she is the best writer I know, so that her editorial insights made for vast improvements. But Claire's deep contribution to this work, the one without which it would never have seen the light of day, was to nourish its beating heart, the life at its core, which is to say my heart. If it was Kevin Blackistone who first named the germ of the project, it was Claire who cultivated it by encouraging, cajoling, coaxing, even demanding, time and again—every time I veered away from it to pursue some possibly interesting but purely abstract and so ultimately sterile cerebral path—that I return to, care for, and write from its heart, my heart. Thank you, Claire.

NUMBERS DON'T LIE

Introduction

TWO BASKETS

#2. December 21

On December 21, 2018, Kawhi Leonard, playing for the Toronto Raptors of the National Basketball Association (NBA), dribbled to the edge of the free-throw line, stopped abruptly, and then, leaning back slightly, jumped and released a shot up toward the basket. The ball barely grazed the back of the rim as it dropped through the net. It was the first of eighty-seven baskets made that night by the Raptors and their opponents, the Cleveland Cavaliers.

I didn't see that game, but I know that Toronto won 126–110.[1] And I have seen Kawhi score that first basket because the NBA incorporates hyperlinks in the play-by-play transcript it publishes on its website after each league game. When I click the hyperlink for that play my browser opens a new tab that displays a video clip replay of the successful shot.[2]

I also know how many baskets each team and each individual player made and how many they attempted. I know how many points each player scored and how many minutes and seconds each player spent on the floor. I know how many offensive and defensive rebounds each player and each team collected, as well as how many personal fouls, assists, steals, blocks, and turnovers they accumulated.

I know too which lineups (combinations of five players on the court for a team at a given moment) played for each team, when and for how long each lineup played, how many points the lineup scored and allowed while on the floor, as well as how many shots each lineup took and made, how many rebounds, assists, turnovers, and steals they got, how many times they blocked shots and had their shots blocked, and how many fouls they committed and had committed against them. Plus, I know all of the same information for each individual player in relation to each lineup that he was part of during the game.

But that's not all. I know how many times each player scored after grabbing an offensive rebound. I know how many opportunities to rebound missed shots they had. I know how often they passed to teammates, and how often they deflected passes, and how many times their passes led to passes that led to baskets. I know how often they set screens that led to baskets and how often they corralled loose balls. I know how many times their shot was blocked and how many times they were fouled. I know exactly the spot on the court from where they took each shot, whether or not they dribbled before taking it, whether they were guarded when they took it and how closely. I know how many times they touched the ball and how many times they dribbled it. I know how far each player ran over the course of the game and at what average speed. In fact, I know what happened on every play of the game.

One hundred twenty-seven years before Kawhi Leonard made the first shot in Toronto's game against Cleveland, around December 21, 1891, William Chase, a student in a class at the YMCA International Training Institute in Springfield, Massachusetts, tossed a soccer ball about twenty-five feet into a peach basket suspended from the railing of a gymnasium balcony, ten feet above the floor. It was the first and only goal thrown in what would later be called, and immortalized as, the first basketball game ever played. I didn't see that game either, but Chase's teacher, James Naismith, who devised the activity for his students that day, made note of the event in his handwritten account of what he saw as an experiment that was likely to fail.[3]

All told, in the December 21, 2018, matchup between the Raptors and the Cavaliers, 2,850 different events in thirty-three different categories were identified and counted, and this excludes minutes played and distance run, not to mention the hundreds of different metrics derived by performing calculations with the totals tallied in those thirty-three different categories. In the first game ever played, 126 years before, one event, in one category, was identified and counted (see fig. 1).

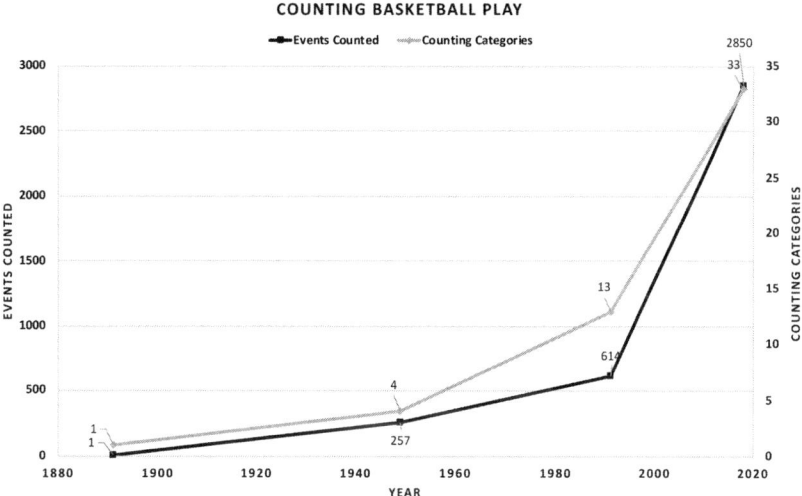

FIG. 1. Growth of counting in basketball.

Here is the question that gave rise to this book: How did basketball go from counting one thing to counting thousands?

The short answer is basketball analytics, or, as I prefer, borrowing a phrase from a leading figure in the field, "the science of moving dots." This combines digital data production, processing, and presentation technologies with statistical methods to create quantitative—descriptive, diagnostic, predictive, and prescriptive—models of basketball play.

In trying to understand the science of moving dots and how it has come to play such a large role in contemporary basketball, I found myself exploring a thicket of new questions, beginning with questions about basketball itself, but quickly proliferating, mutating, and extending into questions about sport more generally, about counting, measurement, and calculation, about statistics and probability, about knowledge, science, and technology, about data and artificial intelligence, about business and pleasure and work and play, about morality, ethics, and politics, about risk, chance, and uncertainty, about emotion and pleasure and beauty, about value and—most unexpectedly—about myself.

#3. Adventure

In early modern Europe, long before our modern ideas of proper science had crystallized, there was among the various types of experiments a kind of experimental activity known as "an adventure," which was especially prevalent among early alchemists.

The adventuring alchemist, Ian Hacking writes, "heated and mixed and burnt and pounded" but was "guided by no good theory" so that he could only guess what would happen. The adventure "might suggest an hypothesis that [could] subsequently be tested, but adventure [was] prior to theory." And though the alchemist might have had an ultimate aim such as making gold, the activity was done for its own sake so that "an adventure," he concludes, "[was] an end in itself."[4] Needless to say, such adventures were fraught with danger and unknown risks. You might get gold. But you might get yourself blown up.

We find in this etymological history of the word "adventure" the makings of quite a story (see fig. 2). This story begins with movement. But notice that in this movement we do more than just move away from a home place or other known origin. We also move toward another place. We may have been to that place before, but because in adventure we are also moving in time—away from the familiar past and present and toward an oncoming future—that place to which we draw closer remains unknown. And in the course of that movement in space and time, we encounter risks and perils, marvels and wonders, mishaps and misfortunes placed in our path by those obscure forces that we may call chance or luck or fortune, destiny or fate or randomness. In adventure we move away from the familiar in space and time and draw closer to what we do not know.

I see basketball play as an adventure, and I want my approach to the sport to be one as well. I want to highlight in basketball the movement of players—every single bounce of the ball becoming a risky encounter with the unknown. And I want my writing to move with them so that it moves me, moves you, closer to what we do not know.

After all, uncertainty about the future, chance, fortune and luck, risk and peril, and wonder or marvel: basketball, at its core, involves all of these elements. As sociologist David Goldblatt put it, one of the distinctive features

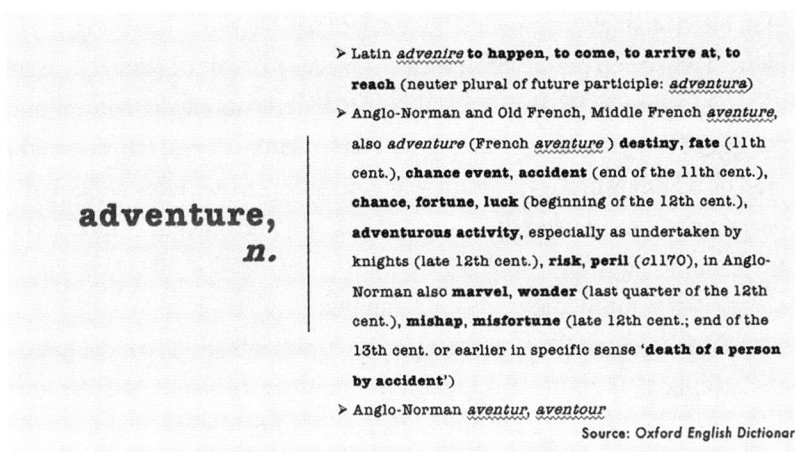

> Latin *advenire* **to happen, to come, to arrive at, to reach** (neuter plural of future participle: *adventura*)
> Anglo-Norman and Old French, Middle French *aventure*, also *adventure* (French *aventure*) **destiny, fate** (11th cent.), **chance event, accident** (end of the 11th cent.), **chance, fortune, luck** (beginning of the 12th cent.), **adventurous activity**, especially as undertaken by knights (late 12th cent.), **risk, peril** (*c*1170), in Anglo-Norman also **marvel, wonder** (last quarter of the 12th cent.), **mishap, misfortune** (late 12th cent.; end of the 13th cent. or earlier in specific sense '**death of a person by accident**')
> Anglo-Norman *aventur, aventour*

Source: Oxford English Dictionary

adventure, n.

FIG. 2. Etymology of adventure.

of a ball sport like basketball "is the degree of uncertainty and chaos and spontaneity that putting a bouncing ball with human limbs creates. That's above all what balls bring: spin, uncertainty, variation, bounce."[5]

Indeed, isn't the original, driving quest of basketball players—going back to the sport's invention in 1891—to get the ball to do what they want it to, which means also to get their bodies to do what they want them to? Early instructional materials are filled with elaborate instructions—often illustrated, sometimes informed by geometry and physics—about how to do just that.

But then, I muse, perhaps that is the fuel source buried deep in the existential core of the science of moving dots: the anxiety that comes with caring—but not knowing and having limited control over—whether or not a body will get the ball to go where it wants it to.

When I think of it that way, one of the most powerfully alluring dimensions of basketball analytics stands out in gleaming relief: its promise to tell us what will happen. Or at least to tell us what is most likely to happen so that we can hedge our financial and emotional bets and minimize our financial and emotional losses. Basketball analytics sells us the fantasy that calculation provides a safe haven from the torment of loving something—a possession, a team, a vocation, a career, a life—and not knowing what will happen to it.

I'm often strongly compelled by that fantasy. No more worrying about whether I will be up to the unforeseen challenges around the bend. No more paralyzing agony over decisions. No more regrets about the failures and mistakes of the past. How much more relaxed and free and lighthearted I would be if I knew how everything was going to turn out. How confidently I would proceed, relieved of the fear of risk and peril that may lurk in the murky, unknown future.

I *definitely* want to know what will happen.

But I don't get too far down that path in my imagination before I pause, then backpedal, then turn and sprint in the other direction. What a horrifying prospect! I'd be an anonymous cog in some universal clockwork, blindly turning; only worse, I'd know it to be so. My very humanity and my freedom, I defiantly proclaim to myself, depend on my ignorance of the murky, unknown future.

I definitely do *not* want to know what will happen.

I am, in other words, ambivalent.

I experience this concretely, within myself, as a chattering crowd of voices rising in murmurs and shouts from the deepest parts of my memory. They call me to count, measure, and calculate, promising that if I do so properly, if I can reduce the qualitatively experienced material phenomena of my life to a number, I will be able to manage it and improve it. Most of all, these voices demand that I account for myself and report on my progress toward an ever-receding horizon of perfection. In this way my ambivalence manifests as the conflicting desires to drive these voices away, like the raucous taunts of devils, and to invoke them, like the tender whispers of my guardian angels.

But either way I have found that these voices dissolve into one voice, the voice of my late father, and thus they lead me back to my experiences as a basketball-loving American boy raised by a Spanish immigrant scientist with an authoritarian streak and a mania for measurement.

Such strong personal feelings, let alone the memories that fuel them, I worry, have no place in scholarly writing. And I never know where they will lead me or what will happen when I share them. I often wonder if I am making gold or am about to blow myself up or, perhaps worst of all, am just going to wind up with the same dull, cold lead I had to begin with. But such fears notwithstanding, I find it impossible to ignore these feelings.

Hence I undertake this writing as an alchemical adventure that I hope to navigate not only with clarity but also with the integrity to manage the uncertainty and risk attending these unexpected collisions of the intellectual and the affective—the scholarly and the personal—and perhaps in the process allow for something new to emerge.

#4. Basketball

Is there really a kind of existential core of basketball consisting of the emotionally charged uncertainty about whether—once you let it go—a bouncing ball will end up where you want it to? Maybe. Probably.

But even if this is true in some sense, it's also true that what we call "basketball"—rules, equipment, venues, organizations, fundamental skills, techniques, tactics, strategies, games, and, of course, players—has changed dramatically since its invention and even today encompasses many different forms of play. So even if that core experience of uncertainty does exist, and even if it spans all these variations, it's likely experienced differently across the many different settings in which basketball is played, from the solitary child shooting a ball on a playground to the elite professional setting of the NBA Finals.

In this way philosophical musings on the essence of basketball quickly become inseparable from historical and social issues. And these, in their turn, quickly become inseparable from cultural and psychological questions about how we relate to basketball: How have the underlying, individually and collectively held assumptions and expectations we bring to the game varied? How about the purposes for which basketball has been played, organized, or watched? And what meanings have players, coaches, administrators, educators, investors, journalists, and fans derived from basketball play? How have these changed over time and in different settings? What have we invested in basketball? And what have we wanted to get out of the game?

As I (and others before me) have argued elsewhere, basketball has never been "just a sport."[6] Rather it originated out of an interplay of social developments and problems, cultural agendas, and individual desires. And ever since, it has been traversed, impacted, and shaped—indeed, partly constituted—by impulses toward physical development, moral improvement, social reform, political discrimination or empowerment related to gender, race, ethnicity and national identity, personal enjoyment, social bonding, community pride, spectator entertainment, competitive supremacy, creative expression, emotional gratification, and financial profit. Some involved in basketball may imagine that the sport once existed immune from the influence of such forces and that it was only over time that they seeped into the sport. But this is at best a naive fantasy, at worst an ideology, sometimes cynically wielded for coercive or exclusionary purposes. All the elements I just listed above have always been as much a part of the sport as—well— baskets or balls.

But these elements have not always been part of the sport in the same way. Different agendas and desires have fluctuated in their importance and influence on the sport at different moments in history and in different settings. Like the bubbles in water brought to a boil and then left to simmer, some investments have risen to the surface, pervaded the sport, and then receded to the margins. Moreover, the relationships among these agendas and desires have varied so that at any given moment each of these agendas has influenced the others in different ways. Finally, our *understanding* of these agendas and desires and the ways they manifest has changed as well. And all this, of course, has changed how the sport has been imagined, taught, played, organized, administered, coached, sold, covered, photographed, filmed, and watched.

Basketball, in short, is not only not "just a sport": it is not, ever, just one thing. Or, if it is one thing, then that one thing is something like an ever-shifting, four-dimensional kaleidoscope comprised of embodied imagination and activity, cognitive effort, moral frameworks, emotional intensities, financial investments, cultural norms and attitudes, and social and political forces, and the relations among these. Better not to think of basketball as one thing. And better to greet with skepticism the claim that it has a spirit or nature that persists unchanged over time and spans all forms of play.

The agendas, investments, desires that we bring to the game shape therefore not only basketball play but also what we look for and what we see when we watch basketball. And this, in turn, shapes how and what we record, report, and discuss about the games we see. In short: what we want shapes what we look for, what we look for shapes what we see, and what we see shapes how we represent basketball. From water cooler conversations to big-budget pregame shows, from rulebooks to institutional policies, from pregame pep talks to postgame interviews, from instructional manuals to how to videos, from media recaps to DIY YouTube highlight videos, we represent basketball in words, images, and, of course, numbers.

It is this last form of representation—numbers, or quantification—that currently fascinates me. By "quantification" I mean the process by which we render our qualitative perceptions and experiences into numbers—through activities such as counting, measuring, and calculating. The quantification of basketball—from scoreboards to scorebooks to the advanced statistics section of the NBA's website and beyond—is the subject of this book.

Quantification, I have found, has played a role in both expressing and managing tensions within that changing network of broader agendas I just described. This process runs from the first decade following the sport's invention in the late nineteenth century through its institutionalization as a major high school and then commercialized college sport in the years leading up to the Second World War, to its massive expansion as a multi-billion dollar, multi-sector global industry in the 1980s and '90s, and it culminates in the last twenty years, which have seen the most significant expansion in the role of quantifying techniques.

#5. Play

Then, from yet another perspective, the history of basketball is also the history of individuals and groups experiencing, mobilizing, harnessing, repressing, and releasing a desire to play. But, play too can mean many different things depending on the player and the circumstances. Discussions about whether or not (or how) to quantify basketball play are not only discussions about what it means to play *basketball* but also discussions about what it means to *play* basketball. In other words, the stakes at the intersection of quantification and basketball include different, sometimes conflicting and competing, desires with respect to the role of play in the sport.

TABLE 1. Rhetorics of play

Play rhetoric		
IN GENERAL	IN BASKETBALL	Keywords
Fate	Gambling	Animism, divination, chance, chaos, complexity, uncertainty, magic, luck, fortune, risk, probability, control
Power	Competition	Contest, skill, strength, strategy, victory, status, politics, war
Identity	Fandom	Tradition, ritual, community, festivals, parades, spectacle, media, mega-events
Progress	Moral improvement	Enlightenment, evolution, development, growth, socialization, utility, games, sportsmanship
Imaginary	Creativity	Romanticism, imagination, improvisation, flexibility, art, fantasy
Self	The Zone	Romanticism, individualism, freedom, flow, optimal experience, enjoyment, ecstasy, leisure
Frivolity	Fun	Work ethic, Protestantism, nonsense, comedy, jokes, tricks, pranks, uselessness

Accordingly, on occasion in the pages that follow I'll refer to and reflect upon various notions of play. Because of this, I want to introduce you to them briefly as they pertain to basketball. In doing so, I've adapted play historian Brian Sutton-Smith's typology of seven "rhetorics"—or ways of thinking and talking about the nature and purpose of play—to better convey how they appear in basketball culture (see table 1).[7] Some of Sutton-Smith's rhetorics are ancient in origin, others more modern. Some will appear very obviously and directly relevant to basketball, others less so. But I contend that every play rhetoric or form that Sutton-Smith describes manifests itself to some degree in NBA basketball.

In the rhetoric of play as fate or gambling, we are not the players but the played, pawns in a game being played by some external agent vastly more powerful than ourselves.[8] Many readers will be familiar with the notion of basketball gods, unseen forces who decide the fate of our shots and our teams. But this rhetoric also encompasses our attempts to retake some agency by playing the odds, aided in our time by the distinctly modern science of fate: the mathematics of probability theory.[9] "Modern methods of dealing with the unknown," announces Peter Bernstein, "start with measurement, with odds and probabilities. The numbers come first."[10] In basketball, not only professional gamblers and fantasy league "owners," but also real owners, general managers, coaches, and players all take risks and make "bets" that a complex web of forces beyond their control will converge in such a way as to produce a favorable outcome: a made shot, a successful play, a win, a championship, a luminous career, more fans in the seats, jerseys sold, eyes on the screen. Within the context of this rhetoric of play, we might view basketball analytics as a contemporary method of divination, a way of discerning and harmonizing our actions with the will of the "basketball gods."

Within the second rhetoric of play as power or competition, play represents (and originally aimed to prepare one for) a real struggle for power and status.[11] Historically, this mutated into athletic gatherings (Greek: *agones*), games, or festivals, such as the ancient Olympics. In this setting, the competitive element (Greek: *agon*) tested virtuosity (Greek: *arête*, a term encompassing strength, prowess, courage, and self-discipline). The display of virtuosity was rewarded with prizes (Greek: *athla*, from which we get the word athlete).[12] These athletic competitions eventually became—through processes involving national cultural needs and agendas, bureaucracies, record keeping and, often, commerce—our modern professional sports like NBA basketball, where championship trophies symbolize not just virtuosity but especially superiority over one's rivals.

Closely related to this, we find the third rhetoric of play as identity or fandom, including "forms of bonding, including the exhibition and validation or parody of membership and traditions in a community."[13] Consider the myriad ways that individuals and groups shape their identity in relation to individual athletes or to teams of athletes, often by way of the city, region, or nation these athletes represent.[14] Wearing replica jerseys to express team loyalty or affective identification with a player, investing in rivalries, attending championship parades, and staging the spectacles that surround sporting events from small-town Friday-night football games to the World Cup, from March Madness to the NBA Finals—all these showcase sporting play as identity-affirmation.[15]

The fourth rhetoric argues that play should aid in human psychological, physical, and moral development.[16] This view of play, as progress or moral instrument, dates to the second half of the nineteenth century. Among its manifestations were a set of interrelated attempts to organize children's play in newly created public playgrounds between 1880 and 1920. "Play professionals," as those spearheading these organizational efforts were called, were often influenced by the ideals of a Protestant religious movement known as "muscular Christianity" that emphasized the moral benefits of vigorous, supervised physical exercise.[17] They believed their efforts could save children by counteracting the dire conditions in rapidly growing cities while simultaneously inculcating in these same (often immigrant) children certain values that play professionals believed were currently imperiled but crucial to the cohesive progress of American society. This rhetoric of play as progress or moral instrument, as I'll explain in chapters 4 and 5, directly inspired the invention of basketball.[18] And we continue to hear its echoes whenever tactical or strategic decisions—such as passing to an open teammate rather than shooting the ball oneself—are described as indicative of moral traits such as, for example, unselfishness or selfishness, cowardice or courage.

The fifth rhetoric of play as imagination or creativity, though also modern, proposes a different account of the nature and purpose of play.[19] Originating in the eighteenth century, play in this rhetoric appears—explicitly challenging the rationalist Enlightenment philosophies of the time—both as an avenue toward more holistic understandings of ourselves and our world and as a higher creative faculty of transforming both. "Man," declared German poet and philosopher Friedrich Schiller, "is only wholly Man when he is playing."[20] Crucial to this view, whether applied to adults or children, philosophers or scientists, artists or athletes, is the paradoxically facilitating role of constraints.[21] "Playing a game," in an oft-cited definition, "is the voluntary attempt to overcome unnecessary obstacles," including rules, opponents, equipment, natural physical laws, and human limitations.[22] Such a situation calls for what one philosopher of sport calls "responsive openness," a stance he argues is especially available to us in play, art, and sport.[23] Though every sport offers these opportunities for play as creativity, some maintain that basketball offers them more intensively.[24]

The inner experience of this understanding of play is emphasized in the sixth rhetoric of play as self or "the Zone."[25] During such optimal experiences—called "flow" by psychologist Mihaly Csikszentmihalyi, the preeminent expert on the phenomena—we feel strong, alert, in effortless control, at peak capability, and unselfconscious.[26] In one sense it seems misleading to call this the rhetoric of "play as self" since a common feature of flow is the *waning* of our sense of self as separate from our activity or surroundings.[27] Most athletes will be familiar with this experience by a different name: Being in the Zone.[28] The key theme that emerges from various studies of flow among athletes is, simply put, freedom; a freedom seemingly paradoxically achieved by having voluntarily submitted to the arbitrary constraints that define sports.

The seventh and final rhetoric of play as frivolity stands in curious relationship to the others. The preceding six rhetorics share the presumption that play is meaningful and important and, in their modern forms, affirm the value of play to counter Protestantism's long-standing prohibition against play as a threatening, even diabolical, distraction from the divine imperatives of work, seriousness, and productivity. The rhetoric of frivolity, according to Sutton-Smith, challenges or, better put, eludes (from *ludere*, the Latin word "to play") this presumption of the importance of play by frivolously— playfully—undermining the seriousness with which they approach play. Whatever aim a given rhetoric asserts as transcendent in a particular form of play, the transgressive rhetoric of frivolity will ironically lay low. In the process, the satirists, tricksters, clowns, comedians, fools, and traitors who embody the rhetoric of play as frivolity imply that play is—finally, simply, and meaninglessly—play.[29] It is, after all, they might say, only a game.

#6. The Knife's Intentions

In the late seventeenth century, in a universe parallel to ours, the learned scholars in the city of Cittagazze experimented with matter and managed to construct a double-edged blade. One side was sharp enough to cut through the strongest of materials as if through butter, while the other side—subtler still—could pierce the invisible fabric separating one universe from another. The bearer of the deadly weapon therefore also possessed the extraordinary power to travel freely between worlds. For centuries the scholars grew wealthy, slipping into other worlds, stealing goods, and returning undetected to Cittagazze.

Eventually, by an obscure twist of fate, this enormously powerful tool falls into the hands of Will, a mere boy. Serious and earnest, Will intends to use the knife to aid his friend Lyra, who appears to be at the center of a cosmic struggle between good and evil, pursued by powerful agents and forces all claiming to want to bring Lyra and Will (and the knife) under their protection. It is confusing and frightening and, as Will and Lyra discover time and again, it is not always so easy to tell friend from foe.

In fact that is exactly the question that comes up when the unthinkable happens and the knife shatters. Bereft of its powers, Will and Lyra are stranded defenseless in a remote world, sitting ducks for those pursuing them. Who can they trust? Fortunately for them, they happen upon Iorek Byrnison, king of the Armored Bears, fierce warrior, champion of Lyra, and master blacksmith. This is perfect! So far, Iorek has proven himself to be the only unwaveringly truthful and reliable ally to the children. However, though Iorek trusts Lyra and Will and admits that he can mend the knife, he is reluctant to do so. The children plead with him.

"You wouldn't believe how important this is," Lyra begins, "—if we can't get it mended then we're in desperate trouble, and not only us—"

But Iorek cuts her off, "I don't like that knife, I fear what it can do. I have never known anything so dangerous. The most deadly fighting machines are little toys compared to that knife; the harm it can do is unlimited. It would have been infinitely better if it had never been made."

Will jumps in, "But with it—"

Again, the usually taciturn Iorek interrupts, "With it you can do strange things. What you don't know is what the knife does on its own. Your intentions may be good. The knife has intentions too."

"The intentions of a tool," he explains, "are what it does. A hammer intends to strike, a vise intends to hold fast, a lever intends to lift. They are what it is made for. But sometimes a tool may have other uses that you don't know. Sometimes in doing what you intend, you also do what the knife intends, without knowing. Can you see the sharpest edge of the knife?" When Will admits that he cannot, Iorek poses a question Will cannot answer, "Then how can you know everything it does?"[30]

Back in our universe, also in the late seventeenth century, during what is usually called "the Scientific Revolution," a group of learned scholars experimented with matter and developed methods and instruments for better understanding nature. Building upon their discoveries, scientists since that time both refined and expanded the means by which we understand and manipulate the natural world; and inventors and entrepreneurs—usually with support from states and private entities—have devised technologies whose power rivals that of the subtle knife of Cittagazze.

Now these technologies have become part of the science of moving dots, which has, as the CEO of a basketball analytics firm once proclaimed, allowed basketball analysts to "quantify what was previously unquantified," and thus provide important insights that can help players improve their performance and even lengthen their careers. In this way, proponents claim, both players and fans can enjoy the game more deeply. Moreover, in some cases the discoveries of basketball analytics can challenge irrational—sometimes racist—beliefs about basketball play and players that have pervaded the sport since its invention.

I embrace the scientific method. I support empowering players, enhancing the joy of playing and watching basketball, and combatting racism. And I recognize that basketball analysts—just like Will and Lyra—may indeed have good intentions. But I still have misgivings about what Iorek might term "the knife's intentions"—the unforeseen, and possibly unwanted, effects of our use of the science of moving dots, especially as its current use and future development now depend on financial investments from economic actors whose intentions may or may not align with the laudable aims I just mentioned. Just as gun rights advocates in the United States defend their claims by arguing that "*guns* don't kill people, *people* kill people"—implying that the tool is inert and therefore morally neutral—sometimes advocates of analytics seem implicitly to argue that "*numbers* don't lie (or reduce, or mislead), *people* lie." Like Iorek, I challenge the validity of the underlying assumption that the instrument is so easily separated from its makers and users and therefore truly inert and morally neutral.

Before making his decision, Iorek insists that Lyra consult her "alethiometer"—an oracular instrument that provides her with deeper insight and, sometimes, advice about complex situations she faces. "Know what it is you are asking," Iorek tells the children, "and if you still want it then, I shall mend the knife."[31] As is often the case with complex matters, the alethiometer's answer is not clear. It seems to encourage mending the knife, though in an ambiguous way that also hints at the hidden costs of doing so. Only later do we, and they, learn the true, terrible cost of using the subtle knife.

In Pullman's trilogy, both instruments—the subtle knife and the alethiometer—are, of course, technological instruments. But where the knife stands for technologies oriented toward narrow aims pursued without regard for broader consequences, the alethiometer stands for technologies concerned with—indeed designed to bring into view—exactly such consequences, especially when they may be obscured by private agendas.

What are we asking for when we ask for the science of moving dots? What kind of basketball future, I would want to ask an alethiometer,—what "rough beast"—are we ushering in with the continued expansion of basketball analytics? Do we really know? Of course, I don't have an alethiometer, but I have the resources of scholarly disciplines and perspectives that, like Lyra's "symbol reader," can provide deeper insight into the complex situations we find ourselves in. We can use these to explore some questions that can help us take better stock of the "intentions" of the science of moving dots.

#7. Counting and What Counts

What in basketball, culture, and society has fueled the rapid expansion of the science of moving dots? What historical tendencies and cultural assumptions give authority to its ideas, methods, and practices? What deeper, unresolved, and perhaps unfathomed preoccupations compel so many of us to turn to quantification? What social and political structures and power differentials influence the use of these methods as well as the purposes to which they are put and the effects they have or may yet have?

Ultimately I summarize the underlying skepticism that drives these questions as follows: Not everything that can be counted counts, and not everything that counts can be counted.[32] Or, to put this another way, I worry about and therefore aim to shed light on the relationship between quantification (counting) and value (what counts) in the science of moving dots.

For reasons that I will make apparent, the science of moving dots ultimately defines value (what counts) in terms of winning athletic and economic competition. And if that is all that counts, perhaps we should welcome the expansion of basketball analytics with open arms. But, for many, defeating opponents and maximizing profit are not the only things that count, even in professional basketball. In fact, the complex history of the sport's relationship to other domains—political freedom, social justice, aesthetic style, pleasure, soul, and feeling, to name a few—seems to me to call for us to incorporate into our conversation about the science of moving dots some alternative frameworks of value, informed by qualitative interpretive methods, that have thus far been largely missing from that discussion. I offer this book as a response to that call.

To this end, the book consists of ninety-nine "adventures": short essays composed in the uncertain, experimental spirit of the medieval alchemists (and ballers) I described above. I have divided these primarily into two parts. In the nine chapters of "Part 1: Counting," I provide a historical account of the nature of quantification in basketball and the various purposes to which it has been put. It is, in short, a history of basketball counting (in chapter 1 and chapters 3 through 8) that encompasses a detailed look at the rhetoric (in chapter 2) and work of the science of moving dots on the contemporary scene (in chapter 9). "Part 2: What Counts" offers four chapters that collect alternative perspectives and frameworks of value that might help us to keep sight of what may count in basketball that is not counted by the science of moving dots.

Interwoven with the thirteen chapters comprising this central framework you will find ten "interludes" (again, drawing upon the Latin *ludere*, "to play") and a coda. These eleven sections consist of autobiographical recollections and reflections relating to my own lived experience at the intersection of basketball and counting. I realize these may add little *information* to the general history of counting and what counts that forms the main part of the book. Accordingly, a reader may choose to skip the interludes and coda entirely and instead read only the chapters comprising the more traditional history of counting in basketball.

But the experiences I recount in these "expendable" sections nonetheless shape my approach to that general history. Now, some believe that to acquire (or produce) knowledge we must set aside or suppress such personal experiences and the emotional charge they carry and that we can't get at the objective truth of things unless we somehow step outside the limitations imposed by our subjective experience. This widely held belief partly supports the cultural authority of quantitative forms of knowledge in particular. However, I do not share this view. Indeed it is partly to challenge it that I have elected to disrupt my own more traditional, ostensibly scholarly history of counting and what counts in basketball with these interludes. At worst, they signal my own biases and therefore help keep me honest about them; at best I hope they will inspire others to do the same.

Introductory Interlude—Records

#8. Percentiles, or, Other People

"*Suéltalo hijo*": my father's voice broke through the stupor of disappointed disbelief. My end of the tape measure scrambled back up to my father's hand in a wild, panicked obedience.

I was disappointed, but all was not lost. I'd been through this before. I knew that the absolute measure was only the first part, and not even the most important one. What mattered more than my height was how tall I was compared to other boys my age.

I followed my father, past the engraved plaque—"Dr. Antonio E. Colás, MD, PhD"—mounted next to the doorway of his den, into the dense, comforting aroma of pipe tobacco mixed with old papers and books. There, in its place on the metal shelving, was the thick, gray, hardbound volume with the words "CIBA-GEIGY Scientific Tables" embossed in red on the spine. I did not know what those words meant. But I knew that inside the book—and precisely where inside the book (because I'd sneaked in here many times to look at it)—there was a page on which two groups of lines gracefully snaked their way from the lower left to the upper right of a graph. The lower group was for weight, which I did not care about. The upper group was for height. At the top of the page was the chart title: "2–20 years: Boys" and below that: "Stature-for-age and Weight-for-age percentiles."

I'd learned what this meant two years before, just before my fifth birthday. Having measured me, my father showed me the graph and carefully put a small plus sign at the point where my age intersected with my height. The plus sign was just above the lowest line of the upper group.

Then, standing next to my father, who was seated at his desk, I watched as he drew a row of ten faceless stick-figure boys on a blank sheet of paper. Each boy was a little taller than the boy to his right. Next, he drew another boy, all the way to the left of the page, who was a little shorter than the shortest boy. Above that boy's head he wrote my name: "Yago." I hoped for a face but did not get one.

Instead, he explained to me that "percentile" allowed me to see how I measured up against all the other boys my age: how many were taller than me, and how many were shorter. He was careful to note that even though his drawing made me look like the shortest boy of all, there were actually four boys shorter than me (out of one hundred), whom he had not drawn. That meant I was in the fifth percentile.

There were also other plus signs on the page, all marked above or very near to the upper-most line. They were for my oldest brother. He was nine years older than me, played basketball, and already had two gold trophies of a basketball player standing tall, reaching high above his head with a tiny golden basketball cradled in his palm. My goal was to have my plus signs bound up the page so they'd be next to his—and also, to get trophies of my own.

Already last year, at six, having shot up six and a half inches from the year before, I'd tasted the thrill of racing past half the boys in the row. Now at age seven what mattered to me even more than being four feet tall, which I was not, was how high my plus sign would climb on that sloping ladder of lines, where I would stand in that row of stick-figure boys.

My father opened the book to the percentile tables and laid it flat on a worktable. He hovered the fine-point pen he'd removed from his plastic pocket protector just above the page, following the line up from the number "7" printed above the word "Age" on the x-axis, while his left index finger moved to meet it from the left-hand side of the page, along an imaginary line just below the number "48." Before he even marked the spot with the little plus sign, I could see where they'd meet: just below the middle one of the group of lines. Not only had I not moved up any lines, I'd actually moved down, from just above the middle line last year to just below it this year.

One of the stick-figure boys shouldered confidently past me, dropping me from fifth place to sixth. I had not grown fast enough. I did not measure up.

#9. The Archive

I am in the basement again. Only now it is more than forty years later. Nobody is there to measure me. My father is dead.

He died about eight months ago. My mom has been deep in the oblivion of Alzheimer's for quite some time and has been in the oddly named Attic Angels nursing home for about a year and a half. My siblings and I have agreed to put the family home up for sale, so my wife and I are using our holiday vacation to go through the things in the house that my parents accumulated over the nearly half century that they lived there.

Over the last two decades, since he retired, my father had been filling this basement. A bookcase now covers the wall against which he used to measure me. In fact, floor-to-ceiling metal bookcases cover all the walls down here. Their shelves are filled with books, of course, but also with old magazines and newspapers, maps, file boxes filled with personal papers and reprints of scholarly articles, photographs, unopened packages of cookies and chocolates and prescription refills, and old household appliances (often in their original packaging and marked with a note giving the date and explanation for their demise). The ping pong table in the center of the room, where my siblings and I used to have heated matches, is piled high with more of the same, and the floor underneath has still more boxes. Four-drawer metal file cabinets, stuffed full, squeeze in wherever they can find room. Though there is no discernible order to the arrangement of these possessions, everything appears neatly arrayed.

My siblings and I call this "The Archive," and we sometimes teased my father about it. The name seems appropriate. The word "archive" goes back to the Greek word for government, as in a ruler, so that an archive is where the records of the government or ruler are kept. Over the past few years, no doubt anticipating this moment, my older brother Juan, a lawyer and judge and so I guess a ruler of a somewhat different sort, repeatedly begged my father for permission to begin to sort the treasures from the trash. My father was unyielding. And the papers and books continued to pile up.

At a basic level, the collection baffled me. Sure, we could dismiss it with a diagnosis: a symptom of my father's obsessive-compulsive personality, a kind of egomania, hoarding. But it's not as though he never threw anything out, and a diagnosis really only begs the question of why he was the way he was. So I wonder not only why he kept so much, but why he kept what he kept. Were there some criteria? Some secret algorithm that determined what was worth keeping, what counted enough to keep? (He devised complex, opaque algorithms, whose secrets he took to his grave, that would decide for him what clothes to put on and what sandwiches to eat for lunch.)

And what, I then wonder, is the relationship between keeping objects and keeping records, between keeping things and counting things?

I just don't know what this collection meant to my father. I can't pretend to know for sure why he saved so much, or saved what he saved: for example, on this day, my wife and I will discover a taxi receipt he'd saved from a professional trip to Colombia in 1957. I know that it was not about sentiment, at least not in the usual sense. These were not merely souvenirs of special moments. They were the tangible records testifying, in minute, unprioritized detail, to his existence on the planet, beginning with his birth in Muel, a tiny village outside of Zaragoza, in the Aragon province of Spain, in the summer of 1928. Perhaps there was some biological basis for this compulsion to accumulate. He might have agreed with that, though when asked he usually offered, with a kind of tongue-in-cheek dramatic flair, a pedantic rationalization for his behavior. But I always imagined that it expressed a deep and urgent need to leave a permanent mark on the world and in so doing to defeat entropy and the chaos of impermanence; to defeat death.

I don't think The Archive directly reflected the scientist in my father. But I do believe that the underlying impulse driving its existence and growth—to defeat the scandalizing catastrophe of death—was also there at the heart of his determination to become a doctor and scientist.

On a hot, sunny mid-April day in the spring of 1938, my father put on a new suit with short pants that his parents had given him. He was not yet ten years old. The dye from the wool suit mixed with his own sweat and bled in rivulets down his bare legs as he stood in the heat during the burial of his fourteen-year-old sister, Sarita.

A week before, the door to her sickroom had been closed to him. He never saw his sister alive again.

Humiliation and boiling rage rose up and swelled in his little body.

Ten years later (November 10, 1948 to be exact), walking around the corner from the family apartment where Sarita had died, he bought a book called *Metodología de las ciencias* (Methodology of the sciences). He had just begun his third year of coursework on his way to a BS in Medicine from the University of Zaragoza.

Inside the book, in blue pencil, he underlined the following passage, which I've translated from the original Spanish: "Science should, firstly, improve the material condition of humankind." And then a couple of lines further down the page, this: "It is best, before all else, to put thought in the service of the struggle against poverty, against sickness, and against premature death."[1]

Was he thinking of Sarita? Or of his own bout with serious illness in the early 1940s? Or of the carnage of the Spanish Civil War, which raged from just after his eighth birthday until just before his eleventh?

Was The Archive a physical manifestation of this struggle, a barricade he erected against death?

I don't know. I do know that the story of Sarita's funeral was the first he told me when we'd set out, years ago, to write his autobiography and that he repeated it many times, especially late in his life. As he was dying in hospice, in April 2014, hanging on despite our efforts to help him let go, we wondered if he was trying to die on the same day as his sister. After he died, my brother even found an original funeral card from that event among my father's things.

Metodología de las ciencias was one of the books that my wife and I rescued from The Archive after his death. It forms one of many slim volumes published by the Barcelona publishing house "Editorial Labor" as part of its comprehensive series entitled Biblioteca de Iniciación Cultural (Library of Cultural Initiation), which promised to offer students and the general public accessible but "absolutely scientifically rigorous" introductions to "the natural treasures, the fruit of the labor of geniuses, and the great ideals of the world's peoples," providing thereby "the cultural instrument needed to satisfy the natural zeal for knowledge, belonging to every man, and systemizing dispersed ideas."

I took all of them home with me—along with some diaries and notebooks, some audio cassettes of telephone conversations he'd recorded, and a manila folder labeled "Baby Santiago." Opening it, I found, among other documents, scraps of paper on which my father had recorded my height at the conclusion of our annual rites of measurement.

#10. First Communion

On November 12, 1972, a few months after I turned seven and learned that I was not four feet tall, I received my First Holy Communion.

I don't really remember the day, except that I was proud to be the first in my Catholic elementary school second grade class to receive the sacrament (I beat Stephen Daugherty by a week), and that I was thrilled to be the center of attention.

But when my siblings and I were going through my parents' things after my father's death, I rescued two photos taken on that day.

In both photos I am standing on a rock in our front yard. It is about two feet high. I was afraid of heights, but I was feeling very big that day. I was in the Zone.

In one photo, my mother stands on the ground next to me. Her head is tilted to the side. We are smiling at each other. With my left hand resting on my left thigh, I bend forward slightly. My right arm is extended, my hand resting on the top of my mother's head. I am taller than her.

In the other photo, both my parents appear, both standing on the ground, flanking me, looking at each other. My hands are resting, one on each of their shoulders. I am looking directly at the camera. My father is still taller than me. I am not smiling.

In both photos, there is a Colorado blue spruce that my father planted next to the rock in honor of my first communion. I always thought of that tree as belonging to me and, though I could never remember the names of natural things, I always remembered what kind of tree that was. The Colorado blue spruce was a childhood friend whose name I never forgot.

In the photos, though it extends a single spindly branch that reaches higher than all of our heads, most of the tree is shorter than all of us.

On the last day I saw it, after we'd already cleared out The Archive and emptied the home to prepare it for sale (a month before my mother died), my friend the Colorado blue spruce was taller than the house.

Now, the house sold to a new family with a young child, the tree is gone.

PART 1 | Counting

1

The Science of Moving Dots

#11. Mountains of Moving Dots

During a March 2015 TED Talk, computer scientist Rajiv Maheswaran showed his audience a digitally enhanced slow-motion video of a basketball player dribbling the ball toward a defender near the top of the key, one on one. "So, what we are doing," Maheswaran explained as the basketball players' bodies vanished from the image, leaving only two dots continuing to move on the floor where the athletes had been, "is turning our athletes into moving dots. So, we've got mountains of moving dots."[1]

Maheswaran is the CEO of a corporation called Second Spectrum, which he co-founded in 2013. According to one iteration of its website homepage, "Data is revolutionizing the sports industry." But given "the challenge of sifting through mountains of data in search of compelling stories," the company promised to "create products that fuse cutting-edge design with spatiotemporal pattern recognition, machine learning, and computer vision to enable the next generation of sports insights and experiences."[2]

By 2015, half the teams in the NBA used the company's services. And by 2017, Second Spectrum became the Official Optical Tracking Provider of the NBA, perhaps because, as Maheswaran claimed the year before, "every word in basketball our machine now knows." He seems to have persuaded many in the basketball world, as he promised in that TED Talk, that with "the science of moving dots we will move better, we will move smarter, we will move forward."[3]

Second Spectrum is a major corporate player in basketball analytics. In its impact on player evaluation and roster-building; performance assessment and improvement; strategic, tactical, and technical diagnosis and adjustment; and media and fan discourse about the sport, the science of moving dots Maheswaran champions has been the most significant development in the NBA in the past fifteen years. Moreover, recently it has begun to make inroads into both the Women's National Basketball Association (WNBA) and men's college basketball as well.[4] And even in settings where the advanced technologies and statistical methods may be absent, such as youth or recreational basketball, the effects of basketball analytics are on display as young players emulate the moves of NBA heroes whose own decisions have been shaped, at least partly, by the science of moving dots.

Of course counting and other forms of quantification have played some role in basketball culture since the first game ever played. Indeed Allen Guttman and other sport historians consider record keeping a distinguishing feature of modern sports such as basketball.[5] But the nature and extent of counting, as well as the purposes to which it has been put, have grown over the 125 years of the sport's history, and never more so than in the extraordinary expansion of quantification—fueled by the use of digital technologies—in the culture of basketball over the past quarter century.

#12. Basic Basketball Statistics

For most of the first century after the invention of the sport in 1891, basketball counting was dominated by the scorebook and the box score. A scorebook is a blank table in which an observer records a tally mark each time a player completes certain actions such as attempting or making field goals or free throws, or committing personal fouls. The tallies are totaled for each individual in the right-hand column of the scorebook and for the team on the bottom row. These totals then appear in "the box score," another table consulted by coaches, players, and journalists after games and published in daily newspapers for fans. A cumulative version of a team's season box score might also be printed in game programs or basketball annuals, and leagues may use these to maintain all-time records.

From the official standpoint of the NBA between 1891 and 1946 the number of categories of actions counted remained relatively stable: field goals made, fouls, free throws made and attempted, and total points were tallied and totaled. Between 1946 and 1979, assists, rebounds, turnovers, blocked shots, and steals were gradually added. Together these tallied totals are often referred to colloquially as "raw stats" or "counting stats."

Some nominally analytical metrics, derived by applying simple mathematical operations to these counting stats, also appeared in official records during this time. They are often referred to as "derived stats." In 1937, at least in some organizations, scoring average began to be calculated on a per-game basis by dividing a player's total points by the number of games in which the player appeared. Likewise, as actions such as assists (1946), rebounds (1950), blocks, and steals (both in 1973) came to be counted officially in box scores, per-game averages were calculated for these actions as well. In 1945 shooting percentage was first reported as a ratio of shots made divided by shots attempted, first for free throws, with field goal percentages following the next year; and three-point field goal percentage appeared in NBA box scores when the league added the three-point line in 1979.[6]

Despite this gradual increase in the number of statistical categories by the 1970s, most experts would have agreed with *New York Times* reporter and columnist Leonard Koppett, who in 1973 cautioned readers against an overreliance on statistics. "The statistics," he wrote, "no matter how elaborate, leave out the very things that count: when, and how."[7] Koppett didn't think that counting per se was bad, just that the things that were counted didn't count for very much. Indeed, he briefly indulged a fantasy in which "it would be possible to count all the things that really matter, such as the 'correct' passes, or defensive play."[8]

Figuratively speaking, we can understand basketball analytics as having emerged to fulfill the desire driving Koppett's fantasy: a desire to count the things that really count. As I'll show below, insiders had voiced this desire long before Koppett, and some had even attempted to meet it. But certain events and trends taking shape at and shortly after the time that Koppett was writing accelerated the emergence of basketball analytics. Professional athletes asserted such labor rights as free agency, which led to rising salaries in professional sports. This in turn made accurate assessments of player value even more desirable to owners. Advances in personal computer technology made historical and contemporary data more widely accessible and easier to analyze. Baseball's so-called Sabermetric movement (also known as "moneyball" after the 2003 bestseller that popularized the movement, about which I will say more in chapter 3) pioneered the effective use of more sophisticated statistical concepts and methods in that sport.[9]

During the 1980s, hobbyists working mostly in isolation sporadically challenged the validity of traditional box score totals as indicators of performance and experimented with new metrics they believed would better reflect context and so better measure player and team performance. The simplest of these, known as "Production Rating," was developed by Michael Manley in 1988. It simply weighted every positive and negative action tallied in the box score equally, added the positives and subtracted the negatives to come up with a player's "credits" for a single game.[10] By adding the credits accumulated over the season, and then dividing by the number of games played, Manley arrived at credits per game, or, production rating.

Others utilized the same basic arithmetical operations but assigned various weights to the different categories of action counted in the box score, reflecting their estimate of the importance of these actions. A point might be weighted by a factor of 1, while an assist would be weighted by a factor .79, an offensive rebound by a factor of .85 and a steal by a factor of 1.20. Once established, these differently weighted raw stats would become variables in linear equations designed to produce a single metric—known as "linear weight" metrics—for evaluating players.

Take this last weighting method example and consider two imaginary performances: Player A scores 12 points, with 3 offensive rebounds, 0 assists, and 1 steal, while Player B scores 4 points but tallies 6 assists, 0 offensive rebounds, and 2 steals. Player A's performance would be calculated as follows: 12 × 1 + 3 × .85 + 0 × .79 + 1 × 1.20, which gives 12 + 2.55 + 0 + 1.20, or a total weighted performance rating of 15.75. Player B's performance, meanwhile, would be calculated with this equation: 4 × 1 + 0 × .85 + 6 × .79 + 2 × 1.20, or 4 + 0 + 4.74 + 4.40, for a total performance rating of 13.14. While a casual fan might just compare the two players' point totals and consider that Player B only contributed to his team one third as much as Player A, the linear weight metric formulas suggest that their contributions were much more similar.

Despite this advantage however, in a retrospective summary of these approaches in 2004, analytics pioneer Dean Oliver dismissed them as "approximate ways of representing someone's opinion about the quality of players. They are 'value approximation' methods. They don't tell you anything about strategy. They don't distinguish between a player's offensive and defensive contributions. They don't add up to points scored or points allowed."[11]

#13. Advanced Basketball Statistics

In 1991, in part to address such deficiencies, Oliver himself, at the time a twenty-two-year-old Cal Tech engineering graduate, broke new ground by observing, counting, and recording basketball play in a new way. In an article posted on his personal website entitled "New Measurement Techniques and a Binomial Model of the Game of Basketball," Oliver introduced "a new scoring method for basketball games that identifies new and valuable statistics for teams and, eventually, players."[12] Instead of making tallies to represent events such as made shots in a table, such as the traditional scorebook, Oliver used a code to record on a single line all the events involving the ball from the moment a team took possession of it until the moment their opponents took possession. It might look like this:

23		LA	32D	4		42	4	32	++B	
	22	D	11D	4D		53	++L			
24		LA	45D	32D	42	F10(2) xo				
	25	D	4D		40			11D	+Y3pt	
24		LA	32D	42D	4		21		-X	
	27	D	10R	4D		23	++R	FB		
27		LA	32		45D	32D	45	32D	-2	32R
	+L	F40(1) O	TIME 1:13							
	27	D	11RD BP		TO					
29		LA	4STL	D		32D	4++R		FB	
	29	D	11D	4D		40	-A	11R	+3	
29		LA	32		-Y	END 1Q				

FIG. 3. Dean Oliver basketball scoring method sample.

Oliver explained how to decipher this excerpted sample of his coded recording of events in a game between the Los Angeles Lakers and the Detroit Pistons: "On the left is the running score of the game. On the first line, the number 23 appears to the left of 'LA,' meaning that the Lakers ended the possession with 23 points. The numbers to the right of 'LA' or 'D' on each line correspond to the jersey numbers of the players as they touch the ball. For example, the first line shows that the Lakers' number 32, Magic Johnson, dribbled (32D), then passed to Byron Scott (number 4), who passed to James Worthy (number 42), who passed back to Scott (4), back to Johnson (32) who made a jump shot on the assist from Scott (4 32++B). . . . A flat line (-) next to a number indicates that the person with that number shot the ball. If the flat line is crossed vertically (+), then the shot went in. If a second vertical line is present (++), then an assist is credited to the player whose number is listed previous to the one who made the shot. The subscript next to the symbol indicating a shot is shorthand for where the shot was attempted on the court" and corresponds to one of nine shooting zones Oliver labeled on a half-court diagram.

But the specific codes Oliver used are not really important to grasp or retain here. What is important is that by representing each possession as a series of interconnected actions among players on the floor, Oliver's new measurement technique offered a picture of, as Koppett might have put it, the "when and how" of basketball plays.

Equally importantly, it enabled Oliver to reframe the elementary unit of basketball play. "The most basic thing to come out of the score sheet," he emphasized, "is the concept of possessions," defined as the interval of play between when a team gains possession of the ball and when it gives up possession to its opponents, which occurs either when it scores, misses a shot that is rebounded by the defense, or when it turns the ball over.[13] By this definition two teams have the same number of possessions in a single game.

He then derived two fundamental analytical measures of basketball play from this conceptual innovation: First, he quantified "pace" as the ratio of possessions per game. This enabled comparison of the tempos of different teams in a single year, of single teams in different years, or of the league as a whole in different years. This in turn permitted meaningful comparison of the offensive and defensive statistics of individuals and teams, regardless of differences in tempo. Second, Oliver measured overall team performance with what he called "offensive (or defensive) rating": the ratio of points scored (or allowed) per possession.[14] Oliver offered this as a measure of "efficiency," explaining that "where a team offense is referred to as good, it is because they are efficient."[15] Oliver thus redefined winning to mean scoring more points than your opponent with the same number of possessions. Economists Dave Berri, Martin Schmidt, and Stacey Brooks subsequently tested the strength of the correlation between efficiency and winning by running a statistical regression analysis and found that "95% of wins can be explained by team's efficiency measures."[16]

Further statistical analysis of historical data using this framework of possessions, pace, and efficiency—known collectively as "possession-based statistics"—led Oliver to identify aspects of game play that constituted high efficiency: making a high percentage of field goals, minimizing turnovers, gathering a high percentage of a team's own missed shots, and shooting (and making) a high number of free throws.[17] These components came to be known as the "Four Factors," each measured by a new statistic: (1) effective field goal percentage, (2) turnover percentage (3) offensive rebound percentage, and (4) free throw rate.[18] While the Four Factors were initially devised in relation to team performance, further research yielded statistical formulas for calculating individual players' contributions to their team's performance in each of the four metrics, as well as overall offensive and defensive efficiency ratings for individual players.

Throughout the next decade, Oliver and a small but growing group of basketball fans with statistical expertise experimented with these advanced statistics, using publicly available data sets on personal websites and in online forums. In 2001, these individuals formed an online forum calling itself the Association of Professional Basketball Research (APBR), marking a more organized, collective effort to develop the field by identifying new areas of inquiry and by sharing and debating data and methods of analysis.[19] Among other things, these analysts devised pace-sensitive, nonlinear, single-number metrics to represent player performance, or value, and refined quantitative descriptive, diagnostic, and predictive models of the expected cost and gain of various elements of individual and team play.[20] In 2004, Oliver published much of the work he'd been doing since the early 1990s in a printed volume called *Basketball on Paper: Rules and Tools for Performance Analysis*, considered by many to be the bible of basketball analytics. Meanwhile sports economists began to use the data to quantify the value of a win in dollars. From there attempts emerged to convert metrics quantifying players' contributions to victory into dollar amounts (on the basis of the dollar value of a win) and then to compare these converted figures to player salaries.[21]

The increased visibility these forums and publications offered, the insights they conveyed, together with the popularization of baseball analytics with the publication in 2003 of Michael Lewis's bestselling chronicle of that trend, *Moneyball*, led to greater institutional and cultural purchase for basketball analytics. NBA franchises took note and began to hire data science experts—including, for example, Oliver himself—to analyze (and privatize) statistical data. Journalists in sports and mainstream media profiled key figures in the movement.[22] In 2007, Daryl Morey (Northwestern, BS, Computer Science; MIT, MBA), at the time a consultant for the Boston

Celtics (and now general manager of the Houston Rockets and, for many, the current face of basketball analytics), helped inaugurate the MIT Sloan Sports Analytics Conference, attracting scholars, NBA analysts, coaches and players, journalists, and industry representatives. Today it is an annual mega-event in its own right whose keynote speaker in 2017 was former U.S. president Barack Obama.

Meanwhile, in the public domain, websites like Nylon Calculus and FiveThirtyEight provided primers on analytics to fans, shared independent research, and even utilized analytic methods to provide probability estimates on the outcome of future contests. The popularity of such independent sites among fans led established corporate basketball or sports websites, such as FanSided and ESPN, to establish formal partnerships with them. ESPN now includes an in-game "win probability" metric on its website and mobile app. As players make or miss shots or turn the ball over, fans can watch their team's chances to win the game bounce around. The media conglomerate also devotes an annual issue of its magazine to documenting the use of analytics by franchises in all four of the major men's professional sports leagues in the United States.

At the same time, scholars founded the *Journal of Quantitative Analysis in Sports* to vet—and thereby enhance the scientific credibility of—basketball analytics research, and some of these same academic researchers published scholarly volumes, textbooks, and books for lay readers.[23] By the start of the 2015–16 season, every NBA club had at least one analytics expert and most had created analytics departments.[24] While most of these first and second generation researchers had degrees in economics, engineering, computer science, mathematics, business, and the like, the up-and-coming generation is more likely to have received specialized interdisciplinary training that prepares them for careers in the science of moving dots.[25]

#14. Big Data Basketball

Personal computers and the Internet had already facilitated the work of basketball analytics pioneers like Dean Oliver in the 1990s and early 2000s. But during the 2009–10 season, a company called SportVU introduced, to six NBA arenas, a quantum leap in digital data production technology. Six cameras installed in the catwalks relayed images to proprietary software that plotted the position of all ten players in two dimensions and of the ball in three dimensions, twenty-five times per second. Soon more teams invested the $100,000 required for the system, and by the start of the 2013–14 season, SportVU was in every NBA arena. Through a contract with SportVU's parent company, Stats, LLC, the NBA and its franchises received full data sets (nearly eight hundred thousand data points per game) from each game.[26]

Stats, LLC also offered customized packages of statistics and reports to teams and the media, while other private firms, like Second Spectrum, offered analytical services to NBA clubs. Second Spectrum, as I noted above, has now taken over as the official provider of the optical tracking hardware and software for the entire NBA. While most of this data is privately held and fiercely guarded by franchises, the NBA releases some publicly on its web page and journalists can apply for subscriptions to access more extensive data sets. Meanwhile, younger analysts hoping to break into the field, or just as a hobby, have created new websites, joining "old" standbys like Nylon Calculus, FiveThirtyEight, and Steve Shea's Basketball Analytics, to provide fans with analytics-driven perspectives on the sport.

Basketball analysts, mathematicians, and computer scientists experimenting with mathematically modeling and simulating basketball play have been working to use this flood of data to address questions that had previously seemed impossible to answer.[27] Where and via what trajectory is a missed shot likely to rebound? How does that vary depending on the shot attempt location and trajectory? Who has the best shooting range? How much does a given shooter's accuracy vary depending on whether he or she attempts a shot directly after receiving a pass or after first taking a dribble, or two, or three, or four? How about depending on whether a defender is guarding them? Or guarding them within one foot, or two, or three or four? For that matter, what is good defense? And how can we measure it? Using computer vision (or pattern recognition) and machine learning of the sort Maheswaran describes in his TED Talk, analysts provide highly detailed descriptions, diagnoses, predictions, and prescriptions to professional franchises.[28]

In chapter 9, I'll consider in greater detail some of the questions occupying basketball analysts today. For now I'll offer just one—somewhat dated, but nevertheless important—example from 2014, the early years of big data basketball. That year Harvard University statistics graduate student Dan Cervone and colleagues presented a paper at the MIT Sloan Sports Analytics Conference.[29] Recognizing that even Oliver's advanced possession-based analytics metrics are "driven by events that occur at or near the end of a possession, such as points, turnovers, and assists," these scholars developed a "framework for using player-tracking data to assign a point value to each moment of a possession by computing how many points the offense is expected to score by the end of the possession." This number, called "expected possession value" (or EPV) "allows analysts to evaluate every decision made during a basketball game" and suggests "a multitude of new metrics and analyses of basketball that quantify value in terms of points." In a graph representing the expected value of a possession, time in tenths of seconds might run along the x-axis and the expected points on the y-axis. You might see the resulting plot line slope down as a player dribbles into a double team and then rise steeply as he completes a pass to a teammate wide open near the basket.

As granular as the analyses promised by these innovations is, the emerging cutting edge of digital data production technology goes still further, using digital biometric devices to bring "the metric revolution to the human molecular level, remaking the bodies of its players through analytics."[30] In addition to various basic physical measurements and tests designed to quantify size, strength, speed, agility, and leaping ability, franchises themselves now conduct, or farm out to subcontractors, a battery of injury diagnosis and prevention examinations utilizing sophisticated data production technologies and employing statistical methods to process the data and to estimate future physical performance trajectories, with particular regard to the likelihood of injuries. Thus, for example, the firm Fusionetics offers what it calls "an athlete management system" that includes tests for movement efficiency, range of motion, recovery and readiness, training load, and performance.[31]

Meanwhile, at Peak Performance Project (or P3)—where "science meets sports performance"—"each athlete . . . is put under the microscope—we take a medical approach—utilizing 3D Motion Capture and Force Plate technology to assess how you execute the movements of your sport." Combining these "thousands of data points" into what it calls a "movement fingerprint," the company prescribes "a very personalized training program to correct biomechanics deficiencies and to optimize relevant athletic needs."[32] The NBA "quietly invited" P3 to test prospects at its annual draft combine in order to get baseline measurements in key biochemical tests and Adidas did something similar for "high school and college prospects." Armed with this data, P3 will have what its founder, Dr. Marcus Elliott, calls "crazy valuable" information about athletes' "propensities for injuries."

But we still want more. Currently, due to resistance by the NBA Players' Association (NBAPA), biometric tracking devices are not permitted during game play. The resulting information gap is why journalist Andy Glockner describes "the Holy Grail of athlete injury prevention and performance improvement" as the integration of all this off-court movement data with "in-game tracking data, practice tracking data, and so-called off-site biometric data culled from tracking sleep, monitoring diets, and taking periodic bloodwork to check players' vital levels." Glockner is talking about adding to the measurement technologies used by P3 and Fusionetics such technologies as wearables (meaning devices utilizing global positioning system and radio frequency identification) and smart-clothing and equipment (garments fitted with pressure sensors to measure muscle activation and joint/limb positioning) that will provide real-time measures of athletes' bodies performing under the stress of competitive conditions.[33]

Even without this Holy Grail, basketball analytics experts struggle to stay abreast of the flood of existing data. But in the meantime the science of moving dots has already significantly impacted the sport. To take only the most evident example of the on-court changes analytics has inspired, the number of three-point shots attempted in the NBA has risen sharply in recent years as coaches and players have assimilated the insight, first put forth by basketball analytics, that on average three-point field goal attempts generate more points per possession than their two-point counterparts within the arc, unless the latter are taken near the rim.[34] And all these changes have coincided with a rapid rise in the values of league franchises and in the league's own revenues.[35]

Off the court, sophisticated individual player metrics developed by basketball analytics, despite admitted limitations, have aided decision-makers in their quest to assemble a cohort of players likely to maximize efficiency (and, therefore, the likelihood of winning) at the lowest cost possible.[36] And some feel that the data torrent unleashed by SportVU (and now Second Spectrum) and the expansion of the use of biometric devices will help remedy deficiencies in these individual player metrics.[37] All of this has unfolded as the NBA has attracted more fans and generated more revenues than ever before.[38] In this way the "science of moving dots" is now utterly integral to both NBA teams "chasing perfection" and to the league as a whole in its own quest for consumer dollars.[39]

Interlude—Rulers

#15. Middleton

Among the thousands of pages and hundreds of folders of all different kinds in The Archive, my wife and I found a plastic folder, letter sized, with openings along the top and bottom. Through the clear cover I could see that it contained a letter, typewritten, on onionskin paper. What caught my eye was the addressee: "Mr. Don Lindstrom, Sports." I knew that name! Don Lindstrom was the (local) sportswriter of my adolescence, his beat: Madison area high school sports.

The letter was dated, flush right, "March 1, 1983." My senior year in high school! Days, in fact, before I, as co-captain, would help lead the Edgewood High School varsity boys' basketball team, figuratively and literally, to Mecca. Figuratively because we had made it to the state championship tournament for the first time in nearly a decade and literally because the tournament games were held in Milwaukee, at MECCA, home of the NBA's Milwaukee Bucks. My father had written to Don Lindstrom!? "Jesus Christ," I groaned silently. I felt a familiar spasm of incipient embarrassment, similar to what I felt when we'd go out to dinner. Between his temper, his heavily accented English, and his, well, just kind of weird way of talking to people, I never knew what was gonna happen.

"Dear Mr. Lindstrom," the letter began. Oh no! I realize that greeting may seem innocuously formulaic. But that kind of formulaic politeness is just how my father would begin before he eviscerated a telemarketer on the phone, a door-to-door salesman, a waitress, my mother, me. But he didn't eviscerate Don Lindstrom, thank God. He simply pointed out that "In the list of scoring leaders . . . two Edgewood players are listed with fewer total points than they actually have" and then he offered the correct data. Not only that, but he concluded by politely thanking Don Lindstrom for his coverage of high school sports and "in particular, for the kind words you had for my son's performance in the Edgewood-Middleton game."

Ahhh! The Middleton game! I have to tell you about Tuesday, February 8, 1983. Unforgettable. Probably—dare I say "objectively"—the peak of my basketball career.

Let me set the stage. Middleton came into our gym with an 11-3 record, hot on a five-game winning streak. We were 9-6 but had just lost two heart-breaking games, each by two points, the last against our hated neighborhood rival, West High. According to the scouting report our coach prepared (and that I, my hoarder father's son, saved), Middleton was "an excellent team that can and will do a lot of different things," particularly with their "two guards with good size and quickness who can both shoot it as well as go to the basket." Of these two, "Zingg (14, 6′2″) is their best. We must stop him from penetrating, from hitting the 15–18-foot jumper. He's a player. Can go right or left, loves to drive vs. Man defense. (Avg. 20 PPG)." Coach Maturi also wrote up our team goals: hold them under fifty points on no more than 42 percent shooting from the field.

At the half, things weren't looking so good as Middleton was up 30–26 and shooting 64 percent from the floor. But then, and I quote from Mr. Don Lindstrom's account of the game the following morning, "Yago Colas became Madison Edgewood's hero—both offensively and defensively—Tuesday night." Shall I continue? If you insist. "Colas, a 5′8″ senior guard whose real name is Santiago, scored eight fourth-quarter points, including four free throws in the final 24 seconds to lead Edgewood to a 56–52 victory over Middleton."[1] But wait. Wait. "It was also Colas who put a second-half defensive damper on Middleton's standout junior guard, Dave Zingg. That, according to Edgewood Coach Joel Maturi, provided the game's turning point." I could go on. Don Lindstrom's article mentions me—count them—thirteen times (not counting the headline—that's right, the headline: "Colas,

Edgewood slip past Middleton"). Middleton was a big enough event that almost a year later, Don Lindstrom would include it (singling me out by name) in his recap of top prep sports stories of 1983 in the Madison area.

At the end of Don Lindstrom's recap of the game, there was a little box score that included the line score (the points by quarter for each team) and then the field goals made, free throws made, and total points for each player. But I know a bit more about that game than just that I made six baskets and four free throws for a total of sixteen points. I know I made those six baskets on nine attempts and those four free throws on five attempts. I know I had two rebounds (both defensive), five assists, no blocks or steals, one turnover, and one foul. I also know my stats for each quarter. How do I know all this? Well that brings me back to the basis for my father's politely helpful letter to Don Lindstrom.

You see, my father kept my basketball statistics for every game I ever played. Well that's not exactly true. He didn't keep them in sixth or seventh grade. But from November 1978, my eighth grade team's preseason exhibition loss to West Middleton Middle School (sixteen points on 8 of 11 shooting, four rebounds, four steals), through March 1983, the last game of my senior season, and my career, an overtime loss to Oshkosh Lourdes in the quarter finals of that state tournament contest on the Mecca floor (nine points on 4 of 6 shooting from the field and 1 for 2 from the line, one rebound, four assists, three steals, two turnovers)—he kept them. For every game he used his ruler to measure out a grid of twelve rows and eight columns on the top sheet of a 5″ × 7″ yellow pad: a row for each of twelve statistical categories, a column for the category name, one for each of the four quarters, one giving the totals for each half, and one for the game total.

For eighty-five games he kept my stats, and then he kept all eighty-five of those little yellow sheets of paper in a folder in The Archive. Did he know that one day, decades later and just a couple of years before his death, I'd ask about them? I was certainly fascinated by them in high school. I pored over them, tallied them. Calculated with them. I played with the numbers because it was enjoyably absorbing in itself. I implored the numbers to tell me I was a good player. But I know now that the numbers were basically a metonym for my father. So I played with them obsessively because I wanted to spend time with him and, above all, I wanted them, and him, to tell me I was good (enough).

In 1982, sometime after my senior season, he got an IBM PC. I didn't really care too much. Our high school had just begun offering computer classes. I didn't care about that either. Computers were for nerds. And though I was a good student and too polite to have put it this way, I wasn't a nerd. My father, however, apparently was a nerd. And I began tentatively to reconsider the value of nerds when sheets of perforated paper with my stats, and my teammates', and our opponents', printed out in neat tables, began to emerge from my father's study. He kept all of those in The Archive as well. And that is how he was able to inform Don Lindstrom of the error in the newspaper's statistics and to provide the correct data.

After he died, I rescued all of this from The Archive. So now I have them. And I've entered them all into a spread sheet in Excel. I named the file "Yago Lifetime Stats."

#16. Rulers

The metal instrument my father laid flat across the crown of my head, perpendicular to the concrete wall of our basement, is called a ruler.

This is no coincidence, explains Witold Kula: "The right to determine measures is an attribute of authority in all advanced societies. It is a prerogative of the ruler to make measures mandatory and to retain the custody of the standards."[2]

And measurement expert David Hand says, "We can count stones, sheep, and people, but we cannot count length, weight, or time. In order to apply arithmetic to continua such as these we have to discretize them: divide them into chunks which can then be counted."[3] These countable chunks are called quanta. Hand continues, "We then assign numbers to represent the magnitude of attributes of a system we are studying or which we wish to describe."

And so, we divide a boy into forty-seven and three-quarters inches. In the same way we divide the collective effort of a group of young people playing a game into 1.035 points per possession.

Measurement and other forms of quantification are ways, Hand elaborates, of "translating our observations about the world into numerical form" or of "mapping from the real world to an artificial one and, in particular, one in which we can apply mathematical tools." In this way, Hand says "the quantitative lifts our discussion from the untidiness of the real world, to a plane which we can manipulate and control, and use to predict and understand." The whole point of the enterprise, he concludes, is to "understand and manipulate the universe."[4]

My father certainly wanted to lift the discussion from the untidiness of the real world and to understand and manipulate the universe. And who could blame him? Before he was ten years old he had witnessed both the public chaos of the Spanish Civil War and the private tragedy of his beloved sister's death from illness. Two decades later, moving his young family to Colombia in search of better opportunities, he arrived in the midst of the carnage known in that country simply as *La Violencia* (The Violence). Is it any wonder that he would develop a mania for measurement and for the rational control of his environment he believed it would provide?

I am my father's son: so I want to tidy and control reality as well, and measuring sounds like a reasonable and desirable way to do it.

But Alfred Crosby, in his history of measurement in early modern Europe, sheds light on the other side of quantification, the dark side of my father's devotion, my devotion, "to breaking down things and energies and practices and perceptions into uniform parts and counting them."[5] Quantification, Crosby says bluntly, is how "we reach out for physical reality, push aside its darling curls, and take it by the nape of the neck."[6]

I am my father's son: so I know this already. I knew it already, at age seven, in the bones of my not-quite four-foot-long body.

Now, my father may have introduced me to numbers and, in so doing, quantified me and, in more ways than one, ruled me. But make no mistake: I wanted my father to measure me. I approached these annual measurements with hopeful anticipation. Sometimes my hope grew into a carefully formulated request to be measured even when the appointed time had not yet arrived. My father always consented, and we marched down the stairs to the basement. Year by year, day by day, my body changed in myriad ways, seen and unseen. Basketball became a love, and the deeper it wove its rhythms into my changing flesh, the more fervently I craved growth, and the precisely choreographed ritual of measurement that would attest to it.

But, why the number? After all I must have had some indication of my own growth, noticed on a daily basis the things I now could reach. I must have stood back to back with my friends and playmates, sliding our hands levelly across the tops of our heads to see who was taller, by how much, and whether or not it had changed. Mike Kessenich is tall, Robbie Hoffmeister is not, Ken McCormick is the same as me. My favorite corduroys from second grade are now flood pants. But none of these carried for me the weight, the legitimacy, the authority of my father's measurement. Why did I not trust my own senses? Why, especially since they were implacably unalterable and so rarely gratifying, did I instead invest so completely in the numbers on the tape measure? In the authority of the numbers produced by my scientist father's precisely choreographed ritual of measurement?

The answers, I guess, or at least the beginnings of some answers, are right there in the question.

I wanted my Dad. And he wanted numbers. So, I wanted numbers. But why did he want numbers?

I know he was curious about the world and that he had a powerful investment in reason and science as a way to understand it. I also know he hated surprises. So perhaps, like many scientists before him, he believed that if you want to avoid surprises you need to be able to predict how something will behave. And to do that you have to know with precision what it is, how it works, and how it behaves. And, finally, if you want to know with precision what it is, how it works, and how it behaves, you have to measure it.

And thus I have an image of my father and I caught in a vast net, both the obedient servants of a different ruler.

#17. How to Maximize Control of Events and Save Time

In The Archive—actually in a drawer in my father's desk—I found a list, printed out in twelve-point Times Roman font and sheathed in a clear protective plastic cover. At the top of the list, printed in bold, underlined, capital letters, was this title:

<u>HOW TO MAXIMIZE CONTROL OF EVENTS AND SAVE TIME</u>.

Beneath the title, the numbered list of twenty-three items includes such tips as "10. Eradicate **dysfunctional** interruptions" or "12. 'What is the greatest **threat** to my **survival** socially, financially, professionally, physically and spiritually?' Take definitive action to minimize those threats" or "19. Delegate with discernment. Instead of having subordinates bring you problems have them bring you the answers. **YOU** ask the questions." Reading that last one, I realize that my father viewed me as a subordinate.

But even without looking at the whole list, the title alone pretty much sums up my father's core values and his voice. I'm struck first by how it resonates with a Taylorist drive for efficiency that was truly important to my father. But this title reveals deeper values too, especially when you think of saving time not only in the everyday sense but as a deeper existential imperative to gather the time of one's life. My father hoarded objects, and perhaps he wished he could hoard his time as well. In that way, to save time is just to maximize control of the biggest, most terrifying event of all: death.

Not only the content but the formatting of the title, too, reflects my father's voice: caps, underscore, *and* bold for maximum emphasis. Once when he was a young academic firebrand, perhaps thirty years old, he was in a faculty meeting that got a little heated. One of his colleagues tried to settle him down: "Calm yourself, Antonio, you're going to get a heart attack." "I don't get heart attacks," my father flatly retorted, "I give them." He told that story often, his big straight teeth bared with a gleeful relish.

When I was small I used to be afraid of my father's voice, which—deep and loud—always sounded impatient and angry. It was hard for me to tell, just from the sound of his voice, whether he was in a good mood, or angry. As I grew into a teenager it still made me nervous, but I also often felt embarrassed by it in public. At my basketball games, even as he kept my statistics, he frequently berated the officials. You could hear his heavily accented bass rise to the surface from under the other noises in the crowded gym, barking with self-satisfied anger—"C'mon! Ref! Are you blind?"—and often with a slight idiomatic error of which he was totally unaware: "What happened to you?! Have you eaten your whistle?!"

It's not that all he did was complain, or that the complaints in themselves embarrassed me. He also cheered and embarrassed me. When I first started writing about basketball about ten years ago, I called my blog "Go Yago!": the phrase my father shouted so often and so repeatedly that my friends would joke about it: "Go Yago! Go! Go Ya Go! Go Ya Go Ya Go Ya!" they would shout, deepening their adolescent voices and trying to turn their nasal Wisconsin accents into my father's Spanish-Scottish hybrid. Eventually the repetition would transform "Yago" into "Goya," the last name of my father's favorite Spanish painter, Francisco Goya, whose grisly depiction of *Saturn Devouring His Son* my father once lovingly sent me as a postcard during a business trip to Spain.

By the time I grew into an adult and would come home to visit my parents, I was astonished by how much and how loudly he talked. Part of it was that his hearing began to go, and he refused to wear his hearing aids. Part of it is that his principal interlocutor, my mom, was beginning to sink into the unresponsive fog of early Alzheimer's. But part of it was just him being the way he always had been, but more: the distillation of the self to its core that seems to come with aging.

But now, looking at the title of this list—capitalized, underscored, and bolded—I don't hear his emphatic voice as angry so much as fearfully desperate to be heard and understood. Perhaps that too was an expression of the desire to maximize his control over death. It is as if I can hear an echo drifting from the distant past, reflecting the secret content of the many things—some terrible, some wonderful—I heard him intone in bold, underscored caps over the course of my life with him.

"I am here! I am here!" the echo shouts, but softly somehow, straining to be heard.

2

The Culture of Moving Dots

#18. The Rhetoric of Moving Dots

The expansion of basketball analytics over the past fifteen years has been impressive, to be sure. And I am certainly convinced that the trend has generated interesting and important novel understandings of many different facets of basketball play. But the array of new concepts, methods, technologies, and metrics generated by the movement in such a short time has also been met with caution, resistance, and at times downright disdain. Perhaps the most notorious of such expressions of the latter came from former NBA player and current TNT broadcaster, the Hall of Fame forward Charles Barkley who called Darryl Morey "one of those idiots" and described analytics "as crap" before concluding that advocates and practitioners of basketball analytics were "a bunch of guys who ain't never played the game [and] they never got the girls in high school." [1]

Barkley's dismissal was rightly met with ridicule. Nevertheless, in the face of such skepticism, corporate entities in the field, as well as individual practitioners, cannot simply point to complex formulas or lines of digital code and expect that basketball players, coaches, general managers, owners, and fans will immediately accept that the knowledge basketball analytics offers is superior to what they already know. Even if they acknowledge that it may be superior, they may yet question whether it will be practically usable. In short, the value of basketball analytics does not speak for itself.

Moreover, for most basketball insiders, let alone casual fans, the quantitative aspects of basketball analytics are, on their face, incomprehensible. The inner workings of digital technologies for data production, analysis, and presentation are highly specialized and obscure, as are the engineering principles, complex statistical formulas, and mathematical models underlying this technology. And it often appears that the deeper bedrock of conceptual principles and assumptions upon which the edifice of basketball analytics has been erected, some of which date back centuries, are unfamiliar even to practitioners and advocates of the phenomena that rest upon them, let alone to the rest of us "stakeholders" in the sport.

So, alongside the dizzying proliferation of sophisticated quantifying technologies and techniques, basketball analytics has also had to evolve an accompanying rhetoric to explain the value of its innovations and to reassure others that their investment—whether financial, emotional, cognitive, or tactical—will return a value greater than the risk. All of this is to say that the numbers of basketball analytics invariably come to most of us garbed in words (and sometimes, importantly I will argue, pictures): dressed in explanations, narratives, and arguments and bedecked with tables, graphs, charts, and sometimes even computer-generated animations.

This cultural corpus—appearing in books, conference papers and journal articles, blog posts, podcasts, media interviews, and biographical profiles—forms the welcoming front porch of that vast, complex underlying network of capital resources, infrastructural hardware, software, past and present knowledge, institutional structures, and social relationships and practices that together comprise the "science of moving dots." The science of moving dots may generate the hard, practical insights of basketball analytics, but it is the front porch—what I call "the *culture* of moving dots"—that makes these insights understandable, inviting, and desirable.

Studying the structure of that cultural "front porch," I've found a framework of elements that I refer to collectively as "the rhetoric of moving dots." By "rhetoric," I mean "the use of words by human agents to form attitudes or to induce actions in other human agents."[2] The rhetoric of moving dots, then, works to generate the allure and persuasive power of basketball analytics. At the most general level the rhetoric of basketball analytics proposes that its methods, technologies, and metrics give its adopters tangible value by providing objective insight into a sport whose essence, after all (in the words of Leonard Koppett), is deception.[3]

To put this another way, the complexity of the sport itself combines with our cognitive biases, emotional investments, and prejudices to create the appearance of mystifying chaos and of a treacherously shifting ground upon which to attempt to form judgments and base high-stakes decisions. In the face of this, the rhetoric of moving dots assures us that the quantifying technologies and methods of the science of moving dots will shear away our distorting biases, penetrate the turbulent, noisy surface of basketball play and draw forth from its depths reliable, efficient, objective knowledge of the true nature of the sport and its players. By applying this knowledge to judgments and decisions regarding physical training, personnel, tactics, and strategy, all basketball decision makers can minimize risks and maximize the value of the return on their investment, whether that investment takes the form of effort expended, shot attempts, possessions, dollars, or love.

I sometimes imagine this rhetoric as the voice of basketball analytics.[4] Of course this is a metaphor: basketball analytics does not literally speak in any voice in the way that an individual human being speaks. But I mean by this metaphorical borrowing to impart some of the concreteness and particularity, as well as the emotional dimensions and power, of what I've been calling the rhetoric of moving dots. When this rhetoric effectively persuades its audience, it does so at least in part to the degree that those who encounter it, in whatever medium, "hear" it as a voice, as the voice of someone who is saying something, and saying it in some way. What does the voice of basketball analytics say? How does it say it? By what subtle tones and inflections does it make itself heard and persuasive?

And, at the same time, by what tics and idiosyncrasies does it reveal what I earlier called "the knife's intentions"—the deep historical forces and broader social agendas that are, possibly without the speaker's knowledge, also making themselves heard? Whose voice does it remind us of? And what qualities do such memories, conscious or not, lead us to transfer to the science of moving dots?

#19. Enlightenment

The rhetoric of moving dots consists of a set of claims, metaphors, and argumentative strategies. At the broadest overarching level these strategies loosely echo those that characterized the eighteenth-century European philosophical, scientific, and political thinkers whose thoughts, writings, institutions, and actions came to be known as "the Enlightenment."

"What was the message of these Enlightenment intellectuals?" asks Isaac Kramnick: "Unassisted human reason, not faith or tradition, was the principal guide to human conduct. . . . The natural universe . . . was ruled by rational scientific laws, which were accessible to human beings through the scientific method of experiment and empirical observation." An integral part of this project entailed "establishing the understanding of numbers as an objective description of reality outside of interpretation."[5] Together, "science and technology," Kramnick concludes, "were the engines of progress enabling modern men and women to force nature to serve their well-being and further their happiness. Science and the conquest of superstition and ignorance provided the prospect for endless improvement and reformation of the human condition, progress even unto a future that was perfection."[6]

"Reason," "science," "experiment," "observation," "numbers," "objectivity," "technology," "mastery," "progress," "improvement," "perfection": Kramnick's succinct summary gathers together the major watchwords of the Enlightenment. But it does more than this. It also highlights the assertions of causal connection that order that word-cloud into a linear narrative. Presented schematically, that narrative looks like this (see fig. 4).

This narrative structured the Enlightenment's supporting rhetorical keywords into a story that was compelling enough to enough people to have shaped the world we live in. Indeed, I wouldn't be typing these words on a computer if I didn't, at least to some degree, believe in it myself.

On the one hand, the plausibility of this narrative depended on the degree to which the descriptions of reality provided by reason faithfully corresponded to the objects they purported to describe; that is, that the discoveries of reason (on the left in figure 4) could be viewed as genuinely objective: independent of and undistorted by any subjective bias or agenda. This crucial claim to objectivity could maintain its credibility only to the degree that it could itself appear to have stripped away subjective interests, or values, from its processes: it had to present itself as value-neutral.

On the other hand, if objective knowledge was to migrate successfully beyond the scientific domain in which it was produced, and if scientists were to receive private or public support for their research, then non-scientists had to be persuaded that the facts of reason were valuable *to them*, which is to say, that they carried value according to their own necessarily *subjective* criteria. This imperative is registered on the right-hand side of the narrative figure 4, which I've amended in figure 5.

We find then a tension running through Enlightenment rhetoric: science must discover objective facts independent of any subjective bias, but its facts must be of value according to some subjective criteria. Enlightenment thought (and we today who have inherited, internalized, and repeated this narrative) has responded to this tension by pretending that there exists in reality a rigid separation between matters of fact and matters of value. Within this view science cannot tell us how we should want things to be. But once that question has been decided either through consensus, compromise, or coercion, science is the best guide to how to get things to be that way. I'm not saying, by the way, that this belief in the possibility of dichotomously separating facts from value is necessarily right or wrong, though in in my view it creates more problems than it solves, I'm just pointing out its fundamental role in Enlightenment rhetoric because the tensions it generates appear also—albeit mostly in unavowed form—in the rhetoric of moving dots.[7]

FIG. 4. Enlightenment rhetoric as narrative.

Now, how do the different specific rhetorics of moving dots, all of which descend from this overarching Enlightenment rhetoric, fit together? Michael Lewis's book *Moneyball* probably did more to advance the agenda of sports analytics than any other cultural document. Lewis explicitly frames his story of baseball analytics as a dramatic Enlightenment tale of "how an unscientific culture responds, or fails to respond, to the scientific method."[8] Lewis is clearly charmed by the irrepressibility of that unscientific culture, particularly as it manifests in the personality of Billy Beane, the poster boy for the "scientific method" in baseball. But Lewis nevertheless appears to subscribe to, and certainly amplifies, sports analytics' Enlightenment rhetoric whereby the bright light of science and reason will usher in a revolutionary era of tangible progress by illuminating the dark shadows of irrational prejudices, emotion, and bias. Indeed, that's why the very title of the chapter in which Lewis introduces the emergence of baseball analytics is called "Enlightenment" and it is followed by a description of the prior state of baseball knowledge in a chapter entitled "Field of Ignorance." Ultimately, in Lewis's account, baseball analytics appears as the heir to the Enlightenment: it discovers facts to augment the value generated by the decisions made by human beings in baseball.

I'll have more to say about *Moneyball* in the next chapter, but I mention it briefly here because Lewis's rhetoric represents fairly the rhetoric of basketball analytics (and sports analytics more generally, and analytics elsewhere in our society), which likewise claims first, that whenever superstition, blind faith, and other forms of irrationality can be replaced with rational observation, the hidden laws and patterns underlying the complex surface appearance of sporting performance can be revealed, and second,

Reason
(Objectivity/Fact)
•Science
•Experiment
•Observation
•Quantification

Technology

Perfection
(Subjectivity/Value)
•Improvement
•Mastery
•Progress

FIG. 5. Enlightenment rhetoric and fact/value dichotomy.

that quantified analysis and problem-solving can better insulate athletes and other decision-makers from the caprice of misfortune and empower them to make better decisions and augment the value of their investments. As Rajiv Maheswaran promised, now that the science of moving dots had "quantified what was previously unquantified," "we will move better, we will move smarter, we will move forward."[9] This intoxicating promise is the dream equation of the Enlightenment narrative: reason + (quantified) science + technology = progress.

More specifically and concretely, basketball analysts sometimes divide the kinds of work they do into four interrelated categories by the primary purpose it serves, which can be indicated by a question the work should answer:

(1) descriptive ("What happened?")
(2) diagnostic ("What is wrong?")
(3) predictive ("What will happen?")
(4) prescriptive ("What should we do?")

The knowledge generated within each type can inform work in the others. And the claims of each type are supported by and presented through overlapping sets of specific rhetorics comprised of keywords and metaphors. While the rhetorics supporting these different purposes can blur together, it is still possible to distinguish certain dominant tropes characteristic of each. I have found it useful to organize this variety of terms and tropes into four sets: the four rhetorics of basketball analytics (table 2).

Descriptive analytics deploys a rhetoric of objectivity, which corresponds to an Enlightenment emphasis on the discovery of *fact*, understood as the objective unveiling of reality as it is. The next three rhetorics stress, in different ways, the *value* to be gained by using those facts to guide decisions. Diagnostic analytics deploys a rhetoric of efficiency, predictive analytics deploys a rhetoric of control, prescriptive analytics deploys a rhetoric of winning.

Two other rhetorical devices often decorate the cultural front porch of basketball analytics, enhancing the persuasiveness of the four rhetorics I just listed. One, which I call "the rhetoric of credibility," entails the use of

TABLE 2. Rhetorics of basketball analytics

Purpose	Question	Time	Basketball analytics rhetoric	Tropes, metaphors, keywords	Fact/value dichotomy
Descriptive	What happened?	Past	Objectivity	Revelation, clarification, illumination	Fact
Diagnostic	What is wrong?	Present	Efficiency	Machinery, improvement, progress, productivity	Value
Predictive	What will happen?	Future	Control	Speculation, investment, risk management, mastery	
Prescriptive	What should we do?		Winning	Competitive advantage, opponency, rivalry, mastery	

visual displays of information to illustrate and make more easily accessible the insights and methods of the science of moving dots. By doing this, they also lend basketball analytics an air of transparency and so of credibility since, after all, we are able to see the results of analytics for ourselves, with our own eyes. The second—which I call the "rhetoric of progress"—often opens discussions within the field by providing a historical narrative, a kind of capsule autobiography of basketball analytics if you will, that situates it as the illuminating front edge of a continuously progressive march toward greater understanding of basketball and so of greater perfection in basketball play.

#20. Objectivity

Like their Enlightenment predecessors, the scientists of moving dots employ a foundational rhetoric of objectivity. And, also like their predecessors, this rhetoric usually operates as a critique of the prevailing state of what they see as pseudo-knowledge based on opinion, prejudice, bias, superstition, and other irrational forms of belief.

"For decades," lament Christopher Baker and Stephen Shea on the first page of their book, *Basketball Analytics*, "National Basketball Association (NBA) fans have been subjected to the same dull, insufficient and often misleading statistics. Our minds have been warped. We hallow the great point scorers and judge defense by blocks per game."[10] David Berri, Martin Schmidt, and Stacey Brook offer their quantitative approach to sports as an antidote to the folly of what they call "conventional wisdom."[11] And Ben Taylor's recent contribution to basketball analytics was given impetus by basketball's misleading narratives, which "are often shaped by a few, simplified ideas that do not accurately reflect its players or teams."[12] Even back in 1989, analytics precursor Bob Bellotti prefaced his then-novel metrics by noting that "current statistical categories tabulated by the basketball establishment are clearly inadequate."[13] Before long though, Bellotti's own erstwhile scientific approach—and those of a half-dozen others—would be characterized by Dean Oliver as "approximate ways of representing someone's opinion about the quality of players" created in "hope of better matching their personal beliefs."[14]

In the face of this, basketball analysts, like Enlightenment thinkers before them, turn to rational, quantitative measurement as a way to achieve an objective perspective that will discover facts and at least come closer to truth. Recall statistics professor David Hand's explanation that "We measure so that we can understand and manipulate the universe."[15] Or, as Lord Kelvin put it in his 1889 *Popular Lectures and Addresses*, "When you can measure what you are speaking about, and express it in numbers, you know something about it, when you cannot express it in numbers, your knowledge is of a meager and unsatisfactory kind."[16]

As for the association of quantification with objectivity and knowledge of facts, our "trust in numbers," according to historian of science Theodore Porter, satisfies a need to believe that descriptions of reality and decisions about it are fair and impartial.[17] But it is not just any form of quantification that can inspire this trust. "In fact," write Lorraine Daston and Peter Galison, in their history of objectivity, "the history of mathematical modeling is strewn with appeals to personal intuitions and metaphysical beliefs" so that "only when quantification is invoked to suppress some aspect of the self—for example, its judgments by means of inference statistics—does the appeal to numbers become a call to objectivity."[18] This, of course, is the way that quantification has been invoked in basketball analytics.

As a specific form of quantification, statistics, explains Chunglin Kwa, "approaches the chaos of individual cases with the aim of extracting a meaningful form of equivalence. Individuals who do not fit the mold are excluded, identified as problems, or made equivalent to one another, at least in certain respects." In this way, Kwa concludes, "the quantitative basis of statistics and its standardized methods inspire confidence in outsiders and offer an alternative to depending on scientists' personal opinions."[19] This would explain why inferential statistics has been, beginning with Dean Oliver, the dominant method by which basketball analytics has aimed and claimed to be able to shear subjective belief away from a bedrock of facts about basketball play.

"We present," declare Baker and Shea, "sports analytics as the objective and efficient counterpart to live scouting and evaluation. Where traditional methods suffer, modern algorithms excel. Analytics will measure a player's production ignorant of how ugly he looks doing it."[20] I know of no basketball analyst who claims that numbers, per se, guarantee objectivity. But all claim that if you formulate appropriate questions on the basis of empirical observation, then properly produced and processed quantitative data will give you objective answers. Though basketball analytics relies on computational power and statistical methods unknown during the Enlightenment, it inherits from Enlightenment statistical science the assumption that, given a large enough set of quantitative data and rational principles for how to interpret it, the numbers can overcome subjective bias and yield a more objective model of reality and thereby remove obscurity, reveal hidden patterns, and discover facts.

#21. Efficiency

However, with the exception of a few scholars, mostly mathematicians, most advocates and practitioners of basketball analytics do not solely support their work with a rhetoric of objectivity pursued for its own sake. Rather, objectivity and the pursuit of truth are the basis upon which to reach further ends, which confer value upon the application of scientific methods and quantification to basketball play. And so, in the culture of moving dots, the rhetoric of objectivity comes to be supplemented by what I call the three rhetorics of value: efficiency, control, and winning.

I already noted that Shea and Baker claimed that basketball analytics offers not only objective but "efficient" tools and strategies for building winning teams. A new sports analytics textbook justifies the importance of its subject matter by noting that "every organization would benefit from executing their business with efficiency, and sport organizations are no exception." "Due to the saturated market," its authors continue, "it is especially important for sport organizations to function with maximum efficiency" and doing so requires the "'extensive use of data, statistical and quantitative analysis, explanatory and predictive models, and fact based management to derive decisions and actions.'"[21] And another argues that "statistical models are essential" to "efficiently extracting relevant information about measurements and their relationships."[22]

In the case of basketball in particular, efficiency is not only what analytics promises those making financial decisions; it has also literally become synonymous with winning basketball play on the court. "Efficiency," you may recall, is a measurement of how many points teams score per possession. Given an equal number of possessions, as occurs in a basketball game, superior efficiency means, simply, winning. "We believe," Shea and Baker state—well, efficiently—"efficient players make for efficient teams, and efficient teams win."[23] And while at that time they could only promise to refine their efficiency diagnostics with optical tracking data that was then just debuting in the NBA, Shea followed up with a second book, *Basketball Analytics: Spatial Tracking*, in which he devoted an entire chapter to efficiency.[24]

So the science of moving dots promises to maximize the efficiency of analysis, financial investments, and possessions. But that is not all. For the cutting edge of the science of moving dots promises to maximize the efficiency of the basketball body. In the rhetoric accompanying the use of biometrical methods and devices to maximize the performance of athletes, efficiency too appears as the watchword. And even where the word efficiency is not used, tropes of improvement and of maximizing outputs from constant inputs appear frequently.

According to Dr. Marcus Elliott, the founder of biometrics consulting firm Peak Performance Project, "the idea of trying perfect athletes in the NBA," he says, "[is] the biggest sort of imperfect market that there is in basketball still," which means, following the underlying lesson of moneyball, using superior analytics to gain an advantage on competitors and exploit that inefficiency. As for the downsides, Elliott pauses: "can you use it too say someone's not trying hard enough? I guess, but," he answers his own rhetorical question with another rhetorical question: "is that a bad thing?"[25] I guess not. Thus Andy Glockner describes the process of "chasing perfection" with the aid of analytics as one in which "it's up to the players—and their teams—to develop and utilize their strengths while diminishing and masking their weaknesses. . . . The concept of players improving," he concludes, "is as old as sport itself, but the current era of Big Data analytics the NBA finds itself in is transforming that process more quickly and aggressively than anything we have seen before."[26]

As a concept, "efficiency" derives from the scientific study of mechanical systems in the late Enlightenment. Devised by engineers and physicists to relate a machine's outputs to its inputs used, measures of efficiency helped drive improvements in industrial technology. But the concept migrated far beyond the mechanical domains and purposes in which it originated. Thus, during the American Progressive Era (from around 1880–1920), when basketball (as I will show in chapters 4 and 5) was being forged in the crucible of muscular Christianity—the rise of sports, and the rationalization of physical education and play—the term efficiency began to be applied, in a wide-ranging way, to human beings, most famously as a measure of worker productivity in the industrial workplace, as in Frederick Taylor's principles of scientific management. Such principles, and the ideal of efficiency in particular, seemed to satisfy the Protestant moral imperative to produce more while using less.

However, in a wide-ranging study of these various applications of the concept, Jennifer Karns Alexander shows that efficiency, "even in its technical form, was a tool of control and not a mere technical measurement, disciplinary at its inception and increasingly political after it had reached conceptual maturity. As a measurement, it has an apparently objective form, but its history is as a tool designed to make the natural and human worlds conform to the way in which they are intellectually understood."[27] Consider that to analyze mechanical efficiency, inputs and outputs must be measured in the same units or in units that are mathematically convertible to one another. But what happens when the machines are connected to human bodies?

Or what happens when, through the metaphor so pervasive in the culture of moving dots, the machines are human basketball-playing bodies? Then, to say the least, the calculations grow more complex and the implications more disturbing. The "human inputs" must be reduced to those components that are amenable to quantification in terms of whatever units are being used to measure outputs. For managers efficiency "offered human mastery, through techniques of surveillance and discipline and through accounting principles to track the use and transformation of materials." But it also meant mastery of other people, who were reduced "the stable and balanced ingredients that managers manipulated in pursuit of growth" so that "efficiency" not only "meant mastery; it also meant being mastered."[28] After all, the biometric device manufacturer Catapult is only the latest in a long line of quantifiers to claim that "what you can measure, you can manage."[29]

#22. Control

Which leads me to the rhetoric of control. Enlightenment thinkers believed that the objective use of reason would allow for a deeper understanding of the hidden but regular laws they believed governed the nature and that this understanding would provide the basis for extrapolating from those laws to predict and so control the course of natural events. Their belief in the ability to do so formed a cornerstone of their rhetoric that Enlightenment concepts, practices, and institutions would enhance human freedom and lead to progress. And key to that belief was the development of the mathematical theory of probability.

Applying this theory to data accumulated through empirical observation would allow for a quantified measure of the likelihood of future events and this, in turn, would allow human beings to manage risk. Whether in finance, insurance, navigation, agriculture, astronomy, meteorology, or medicine, Enlightenment thinkers employed quantitative methods to measure uncertainty, manage risk, minimize loss, and maximize the return on investments. Similarly, and in fact using concepts and methods inherited directly from their Enlightenment predecessors, basketball analysts, and sports analysts, more generally, present their work as a predictive, risk management tool, to borrow the phrase of philosopher Ian Hacking, for "the taming of chance."[30]

Risk appears in sports in many forms, of course. Owners assume financial risks, general managers take risks in making personnel decisions, coaches assume risks in making tactical decisions, and athletes face not only the obvious risk of injury but also the risk of failure that comes with nearly everything they attempt in competition. Every jump shot is, in a sense, a bet laid down by a player. Sports analytics presents its objective, data-driven knowledge as a tool to help all these parties rationally quantify these risks and thereby make decisions that will minimize them. Ben Alamar offers a lucid summary of the "numerous new metrics in a variety of sports that are helping decision makers reduce uncertainty around their evaluation of players and teams" and illustrates the point with a schematic graph displaying "risk" on the y-axis and "information" on the x-axis. As the plot descends from the upper-left corner to the lower right we see that "performance data" provides the most information and the lowest risk.[31]

Rajiv Maheswaran puts this quite concretely in his TED Talk when—glossing a bubble chart representing the shooting tendencies of all 450 NBA players, he explains that "it's really important to know if the forty-seven—[he means the 47 percent shooter]—that you're considering giving 100 million dollars to is a good shooter who takes bad shots or a bad shooter who takes good shots." For winning the athletic and economic competition that is professional basketball today requires teams to minimize risk and maximize the efficiency of bodies, possessions, and financial investments.

But the promised benefit of risk management extends beyond those directly participating in the production of basketball play. Fans in fantasy basketball leagues "draft" teams of players to compete against other fans' teams in a variety of statistical categories, and the major internet venues that host such fantasy competitions provide users with fairly extensive analytics to help fantasy owners manage the risks entailed in decisions about which players to draft, trade, waive, or play on a given night. For that matter, in the less tangible domain of affective investment, analytics may well lead some fans to hedge the emotional risk of rooting for a team. In all these areas, basketball insiders and fans, are, in fact, simply following the long-standing lead of professional gamblers, who have long used quantitative data and probability theory to minimize risk and maximize the return on their bets. Indeed, the emergence of probability theory in the Enlightenment was originally spurred by just such needs among gamblers. And, in the wake of a May 2018 United States Supreme Court decision striking down a federal ban on sports gambling, it seems likely that the powerful, historic nexus between gambling, quantification, and sports will only tighten.[32]

#23. Winning

Because, ultimately, it is about winning, right? "This book," writes Thomas Miller, director of the Predictive Analytics center at Northwestern University, in his sports analytics textbook, "is about building winning teams and successful sports businesses. Winning and success are more likely when decisions are guided by data and models. Sports analytics is a source of competitive advantage."[33] Michael Lewis's best-selling book, *Moneyball*, which introduced baseball analytics to a broad audience, was subtitled "the art of winning an unfair game," which referred not only to the game on the field but to the competition among owners in the labor market for baseball talent. And Ben Alamar asserts that "having access to information that competitors do not has a long history of providing teams and businesses with advantage" so that "understanding the components of an analytics program will help managers maximize the competitive advantage they can gain from their analytic investment."[34] Dean Oliver, the "father" of basketball analytics began his work "with the simple premise that a winning team is the goal of all the methods [he] developed."[35] Even when the methods are pitched to fans, part of the pitch involves winning debates with friends, winning fantasy sports leagues, or winning bets.[36] According to Maria Nibali, a sport scientist and consultant in the sport analytics industry, greater reliance on quantification and computational technology yields greater insights and greater insights yield exponentially greater competitive advantage.[37]

Unlike with the rhetorics of objectivity, efficiency, and control, there is no rhetoric of winning, per se, to be found in Enlightenment thought, so we have to think a bit more broadly about winning and competition to trace the contemporary rhetoric of winning in basketball analytics back to that period. However, related notions of opponency, competition, and mastery are found in Enlightenment notions of human reason dominating nature, fate, and chance. And what is the Enlightenment's promise of perfecting the human condition if not an assurance of the ultimate victory? More specifically, the understanding of business as a series of decisions made by entrepreneurs within a competitive marketplace—as implied by basketball analytics in describing the competitive advantage for economic decision makers able to use information to exploit so-called "market inefficiencies"—is adapted from the influential Enlightenment political economist Adam Smith. Smith's idea that the drive to win in this competition fuels growth of all kinds— economic, scientific, technological—was a vital strand in the Enlightenment's belief in human progress through the use of reason.[38]

In Glockner's account of basketball analytics, NBA franchises are engaged in a "high-stakes game" of "chasing perfection." In this game the drive to win fuels the need to acquire more information; information about the past and present that is unavailable to competitors and that franchises (owners, general managers, coaches, and players) can use to minimize the risk of loss and maximize the productive efficiency of their decisions. Already in 2005, Daryl Morey joined the two meanings of efficiency by explaining to a *Sports Illustrated* reporter that the aim of analytics is "to generate wins for less dollars" by maximizing the efficiency of both possessions and financial investments.[39] And, as in Smith's economic theory, though for every winner there must be, in the short run, a loser, in the long run the rising tide lifts all boats as NBA Commissioner Adam Silver attested to an interviewer from the Wharton School of Business in 2017.[40]

#24. Credibility

"In school," remembers Cole Nussbaumer Knaflic, "we learn a lot about language and math. On the language side, we learn how to put words together into sentences and into stories. With math, we learn to make sense of numbers. But it's rare that these two sides are paired: no one teaches us how to tell stories with numbers." As a result we are "poorly prepared for an important task that is increasingly in demand. Technology has enabled us to amass greater and greater amounts of data and there is an accompanying growing desire to make sense out of all of this data. Being able to visualize data and tell stories with it is key to turning it into information that can be used to drive better decision making."[41] As even my own account of basketball analytics has implicitly demonstrated, a salient and often striking feature of basketball analytics—regardless of the particular rhetoric involved—is the visual display of information that accompanies verbal explanation and argument. Charts, graphs, tables, sometimes interactive, sometimes animated appear in most blog posts, journalistic reports, academic essays, and books describing analytics, proposing new methods or metrics, or applying existing measures to current situations.[42]

But as ubiquitous as these visual aids are in the literature, it is as striking that there is, with few exceptions, very little accompanying public reflection upon, let alone rhetorical justification for, their use. Though authors usually explain to readers how to interpret the visual displays, they very rarely pause to explain why one particular type of visual display was chosen over another, let alone what is gained or lost, illuminated or obscured by the final choice. Which is to say that the subjective element—the choice of this over that, for reasons having to do with clarity or persuasion or artistic taste or some combination of the three—tends to be obscured as well. The visual aids appear therefore as inevitable and faithful illustrations, translations, or representations of the facts discovered through analytics.

The Enlightenment did not invent the use of visual displays of information in scientific contexts, and it is certainly the case that developments in digital technologies since that time have vastly enhanced the ease with which data visualization can be carried out and shared publicly. However, as Edward Tufte's striking histories of visual explanation show, such efforts were important to scientists in that era, and the Enlightenment did, as its very name suggests, acquire a kind of monopoly on the metaphorical equation of clear vision with true knowledge and objectivity.[43]

Basketball analytics shares this penchant for visual metaphors in its rhetorics: muddy things are cleared, hidden things are revealed, blurry things come into focus, obscure things are illuminated, closed eyes are opened. With that in mind, perhaps the ubiquity of visual displays of information serves also to reinforce concretely the link—forged so tightly in the Enlightenment—between sight and truth.[44]

This apparent objectivity of visual accompaniments helps explain why they can play such a large role in basketball analytics despite the more general analytical supposition that our eyes deceive and that numbers do their good work precisely by offering a corrective alternative to vision. In this, data visualizations may be, in a sense, the unassailable keep for objectivity and the authority it carries. Where our senses can play tricks on us, our emotions and cognitive biases lead us into error and poor judgment; where even the language of basketball analytics, rife—like all language—with metaphor and ambiguity and the subjective expressions of personal style can mislead, the chart, the graph, the table, the infographic appears to offer unmediated access to the naked objectivity of quantification.

See for yourself.

Better yet, as with some of the interactive visual accompaniments on many online analytics websites or the software downloads accompanying textbooks: do it yourself. Look at or download the data, filter and sort by different criteria. The proof of the power of numbers, awesome but ultimately benign, is that you'll get the same results. After all, the reproducibility of experiments and so the independent verification of results is the bedrock of the scientific method. But what you may be likely to forget is that the freedom of your ostensibly independent inquiry is constrained by assumptions embedded in the tools you are using. These visual displays, I would argue, may be the most powerful and efficient of the rhetorics deployed by basketball analytics, but only so long as they maintain their aura of objectivity and do not reveal too much about their nature as visual narratives crafted by individuals with, among other subjective biases, preferences in matters of taste.

But of course visual narratives are exactly that: stories told in images by human beings with limiting subjective biases. "Data," after all, "can be boring," writes Nathan Yau. He therefore argues that data visualization illuminates the *stories* hidden in the data and in that way brings us closer to the zones of "real life" frozen in the numbers.[45] Meanwhile, in her book *Beautiful Data*, a history of "vision and reason since 1945," Orit Halpern emphasizes that the ways we observe and analyze the world are shaped by our own collective histories and choices and have culminated, she argues, in a "new aesthetic and practice of truth; a valorization of analysis and pattern seeking" that she calls "communicative objectivity."[46] Communicative objectivity is deeply intertwined with cybernetics, digital technologies, and the accumulation of data. Indeed Halpern describes it elsewhere as a "radical shift in attitudes to recording and displaying information that produced new forms of observation, rationality, and economy based on the management of data."[47]

I see the visual displays of basketball analytics as manifestations of this "new aesthetic and practice of truth." But if they are, then they may also be the most vulnerable rhetorical device of basketball analytics. The very fact that the visual rhetoric of credibility appears as the most objective cultural accompaniment of the science of moving dots and that it therefore bears the burden of vouchsafing the legitimacy of all the concepts, methods, technologies, and facts comprising basketball analytics also means that it is the one whose rhetorical nature must never be revealed, lest the legitimacy of the entire edifice it accompanies be called into question.

#25. Progress

In just the last decade the first few "histories" of quantitative thinking in basketball have begun to appear. Though they are so avowedly cursory that I doubt even their authors would call them "histories." Instead they show up in the footnotes or in sidebars, in flashback paragraphs, or in prefaces and introductory chapters to works by authors whose primary focus lies elsewhere: on new methods, key figures in analytics, or new technologies. However scanty and unintentional they may be, though, they nonetheless constitute basketball analytics' "autobiography," such as it is; its own initial attempts to tell us of its past.[48]

Surveying these histories, as well as more informal historically oriented conversations about analytics in basketball culture, reminds me of the famous image from the cover of the *New Yorker* from May 29, 1976. You've probably seen it, or at least a parody of it, even if you didn't know that's what you were looking at. It's called *The View of the World from 9th Avenue*, rendered in mixed media on paper by artist Saul Steinberg.

Perched high above 9th Avenue, we look down and west. The people on the street directly below us are small, to be sure, but moving limbs are discernible. The shapes and sizes of automobiles are distinguishable from one another, and building windows and storefronts are rendered in detail. But by the time our vision moves halfway up the image, or just one block west to 10th Avenue, buildings are faint shaded-in outlines, cars just blobs, and the people nothing more than thin vertical hash marks. Continuing west (and now two-thirds of the way up the image), we reach and cross the Hudson river. "Jersey" is a thin horizontal strip of brownish orange. Beyond it lies a rectangle (smaller than the two square blocks of New York City in the foreground) representing the rest of the United States. Apart from a handful of geological formations, it is entirely flat, and apart from a few place names (Washington DC, Kansas City, Chicago, Nebraska, Texas, Utah, Las Vegas, and Los Angeles), it is blank. Then, beyond Los Angeles lies the rest of the world, almost an afterthought sketched into the upper quarter of the image: a white strip labeled "Pacific Ocean," and then three thin low humps labeled from left to right: "China," "Japan," "Russia."

These protohistories of basketball analytics, despite some variations, share a quality with Steinberg's picture. Just as the detail in the Steinberg's picture diminishes absurdly rapidly the further away we go from the viewer's perspective on 9th Avenue, so also in these short histories, the level of detail diminishes absurdly rapidly the further away we go from the narrator's perspective in the present of basketball analytics. In fact, you can imagine using Steinberg's image as a way to map, as it were, the terrain of basketball history as imagined within the culture of moving dots. The cityscape immediately below us appears rife with the landmarks of Big Data Basketball, powered by optical tracking and biometric technologies. Just a block away, already growing somewhat fuzzy, are the foundational conceptual innovations of

Dean Oliver. Beyond the Hudson, where Steinberg represents a few famous landmarks of the United States, we might plot a few of the statistical monuments of NBA history prior to the advent of analytics: Wilt Chamberlain's one hundred-point game and his fifty point-per-game season (1961–62), Oscar Robertson's triple-double over his first five seasons (1960–65), Bill Russell's eleven championships in his thirteen seasons (1956–69). But beyond that, the first six or seven decades of basketball history appear as undifferentiated landmasses: "China," "Japan," "Russia."

I don't want to make too much of this. None of the authors whose work I drew upon to conjure that image set out to or claimed to be writing a history of quantitative thinking in basketball. All are focused on different aspects of the contemporary scene and provide what history they provide only as an introduction or backdrop to the figures, events, or methods that are their primary focus. So perhaps it is unreasonable to expect that their historical imagination would look much different than this. But even this tells us something about the importance accorded to historical thought in basketball analytics, so that, intentions and expectations aside, I maintain that my image fairly conveys the relative emphasis given to various periods, figures, and events from basketball's past in these few, and admittedly, mostly cursory, historical accounts of basketball analytics that exist.

Yet, as we shall see over the next several chapters, the history of quantification in basketball prior to the formation of the NBA is quite a bit richer and more varied than the historical imagination of basketball analytics might have it. With that in mind, these quasi-historical texts resemble the myths of the culture of basketball that I analyzed in my book *Ball Don't Lie!*. I do not mean to say they are false. Most include some useful factual information. But most also include factual errors. And all involve distortions of the sort I tried to evoke with my comparison to Steinberg's cover. However, though they therefore may not tell us much about the history of quantification, if we approach them as myths they do tell us something about the underlying beliefs and values held by those purveying them.

The first thing that stands out when viewing these texts from that perspective, as myths, is that they are deeply concerned with the present and with a view of the past as existing in service to and function of the needs of the present. That much might be apparent just from the fact that these historical sketches serve just that role in the works in which they appear. The past appears only insofar as the present has either borrowed from it or broken sharply with it so as to improve it.

It is a narrative of progress, in other words, which we should expect as part of its Enlightenment legacy. And, though my choice of Steinberg's image as a metaphor for their historical imagination and my positioning the texts as expressive of a historical imagination necessarily precludes this, we may suppose that as the past exists as precursor for the present, so the present exists as precursor for what these histories are really interested in: the future; for what lies, as it were, behind the viewer's perspective.

In that orientation, basketball analytics doubles down on the claim to relevance it has already staked. After all, isn't the value of basketball analytics that it can sift through the noisy, inchoate data of the past and use the results to forecast the likelihood of—and even empower us to steer closer to—different futures? Isn't that how it equips us to make better decisions in the present? I'm pointing out that the way in which basketball analytics appears to look at its own past (and to view the act of looking at the past) mirrors the way that the statistical methods comprising it look at past basketball performance.

But in pointing this out I am also pointing out the evident bias that attends and distorts basketball analytics' view of the past. There is irony in this, since the science of moving dots, as we have seen, claims superior objectivity about the relationship of the past to the present and future. Steinberg's own drawing suggests a similar kind of irony by depicting the New Yorker's evidently biased and distorted view as a map, as though the New Yorker didn't realize that his view was just that: his view, rather than objective reality.

The joke then isn't just that the New Yorker doesn't know what's beyond the Hudson River, it's that he doesn't know he doesn't know it. Or that he doesn't care. Similarly, the joke isn't just that the science of moving dots doesn't know the past, it's that it doesn't know that it doesn't know it, or that it doesn't care. Either way, in both cases, the distorted views tell us little about what is viewed but a great deal about the biases of the viewer.

Of course, maps are themselves never neutral instruments for representing reality. Rather they reflect the biases of their makers and of the cultures to which they belong. Moreover, as representations, they have also served the purpose of aiding one peoples' control over the world, including over other peoples. All the more reason to beware of the unavowed—perhaps even unintended—aims of the science of moving dots' historical map of the sport's past.

Interlude—Numbers

#26. Yellow Castle Stadium

We never watched baseball growing up. My father hated it. When, on the weekend, a baseball game would appear on our TV, he would comment with disgust on the out-of-shape pitcher, wad of tobacco bulging in his cheek, gut drooping over his waistband. What the hell kind of sport revolves around players—the pitchers and sluggers he was referring to—who are overweight and slothful? Moreover, the leisurely pace of the game drove him mad with impatient anger, as though with each listless kick of the dirt, the players were burying my father alive.

So we never played catch in the yard, which was mostly fine by me given my own cowardly fear of getting hit by a pitch or a line drive.

But this was America's game, and in my neighborhood of American boys, baseball was king and summer days often included impromptu games in the Greenway down at the bottom of our hill, a half-mile-long narrow rectangle of grass dotted with newly planted trees and bisected by a drainage culvert.

One bright day I arrived to find the boys huddled around a mound of sand that had mysteriously appeared, piled near the unmarked edges of our outfield. One of the older boys, a sixth grader named Mark Currie, was laying out a plan. We would create a home run fence out of sand castles and have a great day. We sprinted home for pails and shovels and set to work, supervised by Mark and the other older boys.

I trotted back and forth between the sand pile and the growing curve of sand castles we'd already built. Working hard, the sun warm against the back of my neck, I was squatting with my pail and shovel when a breeze tilted the bright yellow head of a dandelion into my castle, denting the side I'd just perfectly smoothed. Frustrated, I plucked it out of the ground, stood up, flicking the bloom off with my thumb, and crowed loudly, "Momma had a baby and its head popped off!" Swelling with self-satisfaction at having, for once, said the thing that everybody said, and at the right time, I didn't notice that the dandelion crown had landed on the top of my castle.

But Mark Currie, with his blonde hair gleaming white in the early summer sun, noticed. "Everybody," he commanded, "get as many dandelions as you can and cover the tops of your castles!" We scattered like cats, and in minutes, even as new castles continued to take shape, a curving yellow line marked the home run fence of what Mark dubbed, solemnly, "Yellow Castle Stadium."

I went 0 for 4 at the plate that day and badly misjudged—distracted and afraid—one of two towering fly balls hit in my direction in right field so that I had to chase it, alone, as the screams of the other boys behind me spurred me to a panicked sprint. (The other one Mark raced heroically over from center to catch.)

Still, what a great name! And what a great day! To have done a thing like that.

My excitement, however, turned to mumbled embarrassment as I struggled to convey to my father the magnificence of Yellow Castle Stadium and of Mark Currie.

For starters, I had to do it in Spanish. At family dinners, we had to speak in Spanish or else pay a fine into a soldier-shaped piggy bank named "Crispín" that stood in the center of the table, a dead smile frozen on his face.

Nobody asked, but I tentatively volunteered a report on my day. "*Estuve en el Greenway*"—panicked I looked up to see if that proper name would entail a fine, but it did not—"*con los chicos del barrio. Ibamos a jugar al*"—careful to make sure this came out sounding fully Spanish—"*beisbol, cuando tuvimos la idea de hacer castillos de arena y decorarlos con*"—I didn't know the word for dandelion, so I hesitated—"*flores . . . amarillas . . .*" I added, kind of proud at having thought of a way to convey the brilliant yellowness of

Yellow Castle Stadium even without knowing the word for dandelion. "*Y fue may divertido y*"—I glance at my mother—"*y bonito.*"

"*Que barbaridad!*" my father exclaimed, "*A quien se le habrá ocurrido esa idiotez?*"

The answer was Mark Currie. But I had no answer for the question he was really asking: "What the hell have I done with my Spanish life, and what is this American abomination—fruit of my very loins—taking shape and rising before me?"

"*Tempus fugit.*" He told me, not paying a fine into Crispín even though that wasn't Spanish. "*El tiempo vuela, hijo; vale mucho, y hay que procurar vigilar bien como lo gastas.*" Time flies. I was supposed to capture it, to hoard it. But I couldn't even catch a fly ball. How was I supposed to catch time?

He didn't get it and by the time he was done not getting it, neither did I.

So, most days, after a weekend day spent at the Greenway, or at a friend's house, baseball meant to me a clutch in my chest where the comforting Americanness of playing catch with my (imaginary) American Dad (who would have in turn played catch with his American Dad) was supposed to be.

#27. Juggling Numbers

Let me teach you to count.

First, understand that you were born with what psychologists call a "number sense." That's good. When you were just a few days old, you could already recognize and distinguish between collections of two and three items. And before you turned one, you knew, even if you couldn't say so, that one plus one is two and two minus one is one.[1] You still couldn't count, but that's a good start.

The morning that you clambered onto the school bus for your first day of kindergarten, you probably saw an empty seat, maybe more than one. Whether you thought it or not, you knew then that relative to the number of children there were more seats: that's what mathematicians call *relative number sense.*[2] Also good, but also not yet counting, since you still didn't know exactly how many children or seats there were. You just knew that there were "more," or "less," or "the same" amount of one relative to the other.

To get beyond relative to *absolute* number, instead of comparing two concrete collections of objects like seats and children, you compare one collection of objects to a model collection, which typifies a possible collection. The fingers on your hand could be a model collection symbolizing the concept "five."[3] But notice now that once you've got that, you don't really even need the model collection anymore. You can just use the word: "five." Now you've got a *cardinal* number and you're almost there.

Next, just arrange those cardinal number words "in an ordered sequence, which progresses in the sense of growing magnitude." That's a "number system" and with that you have all you need to begin to count. Just assign to every object or event in your collection a number, in ordered succession, from your number system.[4] LeBron James takes a shot: assign it the number one. A minute later, LeBron James takes another shot: assign it the next number in the sequence: two.

Tobias Dantzig explains that in your fingers you possess "a device which permits [you] to pass imperceptibly from cardinal to ordinal number. Should [you] want to indicate that a certain collection contains four objects [you] will raise or turn down four fingers simultaneously." That is the finger as cardinal number. "Should [you] want to count the same collection [you] will raise or turn down these fingers in succession." That is the ordinal number.[5] From this very concrete observation of an action you might once have used to determine, or to respond to a question about your age, Dantzig offers this expansive conclusion: "Without our fingers the development of number, and consequently that of the exact sciences, to which we owe our material and intellectual progress, would have been hopelessly dwarfed."[6]

Be that as it may, there are things we can't do with our fingers—since we have only ten of them. But let's say that instead of representing a LeBron James field goal attempt with a finger, we represent it with a notch on a stick, a pebble or a shell on a board, or a bead on a wire. Now we can use a larger notch, pebble or shell, or bead to represent a collection of, say, ten smaller notches, pebbles or shells, or beads. (These objects, marks, or actions, by the way, are the source for many of our counting words: "calculate" from the word for pebble, "tally" and "score"—as in William Chase scored the first basket in basketball history—and "compute" come from words for "cutting," as in a notch in a stick.)

Anyway, now that you can count, you just need something to count. You might start with something that matters to you—something that counts. David Hand identifies the social situation that appears to have first led human beings to such discoveries: "Transactions could be recorded by putting the tokens in a closed clay shell. This could be transferred from place to place and broken open to reveal the number. Extending this yet further, a representation of the contents could be scratched on the outside of the shell, and this is the origin of the Sumerian numerals, which appear to be the oldest written form of numbers." Once you've got this, Hand concludes, "numbers have become entities in their own right" so that we can "juggle with the numbers themselves." [7]

Hand is not the first to observe that these early but fundamental advances in quantification were driven by the practical needs of those engaged in trade and commerce. They were seeking knowledge, to be sure, but not so much to deepen their understanding of the world for its own sake as to maximize their economic advantage, which may be why juggling with numbers, for Americans of the nineteenth century, was part of what made them American. To juggle with numbers was to shed the antiquated disdain—shared both by Old World aristocrats and New World Puritans—for the commercial vulgarity of counting and instead to embrace the progress, prosperity, and power promised by arithmetic.

We counted ourselves, we counted our money, we counted our blessings, we counted our runs in baseball and, before long, we'd be counting our buckets in basketball.[8]

The role played by counting in forging an emerging sense of American identity in turn sheds light on a moment that occurs about a half hour into Ken Burns's documentary *Baseball*, as well as on the effect it had on me. The narrator introduces us to Henry Chadwick, inventor of the baseball box score (about whom more in the next chapter), explaining that he "began keeping comparative statistics so that he could compare one player's performance against another." Then, as the camera zooms in on a sepia-toned photo of Chadwick, we hear a different voice: "Because we've been playing it fundamentally the same way for so long, the way that we can find the benchmarks that cross generations and cross decades is to be able to use these statistics as . . . a means by which we can connect to the permanence of this thing." Sports statistics as time travel: it is not only fans who see it that way. One of the first and most influential professional philosophers to turn his attention to sport, Paul Weiss, made a similar claim for the numbers in his landmark treatise: *Sport: A Philosophic Inquiry.*[9] But also sports statistics as the obliteration of time and change, since it connects us to "the permanence"—the putative unchanging, fixed essence "of this thing."

The film cuts to the speaker, Daniel Okrent, a forty-six-year-old editor so esteemed that he would, in 2003, become the *New York Times* first public editor. But despite his graying hair, Daniel Okrent looks boyish. Perhaps I should not be surprised. After all, he is the man who at the age of thirty-one, in 1979, invented Rotisserie League Baseball, the first and still best-known form of fantasy baseball, in which participants—called "owners"—assemble "teams" whose virtual contests are decided by the day-to-day statistical performance of the players they've "drafted."

As the camera frames him tightly, his sensitive eyes, behind the protection of his owlish glasses, searching for contact with his interlocutor—Daniel Okrent explores the heart of his desire for numbers: "I can make that comparison with my father who could have made it with his father on that common language of statistics."[10] He is not the first to speak of numbers as a kind of universal tongue, and usually I find myself cynically irritated by such proclamations.

But in this moment I was touched and understood, for that is exactly how I felt. Across the abysses—land-mined with misunderstanding and explosive resentment—that separated my Spanish scientist father from the American basketball-playing boy that I felt myself to be, "that common language of statistics" extended itself like a bridge. And, as my father and I juggled my numbers together across the kitchen table, I could almost feel what generations of American boys felt as they and their fathers tossed the horsehide back and forth in graceful arcs as the sun set on another honest day's work in the nation's heartland.

3

Counting, America's Game

#28. Counting America's Game

Basketball learned to count from baseball, which in the late nineteenth century first pioneered that quantifying snapshot of sport known as the "box score" and then, more significantly, led the way again a century later by applying advanced statistical methods to sift the wheat of meaningful patterns from the chaff of superstitious noise in one hundred years of baseball numbers. And most of us first learned all this from Michael Lewis's best-selling 2003 book *Moneyball*, later made into a 2011 Oscar-nominated Columbia Pictures feature film starring Brad Pitt in the role of maverick Oakland Athletics manager Billy Beane.[1]

Moneyball, Lewis explained, began with a question: "How did one of the poorest teams in baseball, the Oakland Athletics, win so many games?" In the quest for an answer he discovered a story he fell in love with and felt compelled to write: "concerning a small group of undervalued professional baseball players and executives, many of whom had been rejected as unfit for the big leagues, who had turned themselves into one of the most successful franchises in Major League Baseball."

But this story about a baseball team, he confesses with some surprise, was also at the center of a larger story: "about the possibilities—and the limits—of reason in human affairs. Baseball . . . was an example of how an unscientific culture responds, or fails to respond, to the scientific method."[2] In this way *Moneyball* evokes memories of my own upbringing, my family, my father, where the turmoil caused in his heart and home by the "possibilities—and the limits—of reason in human affairs" caused sometimes violent collisions between "an unscientific culture" and "the scientific method." In those collisions there was nothing I'd want more than to make my father smile, and there was no surer way to do that than to be scientific.

I make this personal aside here, though I have left the details for the interludes and coda, because the emotional investments that the book and especially the movie can trigger are an important part of how the ideas it depicts came to be so influential. That is, though one might presume that Lewis's description of rational methods of analyzing baseball play would persuade because of their apparently objective superiority, the emotional—or irrational, if you will—undercurrents are an important part of how we come to desire quantification, both as the expression of reason par excellence and as a safeguard against the risks of loss entailed by misappraising value.

Even now, as I watch the movie adaptation of *Moneyball*, I'm looking at Brad Pitt's face (at this point, he's not even Billy Beane yet in my mind) and feeling the desire stir in me to make my father smile.

Is there anything better than making Brad Pitt smile? He's not happy now. He seems angry and fed up. But I can see in the muscles of his jaw the effort he's exerting to contain his emotions (because he's not a stereotypical bullying ex-jock with anger issues but rather a kind, sensitive, thoughtful guy; because he's reasonable). His eyes, as he looks around the room at the dimwitted men who can't understand him, are steady, his gaze straight and level as a ruler. He firmly but coolly makes his point.

A few hours later, he's sad. He sits alone in the dark on an airplane remembering how he passed up a baseball scholarship to Stanford University. Two decades earlier eighteen-year-old Brad had been selected, right out of high school, in the first round of the Major League Baseball draft, promised by scouts of the New York Mets that he was their superstar center fielder of the future. He was told that he had all the tools, that he was exceptional, a rare find, a sure thing. That future never materialized. Instead, he played less than 150 Major League games over a six-year below-average career for four different clubs.

His clear blue eyes have gone dark, quavering pools reflecting the past, a bygone fork in the road, a step he can never untake. Is there anything more heartbreaking than sad Brad Pitt? Sad Brad Pitt wonders, same as all of us: How good was I? And how can I know for sure? What if I had known then what I know now? What if I could have seen the future? What would I have done differently?

Back home, still alone, still in the dark, but now in his kitchen, a coffee cup in one hand, a scotch on the table, he's still brooding over the road not taken.

So, he wakes Jonah Hill, whom he has known for only a few hours, with a phone call, rousting him out of bed, out from under the portrait of Plato—pop culture's mascot for Team Reason, it seems—hanging above his headboard:

"Listen," he says, "Would you have drafted me in the first round? After I left, you looked me up on your computer. Would you have drafted me in the first round?"

"I did, yeah," answers Jonah, "you were a good player."

Brad's not having it. He wants the truth. He spits into the coffee cup. He is a man, an American man.

"Cut the crap, man," he sneers dismissively, then repeats, his voice rising insistently, "Would you have drafted me in the first round!?"

Jonah, standing in his Yale T-shirt—official jersey of Team Reason—hesitates before answering.

"I'd've taken you in the ninth round. No signing bonus."

Brad puts the coffee cup on the table and picks up the glass of scotch. The truth hurts.

Jonah concludes, "I imagine you would've passed and taken the scholarship."

"Yeahhh," Brad slurs, before taking a drink.

If that's the answer to his question, it's not as satisfying as Brad imagined it would be. But really, deep down, he already knew the answer. It just hurts to hear it confirmed by someone else—someone he already trusts to be objective. The final dying embers of Brad's irrational hope for a different answer—for a different past with its own different future, which is to say, for a different present, a different life than the one he is living—are snuffed out.

#29. The Unfair Game

Life is unfair.

But Brad Pitt's not crying about it. He's moving forward. He just wants to win the unfair game. And, because he's Brad Pitt, because he's sad, because it's unfair, because he's not crying about it, and because, like him, I wonder, how good I really was—how good I really am, I want him to win it, too. His quest to do so forms the human heart of the story that Lewis fell in love with; the story, remember, "about the possibilities—and the limits—of reason in human affairs."

Just before he hangs up the phone with Jonah Hill, Brad, who plays former real-life Oakland A's general manager Billy Beane, tells him, "Pack your bags. I just bought you from the Cleveland Indians." Hill plays fictional Peter Brand, a Yale-trained economist whose first job in baseball was working as an advisor to the Cleveland Indians (the character is loosely based on Paul DePodesta, the Harvard-trained economist who was Billy Beane's assistant in real life).

In their first meeting after Brand has joined Beane's staff, he explains to his new boss just how they will win the unfair game, by which he means the unfair game that the business of Major League Baseball has become: one in which rich teams (say the New York Yankees) outbid poorer teams (like the Oakland Athletics) for the best players. Standing before a whiteboard divided into rows and columns filled with numbers, he points to a table cell in the upper-left corner in which is written this equation.

$$\frac{\text{runs scored}^2}{\text{runs scored}^2 + \text{runs allowed}^2} = \text{Win\%}$$

"So, using this equation in the upper left right here, I'm projecting that we need to win at least 99 games in order to make it to the postseason. We need to score at least 814 runs in order to win those games and allow no more than 645 runs."

He pauses—the image of a computer spreadsheet fills our screen before giving way to an extreme close-up of indecipherable strings of letters, punctuation marks, and numbers—and Beane asks him "What's this?"

"This is the code that I've written for our year to year projections. This is building in all the intelligence that we have to project players. It's about getting things down to one number. Using stats the way we read them, we'll find value in players nobody else can see. People are overlooked," he continues, "for a variety of biased reasons and perceived flaws: age, appearance, personality. Bill James and mathematics cut straight through that."

Bill James plays a larger role in Lewis's book than in the movie. A graduate of Kansas in economics and English, James was also an obsessive baseball fan. As an early leader of a group of hobbyists who called themselves the Society for Advancement of Baseball Research (its acronym—SABR— became the name of the movement, Sabermetrics, that would become synonymous with advanced analytics in sports), James self-published a series of baseball abstracts in the 1970s whose audience gradually expanded from a cult following to a broad readership among fans and a handful of Major League Baseball insiders. In 2006 *Time* magazine named him one of the one hundred most influential people of the year. Including him in the category "Scientists and Thinkers," the accompanying profile asserted that his principles "infuse our thinking with a perspective that is objective rather than subjective. What James demands is that we take time to listen to what the game is telling us over and above what we are predisposed to believe."[3]

As we watch a montage of close-up shots of printed formulas, graphs, charts, player names, photos, and stats—many from the pages of James's baseball abstracts, Brand cuts to the bottom line: "Billy, of the 20,000 notable players for us to consider I believe there is a championship team of 25 people that we can afford because everyone else in baseball undervalues them."

This is what Brand meant when he said to Billy, back when they first met, "Baseball thinking is medieval." "Medieval," in the universe of *Moneyball* (as in the Enlightenment), means unscientific and inefficient. In an interview quoted in Lewis's book, Peter Brand's real-life counterpart, Paul DePodesta, described that "medieval" thinking this way: "There was, for starters, the tendency of everyone who actually played the game to generalize wildly from his own experience. People always thought their own experience was typical when it wasn't. There was also a tendency to be overly influenced by a guy's most recent performance: what he did last was not necessarily what he would do next. Thirdly—but not lastly—there was the bias toward what people saw with their own eyes, or thought they had seen. The human mind played tricks on itself when it relied exclusively on what it saw, and every trick it played was a financial opportunity for someone who saw through the illusion to the reality. There was a lot you couldn't see when you watched a baseball game."[4]

Sabermetrics promises to cast the bright light of science, objectivity, and reason on baseball and thus dispel the darkness of superstition, pseudo-knowledge, and subjective bias that blinds scouts, managers, and fans. In the book, the movie, and in real-life sports analytics, truth can only emerge from the rigorous use of the scientific method to pierce the deceptive veil of appearances to reveal the "hidden game," the inner workings of the sport. Only the scientific method can level the playing field, delivering to underdogs like Brad Pitt a competitive advantage over the stupid, tyrannical rich, who can afford the luxury of uncritically subscribing to the dogma of traditional wisdom and mystical intuition.

#30. The Desire of America

All the devices we have invented for extending our power to count beyond our ten fingers pale in comparison with the computer. The word "computer" comes from the Latin verb *computare* which means "to count, sum up, reckon together." *Computare*, in turn, comes from a verb meaning to prune, cut, strike, stamp, or score. Thus, though its wondrous powers can lead us to lose sight of the fact, a computer is, at bottom, a counting machine, a score-keeping device.[5] So it should come as no surprise that computers played an enormous role in the efforts of Sabermetricians.

In *Moneyball*, Lewis often makes DePodesta's computer into the grammatical subject of sentences and thereby into the apparently autonomous generator of the knowledge needed to win the unfair game. The computer "spits out names" and "serves up statistics," while old-time scouts consider that it "somehow challenge[s]" their authority.[6] In the film, the mesmerizing visceral pull of the digital screen is exploited as a metonym for disembodied, objective knowledge via numerous montages of, or scenes prominently featuring, computer screens and keyboards, programs seemingly running on their own, liberated from the messy interference of human beings with their passionately held biases, humming along as they spit out their parade of objective and so indisputable evaluations.

From the point of view of the "medieval" scouts, however, that very same computer is not the infallible source of knowledge but a blind alley and the most telling sign of what's wrong with Beane's methods. It's not the scouts who are irrational, but rather the numbers guys: they are the ones who have stopped thinking for themselves, who venerate the illuminated black screen of this box like medieval peasants bowing in awe before an eclipse. Against such obeisance, scouts tout the value of their experience, collective wisdom, and intuition when it comes to assessing the intangibles that make for big league success. A computer can't feel these things. A computer has no eyes to see. Nerds like Peter Brand and Bill James might know how to manipulate the stats, but baseball is more than just numbers, a truth they'd recognize if only they'd actually ever played the game. Instead they let their numbers blind them to the reality on the field that is staring them right in the eyes.

Running through the heart of this intersection of science and sport, then, a complicated epistemological war erupts over the terrain called "reality"; a war that reprises ancient battles over matter and spirit, what is tangible and what is intangible, sense perception and reason, emotion and logic. Each side advances its claim to reality by invoking now one, now another of these dichotomous terms in a complex, sometimes sloppy, high-stakes rhetorical dance of language.

"Field of Ignorance" and "The Enlightenment" are the titles Michael Lewis gives to the two chapters of *Moneyball* in which he chronicles this battle of the dawning of Sabermetrics out of the night of the dark ages, from the illuminating work of Bill James to the moment its warmth first kissed the cheek of Billy Beane. Beane and his aides will thus recapitulate the journey of scientific revolutionaries from centuries past—the journey, indeed, as science itself tells the story, of the human species—in order to win this battle against darkness and the unfair game over which it lords. They mistrust mystical intuition and even sense perception, accumulate relevant data then subject it to sophisticated statistical analysis and apply implacably objective, logical thinking to the results in order to make diagnostic, descriptive, and, above all, predictive inferences about what human beings—baseball players—will do. But we all know, and they all know—which is the point of the story—that seeing the truth doesn't make us believe in it, let alone act according to its guidelines.

That may be why the narrative structure of *Moneyball*, even as it emphasizes the impersonal power of computers, subtly overrides our resistance to that power by cementing our identification with the human being whose bidding they do. Two unresolved conflicts drive that narrative forward: first, the competition among franchises to acquire good players given a wide disparity in the financial resources available to do so; and second, the conflict in views among baseball decision makers about what is a good player. The story of Billy Beane and the Athletics emerges from and unfolds within these two conflicts: the team has far fewer resources than its competitors and, within the organization, Beane struggles to persuade his staff and employer that the traditional methods and criteria by which they have judged the goodness of baseball players are flawed, which is to say irrational and unscientific, not to mention economically inefficient.

But though it is driven by these conflicts, *Moneyball* doesn't actually begin there. Instead it opens with the story of Beane's own failed career, a career he never really wanted but was driven to pursue as a teenager by pro scouts whose irrational, unscientific, and baseless promises about his future come to emblematize the obstacles to resolving the two conflicts driving the book's narrative. In this way the quest to overcome these conflicts gets a human heart and a human face. It would become, in the movie, the face of Brad Pitt. It also accomplishes something even more fundamental. It stokes in us a desire as firmly rooted in the heart of most sports fans as any other: to see the underdog, unfairly kept down by circumstances over which he has no control, come out on top through dint of hard work and intelligence. The desire that sport, and life, be a meritocracy.

It is the desire of America.

Thus stirred, we consumers of *Moneyball* likely accept the invitation to suspend our team loyalties, our class affiliation, our worries about technology run amok, and our feelings about statistics long enough to want what Billy Beane wants: to win the "unfair game." So, yes, we want his team to succeed. But the seeds of desire that *Moneyball* plants into the soil of our hearts yield a more encompassing affective harvest. Because to desire Billy Beane's success is also, given the circumstances within which he must labor to desire the success—whether or not we understand them—of science, reason, and objectivity, of numbers and efficiency, and of the theories, methods, and technologies that will get him there. We want these things because Billy wants them, and we want what Billy wants.

Finally, though, we also want these things because *Moneyball* invites us to believe that these things are what we should want if we want fairness. And don't we all, especially in sports, especially in baseball, especially in America, want fairness? So if Billy Beane says we'll find fairness in a computer, then we'll be darned if we won't give the gizmo a whirl. After all, explains Michael Novak in his meditation on the joys of baseball, for we "Americans, nothing is real until it is counted."[7]

#31. Box Score Patricide

"Someone created the box score," Daryl Morey, perhaps the best-known figure in basketball analytics today, once declared, "and he should be shot."[8] In fact the first basketball box score appeared in the 1890s, well over a century before Morey delivered a death sentence for its creator. And what most people consider the first *baseball* box score appeared another half-century before *that*, on October 22, 1845, when the *New York Morning News* published what it—with a candid descriptive accuracy missing from the reporting of much contemporary sports statistics—called an "*abstract*" of a match held the day before between a baseball club from New York and one from Brooklyn.[9]

The simple table had three columns: players, runs, and "hands out." The rows were filled in with the names of each player, the number of runs that player had scored, and the number of times that player had been put out. What baseball historians have found significant about that table is that even as an abstract it is more suited to capture the significant events of a cricket match than of a baseball game. In cricket, as Alan Schwarz, author of *The Numbers Game: Baseball's Lifelong Fascination with Statistics*, explains, two things can happen to batters: "either being put out or scoring a point by reaching the opposite wicket." As a result, he concludes, "hits that placed a batter on base without ultimately helping him score a run went entirely unrecorded."[10] Because such hits didn't count, in other words, they were not counted.

We don't know who created that abstract, but the person Daryl Morey is looking to shoot, the person most often credited with transforming this rudimentary statistical abstract and, in the process, creating what would be called "the box score," was Henry Chadwick, known as the "Father of Baseball." Chadwick's "influence on baseball's statistical record," writes John Thorn, official historian of Major League Baseball, "is enormous" and, he adds, "in the evolution of baseball and its bevy of associated numbers, no figure was more important than Henry Chadwick."[11] Historian David Voigt goes further, comparing Chadwick to Moses, "destined to show baseball leaders how to fulfill the game's promise as America's national field sport."[12]

But in Michael Lewis's story of baseball counting, Chadwick is no prophetic hero. Rather, the Father of Baseball first appears in *Moneyball*, in the chapter called "Field of Ignorance," as a semi-comical foil for the scientifically sophisticated approach of Bill James. He is an icon, in other words, of baseball's "medieval" thinking. Lewis calls Chadwick "the beginning, and occasionally the end of the answer" to the question: "How could baseball statistics be so screwed up?" For Lewis, Chadwick's box score amounts to a "system of perverse incentives for anyone who trotted out onto a baseball field."[13] The phrase suggests that Chadwick did something more than just count—unduly, but understandably, influenced by cricket—the wrong things. It suggests that the error harbors a moral lapse, either in intention or in effect.

In fact Lewis's problem with Chadwick appears to be that he was not at his core a scientist but rather a moralist. Moreover, he advanced his moralizing agenda by utilizing the methods and representational tools of science. Lewis explains: "Chadwick's stated goal in counting the events that occurred on a ball field was reform . . . He was as upset about the immorality he witnessed on the baseball diamond as he was about the drinking and gambling he found on the city streets." Using his statistical metrics to achieve these ends, Lewis complains, Chadwick "longed to affix blame and credit for baseball plays and . . . grossly oversimplified matters." The perversity of Chadwick's approach to statistics, from Lewis's point of view, lies precisely in the fact that he allowed the judgments of his "moralistic mind" to influence what should have been objective intellectual decisions about how the game works and, on that basis, what should be counted. In this way Lewis's case against Chadwick is that because he forced the science of numbers to serve the ends of moral fervor, he not only perverted baseball but corrupted the purity of science as well.[14]

Is it any wonder that Daryl Morey would have him shot?

#32. Perverse Incentives

Michael Lewis is not wrong or even misleading about Chadwick's motivations. "Like a gentleman," Chadwick wrote of the model baseball player in 1861, "he abstains from profanity, always has his temper under control, and takes matters good humoredly; or if angered, keeps silent. . . . He never disputes the decision of an umpire, either by his words or actions; but, when a judgment has been rendered, he silently accepts the decision. . . . Regarding the game as a healthful exercise, and a manly and exciting recreation, he plays it solely for the pleasure it affords him and if victory crowns his efforts in a contest, well and good; but should defeat ensue he is equally glad to applaud the success obtained by his opponents."[15] Totally absent from the description, you'll notice, are athletic ability, baseball skill, or competitive achievements, let alone efficiency. Chadwick's life and his work as a journalist—including and beyond sports—was indeed driven by a passion for social reform, informed by his Christian values.

And, like other reformers of the period—including some who would go on to play central roles in the invention and development of basketball—Chadwick saw in team sports the potential to foster certain moral values that could mitigate the vices, gambling and drunkenness, for example, he saw increasing in America's rapidly growing cities. "Chadwick's writing," says historian Jules Tygiel, "reverberated with the rhetoric of American reform."[16] He was among the passionate vanguard of so-called muscular Christians for whom sculpting bodies meant sculpting souls into spiritual six-packs and thereby turning sports like baseball into instruments for positive moral and social improvement. And the numbers used to record the actions of players on the field came to be one of his primary instruments in fulfilling that mission.

Though Chadwick may have been among the first to apply the idea to sport, he was not alone in his belief that statistics could be a tool for social reform.[17] The English word "statistics" bears the marks of this purpose. Imported to English in the late eighteenth century from German, it originally referred to "those matters that ought to be known to the statist" (hence statist-ics).[18] Statistics, or "political arithmetic" as it was also called in the nineteenth century, was designed to give an accurate portrait of, well, the state of the state. In the United States, as historian Patricia Cline Cohen put it: "The statistical champions of the mid-nineteenth century were fairly clear about what they regarded as the effects of quantification on social thought. Enumeration focused concern on an issue, accurately described its dimensions and suggested the proper course of action to be taken."[19]

Chadwick's own brother had used statistics extensively to support his argument for reforming sanitary conditions among the working class in England in the 1840s. And so of course Chadwick "pounded his rhetorical fist hardest when discussing the importance of statistics." Of course he wrote, in 1861, that "in order to obtain an accurate estimate of a player's skill, an analysis, both of his play at the bat and in the field, should be made, inclusive of the way in which he was put out; and that this may be done, it is requisite that all . . . contests should be recorded in a uniform manner."[20] Obtaining an "accurate estimate of a player's skill" would mean counting—and by counting, emphasizing—those plays that Chadwick believed best embodied the moral values of the model baseball player.

Consider what is, from the point of view of Michael Lewis in *Moneyball*, the most notorious example of Chadwick's perverting influence: the walk. Chadwick attributed the walk to bad pitching (rather than good judgment by the hitter) and so scored walks as errors, demerits against the pitcher. I imagine that, given his values, Chadwick might have said of a batter taking a walk that "it is hardly manly to lie in wait, like a snake, for the other fellow to misstep. A muscular Christian gentleman makes a fair swing to put the ball in play and then accepts the outcome." Chadwick's moral views could not "let him accept the fact that a hitter would allow himself to be on base unless by a clean ball hit into play."[21]

For Sabermetricians like Billy Beane, however, winning is the point: you have to score to win and you have to get on base to score, and concern—especially unmodified moral concerns—over how you got there is at best a luxury you can't afford or at worst a sign of benighted prescientific and moralistic thinking clouding the mind. From that standpoint a walk is just as valuable a play by the hitter as a clean base hit. Hence Lewis assigns Chadwick to a position in the "Field of Ignorance." By contrast, the story of a different set of incentives, whereby the Oakland A's rewarded players for taking a walk at least once in every ten at bats, appears in the chapter "The Enlightenment."

Chadwick saw a baseball game as a social microcosm. If a team was a social collective, then it made sense to consider the actions of individual players from the vantage point of whether they contributed to the collective, competitive, and moral good of the team or instead detracted from it. Recording these events became a way of keeping a tally of individual accountability. "Many a dashing player," Chadwick argued in 1864, "who carries off a great deal of éclat in prominent matches, has all 'the gilt taken off the gingerbread,' as the saying is, by these matter-of-fact figures, given at the close of the season; and we are frequently surprised to find that the modest but efficient worker, who has played earnestly and steadily through the season, apparently unnoticed, has come in, at the close of the race, the real victor."[22]

Lewis's critique of Chadwick exemplifies a popular argument used to support the expanded use of analytics in baseball and basketball: that it provides an objective, quantitative account of reality and thus offers a unique corrective to moral and other subjective biases. Because of the fundamental importance of this pervasive view to the legitimacy of analytics, I want to stress that the difference between Chadwick and Billy Beane is not, as Lewis would have it, that the former "perversely" saw baseball as a social microcosm and used statistics as a tool to incentivize player behavior he deemed valuable, whereas the latter saw the game as "just a sport" and properly used numbers only for objective purposes. The difference between them lay rather in their view of the purposes of sport (viewed in both cases as a social microcosm) and therefore in which behaviors they viewed as valuable and sought to count and, by counting, to incentivize. After all, the belief that the purpose of competitive sport is victory is no less a subjective, social, and moral belief (and no less perverse) than the belief that the purpose of competitive sport is to foster cooperation and self-sacrifice; and the use of numbers to promote moral virtues is not, in itself, less objective than the use of numbers to promote competitive success and financial value.

For Chadwick and many others of his era, to distinguish between competitive and moral accountability would have made no sense. Indeed such a distinction would seem to echo a dangerous and growing tendency in American society to focus exclusively on competitive outcomes, to value ends independently of the means employed to achieve them. Such a focus would wear away at the moral fibers holding the rapidly changing young nation (already divided by slavery and fractured by the Civil War) together. Statistics could be used not only to compare ends, such as a final score, but to compare and evaluate the means by which players and teams reached those ends. In the process the statistical reformer could exercise an indirect influence on the tactical and strategic decisions of individual players and coaches: the game could be reshaped. Indeed, the very meaning of "victor"—as in Chadwick's passage above—could be transformed to include moral qualities such as earnestness, unselfishness, and steadiness in the workplace.

This, too, is America's game.

Interlude—Thermometers

#33. The Frog: A Dialogue

I played basketball on my school teams from sixth grade through my senior year of high school. And, despite the fact that my father kept track of my statistics for every game from eighth grade on, I still truly have no idea how good I was.

Okay, not no idea. I mean, if you asked me: "Yago, were you poor, below average, average, above average, or good?" I think I'd say, "above average." So sure, I have some idea—if you call being able to answer that question in that way an "idea."

But I am my father's son, so both your question and my answer—my so-called some idea—now lie there like the waxy frog in Sister Angelo's sophomore biology class: pinned, spread-eagle on its back, waiting to be taken apart.

"What do you mean," the voice of my father in me begins, calmly confident, almost bemused, "by 'average'? Average assumes a sample." He and I march in lockstep to the row of dictionaries in the family room to confirm this. You protest that you concede the point. We don't care. We open the dictionary, adjust the swing arm adjustable lamp with the blinding 200-watt bulb so it is directly over the page, and jab our finger at the definition. We're not trying to rub it in. We're just focused on the truth. And we relish the discipline of methodically seeking it.

So, we ask, "What is your sample? Who are you asking Yago to compare himself to? All basketball players ever? Should we compare him to *Weelt Chamberline!?*"

We might laugh—controlled maniacal, as if we were barking through a straw.

"No," you say, "of course not." You're desperately trying to clamber over to the right side of the joke. We've got you now: "Then who? What age group? What position? What interscholastic athletic division? What geographical region?"

You are dizzy and nauseous. You know how the frog felt in its final moments, as the chloroform seeped in.

Let's say you narrowed it down to high school basketball players in the city of Madison, Wisconsin, in the 1982–83 season—my senior year.

We say, "Alright then, very good. Now we have a clearly defined sample." You are relieved. But we're just patronizing you. We've already anticipated the next ten moves, and each of the ten moves that could be made on the basis of those. We have become IBM Deep Blue or, better yet, Google DeepMind. And right now our deep mind is impatiently rubbing its hands together. All we've done so far is made the first incision and pinned the skin flaps back. So you're still not out of the woods. In fact you just got into the woods.

"Now, on the basis of what performance criteria are you comparing Yago to the other players in the sample?"

Maybe you hesitate.

It's hard to know, honestly, if it's better to dive right into the icy water with a stupid answer or to be more tentative, just dipping your toes in with a stalling, rhetorical question. But the very fact that you're even wondering that means we're already in your head too. Because now you're not only wondering how good a basketball player I was, you're wondering how good a thinker you are. And the stakes seem impossibly high.

Maybe you imagine that if you say one thing, we'll say, "Very good!" Or maybe you fear that if you say something else, we'll shake our head in grave disappointment, haul another book off the shelf, grab some scrap paper, and sharpen a pencil and you'll be there for hours—a day wasted, leaving you empty, while the other boys are eating hot dogs and watching baseball with their non-professor, American dads.

Maybe we'll just dismiss you, with shocked anger: "*Imbécil!*"

Either way, you imagine that what you say or do in this moment will have some effect on what we say or do.

You imagine you have some control.

You wish.

You don't.

So, go ahead, just say the first thing that comes to your mind. Is it points per game? That's logical, time honored. Slow and steady wins the race, right?

Or are you feeling perversely rebellious or just counter-phobic? If so, how about cheers received per game? Maybe if you jam your foot on the accelerator, the engine driving our mind will overheat and break down and you'll be free.

No, that's just a fantasy, and the price of indulging it is too high: derisive laughter at the moronic irrelevance of your thought, which will go down on your permanent record, only to emerge years later, when you are yourself a grown man, in the form of a withering remark over dinner on your forty-eighth birthday about your lack of discipline, about how you are a dreamer, unrealistic.

Let's go with points per game. And to make this illustration simpler, let's say we have the figure for Yago and for the rest of the players in the sample (and let's say we trust those figures to be accurate). It seems like a reasonable metric, right? I mean, the object of basketball is to score more points than your opponent, so the player who contributes the most points to that effort must be the best, right?

But what if Yago scored the most points per game (he didn't) but took so many shots in order to do so that he hurt his team (he didn't)? Or what if he scored the least points per game (he didn't) but scoring wasn't his role on the team (it wasn't)?

You see where this is going? I think it's called an infinite regress. Actually, probably not. I don't know. But whatever the name for it, you're in a situation where the questions never fucking stop.

And what I do know—what I feel to this day in my flesh, in the hardening pit of my stomach—is that my father was like the love child of Socrates and M. C. Escher, so that a discussion with him felt like a panicked panting sprint through an unsolvable maze, while the minotaur marched patiently at my heels, holding an enormous dictionary, asking questions only he knows the answer to: there was no way out and there was no way in.

Maybe he was just trying to teach me how to think critically, in a disciplined way, like a scientist. Maybe he wasn't trying to teach me anything and instead just couldn't help himself.

#34. Thermometers

I think my father's desire to measure was driven by complex undercurrents, motivations of which he may not always have been aware. I've already indicated as much by suggesting that at some level he was using measurement to order a turbulent, threatening world.

But it's not that I think my father measured me just to keep the demons of death at bay. I don't even think he kept those records of my height in The Archive for decades for that reason. I know that it's not that simple. The rage and humiliating impotence provoked by his sister's death, not to mention his early childhood experiences of the Spanish Civil War, his adolescent commitment to putting his mind and life in the service of science's struggle against death, and his paternal measurements of his youngest son's small body are like isolated beads arranged along a string of various threads of other complexly interwoven public and private events, trends, ideas, and motivations.

I find in some of the other evidently cherished volumes from his library some signs of these, registered in marginal notes and exclamation points and underscores—these last, beneath important passages, drawn carefully along the edge of a ruler. From these I know he understood scientific research to be the pursuit of the truth of how things in the world actually work, regardless of what we might have imagined—or wished—to be the case. He believed that the scientist must be an independent and imaginative yet rigorously logical thinker, as well as a meticulous observer of phenomena.

All of this, including the more specific instruments, methods, and techniques that comprise the modern practice of science my father consciously cultivated and deployed, ultimately, to understand nature so as, where possible, to control it or, if not, then at least to predict its behavior; and all of this to serve that ultimate aim of improving human life. To know—the world (and oneself)—accurately and objectively, so as to manage it (and oneself) and thus prevent the calamities caused as much by superstition, emotion, and irrationality as by the caprices of nature: I believe that is what it meant to my father to be a scientist.

Perched precariously between an intense love of being alive and traumatic memories of death, between a profound appreciation for life and its processes and a profound understanding that its processes lead inexorably to death, my father experienced the present as risk—as a teetering tension between a chaotic past and a future fraught with danger. And his commitment to science expressed, I believe, a desire to understand and discern the order within the chaos of the past as a means to elude, through decisions made in the present, the perils of the future. His commitment to science was, at bottom, his way of minimizing to a tolerable degree the risk and uncertainty inevitably attending our lives in the present. He was, in this, a grateful inheritor of the Enlightenment conviction that "once the proper scientific method was recognized and applied, a steady enlargement of human knowledge and a steady improvement of the human condition would be the inevitable result."[1]

Passion—in the form of curiosity, the thirst for discovery, and the love of truth—was certainly an indispensable part of the successful scientist's psychological equipment: he underlined those passages in his books as well. But that passion could also become a perilous threat if it was not mercilessly subordinated to the objectivity of rational methods. And my father was nothing if not passionate, so that his war against entropy in nature was also a war against the tectonic stirrings and volcanic eruptions of irrationality and emotion within himself; a kind of Cold Civil War maybe, which, when it got too hot to manage internally, he projected outwardly, onto those around him, those he loved most: his mystical, stubborn, loyal wife and his bafflingly independent children, whom he often described as "subrational," and in whom he simultaneously, forcefully encouraged and ruthlessly domesticated expressions of the wildness within.

These large-scale commitments entailed myriad daily and mundane skirmishes—collisions, Michael Lewis might say, between "the scientific method" and "an unscientific culture"—that my father carried out in the household in which I grew up. He measured and fanatically regulated the temperature in the house at all times. We had no screen doors and the windows were never open. We did have central air conditioning. The mercury thermometers he placed in every room in the house in the early '70s gave way to digital models in the '80s, which in turn gave way, by the 2000s, to wireless indoor/outdoor thermometers with forecasting capabilities that were also wirelessly synced to NIST-F1, the cesium fountain clock at the National Institute of Standards and Technology, which serves as our nation's official scientific timekeeper.

When I said I was cold, he would point at the thermometer and report, matter-of-factly, that my feeling was impossible since the temperature was exactly seventy-two degrees Fahrenheit (22.22 Celsius). (And today, when I'm asked how I slept, I freeze momentarily, nervously uncertain, until I check the app on my phone and report my answer as a percentage that the app tells me indicates the quality of my sleep.)

In 2013, when he finally conceded that my mother would receive better care in an assisted living facility, he even installed one of these in her room, next to a portrait of the Virgin Mary. He couldn't control the temperature in the facility, but he could at least complain to the staff that it was too hot or too cold, or fluctuating wildly, and point to the giant display on my mom's wall as proof.

He measured to predict and prevent problems before they arose. So perhaps he measured me to help predict and prevent problems with me before they arose.

I often did not understand my father. I did not understand why things had to be done *this* way, and not *that* way; why I had to be *this* way, and not *that* way. At some point, I know, I stopped asking. But I understood well, and feared, the explosions of anger into which he would be thrown when I did things *that* way, when I was *that* way.

From his commitment to science I took many wonderful things: curiosity, delight in the intrinsic rewards of investigation, respect for and joy in learning, love of books. But from the confusing, irrational intensity of his commitment to reason and quantitative assessment, I think, I learned to doubt myself reflexively. And along with that I took a desperate and deeply held—but only dimly sensed and therefore slavishly obeyed—need to control myself and my environment in order to minimize risk and thus stave off the catastrophe of surprise, of the terror of his cold disapproval or his hot rage, and ultimately of death, ruler of us all.

The last time I saw my father's face in person, I was pushing his cold embalmed body along two cardboard rollers into a crematorium.

The temperature was three thousand degrees Fahrenheit (1648.889 Celsius).

4

Counting America's Bodies

#35. The Ideal Man

In 1915 physical educator, childhood friend of basketball inventor James Naismith, and sculptor, R. Tait McKenzie published a book in which he included a photograph of one of his sculptural creations. He announced that it represented the "culmination" of the "search for the ideal man."[1] Cast in patinated bronze in 1903, the sculpture represents a nude male, standing, head tilted down and to his right, and with his left hand lowered across his body where it joins his right hand just above his right hip. McKenzie explained that the figure embodied "the proportions and girth of the physically ideal American student of twenty-two." But who was the model? And where did McKenzie find him? The answer is that the student did not exist. Or, more precisely, that McKenzie found "him" in printed tables of numbers: as the average of hundreds of measurements of (male) college students taken by Dr. Dudley Sargent at Harvard University over a period of eight years.[2]

Sargent had been at the forefront of an emerging late nineteenth century obsession with anthropometry, the measurement of the human body. In 1886, at the second annual meeting of the American Association for the Advancement of Physical Education (AAAPE), Association President Edward G. Hitchcock Jr. told his audience why. "In the Divine mind," Hitchcock explained, "there is the ideal or plan not only of the great groups of animals but of man also" and that "we are left to study and work out what this plan may be."[3] That is the work, he said, of anthropometry, whose "ultimate and philosophical aim . . . is to ascertain the ideal or typical man" so as to "be able to tell normally developed people what deficiencies they have, if any, and how their best development can be brought about."[4] Sargent's work and Hitchock's rhetorical support for it constituted the first institutional expressions in America of a systematic ambition to set physical education on the secure scientific foundation of measurement and statistics.[5]

One year later Dr. Hitchcock emphasized the same theme, challenging attendees at the 1887 convention to use measurement to discover "what was the ideal form and proportions in the mind of the Creator when he said, 'Let man be formed in our own image.'" The statistical tool that would be used to fulfill this aim was the average. Given a large enough pool of individual measurements, one could determine the average height in a population. Then, according to Hitchcock and others, this average could be used as a standard against which any individual could be measured. Concretely, Hitchcock introduced the "advanced idea" that anthropometrics could "furnish a series of charts or tables of different heights . . . By which any person may see at a glance whether he corresponds or not in certain bodily measurements and tests to the averages which these charts represent." This would be one way in which educators could "tell normally developed people what deficiencies they have."[6] The average, in other words, provided the ideal.

Baron Quetelet (1786–1874) may have been, as Hitchcock acknowledged, the Father of Anthropometry, but that is not primarily why he is remembered. More than anyone else, Quetelet was responsible for applying to human populations statistical methods used by scientists to discern patterns in nature.[7] The centerpiece of the work was his concept of the "Average Man." "Everything," declared Baron Quetelet, "differing from the Average Man's proportions and condition, would constitute disease. . . . Everything found dissimilar, not only as regarded proportion or form, but as exceeding the observed limits, would constitute a Monstrosity." And by contrast, Quetelet asserted "All the qualities of the average man, would at the same time represent all which is grand, beautiful, and excellent."[8]

But that's not all: for Quetelet and Hitchcock, by embodying this physical ideal the average man necessarily also embodied a moral and aesthetic ideal as well. Correspondingly, physical education was seen as a means to a higher end. As President Hitchcock reminded members in his opening remarks in 1887, "the body is not the ultimate end of all our study. . . . . Let the thought be eminent and predominant with us that the highest aim of all our special work is to develop the most perfect type of man and woman in body, soul, and spirit,"[9] Hitchcock's reminder reflected several important tendencies in late nineteenth century American society—muscular Christianity, modernization, the study of the human body for military and industrial purposes, and scientific professionalization—whose convergence had inspired the formation in 1885 of the association whose members he led.

All these threads came together at the 1885 Brooklyn gathering of physical educators, who formed the AAAPE and, in doing so, initiated the first formal, collective efforts to institute a scientific physical education here in the United States. The basis for their assessments of different exercise systems were a combination of anthropometric and performance measurements. Shortly I will describe how, by the turn of the century, they would shift their emphasis from anthropometry to the measurement of the functional effects of exercise.[10] But beyond such shifts in emphasis and internal debates, everyone working in the field would have agreed with the sentiment voiced by the Englishmen Sir Francis Galton in 1891—a few months before basketball was invented—that "the replacement in all scientific work by numerical values, in the place of vague adjectives, is a gain of first-class importance."[11]

This work—and the belief motivating it: that numbers and measures, or rather the right numbers and measures, rightly recorded and interpreted, could serve as indices of physical and moral excellence—was just a somewhat more scientific, systematic, encompassing, and more firmly institutionalized expression of what Henry Chadwick was already looking for with his box score. Much like for Chadwick at the time that he invented the box score, for these physical education professionals, physical excellence (or competitive success in athletics, for that matter) was meaningless and even dangerous if pursued without regard to the morality of the means by which it was pursued. For the ultimate aim was the development of each individual toward the holistic ideal conceived in, as Hitchcock put it, "the Divine mind." And to steer individuals toward that ideal, you had to begin by measuring them.

#36. The Efficient Body

The roots of the quantifying efforts of anthropometrists may extend far back into ancient history and even have more direct antecedents in the period between 1250 and 1700. But most of the methods, concepts, practices, and disciplines begin to take recognizable shape over the course of the eighteenth and nineteenth centuries. It was during this period that, concomitantly, the dream of pantometry that first appeared in Renaissance Europe between the fifteenth and sixteenth centuries began to seem within reach. "Establishing the understanding of numbers as an objective description of reality outside of interpretation was a project of modernity," writes Sally Engle Merry in her study of the use of quantitative indicators in formulating and assessing human rights policy, and "the idea that numbers guarantee value-free description is still pervasive."[12]

Within this broad context, the scientific study of athletes was spurred by social agendas relating to national identity, gender, and race and ethnicity, and these, in turn, were inflected by notions of the moral purpose and effect of athletic activity.[13] Among the ways this complexity manifested was through the metaphorical language in which researchers conveyed the nature of their efforts and, especially, their aims.[14] On the one hand, the nation was seen as an organism, a living body whose health and survival depended on the health and vigor of the bodies of its citizens. But, on the other hand, the athletic (or military) body was understood as a mechanical device—an apparatus, machine, or engine—and indeed was studied, in the words of medical historian Georges Canguilhem, "to discover how far it can be transformed into a mechanism."[15]

In doing so the pioneers of sports science were the heirs of the mechanistic philosophy characteristic of the scientific revolution according to which nature operated according to fixed laws, like a clock. These laws could, if one took the mechanism apart and analyzed it scientifically, be discovered. Its constituent parts and their operation could then be modeled mathematically. And these models would facilitate prediction and control.[16] As early as 1747 the Enlightenment author Julien Offray de La Mettrie first published his materialist tract *Man a Machine*, provocatively applying mechanistic philosophy to every domain of human experience. Today, in one textbook of sports performance measurement and analytics, the author declares from the outset that her objective is "to help the sports data analyst, as well as athletes themselves, understand the human body and how its *machinery* functions during athletic events."[17] And, of course, it is commonplace for fans and journalists to refer to a superior athlete as a machine.[18]

The early anthropometrists of the AAAPE laid down the foundations of this way of thinking, at least as far as American sport and physical education is concerned. Already in the 1890s, but especially after the turn of the century, major figures in the association voiced agreement that understanding and improving human physical efficiency should be the main focus of their profession's efforts. As efficiency became a central concern, the older anthropometric practices of taking myriad structural measurements gave way to a search for ways of measuring the functional capacity of the body in terms of physical efficiency. In articles and books—including one, which I'll describe in a moment, by an individual directly involved in the invention of basketball—authors introduced and debated a variety of tests by which to measure it.

Emblematic in this regard were the remarks of George Meylan, shared with members of the Anthropometry Section at the association's annual meeting in April 1905. Arguing for the importance of differentiating among men on the basis of physical efficiency in other domains such as the military and manufacturing, he claimed that physical educators should bear primary responsibility not only for developing physical efficiency but for assessing it. "Is it not essential that we devise some means by which we can assign marks after an examination on the degree of efficiency reached by the students?"[19]

Meylan was a bit vague about just what he meant by physical efficiency. He first canvassed a range of prior historical conceptions, then equated it with "vitality" at one moment, before settling on: a "healthy, vigorous body, with perfect subjective and objective control."[20] Such uncertainty was common in these discussions. But though physical educators may have been somewhat unsure of just what constituted physical efficiency, they were of one mind about its vital importance, not only as the goal and main index of physical health, but as vital to an individual's overall happiness and integral to the well-being of the nation.

This view that the measure of the organism's health was productivity and, more specifically, efficiency as well as the underlying metaphorical understanding of the human organism as a machine is unsurprising given the rapidly industrializing context in which physical education professionals worked. Modern American sports—perhaps none more than basketball—were generated out of this matrix of modernization, rationalized efficiency, Protestant morality, and the ascendancy of a heavily quantified science of physical performance. "Bodies," sports scholar Tara Magdalinski states succinctly, "were thought to be fixed entities that, like machines, could be improved upon to elicit a greater level of efficiency."[21]

In Debra Shogan's account of what she calls "sport discipline" in the "making of high-performance athletes," she offers a nuanced description of the complex webs of differential power relationships at work in contemporary athletic training and performance science. Athletes are not merely the passive dupes of such systems, she rightly observes. Indeed, Shogan astutely points out that by identifying them as such (while simultaneously exempting other groups—such as, for example, intellectuals, whose performance is also subject to measurement—from such characterizations) we mobilize and reinforce dualistic philosophies that hierarchically separate mind from body, just as is done in those quantifying sciences of sport performance that some of those same intellectuals wish to critique. Whatever one's intentions, in other words, failing to recognize the agency of athletes dehumanizes them in a manner similar to those who see them as performance engines.

Of course it's also true that for an athlete to realize that agency as fully as possible depends, at least in part, on understanding as fully as possible the system in which he or she is participating, including its implicit presuppositions, its social and historical ramifications, and its unstated aims. Athletes occupy a unique vantage point for acquiring an adequate understanding of that system. But their very same position, together with characteristic operations of that system, also places limits on their understanding and agency.

It's in the spirit of facilitating such understandings and augmenting that agency, in fact, that I'm writing this book, hoping thus to respond affirmatively to Shogan's exhortation to recognize and amplify the ways that athletes, as agents, implicitly and explicitly question "the demands of high-performance sport" and refuse "those demands that contradict other important values."[22] Play, at least in those senses of the term conveying aesthetic creativity; individual self-fashioning; the cultivation of freedom; and the unique markers of individual style; not to mention the emotional responses these provoke in us spectators, may be among those other important values in whose name we may wish to question and refuse some of the demands of basketball analytics, even as we avail ourselves of some of their insights.

#37. Playing a Team Game

Among those listening to Dr. Hitchcock at the AAAPE Convention on that Thanksgiving Day in 1887 at New York's Adelphi Academy was a young NYU medical student named Luther Gulick Jr. The son of Presbyterian missionaries, Gulick was no doubt stirred by Hitchcock's words. Indeed, not long after this, he would design the famous logo of the YMCA: a triangle symbolizing the unity of body, mind, and spirit. But Gulick was also a physician in training and a scientist. So as much as his loftier spiritual and moral ambitions were stoked by Hitchcock's exhortation, he would have been as keenly interested in the president's observation that the "the prominence of Anthropometry in athletes and physical education . . . is not the least valuable and ornamental work in our Association."[23] "Educators," Hitchcock continued, "and hard common-sense business men are determined to know all they can about the proper and normal proportions of the body, and what it can be expected to do and what development may be obtained.[24]"

At the time, Gulick was paying for his medical education at NYU by working as the head of the physical education, or "gymnasium," department at the relatively newly founded Springfield YMCA Training Institute. By 1889, MD in hand, he would publish his own volume *Physical Measurements and How They are Used*. The following year, 1890, he would present a paper at the organization's fifth annual meeting outlining "Physical Education: A New Profession" as an inviting field in which "every man may expect to do that scientific work which will be not merely original with him, but original to the world."[25]

He defined physical education broadly: "to draw out and train the physical powers, to prepare and fit the body for any calling or business, or for activity and usefulness in life" and accordingly believed it an essential component of training for any vocation, including all the fine arts. "It is the purpose of physical education," he wrote in 1891, "so to train the body that it can and will obey readily, accurately, and thoroughly the dictates of the mind. By these means the mind, also receives a training which enables it to act with more efficiency."[26]

We citizens of basketball may remember Luther Gulick best for having challenged James Naismith to invent a new game. But this appears as a relatively marginal detail to his biographers against the background of a short but enormously productive and impactful career dedicated to fusing ideals of muscular Christianity with scientific principles and practices and putting this fusion to work through rationalized modern institutions.[27] Perhaps foremost among the domains on which Gulick left this mark was the playground movement that emerged around 1880 and continued to flourish through 1920. "Play professionals," as Gulick and others spearheading these organizational initiatives came to be known, believed that play could serve as an instrument of moral progress and even social reform in the context of immigration, urbanization, and the widening gap between rich and poor.

The growing popularity of sports, particularly team sports, along with the observed inclination of urban youths to organize themselves into gangs, led play professionals to try to harness and temper or redirect the unbridled competitive spirit pervasive in both business and in the increasingly sport-crazy American public during the Gilded Age. Thus, where the "sporting craze" emphasized victory and increasingly aimed to draw paying spectators, play professionals discouraged spectatorship and the pursuit of victory at all costs. In other words, concerned with manifestations of the rhetoric of "play as power," Gulick and others developed a theory of play as a tool for individual and collective progress.

The basis for the program was their belief that there was no hard and fast separation between cognitive, moral, and motor faculties and, in fact, that "muscles and muscle control were the primary links between the child's 'inner' realm of idiosyncratic feelings and his 'outer' world of social encounters."[28] Therefore, they reasoned, if they could control the muscles of children they could control the minds and consciences of children.[29]

We can, in view of this, see why physical efficiency, in the sense of "perfect subjective and objective control" of a "healthy, vigorous body" became a focus of scientists and, more particularly, of their quantifying efforts. Then, avowedly aiming to model their field on modern; scientific; and rational research disciplines and social institutions, they sought to rationalize play processes (the games themselves); programs (playgrounds and equipment); and people (the players) in order to create "the ideal twentieth-century American citizen"—an efficient team player who would embody a new balance between individualism and cooperation; initiative and caution; reason and intuition; personal freedom and social responsibility.[30]

The complex intertwining of these various aims and initiatives can be grasped by juxtaposing the titles of Gulick's two most influential books: *The Efficient Life* (1913) and *A Philosophy of Play* (1920). At first glance they may appear to be at cross-purposes. Certainly, depending on which rhetorics of play (or of efficiency, for that matter) we mobilize, there will be more or less tension between the two. But for Gulick they went hand in hand. Thus, in recommending exercise in support of "the efficient life," Gulick advised that "the kind of exercise that hits the mark is the kind a man likes for its own sake; and the kind a man likes for its own sake has something of the *play-spirit in it*—the life and go of a good game."[31] Gulick viewed such affirmations of the value of play as simply the flip side of his claim that "to live the positive life—the life of affirmation—is to live the life that carries on *efficiently* its part in the work of the world."[32] Putting these together, Gulick argued that while "play, in itself, is neither good nor bad," the kind of play that he advocated and was so instrumental in institutionalizing—organized, supervised play—he saw as fundamental to maximizing workplace efficiency and, moreover, fostered a kind of freedom which was "the type of freedom on which democracy rests."[33]

"It is pleasant," Gulick observed more concretely, "when playing basketball to make a brilliant play for oneself; it is pleasant to be the hero who makes the home run in baseball. But no team that is made up of individuals looking for their own glory ever wins in any of the great collegiate sports—any more than a community can succeed where each citizen works solely for personal interest. This lesson the boy must learn by experience; and he learns it, partly at least, in playing a team game."[34] Perhaps Gulick imagined that in the process the basketball-playing boy was harmonizing the freedom, individual self-expression, and enjoyment of the play-spirit with the imperative to efficiency and self-sacrifice demanded by modern life. And perhaps the boy was doing just that, whether he knew it or not.

Interlude—My Basketball Soul

#38. My First Basket

Sometime around my fourth birthday my father and oldest brother dug a posthole next to the driveway, poured concrete, put in a pole, and climbed high on a shining silver ladder to attach a backboard and rim.

My father documented the event with a photo. I appear in the lower-right corner, the shortest person in the picture. I am three feet three and one-quarter inches tall. I am standing next to my brother Juan, the second oldest, who would have been twelve at the time. The ladder rises up toward the stiff white net. Next to the ladder is my sister Chinca, two years younger than Juan. Holding the ladder is my oldest sibling, Tony, who is thirteen. And, atop the ladder is my mother, who has just made the very first basket—a slam dunk, no less—on our very first basketball hoop.

I was there, but I don't remember the first basket made. I know of it only from photos and stories.

But I do remember, at some point, staring up from directly below: the still stiff white net, circled by the bright orange rim, both crisply set off against a perfect blue sky. And I remember adjusting my position, trying to stand just perfectly, so that as I stared straight up the halo of the bottom of the net and the higher halo of the rim—ten feet above our poured concrete driveway—were aligned concentrically above my head, framing the infinite heavens to which these twin halos both beckoned and connected me.

#39. Soul of a Scorer

Like novelist Pat Conroy, in my childhood I too "fell in love with the smell and shape of a basketball"; I too "long[ed] for its smooth skin on the nerve endings of my fingers and hand;" I too "lived for the sound of its unmistakable heartbeat, its staccato rhythm." I too know the comfort of that feel and sound: the sense of absolute, easy, effortless control that came with dribbling a basketball. Casually dribbling, then springing into motion, intensifying the rhythm of the ball, which accompanied me, following my bidding like a cheerfully obedient pet, my vital, lively animal familiar.

Experimenting with varying and controlling the rhythm of the ball hitting the pavement or the floor, I felt the pleasure of a virtuoso percussionist—the ball and pavement my instruments. And more than once I dribbled around the driveway laying down the track of the bouncing ball over the rhythms of Earth, Wind, and Fire blaring out of my father's big Sony boom box (which, to my boundless amazement, he'd allowed me to take out to the garage).

As the only native-born American in our immigrant family, I was frequently reminded that I was the first Colás who could become president of the United States. Spain, my parents' native land, loomed large in our household, in visits to relatives or theirs to us, and in the Spanish language, which we were required to speak at home. So that in my childhood, besides attending fireworks shows on Independence Day, basketball was, to me, the most American thing we did together as a family.

I developed and refined my handle in heated competition against my older brothers and my father in our driveway, probably starting around the summer I turned five. My eldest sibling, Tony, as his American friends and, eventually, I myself, would call him (though his given name was Antonio, like my father, or just Toño for short), was the best athlete and most skilled; my father was the most unforgivingly physical; and Juan, the second oldest, was, though less athletic, the one who knew how to wear me down psychologically. But the truth is, however I classified their differences, they were all bigger, faster, and stronger than I was. I couldn't shoot over any of them, and I couldn't back any of them down. They were all three aggressive defenders who got up in my chest, suffocating me, and they all three got under my skin.

I was born with them under my skin.

If they took it easy on me on account of our age and size differences, they were masters at disguising it, or I was a master at concealing the fact from myself. So, my game became protecting the ball, and using its motion as I protected it to create an opening, a passage, a line of flight through which I could burst on my way to the hoop.

But all that, exhilarating though it may have been, was just a prelude to what I lived for: making baskets, getting buckets, cashing out. Bang Bang. Ching Ching.

I was small, but before long, near the hoop at least, I could get the ball up and over the rim, just like the grown-ups. So, it was all about lay-ups for me, about earned lay-ups crafted in traffic, under duress. My enemies never relented; even when I'd created my half-step margin, they rode on the back of my hip, the steel bar of a man's arm across my chest, a sharp knee in my thigh as I pushed past. But with the ball in my hands, my bones and muscles and surging blood knew—even if my mind was never sure—that the path to the hoop was mine, a thing I had made and that I had a right to. The narrow passage was my realm, my kingdom, and my Eden.

And I would protect it. For even when I got my step on them, I knew it wasn't done. Their heavy shadows loomed behind me. I could hear the sound of their breathing and feel the impending weight of their bodies. They could easily block my shot from behind, frequently did so, and in doing so ejected me from my paradise, crushing the sense of power and autonomy I had labored so earnestly to craft.

So I developed through trial and error the knowledge of using my body and the hoop to protect the shot, to protect the space I had created—my space—and to extend that space all the way up and over the rim: a tube through which I would, with all my strength, launch the ball. I watched and emulated and imagined myself to be Tiny Archibald, a six foot, 150-pound NBA player who was, around that time, becoming the first and only NBA player ever to lead the league in both points per game and assists per game in the same season.

I learned to stop on a dime, fake a shot, and when my father or brothers (too big to stop so suddenly) had committed to go for the block and gone up or by me, I would toss it up softly off the board. But I also came to learn that I didn't have to be set and in control when I shot. I learned that I could go under the basket to shoot the reverse. I learned to change my shot in mid-air. I learned to improvise.

Two points.

Because we kept score. Initially, as I recall it, we kept score by twos (there were no three pointers at that time and, as I said, no free throws) until someone (usually one of my opponents) grew bored of the game or I erupted into frustrated raging tears at the impossibilities presented by my being small. Later we would adopt the more conventional playground custom of counting each basket as one and playing games to fifteen, which you had to win by two. Two points, one point: what did it matter? What counted was the sound—the sound!—of the ball slipping home through the fluttering, grateful net. The sound of accomplishment. To this day, sitting at a desk far from that time and place, far from any hoop, just recalling that sound causes my whole body to relax.

I may not have cared how they were counted, but after the games I would sometimes retreat to my room and record the scores in a notebook, thus creating a most unsystematic record book of our competition. I don't remember if I ever referred to these, or studied them, but I know that later, as I got a bit older, maybe ten or eleven, and began to play one-on-one games with friends, I became more detailed in my record keeping, and that recording scores and shooting percentages (as best I could recall them) and then studying them later, looking for interesting patterns, was a way of extending the fun of playing basketball.

The driveway was my pragmatic academy in ball and life, fed by the chaotic urgency of my small body and my large desire to keep up, my will to be grown and seen as equal (at least) to those around me, bosses of me everywhere but on the court.

I never felt intimidated or afraid. I was anger and determination.

I was that ball on a string. I was control.

I was the joy of life beating in that ball and what its movement, mysteriously connected to my own, lent to me.

It was my friend.

I was the laws of the physics and geometry within which I operated.

And in the beginning—from the beginning and still to this day (on a good day)—I was that crazy, intuitively calculated prayer tossed up off the board at the end.

I was the happy net.

I was two points.

I was a scorer.

#40. Bango!

On Sunday, March 23, 1969 the Milwaukee Bucks of the NBA ended their first season ever with a 128–118 win over the Phoenix Suns. I'm not sure if this is why we put that hoop in our driveway in 1969, in what looks to me from the photo to be the early spring, around the time the Bucks finished their inaugural season. It may have been a coincidence, but it must have been around the same time. So that in my mind and memory the appearance of a basketball hoop in my driveway and of a professional basketball team in Wisconsin were two sides of the same basketball coin: playing and fandom. Indeed most of the driveway games I would play over the next decade and a half, whether solitary or with family members or friends, were—in my imagination—Bucks games.

I learned to narrate these imaginary games from listening to the voice of the Bucks, Eddie Doucette, who provided the play-by-play for radio broadcasts of the games that I would listen to in my bed at night on a little transistor radio that was molded and decorated to look like an oversize red die. I lived to hear the word "Bango!"—his signature call for a Bucks basket, so notable that it became the nickname for the team's mascot. And, even as his call would serve as the template on which I'd base my own solitary adventures on the imaginary hardwood of the poured concrete driveway, it also helped drown out the disturbing voices of marital and familial conflict that would drift into my room from downstairs once everyone thought I was asleep.

During their first six seasons the Bucks played a few games a year in Madison, at the Dane County Coliseum. I don't know how many games I attended, nor do I remember exactly which ones. Most of those memories have faded or become confused with historical highlights I have seen, but one has remained vividly present for me. On March 2, 1972, the Los Angeles Lakers and their marquee stars Wilt Chamberlain (known as the "Big Dipper") and Jerry West (whose silhouetted image had that season become the NBA's logo) came to my town, Madison, Wisconsin, to take on my defending champion Milwaukee Bucks with their marquee stars Kareem Abdul-Jabbar (still today the league's all-time leading scorer) and Oscar Robertson ("the Big O," who averaged double figures in points, rebounds, and assists over his first five years in the league, an achievement unmatched to this day).

Both teams were assured a playoff spot by this point, but playoff intensity was still in the air and, though records show that game to have been a sellout, I remember it as if the Coliseum were half-empty. Maybe that's my mind's way of registering how special I felt being there that night: as if I were in on a secret that most of Madison missed out on, as if the game were being played just for me.

Back then I felt somewhat ashamed to be in the minority among my friends in Madison as a basketball fan. They were baseball and football and hockey fans, and basketball hadn't gripped the imaginations of my suburban, almost all white friends. I often wished that I could love baseball and football and hockey as much as they did. I wished that my father loved them, too, and that he was knowledgeable about and adept at those sports like their fathers always seemed to be. I wished that I wasn't afraid of a pitch, wasn't afraid of a collision in football, wasn't afraid of falling on the ice. I wished to be more clearly an American boy. But it wasn't that way: I played soccer (when almost nobody in my town played it) and basketball, and my father was never very good at either of them. So, for a few years at least, I felt that I was the only kid in Madison who loved and played basketball, and I was certainly the only one of my friends to see the Bucks and the Lakers that night.

That Lakers team was named one of the top ten teams of the NBA's first fifty years. The Bucks team of the previous season, for that matter, substantially the same team I would be watching that night, could easily have been included in that list—in fact, by one reckoning the 1970–71 Bucks are the most dominant team of all time. In any event, among the ten players who started that game for their respective teams were five who would be inducted into the Hall of Fame as players, and the four I mentioned would be named to the list of the fifty greatest players in the NBA's first half century. Indeed I'd say most honest fans would put those four on their list of the top ten players in NBA history.

I don't remember very much about the game, almost nothing in fact, except for the quick, swirling movements of West and Robertson on the perimeter, and, especially, Kareem posting up Wilt near the hoop, their massive legs like tree trunks straining at eye level in a duel for position, like my dinosaur books with images of triceratops battling tyrannosaurus rex to the death. To this day, I'd argue that you haven't seen a professional basketball game unless you've seen one in person and, at least for a couple of plays, gotten yourself down to see it from court level: that's the only way to let the breaking waves of size, speed, grace, and skill really knock you into wonder.

I remember that the Bucks lost a close one. So I looked up an old newspaper account and found that the Bucks had taken a four-point lead into the fourth quarter, extended it to five with just over a minute to play, but had then blown the game in the final minute, losing by a point on a Gail Goodrich—my God I hated him!—jump shot with four seconds to go. Chamberlain had missed three free throws with the Lakers down by one, but the last was rebounded by Lakers forward Happy Hairston, who passed it out to Goodrich for the game winner.

I doubt that in the excitement of what I'd seen I cared very much about the loss. About a month or so later the Bucks would lose in the Western Conference Finals to the Lakers, who would in turn go on to defeat the Knicks for the championship, Wilt's second as a player. Before too long Oscar would retire, Kareem would be traded to LA, and I would struggle to maintain my love for the Bucks especially as they stopped playing in Madison and their roster was now populated with mere mortals rather than the mythical heroes of my early years.

But that night I lay in my bed dumbly trying to assimilate the magnitude of what I had witnessed: Oscar Robertson and Jerry West, Kareem Abdul-Jabbar and Wilt Chamberlain, the greatest players ever. So big, so fast, so skilled, so cool! They seemed to be able to do anything! And then, the next day, as on so many days after that, I would ask my father to move the car out of the driveway, put on several layers of clothes, grab a rubber Wilson basketball out of the garage, my fingers already growing cold (they would soon be numb), and try desperately and joyfully, through practice and imagination, to grow my very ordinary, undersized self to the cosmic magnitude of what I had witnessed, to the extraordinary dimensions of the Big Dipper and the other stars I'd finally been close enough to almost touch.

5

Counting for Character

#41. The Experiment

In December 1891—eighty years before I saw the Big Dipper, and even two decades before Luther Gulick Jr. could effectively conjure for readers that image of the basketball-playing boy as a natural and recognizable element of the playground landscape—the sport was still so new that nothing was what it was supposed to be, and nothing was named.

The first basketball hoop wasn't a basketball hoop but a peach basket that was supposed to have been a box. The first basketball wasn't a basketball but a soccer ball. The first basketball players weren't basketball players but secretarial students. Shots weren't shots, but throws. The first of these to make it into the basket wasn't called a basket, but a goal. And nobody bothered to record it when it happened.

Basketball itself was not basketball. It had no name at all.

James Naismith recalled the scene: "[I] told them that I had another game, which I felt sure would be good. I promised them that if this was a failure, I would not try any more experiments."[1]

Basketball was so new that on that December day in 1891 James Naismith didn't even watch a basketball game. He nervously watched an experiment: "I felt that this was a crucial moment in my life as it meant success or failure of my attempt to hold the interest of the class and devise a new game."[2]

Later in life, Naismith would describe the experiment as an "attempted solution to a problem" in the field of physical education. In a way this is true:

there was a problem and basketball was undertaken as an attempt to solve it. But it is also misleading in that the problem was at the time primarily experienced as a local one, and the solution discovered as much out of chance and necessity as out of a reasoned scientific process. Basketball, in other words, first emerged as the byproduct of an adventure.

The "problem," as Naismith would later formulate it, was the lack of indoor physical exercise that would appeal to a generation of youth accustomed to participating in outdoor competitive sports and therefore were bored by and resistant to prevailing forms of indoor exercise such as calisthenics and gymnastics.[3] But that came only after basketball had become basketball, only, in fact, after it had solved the problem at the local level. Before that, before he articulated the general implications for physical educators of what he'd created, Naismith's experiment was an attempt to solve a different, most local, immediate, and urgent problem.

Just a few weeks before the first basketball game, in the late Fall of 1891, his boss, the young but already eminent and influential physical educator and play professional Luther Gulick, challenged Naismith to take over a physical education class that had so vehemently resisted the current forms of indoor exercise that two instructors had already given up. Gulick, we know, believed that for exercise to provide physical, mental, and spiritual support for the "efficient life," it must be rooted in two principles: first, it must tap into and harness "play" and other "natural instincts," and second, the process of studying and designing exercise should be scientific—meaning empirical, experimental, and rational.

Naismith took his cue from this and began experimenting with the class of so-called Incorrigibles by trying out in succession a series of simple, playful, active school yard games. Fail: the students quickly grew bored with the childish activities. Naismith then switched tactics, trying to adapt popular outdoor adult sports—cricket, baseball, football, soccer, and lacrosse—for indoor play. Fail again: the students liked them, but all proved too dangerous for indoor use.

"Discouraged and disheartened," Naismith retreated to his office and "began to study games from the philosophical side": in other words, a thought experiment. Systematically and pragmatically he examined the basic elements of sports, mentally testing whether, how, and at what cost they would fulfill the conditions required for the new game, which must be (1) easy to learn and absorbing, (2) playable indoors by a large number of players, (3) a good form of all-around exercise, and (4) free from roughness.[4]

From that pragmatic point of departure Naismith determined the kind of ball to be used (large: to prevent players from hiding it, which he believed encouraged roughness), the sorts of movements permitted (no moving with the ball: to discourage tackling), and the type of goal (elevated and horizontal: to encourage precision and accuracy over brute force in goal scoring). The next morning before class Naismith jotted down thirteen rules that, reflecting these principles, would govern play. In the process, he constituted the parameters for the next experiment.

It was so new, there was no data to draw upon.

He could only guess what would happen.

#42. The Record

Nearly fifty years after devising the experiment that would become basketball, when near the end of his life he agreed to pull together all his lectures, publications, and notes about the sport into the (posthumously published) book *Basketball: Its Origin and Development,* Naismith told the story this way:

> They made a great many fouls at first; and as a foul was penalized by putting the offender on the side lines until the next goal was made, sometimes half of a team would be in the penalty area. It was simply a case of no one knowing what to do. There was no team work, but each man did his best. The forwards tried to make goals and the backs tried to keep the opponents from making them. The team was large, and the floor was small. Any man on the field was close enough to the basket to throw for goal, and most of them were anxious to score. We tried, however, to develop team work by having the guards pass the ball to the forwards.
>
> The game was a success from the time that the first ball was tossed up. The players were interested and seemed to enjoy the game. Word soon got around that they were having fun in Naismith's gym class, and only a few days after the first game we began to have a gallery.[5]

By looking at what Naismith thought important to record—and what he omitted—from this, his final account of the first game, of the experiment that was not yet basketball, we may gather an indication of what he valued. The players were "anxious to score," but Naismith makes no mention of the only basket or who scored it. In fact, he never mentioned the first basket made in any of his public lectures or published accounts of the first game. Indeed, the first typed copy of the rules neglected to mention even that a goal was scored by putting the ball in the basket so that Naismith had to add that detail in by hand. And though, sometime after the game, Naismith composed a handwritten account of the experience in which he briefly noted that William Chase scored the first and only goal, he never included this in any published accounts of the game. Even in his last published word on the sport he'd invented he left Chase and his basket out of the official record.

On the contrary, in the passage above the word "however" suggests that despite the players' own eagerness to score, Naismith tried to emphasize something else: encouraging them to "develop team work by having the guards pass the ball to the forwards." In other words, if for the players scoring was what counted (and so perhaps what should be counted), for Naismith it was not important enough to warrant a mention, except as the name for an "anxious" desire to be countered by emphasizing teamwork. Naismith may have invented basketball and even counted the first basket, but at that point, neither baskets nor counting counted most to him.

This "new game of ball" was introduced publicly on January 15, 1892 in what would be the final issue of the Springfield YMCA Training Institute's publication *The Triangle*. In the rules included in the article, Naismith specified that the object of the game is to throw the ball into the opponents' goal. While the rules do not stipulate assigning point values to goals, rule 13 does specify that "the side making the most goals in that time [two fifteen minute halves, per rule 12] shall be declared the winner."[6] Naismith must have imagined that someone would be counting the number of goals scored by each team. Additionally, because rule 7 penalized a team committing three consecutive fouls by awarding a goal to their opponents, someone must also have counted each team's fouls and added, when necessary, the stipulated penalty goal to the opposing team's goal total. All to say that counting evidently formed an essential part of basketball from the beginning, but also that—apart from these simple tallies—Naismith did not appear to give too much thought to the role of quantification in the game.

What Naismith did appear to give thought to, even in this very first article on the sport, was how to keep the game both interesting and free from roughness, and the key to achieving this seemed to be what Naismith called "scientific" play. Naismith exhorted his readers to "let it be played as any other game of science and skill," while also warning that "there is neither science nor skill in taking a man unawares, and shoving him, or catching his arm and pulling him away, when he is about to catch the ball. A dog could do as much as that."[7]

Scientific play appears as a bulwark against roughness; and avoiding roughness, in turn, seems to be essential to keeping the game truly human. This makes sense considering the YMCA's emphasis on cultivating physical activity as a holistic endeavor aimed at developing not only body but mind and spirit as well. From this standpoint "science and skill" seem to refer to the activity of mind, tempering the potentially dehumanizing impulses toward brute force harbored by the undisciplined body. Scientific play keeps us from playing like dogs.

Moreover, scientific play, as Naismith saw it, was also essential to tactical success and hence to player and spectator interest. "This game," he wrote, "is interesting to spectators as well as to the players, and may be made quite scientific by good judgment combined with good co-ordination. Several good points have been scored by two or three players working together." The point of the sport, and the responsibility of those teaching and administering it, must be to show players "that science is superior to brute force." On the other hand, he admitted, "the more players the more fun, and the more exercise for quick judgment."[8] With this final equivocation Naismith indirectly registered a tension. Scientific play may make the game more interesting for players and spectators, but some of the spontaneity and chaos (and roughness) that might arise with more players, he seems to recognize, make it more fun.

In this way Naismith anticipated certain elements of basketball discourse that would be prominent throughout the 1890s and—albeit with shifting meanings and forms—beyond. The tension he registers between "scientific play" and "fun"—which faintly echoes Gulick's tension between "efficiency" and "play"—anticipated three broader axes of tension between competing desires at work in basketball: first, between the individual player's competitive desire (to score) and the administrator's moral desire (to develop teamwork); second, between the spectator's aesthetic desire (for violence) and the administrator's moral desire (for cleanliness); and third, an internal tension within and among administrators between an institutional desire to expand the mission of the association (by attracting players and spectators through basketball) and a moral desire to maintain the purity of the mission of the association (by restricting who plays and how). In registering the tension among these particular conflicting competitive, moral, aesthetic, and institutional desires Naismith exposed another deeper tension brewing in the creative, and troublesome, heart of basketball: between the individual (desire for freedom) and the collective (desire for order).

#43. Basketball Fever

I mentioned that basketball was first introduced in the final issue of *The Triangle*. Two months after that, Gulick and Naismith launched a new publication, *Physical Education*, in order to promote the YMCA's core belief that physical education was an essential "antecedent to the normal development of the mental and spiritual." Opposed both to the pursuit of athletics for the sake of competitive success and to exercise undertaken for the sake of physical health as an exclusive end in itself, the YMCA defined physical education as "the science and art of perfecting the bodily functions, and subjecting them to the will." For, as Gulick had put it back in May of 1891, modern men (and, to a lesser extent) women whose "lives are more rapid and intense," demand "a better body, not necessarily bigger and stronger muscularly, but more enduring."[9]

To fulfill their mission of promoting physical education, Gulick and Naismith sought to develop and promote activities that improved the capacity of human beings to fulfill certain desirable and natural functions that improved, in other words, human efficiency. And, as they also noted, in order to interest a broad sector of the population in such exercise, the activities should be fun, since "there is no strain on the will in following one's desires."[10] They sought to steer the ship of physical, moral, and social goals on the currents of the desire for competitive sport as fun and entertaining. And, when the course proved difficult to navigate—as it would before long—they would turn to quantification as a steadying rudder.

Basketball was the promising centerpiece of this mission, and much of its early history was chronicled first in the pages of *Physical Education*. Reports poured in from far and wide testifying to the sport's rapidly burgeoning popularity as "basket ball fever" swept the country. By March of 1892, what is believed to have been the first public game of basketball drew two hundred spectators to the gallery at the Springfield Y.[11] And, according to one historian, by December of 1892 the game was being played by members in at least one local YMCA in "Arkansas, Illinois, Maine, Maryland, Massachusetts, Michigan, Minnesota, New Jersey, New York, Ohio, Oregon, Pennsylvania, Rhode Island, Vermont, and Wisconsin."[12] By February 1893, *Physical Education* published the first enthusiastic reports of the game from Philadelphia, Albany, New York, Pawtucket, Rhode Island, and Springfield, Ohio. And though the players from Albany lamented that their losses to the West Troy team showed they were "in need of more scientific playing," all shared the enthusiasm of the Springfield, Ohio, reporter who called it "one of the best indoor games extant."[13] The currents of competitive zeal were pushing the ship of basketball forward rapidly.

The very fact that the Albany Y was already competing against players from a neighboring association branch indicates one effect of the sport's rapid spread and wild popularity. Play shifted from *intra*-association recreational competition designed to promote overall development and attract new members to *inter*-association games that fostered, among other things, local pride and competitive zeal, complete with "trash talking" correspondence.[14] For example, the YMCA teams from Providence, Rhode Island and Attleboro, Massachusetts competed in a game in January of 1893 that was reported in the March issue of *Physical Education*. While intra-association recreational games involved varying numbers of players with wide-ranging levels of skill and athletic ability, the sentiments stirred by games such as those between Providence and Attleboro led to the formation of select teams to represent local branches in inter-association competition. And these teams, in turn, increasingly tested their abilities in games against non-YMCA teams representing colleges, military units, and independents.[15]

During these first few feverish years following the invention of the sport, quantification of basketball play was generally restricted to the minimum amount of counting necessary to determine a winner as per the rules. On the one hand, this seems surprising since even before the invention of basketball, under Gulick's leadership, the YMCA had developed, printed, promoted, and sold forms for scoring competition in track and field and gymnastics, and the pages of *Physical Education* were filled with instruction, discussion, and publication of anthropometric measurements. So, the value of quantification was certainly seen as consonant with the YMCA mission. But on the other hand, basketball was new, and the competitive component of the sport was initially permitted only as a lure to attract players, but one that needed to be deemphasized and carefully controlled. Once young men were drawn into playing, how they played (scientifically or not) and what they got out of playing (moral improvement, exercise, and enjoyment) counted much more, at least to game stewards, than who won.

Even what might be considered the first basketball "box score"—of that Providence vs. Attleboro game, printed in the March 1893 issue of *Physical Education* at the conclusion of a report on "basket ball fever"—contained minimal quantitative information. It consisted of a roster for the two sides; a list of the goals scored, who scored them and when; the number of fouls committed by each individual player; and the final score. And it would be almost another year before the official rules published in January 1894—a full two years after the first article announcing the invention of the sport— reflected even basic attention to the scoring process by introducing a minor change. Newly added rule 14 dictated that: "The score shall be counted by points. A goal shall count 3 points, a foul 1 point for the opponents. A majority of points shall decide the game."[16]

#44. First Fans

But a month later, in February 1894, a brief note in the "Personals and News" section of *Physical Education* reported an occurrence that would play an important role in intensifying interest in quantifying basketball play. The item informed readers that "The Hartford Young Men's Christian Association had organized a basket ball league, comprising five teams of their own members." Double headers would be played every Saturday evening through March between teams organized by profession ("Bankers," "Insurance," etc.).[17] This much was not out of the ordinary, nor was the fact, as reported several months later, that "nothing has so interested the general public as has the League games."

However, one detail included in that second report in June 1894 was unusual, though not because of anything that happened on the court. "The executive committee," Allen reported, "thought it best to have admission free to all games and for awhile the seats placed around the running track and visitor's gallery were free also, but such a demand came for reserved seats that a nominal price of 10 cents was charged." The price may have been nominal, but as Allen noted, "In many cases the seats would sell two weeks ahead, while others had a standing engagement for ten or a dozen seats throughout the season." In all, Allen wrote with pleasure, "10,000 has been the total attendance and our average audience about 550." This turnout yielded great publicity for the association and no less importantly, a much-needed surplus, after expenses were paid, of $250.00 to support outdoor sports.[18]

Allen had evidently hit upon a recipe for how to put the intrinsic appeal of basketball to work to solve other challenges facing YMCA administrators. As Dr. A. T. Halsted summarized the formula a month later, with reference to the Hartford experience, competition stimulated rivalry, rivalry stimulated player and fan interest, and fan interest could be turned into a revenue stream to support an expanding structure of competitive leagues, not to mention the other services the Y sought to provide. As he put it, the Hartford experience had revealed advantages such as "increase of membership and general support resulting from the greater publicity of the work of the association; payment of all expenses and a good balance in treasury, from the very thing which involved no additional expense; and the vast amount of good necessarily accompanying the relaxation and enjoyment of these healthy games, both to participant and spectator."[19]

But others were not sold; while this recipe certainly seemed to promise to solve problems of membership and finances, it introduced new tendencies that worried many YMCA directors and the game's administrators. Gulick, Naismith, and others obviously hoped for the sport to be played and even intended for it to be used by administrators for various purposes, and they certainly played an important role in promoting it. However, the very success of these efforts—the force of the desires they'd tapped into and stimulated, in other words—led to changes in basketball play that reflected the diverse motives, needs, and aims of those who felt driven to play it. Even before the Hartford experiment, game administrators worried that the growing competitiveness and rowdy fan bases (as well as the roughness, individualism, and athletic specialization associated with these) were corrupting the moral core of basketball. After Hartford, these worries took center stage. "Is basket ball a danger?" asked the editors of the YMCA publication *Young Men's Era*, inviting physical directors from around North America to weigh in over two issues in late August of 1894. Some claimed the sport should be banned.[20]

In particular, the worries of Gulick and others centered on the corruption of the amateur ideal of playing for the love of the sport. That a few teams, around this time, had broken away from restrictive YMCA policies by forming professional clubs only confirmed their fears.[21] They saw professionalism as feeding an overemphasis on winning, which they believed tempted players to rough and dirty play. This, in turn, they linked to the rowdy behavior of overzealous fans who both incited and were themselves incited by violent, individualistic play. Brute force and individualistic play, in the eyes of those concerned, undermined the sport's core purpose of the overall development of physical well-being, moral virtue, and intellectual capacity. By violating the spirit, and often the letter, of the rules of play, rough players circumvented the very constraints that would otherwise require successful players to use intelligence to make quick decisions, sacrifice their individual interests to those of the team, develop trust in their teammates, and utilize a variety of physical capacities other than brute strength.[22]

Around this same time, in the late summer of 1894, the third annual conference of YMCA physical directors took place. Among the committees constituted during the meeting was a group, which included James Naismith, studying the possibilities of creating an association-sponsored National Athletic League. Its work rested on the premise, as stated in the report, that "the object of athletics in the Young Men's Christian Association differs from that of any other organization in that the Association aims to develop the individual, and in order to encourage the all-round system of physical training, to foster loyalty to the Association." On this basis the committee recommended the creation of an "organization which shall arrange for and have charge of all contests, settle all disputes, and such other work as is usually done by such organizations." It would regulate eligibility, institute and regulate physical tests, and oversee all association athletic competition.[23] Clearly the physical directors of the YMCA were not content simply to voice opinions about basketball (or other competitive sports) but were ready to back these opinions with the force of institutional regulations and sanctions. They might not be able to control the wildfire that basketball play had become, but they could and certainly would build a firebreak around YMCA basketball.

It's in this context that calls for "scientific play" took on greater importance. For, as we have seen, already in Naismith's first descriptions of the game, scientific play was synonymous with playing the sport the way its founders intended: as a means of physical, moral, and intellectual development. If one followed the letter and spirit of the rules, the only way to succeed in basketball was by quickness, agility, intelligence, self-sacrifice, and team play. This much was already emphasized even in articles that were helping to promote the popularity and spread of the game.[24] In January 1894, Naismith had reiterated that "the secret of Basket Ball is in team play" and that "there is no game in which individual play will do less and team play more than in Basket Ball."[25] Team basketball "was scientific basketball," wrote W. E. Allen in one of a series of instructional articles he published in *Physical Education* early in 1895.[26] From this point of view the disturbing emerging tendencies exhibited by basketball players run amok threatened not only basketball but, because of the complicated chain of values invested in the sport, science and morality as well.

#45. Scorebook Cure

With so much invested in and therefore at stake in the future of the burgeoning young sport—nothing less than the moral and social values of America—it's no surprise that Gulick and others would push back, and with more than just opinion. They beefed up rules curtailing roughness and began instituting complex eligibility requirements to ensure amateurism.[27] And, in the November 1894 issue of *Physical Education*, just five months after reports of the Hartford experiment, the significantly expanded *Official Basket Ball Rules for 1895* added a new stipulation. Rule VIII identified a "Secretary," specified his responsibilities ("He shall keep account of the following points in all match games: Number of goals made, by whom goals are made, by whom fouls are made, nature of the fouls made, number of goals made from free throws, length of time of halves, names of all players, names of all officers, names of the teams."), and decreed that "Official games shall be scored according to the details in the score book published by the International Committee."[28] Expanded, uniform, regulated counting would be a way of safeguarding what counted: character.

At the Springfield Y, Naismith himself dutifully fulfilled that role by maintaining a notebook in which he recorded the results of the seven games played by each of the eight teams in the "Y.M.C.A. Training School Basketball League" during its 1894–95 season. For each game the secretary tallied on a table the free throws, field goals, and fouls for each player. Though individual totals were not given, Naismith recorded the team totals and final score of each game.[29] While the tables Naismith used were hand drawn (albeit neatly, with a ruler, of course), they were prototypes of the official score blanks that, by the very next season, the Association's International Committee would require (and print and sell) for use in sanctioned competition.[30]

Yet, despite these regulations, it seems that adoption of the score blanks was slow, or at least too slow for Gulick's taste. In his capacity as editor of the September 1898 edition of the Spalding Athletic Library's *Official Basket Ball Guide* (which included the rules for the upcoming season), Gulick explicitly lamented that "Many basket ball teams did not get down to doing as scientific a work as they should have last year" on account of "a failure to understand, or to use, if they understood, the official score book."[31] "This score book," he continued—whose use he explained and recommended "heartily . . . to all who wish to play a scientific game"—"is almost a necessity to the manager of a team who wishes to keep accurate record of all his players."[32] Institutionally sanctioned and regulated quantification, in the form of official scorebooks, was seen as ensuring scientific play and therefore, by association, as a means for exercising control over the uses to which players were putting basketball.

This institutional control of basketball continued to intensify and expand over the turn of the century, so that before too much longer Gulick's plea seems to have been heeded and he was able to reverse his earlier position lamenting the lack of use of score books. In the Spalding *Official Basket Ball Guide* for 1903–4, Gulick began essentially the same article, also entitled "How to Score Basket Ball," and accompanied by the identical sample score book page, not with a complaint but with the satisfied declaration that "the increased use of the score book last year resulted in teams getting down to more scientific playing. Better records were kept, and the managers were able to size up their men more accurately."[33] And, just a few pages later, ad copy for the "Spalding Official Score Book" boasted that it had been "prepared to meet the demand of the intelligent players who wished to keep record of goals and fouls, their nature and by whom made. This book enables the manager to tell at a glance how many fouls and goals each man made and serves as guide for him in coaching his team."[34] Of course the sales pitch was hardly necessary since a few pages before Gulick's article, rule VIII, section 3 stated: "Official games shall be scored according to the details in the official score book."[35]

In this way, through the combined force of Gulick's persistent influence, commercial persuasion, and consolidated institutional power, the practice of counting those events in basketball play that, by the logic of the rules promoting scientific play, should most directly influence the outcome of games (field goals made, foul goals—or free throws—made, and fouls committed) became standard practice. Perhaps Michael Lewis would characterize this as another instance of "perverse incentives" generated by the ignorance of "medieval" thinking.

But while records were dutifully kept and reported to sponsoring organizations, which published scores and even sometimes individual statistics in annual recaps of the preceding season, observers appear not yet to have been sure how to integrate quantitative data into their qualitative assessments of teams and players. Take the first of such statistical tables, which appeared in the Official *Spalding Basket Ball Guide* for 1905–6, reprinted from a March 1905 item in the *Philadelphia Press* and introduced to readers, in an indication of its novelty, as "the following interesting table," which shows points, field goals, free throws, and games played for each player in what was then called the Eastern League.

From a quantitative perspective, if what was being counted in the official scorebooks is what actually counted, we might conclude that the top five players in the league that year were Fisher, Hyatt, Flint, Dickerman, and Kunkle. But that was not the conclusion reached by Charles E. T. Scharps of the *New York Sun* or F. J. Quigg of the New York Athletic Club in naming their respective five-player "All-America Basket Ball Selections." The two concurred in putting Fisher and Hyatt on their teams. But neither selected Flint, Dickerman, or Kunkle. It may seem obvious to us today, immersed in a world where seemingly everything is counted, that the scanty quantitative indicators available would (and should) not be used as sole indicators of player value. We have developed myriad sophisticated analytical metrics, incorporating a far richer and more encompassing data set, to gauge who is best.

But Scharps and Quigg didn't live in our time, and so it can be instructive to examine why they left the 3rd, 4th, and 5th leading scorers in the league off their lists. The first, most evident reason, is that among the top five scorers all but Hyatt were forwards, and then, as now, the team-oriented culture of the sport requires that even the purely imaginary exercise of constructing an "All-America" team should include players from each position. But while that explains the inclusion of lower-scoring guards on each list—especially since guard was at that time primarily a defensive position—it does not explain why all of the high-scoring forwards I have mentioned were passed over for the two forward spots. The problem may have been that the three played for the two worst teams in the league. To reward their individual accomplishments when those accomplishments apparently did not lead to team success would be to undermine the prevailing emphasis—justified on both moral and tactical grounds—on the importance of teamwork.

Perhaps what was being counted for individuals was not what counted for teams. Or, at least, the measures of individual success somehow did not add up to team success. In any event, though novel, at this point the officially sanctioned forms of quantification were still marginal and exerted little influence on how knowledgeable observers assessed game play, even when the assessment criteria, as above, included the qualities—scientific, clean, team-oriented play—that quantification was implemented to incentivize. It seems that at this point what *really* counted to those viewed as knowledgeable observers was not being counted.

Indeed, already by this time, as early as 1900, an anonymous author proposed tallying no fewer than thirteen different kinds of events (including passes and correct passes, catches and fumbles, dribbles and correct dribbles, shots and missed shots, steals, rebounds, and follow-up shots, and even pivots and reverse turns) as a means of showing "wherein the man or the collection of men . . . is weak."[36] But perhaps because the proposal emerged from outside of the institutional framework that was so tightly controlled and influential by this point, observers who may have sought more nuanced quantitative accounts of the sport were out of luck.

Interlude—One on One

#46. Mano a Mano

My father, as I said, was one of my earliest opponents on the basketball court. He loved to watch basketball and was an intelligent student of the game's more subtle dynamics. But, as a Spanish immigrant to the United States, he was neither experienced nor skilled as a player. Moreover, around the time I was eight or nine, he suffered a back injury that made it impossible for him to run and jump. Most of my memories of playing against my dad come from that time, when he was grounded but still willing—somehow—to come out and play with me.

What a complex classroom in basketball and in life those contests would be. I say he was inexperienced, unskilled, and hampered by injury, but my father, as I recall his game, possessed some natural athletic ability. I don't remember him jumping, but I imagine he had pretty good hops in his day. Around five foot nine with a medium build, he had wiry strong muscles in his legs and arms.

And he was an aggressive, determined competitor. At the time, I appreciated that. For me, playing ball was about playing against grown-ups and thereby feeling like less of the family baby. I couldn't tolerate the idea of someone going easy on me. I'm aware now that the grown-ups were both probably going easy on me and, at the same time, protecting me from the knowledge of that. But I still remember each game as an all-out war of bodies and minds.

Offensively, my father had a somewhat limited repertoire. He had a fairly accurate one-handed set shot, given the time to set it up. He had a pretty quick first step to the basket, but he needed to look at the ball to dribble, which slowed his drives to the hoop. He also had this methodical way of backing in toward the basket, keeping his dribble alive, and then, finally close enough, tossing a quick turnaround half-shot, half-hook off the backboard. That was tough for me to stop because he was bigger and stronger. I still remember feeling the dread of the inevitable as I desperately dug in, trying to hold my ground.

But what I remember most viscerally is his suffocating style of defense. My father gave new meaning to the phrase "man up." I see him, feet wide apart, crouched low, back ramrod straight, playing torso-to-torso defense. He got as close as he possibly could without touching, his hands stretched to the side or straight up in the air, depending on whether I was shooting. As I'd begin to dribble, his arms would come together in a kind of stiff-armed hug. I'd press my drive around him and it felt like I was trying to enter a turnstile the wrong way—a little give, but no way to get through. I imagine that we acknowledged fouls in those games, but I don't actually remember any.

I do remember the combination of frustration and determination that his intense defense used to provoke in me, as well as the elation and triumph I'd feel when I scored. Sometimes I felt so beaten and trapped that I wanted to cry in frustration and complaint. Sometimes, I'm sure, I did (I cried easily as a boy). But sometimes I found that my father's will to stop me seemed to infect me, and I'd feel the germ of my own unshakeable will not to give up until I got past him. Then, no matter how many times I slammed into that turnstile, I'd backtrack my dribble, try a still-emerging crossover or fake, and try to get around him on the other side. Or I'd try a wider path to the hoop, hoping to elude his reach entirely. More than anything, what stays with me is the sense that I lost myself. And in that tiny, intense battle for a swath of poured concrete, that felt good.

Those times I drove past him, I felt elated, proud, relieved, but also a little anxious. I couldn't tell what my dad felt, and that worried me. Was he proud? Hurt? Angry? All I could be sure of was that he was determined and serious. Probably, I was wrong even about that. Maybe all he was doing was trying to endure the pain caused by the herniated disk in his back. Maybe he was thinking about something else entirely. Yet it never felt that way. It felt like he was all there, all about stopping me by hook or by crook. It felt like we both had something personal at stake.

Sometimes this was confusing and unsettling, but most of all I remember those games against my father as strengthening. They built my confidence, not to mention certain skills and qualities in my game that I still notice today when a stronger, bigger, more physical player guards me. I still usually respond by going to the basket with extra determination. I still do my best to bang underneath and to hold my ground when he tries to post me up. And so, above all, I feel the surging and energizing desire to win—more, to vanquish. And if I do, when I do, I feel it has so much to do with will, with wanting it more. I think of my father and feel sure that nobody but him could have instilled that in me.

I'm reminded of Dave Hickey's excellent essay "The Heresy of Zone Defense" from his book *Air Guitar*. Hickey opens with a description of this play:

> Julius [Erving] takes the ball in one hand and elevates, leaves the floor. Kareem [Abdul-Jabbar] goes up to block his path, arms above his head. Julius ducks, passes under Kareem's outside arm and then under the backboard. He looks like he's flying out of bounds. But no! Somehow, Erving turns his body in the air, reaches back under the backboard from behind, and lays the ball up into the basket from the left side.[1]

Hickey thinks about the joy the play elicits and decides that its perfection is as much Kareem's doing as Dr. J's. Kareem's perfect defense elicited Dr. J's perfect response. I now think of my father as my Kareem, the one whose perfect intensity and, ultimately, respect for me as his opponent elicited my best. He brought out my technical skills and most intense determination. Playing against my father gave me the ability to transform feelings of frustration and anger into a combination of focused desire and intelligent calculation.

#47. Pugilismo

One of the photos of my father that I find most fascinating shows him wearing boxing gloves. It is undated, but judging from other photos I have of him, I would guess he must be around seventeen or eighteen. It was probably taken around the time that he bought an introductory guide to boxing—*Pugilisimo*—that I rescued from The Archive. Apart from the usual inscription with his name and the date of the purchase, there are no markings anywhere in the book. I wonder if he read it.

In the photo his shadow extends, taller than him, along the ground behind him. It seems to be late afternoon. A line of trees, trunks painted white, extend bare spindly branches up toward a pale gray sky, flanking a field of short grass.

In the foreground, in a rectangular patch of dirt or fine gravel, my father stands, wearing tennis shoes, floppy athletic socks, shorts, and a sweater. His weight is back on his right foot, which is turned out and slightly behind his left. Both knees are flexed, ever so slightly. His right shoulder is dipped below his left, his elbow bent and tight against his right hip, the gloved right hand up in front of his chest. His left arm is also bent, but the elbow is higher and the fist of the glove extends slightly forward toward the photographer.

His chin down somewhat, my father's open eyes look out from under his brow, directly at the photographer, a slight smile on his lips. He looks happy to me, playful, and innocent. Like he couldn't hurt anybody.

But he did. And maybe it's the fact that the young teenager posing in that image would grow up to hurt me that makes my perception of the image flicker and shift.

His innocence becomes smugness. The slight smile betrays a stupid vanity, a lack of awareness of how awkward and unathletic he is, that he will never be even an average athlete. He appears to me arrogantly unconcerned with his own flaws and limitations, as with the damage he will do when he rails in rage at the world—his family, his youngest son, for failing to meet his impossible expectation that they force themselves into a pleasing mirror image of himself.

Was this the beginning of my rage at the use of numbers as an implacable tool to determine our value? My value? My father obviously wasn't quantifying me when he came home from work one day to find me messy and crying and decided that the best move was to smack me across the face. But still, in his anger and in that hard crack of his hand against my cheek, I find, as I look back, a related, implicit tendency to assess my being and find it wanting—disorderly, unpredictable, chaotic, irrational—and to discipline me for that.

There was no limit to his vigilance or his corrective measures. When I was around four, I used to get constipated. I don't know if he was monitoring my shit, or if I voluntarily reported it, or if my mother, in whom I perhaps confided, had snitched to him. What I do know, and remember with painful vividness, was the terrible remedy that would arrive without warning: my mother would hold me down—as I howled and thrashed like a caught fish—on their big king size bed, my pants and underwear down, while my father shoved a suppository up my ass. It always worked to his satisfaction. My bowels would move. Order was restored. But over time, despite the torture I knew awaited me in response, I started to willfully hold back my shit. The cycle would start again. We fought that shit war for several years, I think, before we moved on to others.

#48. Must You Always Win?

One summer day, when I was perhaps nine or ten, my father and I had just finished a particularly heated series of one-on-one games in the driveway. I have no idea who won. Usually we'd go inside together by way of the garage. Maybe my father would go upstairs to shower before going down to his basement study. Maybe I'd get something to eat. But not on this day.

Somehow (the memory of just how is lost) we found ourselves tossing chest passes back and forth in the narrow walkway that led from the driveway to the front door of our house. Somehow (again I have no memory of how this happened) the passes gradually began to acquire a bit more zip. I see in my memory the look on my father's face: a mix of suppressed glee and grim determination. I feel in my memory the same look on my face. We had each slipped silently into a new kind of competition, escalating the force of passes with the new, never stated goal of causing the other to drop the pass.

I could feel the growing sting in my palms as the ball hit them. I could feel, too, a familiar knot forming in my stomach. He looked angry. I never knew, when he was angry, what might happen next. So when he and my mother or he and my siblings were fighting, or just when he came home from work in a bad mood, or, eventually, just when I heard the groan of the automatic garage door opener signaling his return, I did my best to stay out of the crossfire. But now, with the same angry look on his face, I was literally in the line of fire. He was bigger and stronger than I was, after all, as the graph's chart of his height and weight on the wall of his basement study demonstrated, and as he whipped bullet after bullet in my direction, I felt that knot grow.

As the ball rocketed back and forth across the distance between us there seemed to be no end to this battle. Who would grow tired first? Who would lose concentration? Who—especially this—who would be willing to throw the ball harder at the other? Hard enough to hurt? What deep feelings were compressed into that competition, into our desires to win? Did we want to vanquish the other? To kill the other? To be feared? Respected? To be loved?

Then, growing warm alongside that cold knot of anxiety, I felt grow too something else, something hot like a fire sprung to life: a determination of my own, a desire to throw the ball so hard that he would drop it. A desire to win. He may have been stronger, but I had better technique. I knew what he did not know: that a chest pass is misleadingly named. For though the ball is released from your chest, most of the force of the pass comes not from your upper body but from the step forward you take when you deliver the ball. And I knew, too, that if you stepped forward into the oncoming pass, you could then step back on the catch and absorb the force. My father, though he knew infinitely better than I the laws of physics governing this technique, knew none of this. He stood there, legs apart, feet firmly planted, a statue of strength steeled for the effort of the throw and, equally, against the impact of the catch—rigid and inflexible. For my father was no athlete and so lacked what was already budding within me: a soft, pliable, ineffable feel for the ball. He had no touch.

Eventually one of my passes ricocheted off his stone palms, bounced onto the walkway, and rolled into the front yard. "I win!" I exclaimed. But my father, as he walked sullenly past me toward the front door, said only, "Must you always win?"

Crushed, confused, and enraged, I had no response. Somehow, by winning, I had nevertheless lost.

But I got him back. Forty years later, his cancer—he'd be dead in a month—reducing him to skin and bone, I helped him into bed for what would be the last night he would spend in the home he'd lived in for nearly forty years. It was the night before daylight savings time. He became obsessed with making sure all the clocks (those *not* linked to the international space station or whatever they were linked to) would be changed. I told him I'd take care of it. He questioned whether I would know how. I became annoyed. He noticed and laughed, baring his teeth: "Oh, little boy is becoming angry?! Maybe you want to fight?" He kicked a skeletal leg out toward me. I caught his ankle in my hand and held it. He struggled feebly against my grip. "Do *you* want to fight old man? Cause I'll kick your fucking ass." My wife and sister stood watching, aghast, from the doorway of his bedroom. The muscles in his legs relaxed. His face suddenly went slack. I let his foot fall back down, onto the bed.

I had won, again. And again, somehow by winning I had nevertheless lost.

I guess he got me back.

Must he always win?

6

––––

Counting for Competition

#49. Quantifying Quality

From the turn of the century through the 1940s basketball's popularity among Americans with interests in recreation, sport, and entertainment expanded almost geometrically. While the professional game grew during this period, it remained a regional affair until after midcentury. And while youth basketball in YMCAs and other community organizations remained popular, its importance as a driver of basketball culture began to wane by comparison with basketball in educational institutions. The sport grew both in high schools and in colleges and universities throughout the period. However, during the 1920s the expansion of high school basketball was more pronounced, while, partly as a result of this foundation, the growth of college basketball was more significant in the 1930s and 1940s. And this, in turn, would help establish a commercial market for the foundation of a national professional basketball league.

Spanning that period, newspapers and institutional annuals continued to publish fairly standard box scores for the interest of growing legions of fans. And during the 1910s and 1920s especially, this remained the dominant form of quantification in basketball. But from the perspective of contemporary basketball analytics, more significant (not to mention more varied and innovative and therefore more interesting) developments appeared outside these venues. In the pages of professional or trade magazines for coaches and scholarly journals, two paths of inquiry into the possibilities of quantifying basketball play unfolded. Initially parallel, by the 1940s these paths began to wind together and even merge.

Thus, during the 1920s, magazines for coaches, especially high school coaches, appeared, filled with tactical, strategic, and psychological advice for coaching young players. What is good basketball, they were asking? How do we know it when we see it? Are the elements constituting good basketball the same for individuals and for teams? The same for individuals playing different positions? Are they the same regardless of the setting? How do we teach it? How do we describe it? Even as several popular books authored by notable college coaches expounding their "scientific" or "progressive" philosophies of basketball ignored quantification almost entirely, by the end of the decade high school coaches were sharing experiments in using counting, measurement, calculation, and statistical analysis to help answer these questions.

Most such experiments appear to have been uninformed by contemporaneous research developments in physical education and exercise science. But as many high school coaches were also physical educators, they would surely have been aware, if only at a general level, of the importance of measurement in their field. We saw previously that already in the 1910s tests of functional physical efficiency were replacing anthropometric measurements in physical education. By the 1920s, because of the popularity of the sport as a physical education activity in both high schools and colleges, research in this area increasingly focused on basketball. What is the best way to test and so measure basketball ability and achievement in students of physical education? And what are the physiological and even psychological effects of basketball play? The results of answers to these questions were published in professional and scholarly journals throughout this period, but usually with only a passing, superficial reference to the applicability of the results for competitive play.

But gradually these parallel paths intersected and sometimes merged. First a series of master's theses in education, from the 1930s and early '40s, applied methods of testing, measurement, and statistical analysis from physical education to investigate practical questions of interest to coaches, such as the best method for teaching fundamentals, or for shooting free throws.

At the same time, perhaps motivated by the growing national attention the sport drew through newly inaugurated national tournaments and other highly publicized interregional competitions, some of the same coaches who appeared to have ignored counting in the 1920s, along with some newcomers, began to explicitly incorporate more novel quantitative methods of performance evaluation—sometimes working in collaboration with exercise scientists or physical educators—into their writing about the game.

#50. Scores before Skills?

As the first decade of the new century gave way to the second, basketball continued to develop in ways that challenged the values that game administrators like Gulick had hoped it would foster, and with them, the original forms and purposes of quantification he'd developed to support those values. In short, as basketball in colleges and universities became the most visible and popular form of the sport, competitive success began to displace—in practice if not always in preaching—the older values and purposes the sport had been designed to serve. And as an accompaniment to this transformation, quantification grew somewhat more complex and, more importantly, came to be used more centrally as evidence in investigating and assessing—not to mention improving—the quality of both teams and individuals. Two roughly contemporaneous texts of the period indicate this uneasy transition.

Speaking to delegates gathered in December 1913 for the annual meeting of the relatively recently formed National Collegiate Athletic Association (NCAA), James Naismith himself claimed that feeding spectator enthusiasm for competitive success imperiled not only the moral values of the game but also its aesthetic qualities. To support this claim, Naismith redefined two long-standing keywords of basketball culture: science and teamwork. In his speech he equated what he called—now disapprovingly—"science" with study, planning, and the mechanical execution of a preconceived plan rigidly imposed by a coach. In opposition to this, he advocated what he called "skill," equated with openness, fluidity, spontaneity, improvisation, and grace. It appears that in the twenty years since Naismith had first championed "science" in opposition to "brute force," something—perhaps the developing talent of players, perhaps the nascent industry of college basketball, perhaps broader transformations in American society—led him to make a conceptual shift, whereby he created a third category of basketball movement: essentially an aesthetic experience of motion that was *skillful*, and that avoided both the mechanism of science and the chaos of brute force.[1]

Working from this opposition between "science" and "skill," Naismith superimposed a further distinction between two kinds of team work, which he labeled "machine" and "cooperative." He lamented a growing tendency toward the former, which he equated with a rising emphasis on competitive success ("points" in this speech), the expanding authority of coaches, and the rote implementation of their schemes. "Machine" teamwork, like the scientific approach it embodied, he argued, stokes partisan passions, and in this way draws spectators, players, coaches, and administrators away from the elements of the game that Naismith valued for their broad, holistic educational importance for "life of the twentieth century": namely, "initiative, activity, quick judgment, adaptability to conditions, self-control, perseverance and concentration."[2]

"Audiences," he urged, "must expect to appreciate an exhibition of muscular activity, grace of movement, and immediate response to varying conditions rather than to see their team defeat the other. . . . The main interest in basket ball lies in watching the activity of the players and the kaleidoscopic changes which take place."[3] The responsibility for fostering this, Naismith lay squarely at the feet of institutions, like the NCAA, that must "learn to judge the success or failure of a team as much, at least, by the manly attributes exhibited, as by the score.[4]"

The normally taciturn Naismith, not known for his verbal artistry, even indulged in a quasi-poetic rhetorical flight of alliteration, hoping to persuade delegates of his view that only a narrow mind "puts goals before grace, scores before skill or marks before manhood."[5] It is as though his description of the graceful delights of basketball play inspired him to echo in his own prose the aesthetic values he was hoping, against the rising tide of score-obsessed competition, to advance in basketball.

And yet, when it came time to find a solution, Naismith could only turn to the scorebook, challenging his audience "to discover some method of scoring that will include the attributes of skill and self-control."[6] It's true that Naismith sought to shift what was to be quantified, but the underlying view that a properly kept scorebook could be used as an incentivizing instrument in a program of moral education was decidedly not new: it was present, as I showed earlier, in the baseball box score of Henry Chadwick, and it was behind Gulick's call for proper scorekeeping in the late 1890s. This was a defense of counting for character.

#51. Back to the Figures

In fact, Naismith's call for a reinforcement of the moral use of quantification by reforming scoring methods would be ignored. But the tacit invitation to expand the use of quantification in the game would be enthusiastically taken up in a second text I find indicative of the transition to counting for competition. Spalding's *Official 1915–1916 Basket Ball Guide* forms a landmark in its own right since for the first time it was "Codified and Adopted" by a joint "Rules Committee Representing the Young Men's Christian Association, the Amateur Athletic Union of the United States, and the National Collegiate Athletic Association": indicating the consolidation of institutional control over amateur basketball by merging the efforts of the three major governing bodies for amateur athletics in the United States. And, in this document of institutional control, we find, for the first time, that quantitative data explicitly informed the qualitative account of the preceding season.

"Competition," in the Eastern Intercollegiate League in the 1914–15 season, Ralph Morgan tells us, "was never keener." How do we know? Morgan explains: "Looking over the figures of the competition, one sees the astonishing fact that eighteen out of thirty championship games played were decided by five points or less." Morgan included a table to provide "an illuminating picture of the race" which listed the results of each game by point differential so you could see how long the list of games decided by five points or less was. Though subtle, it is worth highlighting the use of the Enlightenment metaphor of "illumination" to indicate the benefits of quantification. In addition, it's notable that Morgan is using the numbers to drive home a point—contrary to Naismith's—about how keen the competition was and, therefore, how exciting to spectators.[7]

But that was not all Morgan did with numbers in his season recap. He also used them to prove, by analyzing the statistics, Yale's excellence over the course of the season. According to his analysis of the statistics, Yale "possessed an unerring eye for the basket and an ability to play the game without fouling," explaining that the first was important "because it is the principal method of scoring" and the second because "not only is it a better game with few fouls [for spectators, that is] but it also prevents the other fellow from marking points against you from free throws."[8] Then, as if he (or his imagined reader) would grow impatient with such elementary explanations, Morgan transitions: "But to get back to the figures," and the next seven paragraphs consist of an enumeration of the quantitative data found in the "illuminating" table.

Finally, the numbers also explicitly informed his all-league selection according to criteria of "offensive power, defensive power and general all-around play." Though "judgment and experience" were required to evaluate the last of these three, Morgan also asserted that "For the first two abilities the league records speak for themselves."[9] Accordingly, he let the numbers tell him who the top five offensive and defensive players were, respectively, before combining the two lists and rounding them out with a more subjective and quantitative assessment of general all-around play. In the end, for the first time, the list of the players he selected to the first, second, and third all-league teams included their points; field goals; field goals against; free throws; free throws attempted; technical fouls (what today we would call violations, such as traveling); and personal fouls.[10]

I take Naismith's address and Morgan's article as indicators of the beginnings of a shift in the way that numbers were used in the context of a broader shift, already well under way, in the way the game was being used. By this time competitive college basketball was just beginning its ascent to center stage in the nation's basketball landscape. In that context Morgan's article presages a trend of observers and coaches using quantification to evaluate the quality of game play, not in terms of cleanliness or teamwork taken as moral desirables, but rather of these and other elements as integral to competitive success. To do so they not only used the numbers provided by the standard box score in novel ways but also began to wonder about, and to experiment with, methods of quantifying elements of game play not counted in official score books.

It is as though, having successfully secured a place for basketball as a morally and physically educative game, then having stabilized the institutional framework by which that game became one of the country's fastest growing competitive sports, key figures in the sport stopped asking *whether* to play basketball or *how* to play it properly and started instead to ask *how to play competitive basketball successfully*? Numbers were not the only instrument they used to answer that question, and, in some cases, numbers were not used at all. But when numbers were used in the period whose arrival Naismith and Morgan implicitly announce, they were used for this purpose.

#52. Coaches Counting

After the end of World War I, college basketball received an influx of talent: experienced players returned from service abroad and new, well-trained young players emerged from the high school ranks. At the same time, high school basketball continued to expand as more and more youngsters followed in the footsteps of their local heroes by taking up basketball as a competitive sport. The postwar acceleration of basketball's steady expansion together with economic growth and increased leisure time in the 1920s spurred, in turn, something like a boom in basketball literature. Long-standing annual guides, like the Spalding series for amateur players, grew fatter as more and more teams and leagues sprang into being (and more and more specialized sporting goods were manufactured and advertised), magazines for coaches, like the *Athletic Journal*, appeared, and a spate of books, authored by former players and coaches, offered increasingly detailed advice on how to compete successfully in basketball.

In this context we encounter an emphasis on using and refining the existing score blank first championed by Luther Gulick back in the 1890s. Two book-length manuals from the early 1920s, for example, include chapters on how to score basketball. Both include sample score blanks that, while making some minor modifications, are essentially those promoted by Gulick twenty years before. One argues that the scorebook "is a great aid to the coach or manager who desires to keep an accurate record of the work of his team," while another observes—echoing the shift toward "science" lamented by Naismith in 1913—that "the score book is of greater importance as the game progresses in scientific development."[11] Though there was nothing new in the content or method of the counting they advocated, we can see registered in the remarks of these authors the shift in the purpose of counting as it became an aid to the coach in assessing the player's value as a competitive asset.

Sometimes new recording methods were introduced in the same spirit. The editors of the *Athletic Journal*, on the first page of the first issue no less, introduced to readers what they called a "scouting chart." It showed a diagram of half of a basketball court on which player field goal attempts were represented by a player's jersey number written on the spot from which the attempt had been made. Successful attempts were circled. Today such charts, known as "shot charts," are common, whether created by hand with pencil and paper, by using an app on a mobile device, or by using digital optical tracking devices. But this should not lead us to overlook the innovation it represented at the time. The shot chart added an additional layer of analytical power to the data already provided in the scorebook. Previously a coach might know only that a player had made three of twelve of his field goal tries. With a shot chart, a coach might find that all three makes were from the same area of the court. In this way the chart would, as the editors promised, "give a coach much valuable information": the discovery of hidden strengths and deficiencies could lead to new strategies and tactics or even to further investigation; and all of it, again, was explicitly in the service of competitive success.

Charles Wardlaw and Whitelaw Morrison directly took up the question of competitive success in their attempt "to analyze the game scientifically." Describing the process of player selection, the authors pondered the tension between individual ability and teamwork, insisting that "the player's value is to be considered not from the standpoint of the individual but from the standpoint of the team."[12] But how can you know if a player is valuable to the team? After all, in a properly functioning team, individuals will not stand out, so individual contributions to team success will be difficult to isolate. At the same time, the traditional scorebook, counting only those individual actions—points and fouls—that could both be easily counted and, because of the rules, most directly and obviously impacted the outcome of contests, would be of limited utility in considering individual value, as Wardlaw and Morrison advised, "from the standpoint of the team." What were scientific minded basketball thinkers to do?

It is indicative of the inroads quantification had already made that this dilemma did not lead the authors to reject the usefulness of quantitative data but instead to recommend *more* counting. Wardlaw and Morrison counseled coaches to have "some one keep account of the number of times a man shoots for a basket during a game and how many goals he makes, what proportion of his passes are good, the number of passes he recovers and how many he fails to catch, how many times he misses the signal, and so on with all the important aspects of the game which can be measured quite accurately."[13] Wardlaw and Morrison proposed, in effect, expanding the scope of quantification, extending it beyond goals and fouls to include caught and dropped passes, blown plays (i.e., "missed signals"), and even relatively subjective elements such as good passes.

Equally significant as an indicator of the changing role of quantification in basketball is the use to which they proposed putting the resulting "valuable information." For example, a coach may discover he was "mistaken in his original opinion regarding a certain man." Or he may find out "that the record of a certain player shows him to be the best shot on the team" and so "should make it possible for this man to shoot more often, and at once, if all other factors are the same as before, the team becomes stronger."[14] By counteracting biases and exposing hidden patterns, quantification would improve the coach's effectiveness, not so much as a molder of character, which had been emphasized two decades before, however, but rather as an architect of victory.

Still it is important to keep in mind that these innovations, though indicative of a growing attention to how and why to quantify quality basketball play, were still marginal, significant mostly for prefiguring an awareness of the tension between counting and what counts and for certain ways of trying to resolve it for the sake of winning basketball.

More characteristic of the years immediately following World War I is

Ralph Morgan's recap of the 1921 Eastern Intercollegiate League season.[15] As in previous years, Morgan worried over the relative weight to give the "eye" and the "record," particularly when it came to assessing an individual's contributions to team success. And, as in previous years, he found ways to draw upon quantitative data to support his explanations of team successes and failures and, even more so, to make his all-league selections. But the public data available to him was, ultimately, still limited to the tallies—of field goals, free throws, violations, personal fouls, and field goals given up—made in official score blanks over the course of the season. Until innovative approaches to quantification like the shot chart, or the more encompassing tallies proposed by Wardlaw and Morrison became the publicly available norm, and indeed were enhanced by newer methods, the numbers would be of limited value to seasoned basketball thinkers attuned to the complexities of the game.

#53. Counting Complexity

The challenging complexity basketball posed to quantitative abstraction may be why none of the three major book-length treatises on the sport authored in the 1920s by some of the most legendary coaches of all time— Nat Holman of City College of New York, Walter ("Doc") Meanwell of the University of Wisconsin, and Forrest ("Phog") Allen of the University of Kansas—make any reference at all to quantification despite the stress each coach lays, in one form or another, on the importance of approaching the game in a scientific manner.[16] All three authors understood "scientific basketball" to mean approaching the game as a complex system of cause and effect relationships that could be rationally analyzed and studied. By breaking individual and team play down into constituent parts, the best methods for executing both technical skills and tactical plans could be devised, practiced, and then implemented. If quantification did not warrant the attention of these basketball thinkers, it was not because they were opposed to rational analysis, but rather the contrary: their rational assessment of the complexity of the sport led them to take a more qualitative approach given the poverty of the quantitative record available at the time.

They were not alone. By 1927 J. M. Carow, a high school coach in St. Petersburg, Florida, could state the problem flatly in the pages of the

American Physical Education Review: "In order to develop a good basket
ball team it is necessary to know what each player is doing on the floor and
to give proper credit to each player, including the standing guard. Obviously,
the usual method of scoring does not meet these requirements."[17] Carow
went on to enumerate the limitations of Gulick's scorebook in terms that
strikingly prefigure critiques of the box score made by basketball analysts
seventy years later: "The usual score sheet shows the goals and fouls, but
fails to show whether the goals were from long or short shots; the number
of missed shots from the field; the assists; the intercepted passes lost or
won; who is putting the ball out of bounds, getting it off the bounding
board, or receiving it from the tip-off from center, from held balls, or from
out of bounds. From the usual score sheet, it is impossible to calculate the
percentage of goals to total shots, the good plays to errors, the activity or
the relative efficiency of the players."

"Goals and fouls" may have been all you needed to know when the point
of the sport was exercise and moral improvement. But if you want to win,
and you have been around the game, you know that goals and fouls, though
obviously relevant to the outcome of games, are only the beginning of what
you need to know. But unlike his more celebrated counterparts, Carow
responded by doubling down on quantification. After all, he wrote, "Basket
ball coaches recognize that the more they reduce the play to paper the better they can direct it, correct the errors, and develop the players." Carow's
optimistic formulation of a solution was as impressively prescient of contemporary approaches as his understanding of the problem. "In baseball,"
he explained, "a system of scoring has been developed and standardized
which quite accurately shows the players' relative efficiency. It is possible
to determine this efficiency even more accurately than in baseball."

First, an observer would create a simplified transcript of game play
according to a shorthand code similar to what Dean Oliver would develop
decades later (see table 3).

With these symbols, the scorer might use a string such as the following: "#
A B ---- C O ---- /\/\/\/ ---- A B / bo ---- H C." This would signify, according
to Carow, "Ball goes up in center; A gets tip-off to B; it is intercepted by C,
who puts it out of bounds. It is put in by opponent, who passes, dribbles,

TABLE 3. J. M. Carow scoring shorthand

Code	Play represented
A, B, C, D, etc.	Initials of players
----	Plays of opponents
#	Play starts at center
O	Out of bounds
H	Held ball
/	Short shot (Inside radius of 15 ft)
$/$	Long shot
$\wedge$	Short goal
$\wedge$	Long goal
Bo	Ball hits bounding board
fu	Fumble
MWW	Dribble
(Ap—)'	Personal foul by A, shot by —, who makes it
(—pA)°	Personal foul by — shot by A, who fails
(At)	Technical foul by A

and passes. It is intercepted by A who passes to B who tries a short shot and misses. Ball strikes bounding board and is recovered by opponent, who passes to another and C gets held ball." It's clear that the code, though still necessarily reducing basketball play, registers more complexity than even modified versions of Gulick's score blanks.

But quickly and accurately recording complex action is only the first step and is not yet quantification. That happens in the second step, when the actions of each player that are represented by these symbols are totaled up. Even then, however, the system would be limited. Though you would have totals in more categories, you'd have no way to relate these totals to one another. Merely to compare these totals—say player A's three baskets made with player B's three interceptions—would be to presume that each action contributed equally to team success or, in other words, that it had the same value.

Carow addressed this problem by adopting the same method that would be used later to construct what basketball analytics would come to call a linear weights formula, where each positive and negative action is assigned a different weight in a linear equation—depending on what the analyst judges, hopefully based on an adequate sample of historical data, is the value of its contribution to victory. The actual number of times the player completed each action in a game would be multiplied by the weight factor and the totals summed together. Carow's method differed in detail but followed the same principles.

He assigned a different positive or negative point value to each recorded play and then entered the totals for each—he called them "credits" and "debits"—on a table. He then divided the credits by the sum of credits and debits to get a credit percentage. Finally, Carow further adjusted the credit percentage in two ways—to account for playing time and for the team's average—in order to arrive at each player's "relative efficiency," as he called it, prescient even in his use of the watchword for mechanical and economical productivity that would form the conceptual cornerstone of basketball analytics. In essence, through Carow's final statistical adjustments, relative efficiency would indicate how much a player had done (credit percentage) relative to the average for his team and to the amount of time he'd spent on the floor.

Though Carow's "standardized scheme for scoring in basket ball" did not revolutionize basketball quantification and in fact, as far as I can determine, exercised no influence at all on the history of counting in basketball, it nevertheless is indicative of certain attempts to quantify basketball performance over the next decade and, indeed, augurs key features that would characterize, many decades later, basketball analytics.[18] First, Carow sought to acquire a larger mass of data from game play. From his "shorthand" to Oliver's "new method of scoring basketball" to the optical tracking system of Second Spectrum, the impulse is the same: to capture and count as much as possible of what (according to the value system of the counter) counts. Second, Carow applied mathematical and statistical principles and methods to try to quantify and make objective necessarily subjectively determined qualitative differences in the value of different contributions to team success. Third, Carow, using a vocabulary of "efficiency," "credits," and "debits," prefigured the tendency in basketball analytics (and sports analytics more generally) to employ metaphors drawn from engineering and business to think about the quality of basketball players and about the relationship of individual players to the whole team. In these ways it was a sign of what was to come, in some respects, in the very next decade, as college basketball became a commercialized national extravaganza.

Interlude—Measuring Sticks

#54. Clyde and the Doctor

Until I met Danny Johnson, the only basketball players I ever wanted to be were either my brother Tony or a pro. Like Walt Frazier, for example, who played for the New York Knicks around the time that I was first going to Bucks games in Madison. I loved him with the same unalloyed intensity with which I hated Rick Barry. I loved that Frazier was smooth and fluid, fast but unhurried, creative but cool, and apparently effortlessly effective. Walt Frazier's nickname, after all, was "Clyde the Glide": What could be smoother than that? Feel that rolling off your childhood tongue. In contrast, Rick Barry, whose name was not so smooth, seemed rough, scurrying, emotional, clumsy, scrappy, and unhappily effective.

Rick Barry reminded me, in his clumsy, complaining unhappiness, of my father. But also, with his manifestly visible effort, I think he reminded me that, as the smallest in the family by far, I always felt like I was trying, and trying too hard: trying to keep up, trying to be good, trying not to be a crybaby. I hated myself for the effort I had to make and so I hated also the sweaty, panting, grimacing evidence of effort apparent on the faces of my hated players. So in hating Rick Barry's matted sweaty hair, his foolish-looking—if incredibly effective—underhanded free-throw shooting style, his shoving and holding on defense, his petulant whining to the refs, I was hating my dad, and my family as a whole. And I was hating myself.

Naturally I chose instead to be Clyde the Glide. I even once got permission from my mother to transform an old white undershirt of mine into a Knicks jersey by painting "Knicks" on the front and the number ten below the name "Frazier" on the back. Then, in a fit of imaginative inspiration and artistic license (which, as with all such gestures, I undertook without seeking permission), I took the same black tempera paint and gave myself the beard and sideburns that I thought looked like his. Clyde and my other beloveds were a desired possibility, another way to be. Differences in talent, size, age, or race made no difference to my imagination, which hurdled those gaps with ease. I think I was ten years old before I realized, really realized, that the players I loved were almost all black and I wasn't. Even after that it usually didn't matter since anything could happen in the universe of basketball.

Take, for example, what happened in January 1976, in the frozen dead of winter in Madison, Wisconsin. I was ten years old and sprawled with my best friend Robb, who was eleven, on the shag rug in my parents' living room. We were watching the American Basketball Association (ABA) All-Star Game (more on the ABA in chapter 8). Though the upstart and now defunct league was bankrupt and this was to be its last season, it had already captured our youthful imaginations with its bright red, white, and blue basketball, its three-point shot, and, above all, the acrobatic play of its biggest star: Julius Erving, known as "Dr. J."—because of the way he operated. Normally, boring halftime was when Robb and I would go out to play some one-on-one, careful to avoid the patches of ice in my driveway. But that day the ABA had advertised something that had never happened outside of our imaginations and maybe not even in them: a slam dunk contest. A handful of players—including Dr. J.—would take turns throwing down creative dunks, showing off their imagination, leaping ability, power, and skill.

Just before his final turn in the contest, Erving stood at the free-throw line facing the basket. Then, palming the ball in one hand, he dramatically turned and in loping strides measured his steps to the free-throw area at the other end of the court. Robb and I watched, confused and breathless with anticipation. Dr. J. then turned back to face up-court, paused, and with the ball still held firmly in his right hand, he sprinted back toward the original basket. When his left foot hit the free-throw line, he took off, soaring toward the hoop, high blowout Afro shifting slightly backward in the wind;

raising the ball up and back with his right arm, like "Lady Liberty holding her torch," as he later recalled, he jammed it down through the basket as flashbulbs popped.[1]

Robb and I sprang to our feet, laughing and shouting and shoving each other. The play counted for zero points, but Dr. J.'s imagination and freedom raced like a warm current of infinity through our young bodies and minds and hearts and souls. Moments later we took turns imitating the dunk on the improvised hoop in my basement. In our one-on-one games in the driveway over the next few years, Robb usually got to be the Doctor. It wasn't because I didn't want to be the Doctor, too, probably just as much as Robb. It was because, I guess, by that time—a few years after I'd so innocently become Clyde Frazier—something inside me told me that the Doctor, who was black, belonged more to Robb, who was also black, than to me. So, in those games, I'd be the (very white) Portland Trailblazers, which was mostly okay with me because (a) I was born in Portland and (b) they had beaten the Doctor's Philadelphia 76ers in the 1977 NBA Finals. But inside, I still wanted to be the Doctor.

A few years ago I was teaching students about the ABA and somehow, I don't recall how, the word "psychedelic" popped out of one of the kid's mouths to describe the league. Psychedelic in the original Greek means "soul manifesting." If that is so, then when I drift back into that soul space of Robb and me witnessing then trying to emulate Dr. J's *worthless* dunk— perfectly inefficient: it was worth exactly zero points—I think to myself that there may be no better emblem for the psychedelic soul-manifesting potentialities basketball held for me.

#55. Danny Fucking Johnson

It was probably around that time that I first encountered Danny Johnson, the first player my own age—and the first opponent—I wanted to be instead of being me. Let me be clear: I knew nothing about Danny or his life off the court. I just knew this: on opening day of the 1978–79 Madison Parochial Sports League Boys Basketball season—eighth grade for both Danny and me—I had fourteen points and thirteen rebounds in a two-point loss to eventual, undefeated league champion Blessed Sacrament. Not bad. You know what Danny did on opening day? Keep in mind we only played twenty-four-minute games and there was no three-point line. Twenty points? Nope. Higher. Twenty-five? Try again. Higher. Thirty? Uh-uh. Higher.

Thirty-five points! Thirty-five fucking points in twenty-four minutes of play. A new opening day record! It was unthinkable. That would be seventy points in a forty-eight-minute NBA game. Know how many times in the NBA's seventy-year history a player has scored seventy points or more in a single game? Eleven. Not even Michael Jordan scored seventy points in a single game. And if you take away the games where the three-point shot was in effect (since Danny didn't play with one), you're down to eight. Of those eight seventy-point-plus games, seven were done by one individual: the Big Dipper, Wilt Chamberlain.

Maybe I should've expected it. Two years before, when I was a sixth grader on my school's "B" team, Danny was already the leading scorer on his "A" team and the eleventh leading scorer in the league. The next year, Danny, now a seventh grader, was third in the league in scoring. So, though I felt confident in my abilities as a scorer and had high hopes going into the season, the numbers had already told me—had I but listened—that it would be Danny's year. Looking at the fifteen points a game he'd put up as a prepubescent seventh grader, I should've predicted the thirty-five he'd get on opening day, or the twenty-six, or the all-time single-game record thirty-seven (twice!), or the twenty-eight and the thirty-two—against all of which a twenty-two and a season-ending twenty-three, though higher than I ever managed, seemed pedestrian. All in all Danny missed two games that season and still scored 266 points, averaging almost twenty-seven per game. Playing in all twelve of my team's games I scored 150 points, good for second in the league. But my 12.5 points per game weren't even half of what Danny put up.

Now, I should have been satisfied with the fact that my team went 7 and 5, good for third place, while Danny's St. James Spartans finished 6 and 6. I should have been satisfied that we beat St. James both times we played them. I should have been satisfied that in those two games, when Danny and I guarded each other, he averaged only thirteen—less than half his season average—and I averaged eleven, just a little below my season average.

So, I should've been satisfied with all that. But my scorer's soul—and my counting heart—just could not be.

It wasn't just because of the vast disparity in our overall season numbers. The numbers mattered to me, sure. But they were just a sign of something else. When I go back to those cramped, dimly lit parochial gyms, with a faint Wisconsin winter sun barely casting light through high windows onto ancient floors, I can feel that something else rise to the surface again: "fuckin' Danny Johnson!" As a (very) good Catholic boy, I never would have put it that way at the time, but his ability to score left me stupefied: "How the fuck did he do it?" This was not gracious, sportsmanlike admiration I felt. It was bitter, bilious, burning jealousy and roiling resentment.

Here comes Danny approaching half court on a fast break, wait, what? He pulls up just across the line and flings the ball up from his chest: swish, from just across half court—years before Steph Curry was even born. Or there he is, maybe 'cause that first shot was too easy, weaving through a team full of defenders like they were traffic cones on his way to an uncontested layup that he—unlike me—never missed.

Now, I was five foot five in eighth grade. But we were a small team, and so mostly my coach had me post up on the low block. I had three moves that I can remember: (1) a right-handed hook shot (like Kareem's skyhook!—but not), (2) a fadeaway that I could hit drifting toward either baseline (my favorite!), (3) a good pump fake that got me to the free throw line pretty reliably or else gave me enough space to get off my jump shot in the lane (hard work!). Nothing special, I know, but I worked my ass off on those moves the summer before eighth grade, and with them I busted my hump to what should have been a respectable 12.5 points per game.

By contrast, Danny had one billion different fucking ways to score and none looked to me like they required any fucking effort on his part. That's the thing. Danny moved through our basketball world with a carefree ease I felt only in my best dreams, where everything I threw at the hoop went in and the crowd went crazy and everyone told me to just keep shooting, keep shooting. So yeah, I wanted to be Danny. I wanted his twenty-seven a game, and I wanted his ease and his cool. I know, I know: Danny was probably working his own ass off the summer before eighth grade (and before seventh

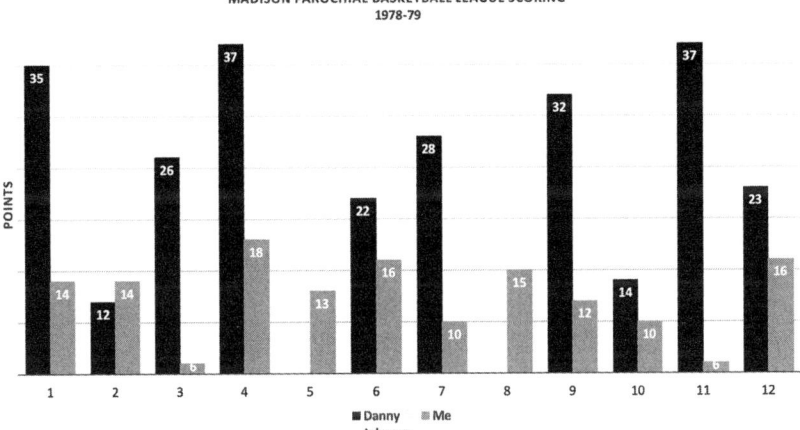

MADISON PAROCHIAL BASKETBALL LEAGUE SCORING
1978-79

FIG. 6. Statistical comparison of Danny Johnson and me.

and sixth), but I was thirteen. I didn't think like that then. I didn't see his effort; I saw only his spectacular and graceful results—Clyde the Glide and Dr. J come to life on my own court and, it turns out, I was not either of them. I was not even Danny Johnson. Hell, despite my unseemly effort and my craven craving to be great, I wasn't even Rick fuckin' Barry (fig. 6).

I was just Yago Colás. I was already a distant second to my dreams, and the gap was only growing wider.

Numbers don't fuckin' lie.

7

Counting for Commerce in College Basketball

#56. Electrical Pursuit Apparatus

The story is told that in 1905, when Phog Allen informed his mentor and basketball instructor at the University of Kansas, James Naismith, that he had accepted an offer to coach the basketball team at Baker College, the inventor of the sport laughed at him: "Why, Phog, you can't coach basketball, you just play it!" Whether or not this actually occurred, and though the two remained fast friends until Naismith's death, the exchange symbolically captures the two very different ways of thinking about basketball that their lives in the game and even their public positions, at times, would come to embody. While Naismith—famously the only coach in Kansas basketball history with a losing record—remained steadfast, as we've seen, in his commitment to the sport as an accessible, educational recreational activity best used to cultivate physical, moral, and mental health, Allen's name would become nearly synonymous with the big-time college basketball coaching profession.

Indeed, Allen would return to Kansas to replace Naismith as basketball coach and go on, over the course of four decades, to preside over a dynasty of championship-caliber teams, some of whose members would themselves go on to become legendary coaches. Allen, it is no exaggeration to say, is the trunk of the college basketball coaches' genealogical tree. But beyond his work as a coach, Allen also impacted the sport by founding, in 1927, the National Association of Basketball Coaches (NABC), in part to galvanize an ultimately successful campaign to reverse the Joint Rules Committee's decision to severely restrict dribbling. And it was in his capacity as president of the NABC, that in April of 1929 he delivered a speech to the delegates gathered for the association's third annual convention, in which he called for the formation of a research committee, appointed by the NABC, that would coordinate physiological research into the effects of basketball and thereby "answer in a most definite manner the people who say that basketball is too strenuous for the average athlete."[1]

Allen cited work that his mentor and friend, Naismith, had been doing already along these lines as a physical education researcher at Kansas. And, indeed, Naismith had previously published the results of an innovative, quantitative study of the strain experienced by female basketball players, concluding—in the face of game administrators who hoped he would corroborate their claim that the game was too "injurious" to be played by women—that there was nothing inherent in the game that should cause it to be injurious to women, or anyone else.[2]

As Allen knew, Naismith was neither the only nor the first to be conducting such research. As early as 1914, studies were being conducted to assess the psychological and physiological effects of basketball play.[3] In some ways this work was just a specific application of research that physical educators and exercise scientists had already been conducting over the first two decades of the twentieth century into the characteristics of physical efficiency and how to measure it. But as basketball occupied a more central role in the physical education programs of both schools and community organizations, it came also to draw more attention from researchers.[4] Out of these efforts, and spurred by the sport's growth over the course of the 1920s, exercise researchers in the 1930s explored ways to quantify aspects of basketball play and to measure basketball ability in greater detail and with greater precision than ever before.

To take just one example, in 1931, Lloyd Messersmith of DePauw University asked himself how far basketball players ran over the course of the game. Today of course, Second Spectrum's optical tracking system provides the distance run by each player. But Messersmith had no such technology available. To determine the answer he constructed an "electrical pursuit apparatus." This consisted of a small, electrified scale-model of a basketball court connected to an impulse counter. An experimenter would trace with a brass wheel on the model court the movements of a player on the real court. Markings on the wheel would transmit signals to the impulse counter which would then register the distance traveled. Messersmith then used the scale ratio to convert the distance covered on the electrical pursuit apparatus to the actual distance covered by the corresponding players on the court.

Messersmith announced his intention to examine the relationship between distance run in various sports with weight loss, speed of player, and so forth, presumably to address issues of the physiological effects and health benefits or risks of sports. Over the next dozen years, Messersmith and his colleagues measured distance under different circumstances (before and after rule changes, men's games vs. women's, college vs. high school courts), eventually submitting his research as a doctoral dissertation in the School of Education at Indiana University in 1942.[5] Despite his original intentions, Messersmith's conclusions are consistently limited to merely reporting the distance run.

Though Messersmith's experiments in movement quantification certainly anticipate the kinds of questions, investigations, and measurements that later kinesiologists, aided by far more sophisticated equipment, would pursue more fully, at the time, a more common and immediately practical use of quantification by physical education scientists in relation to basketball pertained to the measurement of skill acquisition and achievement. Though these studies were mainly conducted in order to refine instructional and assessment methods used by physical education teachers, as the results began to pile up by the late 1930s, researchers increasingly registered, in different ways, an awareness that the effort to measure proficiency in order to determine whether a player was learning a skill was closely related to the process by which a coach might look to assess player abilities in different areas of game play in order to assemble the best team.[6]

#57. The Player's Whole Game

Given the steady appearance of these studies in the 1930s, together with the experiments by coaches like Carow with different practical methods of quantifying player performance, it's not surprising that in July 1938, Harold Dimick would submit a master's thesis to the School of Education at the University of Southern California entitled "Formulation of a Basketball Scoring Method that Will Measure General Offensive Efficiency." If only symbolically, Dimick's thesis is a landmark in that it represents the first formal intersection that I have found of these two main, hitherto parallel, paths of basketball quantification in the interwar period: coaches searching for competitive advantage, and scientists and educators seeking a better understanding of basketball skill acquisition and performance.

"The writer," Dimick confesses, "has constantly been in an experimental frame of mind, and it was in this spirit that the present problem was undertaken. The coach, in his effort to mold players into a team, has long been in need of some motivating agent for all-around play rather than for points alone. It was this urge for a statistical or graphic picture of the player's whole game that prompted this experiment. Another element involved was the need to overcome the public hero-worship and the newspaper estimates of star performance."[7]

Dimick was himself a former college player and a basketball coach, and the motives he avows for designing a better scorebook are all specific to basketball: aiding coaches in player performance evaluation and diagnosis, educating a "score-happy" public as to the complexity of the sport, motivating players to accept the importance of, and to cultivate, all-around skills within a team context. But to solve this task he approaches the basketball scorebook as an instance of the more general problem of the construction of valid, reliable, and objective tests to measure performance in physical education. Indeed, the thesis is as much a general study of test construction in physical education—with chapters devoted to "validity," "reliability," and "objectivity" and numerous appendices, tables, and graphs attesting to these—as it is a specific attempt to devise a quantitative, objective test of offensive efficiency in basketball.

Still, Dimick's solution is relatively straightforward and strikingly similar to the fundamental insights that catalyzed basketball analytics in the early 1990s. If the overall object of basketball competition, he reasoned, was to score more points than one's opponent, then the narrow objective of each possession should be to get the best shot possible. To measure offensive efficiency Dimick took stock—in part by consulting the qualitative treatises of basketball published by coaching legends like Holman, Meanwell, and Allen in the 1920s—of the factors that cause teams to lose possessions (i.e., chances to score). He defined as "errors" "any misplay that caused a loss of possession" and created an equation with errors and field goals attempted in the numerator and field goals made in the denominator. The resulting quotient was basketball efficiency (lower would be better, which is, at least from the modern vantage point, one of the confusing peculiarities of Dimick's system—the others being the omission of free throws and rebounds from the data recorded).

Nevertheless, Dimick's thesis is noteworthy in several respects. In terms of the development of quantifying methods in the sport, as I've said, it brings together what had been two parallel paths in basketball quantification: the use of scientific methods to develop tests of basketball ability for educational purposes and the development of amateur scorekeeping methods to give coaches and players a competitive edge. Moreover, with his attention to how possessions were used as a way to counter a misleading emphasis on points, Dimick anticipated the groundbreaking insights of contemporary basketball analysts such as Dean Oliver. And, Dimick's decision to utilize the metaphor of "efficiency," to describe the desirable quality he was seeking to quantify, forms a link in a chain connecting Gulick and his contemporaries' concerns with physical efficiency and Oliver and other basketball analysts' emphasis on efficiency as the central measure of team quality.

But there are, in addition, two other noteworthy elements to Dimick's work that suggest yet another aspect of the context in which he was writing. First, Dimick decidedly tilts the "efficiency" metaphor away from engineering and toward business and economics. As he puts it: "Points are the offensive objectives of the game, but in order to get a true picture of offensive value, the cost of points in team scoring chances must be measured. Points obtained at too costly a price do not represent true excellence."[8] Second, and possibly related, Dimick introduces a new purpose to the improved scoresheet. Where Gulick had advocated scorekeeping for moral purposes, and the next generation had used it to aid coaches and players in improving performance, Dimick also registers an awareness of fans and the media when he suggests that the scorebook "would tell a better story of the game than the usual point and foul summary" and thus would help "re-educate" fans who currently unjustly judge a player's worth by the point and foul totals printed in newspaper summaries.[9]

We can glimpse then, between the lines of Dimick's thesis, the welding together of competitive value and economic value. For Dimick this may have been merely metaphorical, but the metaphor may have impressed itself upon his imagination because by the time he was conducting his research, college basketball play had recently—and spectacularly—proved a profitable commodity in the entertainment industry, with media reports of double- and triple-headers featuring national powerhouses and individual stars exhibiting their talents before tens of thousands of fans packing Madison Square Garden and other prominent arenas.[10] The success of these events led Allen's NABC to stage the first-ever National College Basketball Tournament, in 1937. And the success of that led to the foundation of two other national tournaments that would become national institutions: the National Invitational Tournament (NIT), sponsored by New York City sportswriters and, in 1939, the NCAA Men's National Basketball Championship, which would become, over time, the billion-dollar extravaganza known as "March Madness."[11] Together with a 1937 rule eliminating the center jump after every made basket, which sped up play and changed tactics and positional assignments, these tournaments helped usher in college basketball's first golden age.

#58. Progressive Basketball

If these events and the broader tendencies toward the commercialization of big-time college basketball they emblematized were not foremost on Dimick's mind, I suspect they may have been nagging at the coauthor—none other than the James Naismith-protégé, celebrated Kansas head coach, Forrest C. (Phog) Allen—of what was at the time of its publication, in the scholarly journal *Research Quarterly of the American Association of Health, Physical Education, and Recreation*, in 1941, probably the most ambitious and sophisticated attempt at a systematic, quantitative evaluation of "team and individual performance in basketball." Allen, as president of the NABC had led the organization to stage the first national tournament and—over the objections of his mentor, the sport's inventor—had pushed through the elimination of the center jump after each made basket. If Dimick, a graduate student, approached the intersection of coaching and science more as a scientist, then Allen approached it as a successful and prominent coach experienced in institutional matters and evidently aware of both the sport's potential to entertain and its burgeoning commercial power.

That Allen appears as an author is not, of course, surprising, since nearly two decades before, he'd already published his four-hundred-page basketball "bible." What I do find surprising is that Allen should appear in the pages of a scholarly journal as a coauthor of a scientific examination of quantitative methods of performance evaluation when his earlier influential work had made no mention of statistics or score books or any other form of quantification. However, perhaps this should not be surprising since Allen himself had already called for more scientific research into the sport. Moreover, as (Dr.) Allen (MD) and his coauthor, Kansas professor of physical education Dr. E. R. Elbel (PhD), point out, "There is quite general agreement that the box score does not give a very complete statistical picture of the game and is consequently of little value to coach or player from the standpoint of game analysis."[12] Perhaps, then, Allen's earlier silence on issues of quantification reflected this same belief.

The problems are familiar: the box score imagines a game in which only one positive thing (scoring) and one negative thing (fouling) count enough to be counted. But for Allen and Elbel this misses the many other mistakes that can bring a team down as well as the many non-scoring contributions that may secure a victory. In other words, they might have said, much that counts in basketball was not being counted, and, as a result, what was being counted—points and fouls—probably counted proportionally less than most people would have assumed just from the fact that it was what was being counted.

Allen and Elbel devised the most elaborate offensive and defensive linear weights formula to date for what they, too, called "efficiency." (It is striking, but rather typical of the literature of quantification in basketball, that Allen and Elbel cite no other authors in their article, despite the fact that others— such as J. M. Carow, whose system I described above—had published, in

TABLE 4. Allen and Elbel linear weights

Offensive				Defensive			
POSITIVE		NEGATIVE		POSITIVE		NEGATIVE	
Field goal	+10	Foul	-8	Block	+4	Fouling opponent with ball	-8
Free throw	+5	Violation	-5	Rebound	+4	Fouling opponent without ball	-8
Immediate assist	+4	Pass stolen	-4	Steal of dribble	+3		
Secondary assist	+3	Pass out of bounds	-3	Steal of pass	+2		
Offensive rebound	+2	Tap out of bounds	-2	Forcing held ball	+2		
Recovers jump ball	+1	Fumble to opponent	-2	Batting ball from opponent's hands and recovering	+1		
Recover's opponent fumble	+1	Fumble out of bounds	-2	Batting ball from opponent's hands and not recovering	+1		
Good pass	+1	Held ball	-1	Deflected pass	+1		
Catch	+1	Error of omission	-1				

well-known publications of the time, efforts to amend the box score using a similar, if less comprehensive, method.) In their case, they came up with a list of nine "positive" offensive items, nine "negative" offensive items, eight positive defensive items, and two negative defensive items and then weighted each item according to their subjective judgment of its importance as a factor contributing to team success or failure (see table 4).

Having tabulated several seasons' worth of University of Kansas game data and then analyzed anomalies and trends in different areas of individual and team play, the authors confidently concluded: "Much information which could be helpful, and is readily available in basketball games, is not used." In particular they claimed to have shown that certain factors important to winning receive little recognition. While some of these are mistakes that "occur so frequently that they appear to have little effect on the outcome," others are important enough that they "readily offset" scoring ability. On the positive side, they proved the "importance of team play" and of "the player who is an important factor in the scoring by his teammates, though he secures few points himself."[13]

The link between the establishment of college basketball as a national, commercially successful competitive sport and the use and promotion of quantitative thinking also appears in the work of Stanford coach Everett Dean, who capitalized on having led his squad to the NCAA championship in 1942 with the publication, later that year, of the book *Progressive Basketball*. Dean's philosophy is announced right on the cover, not only with its title, evoking Enlightenment ideals of progress through knowledge, but even with its simple cover art depicting in four simple drawings the successive stages of a player executing a chest pass, which brings to mind evolutionary iconology, as the images ascend from left to right, and the player's posture shifts from crouched to erect and extended.[14]

Unlike Dimick and Allen, Dean spends little time describing, let alone arguing the merits of, the scorebook he uses. This is not because quantification plays no part in his successful coaching system, but rather, on the contrary, because quantification plays so pervasive a role in his coaching methods that the indispensability of counting to "progressive basketball" is a given. In fact, the scorebook he uses appears from his brief description to capture more or less what Allen and Elbel, Dimick before them, and Carow before him were hoping to capture: a shooting record including the shot position and errors such as fumbling, violations, bad passes, and the like. That Dean (unlike his predecessors) foregoes the elaborate methodological description or epistemological argument for this scorebook may be a sign of how widely accepted the value of such quantifying perspectives had come to be.

Moreover, along with the scorebook, Dean recommends using a number of other quantitative records such as shooting charts, rebound statistics, and jump-ball statistics. Dean seems not to be looking for a single-number metric to assess his players. Instead his approach indicates a recognition that the complexity of the sport requires an equally complex quantitative apparatus. Finally, in addition to this data, in order "to set up some standard with which to measure in a more objective way the different abilities of basketball players," Dean recommends no fewer than a dozen tests of technical skill and physical ability along with a "knowledge test." In summarizing his recommendations, Dean concludes that the tests "provide the coach with scientific data concerning the group of young men with whom he is working," that the tests can help a coach identify "latent abilities of prospective athletes" as well as previously unknown physical "defects," and allow him to check his own biases by comparing his subjective judgments with the objective measures provided by the data. Ultimately, Dean says, "As the game of basketball becomes more and more scientific the coach of this very popular sport should adopt a scientific attitude toward the game."[15]

#59. Scientific Basketball (Again)

When Oregon defeated the Ohio State Buckeyes in the first NCAA championship game in 1939, the Ducks (or Webfoots as they were called at the time) were coached by Howard Hobson. Ten years later Hobson had moved on to Yale University where he transformed that mediocre program, leading it, in just his second year, to an Ivy League Championship and its first NCAA tournament appearance ever. So it was with some authority that Hobson, apparently taking Coach Dean's scientific method to heart, published *Scientific Basketball for Coaches, Players, Official, Spectators, and Sportswriters*, by which he intended to show that factors such as shooting percentages, bad passes, violations, turnovers, and rebounds "may be objectively measured, and that it will be possible to establish, by analysis, a relationship between these factors of performance and the success or failure of the individual player and of the team."[16] Hobson amassed quantitative data from 460 college games in order to establish standards of performance that would facilitate the effort to identify significant relationships between objectively measured factors of performance and game outcomes.

Perhaps much of this was implicit in all the quantifying attempts I've explored in this chapter, but Hobson's effort, besides being the most comprehensive—the first book-length treatise on basketball centered entirely on quantitative data—was original in several respects. First, Hobson made explicit the steps of his scientific approach: (1) establish methods to objectively measure performance in various areas of the game play, (2) amass a large data set to provide historical performance standards, (3) analyze this data set to correlate individual performance factors with game outcomes, (4) apply the results of this analysis to current game play data. Fifty years later much the same method would be used by Dean Oliver in what was seen as his pioneering work of basketball analytics, *Basketball on Paper*.

Second, by explicitly tailoring the method in different ways to each of the five audiences named in his subtitle—coaches, players, officials, spectators, and sportswriters—Hobson indicated the degree to which the sport had expanded beyond direct participants (coaches and players) and organizing institutions (officials) to become a source of popular entertainment (spectators) and an object of media attention (sportswriters). In this way Hobson's *Scientific Basketball* brought together and articulated the relationship between developments in on-court play, quantifying techniques, and the cultural footprint of basketball since the 1920s. Hobson noted the importance of the Madison Square Garden games, All-America selections, and National tournaments in establishing the "country-wide growth and interest in basketball" so that "over 20 million people play basketball each year in the United States" and, in 1949, 105 million fans bought tickets for basketball games—a full third, he notes, of the 318 million tickets bought for all sporting events combined. No wonder that Hobson envisions that "the future of basketball in this country is truly great." Though Hobson was obviously prescient, even to the degree that he conducted an experiment with a three-point shot as early as 1945, I think even he may have had difficulty imagining what the future of basketball would actually hold.[17]

The very year in which his book was published, a new professional league, the National Basketball Association, would be formed out of the merger of the older National Basketball League, which featured marquee college stars in mostly small markets, and the upstart, more commercially oriented Basketball Association of America, centered on the Eastern Seaboard, whose franchise owners were not "basketball men" but had deeper pockets. After three years of commercial rivalry, in 1949, the two leagues called an uneasy truce and merged to form a new league. Though it would take the NBA a decade to achieve the popularity of the college game, the trends related to quantification that had developed over the first fifty years of amateur basketball would eventually take root, grow, and take their fullest form in men's professional basketball, where they would help establish the league, seventy years after the publication of Hobson's book, as a multi-billion-dollar sector of global entertainment industry.

Interlude—Magic

#60. No. 32

So, here's the thing: though Middleton—at least by the numbers—may have been the peak of my basketball career, it is not my favorite basketball memory. No. Though the statistics say I played efficiently; though Don Lindstrom called me the hero; though my coach and my parents were proud; though my team won an important game; though I am gratified that I played the steady, complete game I was supposed to, Middleton does not make my basketball heart sing. In fact, *because* I played the steady, complete game I was supposed to, Middleton does not make my basketball heart sing. To explain that, and to find the game that does make my basketball heart sing, we have to roll the clock back two years, to my sophomore year, when I played on the high school junior varsity during the 1980–81 school year.

The first thing you have to know is that at that time, at least at my school, numbers on the team jerseys (from 10 to 54) ascended by size (S to XL) and still correlated roughly with position, from point guard to shooting guard to small forward to power forward to center. The second thing you have to know is that by that time I was a five-foot-seven point guard—maybe the third-smallest guy on the team—and so I probably should've worn a number in the tens or at most in the twenties. The third thing you have to know is that the jersey number I chose was 32 (33 for away games). And the last thing you have to know, if you didn't know it or remember it already yourself, is that 32 was the number worn by Magic Johnson, the big, six-foot-nine point guard then starring in his second NBA season for the Los Angeles Lakers.

I knew about Magic before he led the Lakers to the NBA title in his rookie season during my freshman year in high school. I'd seen Magic play in person when I was in eighth grade; talented Danny Johnson was breaking both parochial basketball in Madison and my basketball heart, and Magic was playing in his second and final season for Michigan State. Magic's season would end with a victory in the national championship game that remains to this day the most-watched basketball game ever to be televised; one that turned the already popular college game promoted by Allen and others in the '30s and '40s into the financial and cultural behemoth we know as March Madness.

But earlier that year, State came to Madison to play my University of Wisconsin Badgers in the final regular season game of the season, March 3, 1979. Though middling Wisconsin handed the Spartans their last loss of the season on a thrilling half-court buzzer beater, seeing Magic in person left an even stronger impression on me. And by the next season, as Magic was tearing up the NBA, I was tearing up every newspaper and magazine I could find to paste photos and articles in a hardbound scrapbook dedicated to the Lakers' rookie star (and since recovered from my own archive). Among the items there is a letter I received from the Los Angeles Lakers politely explaining to me that "no, though they appreciated my support, they could not give me Magic's home address."

#61. Joy

Magic was, obviously, one of the greatest and most entertaining basketball players of all time. So, there was nothing unusual about my fanboy love for Magic. I loved the no-look passes, the coast-to-coast, full-court fast breaks, and I loved his smile. Magic broke my mold: he was not "cool" in the sense of aloof and his competitive intensity was obvious, but he did make the game look easy, and though emotionally expressive, he never seemed emotionally out of control. Magic played joyfully. His combination of competitive intensity, effort, ease, effectiveness, and joy was foreign to my basketball experience. But also, by this time, basketball was beginning, at least unconsciously, to provide the metaphorical elements by which I organized my perceptions of myself, my family dynamics, and other interpersonal situations. And in this way, Magic emblematized a way of being in life I had never before encountered, in which I could gracefully and self-assertively and even, when called for, aggressively contribute to the greater good—or, even better, an understanding that the greater good called for me to assert myself. My god! I will wear number 32.

My team sucked. We won four games and lost sixteen that year. I think it's a fair reflection of how good we were relative to our competition. It's true that we suffered some key injuries. It's also true that we lost a half-dozen games by just two points, and that we won two of our last five. But we also barely won the games we won. We didn't have many guys on the squad, our tallest player was five foot eleven, and the only other player besides me whose primary sport was basketball suffered a career-ending eye injury before we ever played a game.

Now, the purpose of junior varsity ball at our school was to learn the offenses and defenses that we'd be expected to use in later years on the varsity, and our coach mostly tried to stay true to that. But given the limitations of the squad, he also gave me a great deal of freedom to improvise and, since as point guard I had the ball in my hands much of the time, I did a lot of improvising. It's not that I was a ball hog; I led my team in assists, and we had great, great chemistry on that team. It's just that, like my new hero Magic, I wasn't afraid to assert myself when I knew that would give us our best chance to win.

I hated losing; don't get me wrong. And I was often frustrated. But the pervading tone of the memories from the year are, well, joyful. I had a blast. I was balling out fearlessly. I have my father's stat sheets for only sixteen of our twenty games. But in those games I averaged almost twelve points a game, shooting better than 51 percent from the floor, and almost five assists and three steals per game. I also averaged almost three-and-a-half turnovers a game, which is horrible for a point guard. Indeed, within a year I would come to live in terror of turnovers. But not sophomore year: I don't remember even once thinking about those turnovers that season. And, if I had thought of them, I'd have figured they were a bummer, but turnovers were just part of the cost of playing the kind of creative, courageous ball I was playing. I was free and I was asking neither permission nor forgiveness.

It was during that season that I once again encountered Danny Johnson, now starring for the Memorial High School junior varsity. It was the last game of our season, Valentine's Day 1981. Memorial was at least twice as big a school as ours, with a lot of skilled athletes. Their sophomore class, led by Danny, was especially good. But outmatched though we were, I loved playing Memorial. They played the kind of aggressively and joyfully improvisational ball that I'd been enjoying playing all year and that I loved best.

But I also always wanted to impress the Memorial guys with my game. I wanted them to recognize me as their equal on the court and their stylistic kin; as one of them. That is why lighting them up for my all-time career high twenty-two points with a 9 for 13 mixture of jumpers, coast-to-coast fast breaks, and twisting layups in traffic (along with 4 of 6 free throws) remains my favorite basketball memory. I don't care that they beat us (59–51) or that it was the sixteenth loss of a terrible losing season. I don't care that I turned the ball over three times. I balled my ass off. But that wasn't even the best part.

After the game, as always, we were shuffling through the line mumbling "g'game, g'game, g'game" for the last time that season, barely looking up from our shoes, when a Memorial player took not only my hand but my arm, stopping me in my tracks. I looked up, and Danny said, with a broad smile, "Great game, Ya-go! See you at the park, right?" I don't know what, if anything, I said. But I still remember that inside my chest, my basketball soul sang, and that on his chest, Danny was wearing number 32, just like me.

8

Counting for Commerce in the NBA

#62. Selling Basketball

What is most striking about the history of quantification in basketball after the formation of the NBA is how irrelevant counting appears to be to the development of the league over the first two decades of its existence, at least if changes to the official statistics are any indication. At the time of the league's founding, official statistics were kept in six categories: field goals and free throws made (which together give points), field goals and free throws attempted, games played, and assists. The next season, the NBA began counting rebounds. And the season after that—1951–52—minutes played were tallied, bringing the total of official statistical categories to eight.

From that time, the NBA made no changes to its official statistics for over twenty years: until the 1973–74 season, when it added steals, blocks, and offensive rebounds to the official tally. The final additions were made by the end of the '70s: turnovers in 1977–78 and, with the institution of the three-point line in 1979–80, three-point field goals made and attempted. A few changes were made in the first few years of the league, and then nothing changed for two decades until the flurry of additions over the course of the mid to late '70s. The timing of the latter additions sheds light, I think, on important underlying issues related to the special role of quantification in the NBA; issues that would continue to shape the use of numbers in the 1980s and then again during the rise of basketball analytics in the early 2000s.

Consider the first of those changes, made in the 1973–74 season: the addition of steals, blocks, and offensive rebounds. What may have prompted the league to make such a change after having gone twenty-two seasons without considering these events important enough to count? I haven't been able to locate any official documents to answer that question definitively, so I do not know for certain. What I do know is that the NBA was not the first basketball organization to count these three events. Just one year before, a rival professional basketball league—the upstart American Basketball Association (ABA)—had begun to count steals and blocks. And as for offensive rebounds, the ABA had been counting them since its founding in 1967. The other two statistics added during the 1970s—turnovers and three-point field goals made and attempted—had also first originated in the ABA back in its first season.

The NBA's addition of these statistical categories may not seem very important and may not in fact have had anything to do with the quantifying precedent set by the ABA. But my research suggests that the opposite is the case. These particular categories, especially turnovers, offensive rebounds, and three pointers, indeed played an important role in the subsequent development of basketball analytics. Likewise, the fact that the NBA only added them after the ABA had done so is indicative of just one of many ways in which the short-lived rivalry between the two leagues impacted the NBA in both the short and long term, especially with respect to quantification. Perhaps the most fundamental of the effects the ABA had on the NBA, though, was financial. And among the financial effects, certainly the most important was that by creating a competitive market for basketball playing talent, the rivalry between the two leagues drove up the cost of basketball labor and that, in turn, placed a premium on knowing as precisely as possible the value of basketball play and, more concretely, basketball players.

#63. The Chairman of the Boards

On August 29, 1974, nineteen-year-old high school graduate Moses Malone did something nobody had ever done before. He signed a contract to play professional basketball without first playing even one game, let alone one year, of college basketball. Malone had been the subject of the most intense and extensive college recruitment effort in a decade (going back to when seven-foot-two New York City prep sensation Kareem Abdul-Jabbar—then Lew Alcindor—entertained hundreds of scholarship offers before choosing to go to UCLA, where his dominance led both to three consecutive national championships for the school and the banning of the dunk from college basketball). And Malone had, earlier in the summer of 1974, initially signed a national letter of intent to attend the University of Maryland: *Sports Illustrated* even featured the news in a short notice accompanying a two-page photo of Malone posing with a new Chrysler Imperial he'd leased. But something must have changed his mind. Maybe it was, as one of his neighbors in mostly black, mostly poor Petersburg, Virginia guessed, that the young Malone didn't "know what's gonna happen tomorrow": in other words, at any moment an injury could end his career.[1]

Whatever the reason, Malone changed his mind and went pro. But he didn't go the NBA. Instead Malone signed a contract with the Utah Stars franchise of the ABA. The ABA had been formed in 1967 by a group of businessmen who hoped that by creating a rival league, they could eventually force their way into the NBA through a merger.[2] Their idea was that the ABA franchises they'd acquired relatively cheaply would, just by virtue of becoming NBA franchises, at least double in value. In effect they'd have acquired lucrative NBA franchises at a cut-rate cost. During its existence, the ABA tried myriad competitive, marketing, and financial experiments— many lampooned decades later in the Will Ferrell film *Semi-Pro*—to keep its head above water in its competition with the NBA. Among these, the three-point shot and the slam-dunk contest held during halftime of the annual All-Star Game are best known to NBA fans today.

But equally important in shaping the modern NBA was the ABA's practice of signing players who left college before the expiration of their four years of NCAA eligibility. They'd first done this with Spencer Haywood, a former Olympian and All-American at the University of Detroit who opted to leave college after his sophomore year to join the ABA's Denver Rockets. The league legitimized the signing by inventing a so-called Hardship Rule whereby underclassmen facing extreme economic adversity could declare themselves eligible for the ABA draft. After an electrifying rookie season,

Haywood accepted an offer from the NBA's Seattle Supersonics franchise. Because he would still have been an underclassman, the deal violated NBA rules prohibiting signing players before their college class had graduated. The NBA sued and, following a flurry of countersuits, decisions, and appeals, the case went all the way to the United States Supreme Court, which in March 1971 ruled seven to two that the NBA's draft eligibility rule requiring four years of college violated the Sherman Antitrust Act and that it therefore could not bar Haywood.[3]

Three years later, then, when Moses Malone signed his contract with Utah, he became the first prep star to avail himself of the opportunity created by that ruling. Covering the press conference at which Malone's signing was announced, *New York Times* writer Gerald Eskenazi reported that "the price of basketball talent was the main theme yesterday." Eskenazi was playing off how Malone's mother—a Safeway grocery packer—had described her occupation: "I put the price on the meat."[4] One hopes the irony—not to mention the disturbing racial overtones—of juxtaposing meat and basketball players had not been lost on Eskenazi. But even if it wasn't, perhaps even he did not grasp, at this point, the encompassing and pointed prescience of his own play on words. For the price of basketball talent *would* be the main theme in the NBA throughout the 1970s and into the 1980s, and economic concepts, principles, and methods for quantifying value drawn from markets would begin to play an expanded role in "putting the price" on that talent.

#64. Pricing Meat

By the time Malone signed his contract in 1974, competition between the ABA and the NBA had already driven up player salaries in both leagues. Concerned owners and executives of the two leagues had been talking about a possible merger to end the bidding war as early as the late 1960s. Their plans had been thwarted by a different antitrust lawsuit brought in 1970 by Oscar Robertson on behalf of the NBA Players' Association (NBAPA), which had led to an injunction effectively stipulating that so long as the "Oscar Robertson suit" was pending, any merger had to be approved by the NBAPA.[5] As late as June 1974, merger talks failed as NBA owners continued to resist the players' demands for free agency—a point ABA owners had already conceded (they had, by that time, in fact, joined the NBAPA antitrust suit against the NBA).[6]

Eventually though, the NBA and its players settled out of court in February 1976, just two months after Malone's Utah Stars went out of business and sold his contract to the ABA's St. Louis franchise.[7] The ABA was down to seven teams and, with the folding of the Virginia franchise not long after, would soon be down to six. By this point there was little to prevent the merger, and the rival leagues soon agreed on the terms: four ABA teams (the Indiana Pacers, San Antonio Spurs, New York Nets, and Denver Nuggets), rosters intact, would pay an entry fee to join the NBA. Meanwhile, players from the remaining two ABA teams—St. Louis and Kentucky—would be made available to NBA franchises in a special dispersal draft.

Then, as prefigured by Eskenazi's grim wordplay two years before, the NBA literally set the prices on the contracts of the players in the dispersal draft, just as Malone's mother stamped price tags on meat at the Safeway. The price tag stamped on Moses Malone was $350,000, which was the third highest, just behind the $1.1 million it would cost an NBA franchise to acquire the rights to Artis Gilmore and the half million for Marvin Barnes.[8] In the draft held on August 5, 1976, the now twenty-one-year-old Malone was selected fifth, by the Portland Trailblazers. Two months later, just after opening night, Portland traded Malone to Buffalo, which, less than a week after that, traded him to Houston.

In the first several years after arriving in the NBA, Moses Malone, who came to be known as the "Chairman of the Boards," excelled, rapidly becoming one of the league's dominant centers and its most effective offensive rebounder.[9] As Malone improved, so too did the Rockets, making the NBA playoffs in the last four of Malone's five years with the team, including a 1981 appearance in the NBA Finals. During that stretch, Malone had led the league in offensive rebounds every season, led the league in total rebounds three times, and in minutes played twice. He'd also been among the top five scorers in the league, finishing second in points per game twice. For these accomplishments Malone had been named the NBA's Most Valuable Player twice, first for the 1978–79 season and then again for the 1981–82 season.

In the collective bargaining agreement signed when the NBAPA and the

NBA settled the Oscar Robertson suit, players gained rights to restricted free agency. Before this, through what was known as the "option clause," NBA contracts bound players to their franchises in perpetuity. When the term of a contract ended, a team could re-sign, waive, or trade the player as it pleased. But beginning in 1980 players ending a contract could pursue offers from other franchises. If their current franchise wished to retain rights to the player, they were obligated to match any offers from other franchises within fifteen days (eventually, that restriction would be removed as well, leading to more or less the form of free agency that exists today).

When the 1981–82 season ended in April 1982, reigning NBA MVP Moses Malone headed the list of sixty-three free agents. And yet, four months later, *Sports Illustrated* writer Alexander Wolff was moved to wonder why Malone had yet to receive a single offer sheet from any NBA franchises. Perhaps, Wolff speculated, the NBA's owners had quietly conspired to begin a league-wide "salary moderation plan."[10] After all, that is just what they had sought from the NBAPA in negotiations over the terms of a new collective bargaining agreement. NBA Commissioner Larry O'Brien, Wolff reported, claimed the league's franchises were losing money, and their payrolls, by percentage of receipts, were significantly higher than their major sports competitors.

It seems the ABA had not been the NBA's only problem. The league had overexpanded during the 1970s, thinning its talent pool and spreading to markets with little demand for professional basketball. High visibility lawsuits and on-court violence—including a highly publicized 1977 brawl that left one player nearly dead and his assailant psychologically traumatized—took a further toll on both gate receipts and television revenues. And all this unfolded against the broader backdrop of white America's backlash against the Civil Rights era struggle for black freedom. As the league came to be 84 percent black by the 1978–79 season, racial prejudice led many white Americans to turn away from the NBA.

#65. FAME

We should situate the NBA's addition of new statistical categories during the 1970s as well as the first wave of statistical attempts to quantify player value (such as those single number, linear weight metrics devised in the

1980s, which I discussed in chapter 1) in this context of the NBA's rivalry and then merger with the ABA, rising player salaries, and declining public interest in the league. Indeed the first such attempt—simultaneously the most farsighted and least influential—a computer program created by an economist named Louis Guth, an Ivy League-trained analyst working for the National Economic Research Associates (NERA), was featured by Wolff in that same article about Moses Malone's free agency.

As chronicled by journalist Andy Glockner in *Chasing Perfection*, Guth began to think about how work he had done in the late 1970s on the valuation of professional sports franchises, "aided by early-era computer technology, could be applied to sports themselves—and more specifically, to the monetary and performance value of players." Guth was aware of the advances that had been made on this front by Bill James and the Society for American Baseball Research, and he knew that comparable work did not exist in basketball, possibly because, in Glockner's words, echoing the quantifying pioneers I have discussed above, "it is much more difficult to accurately assess the value of individuals in a sport of team-based actions." Undeterred, Guth, "set out to examine basketball through the lens of the economic principles that underscored his normal work."[11]

Guth created a computer model that he came to call FAME, for "Free Agent (and Trade) Market Emulator"—it may have been more suggestive, if less appealing, to have called it FATE.[12] Within this model, what Guth called—you won't be surprised by now—"offensive efficiency" measured how successfully teams utilized the opportunity that possession of the basketball presented (and defensive efficiency, conversely, measured how successfully teams prevented opponents from utilizing such opportunities). Guth created simple formulas for offensive and defensive efficiency that factored in the statistics tallied in the box score. For offense he included made field goals and free throws, offensive rebounds and turnovers, while for defense he factored in steals, blocked shots, forced turnovers, missed field goals and free throws, and defensive rebounds.

In terms of quantifying play, FAME was not especially innovative. As I've shown you, over the course of the five decades before Guth, a number of coaches and researchers had sought to isolate and quantify the "building blocks" of successful team play, with many considering these in relation to the outcome of possessions, and some even casting the result in the same language of "efficiency." And, of course, within a decade of Guth's work, Dean Oliver would take a similar, though far more refined approach, in developing his possession-based advanced statistical metrics of what he, too, called "efficiency."

But Guth's model was pioneering in other respects. To begin with, as Glockner rightly notes, Guth's model appears to have been the first attempt to use emerging digital technologies not only for storing and manipulating data but for designing and running algorithms to simulate and project possible outcomes. Secondly, given the context of what subsequent generations have called—problematically, given the racial issues surfacing in the league at the time—the "dark ages" of the NBA, I think Guth's model should also be seen as an augur of the later development and refinement of computer-based mathematical models of basketball play used to help franchises control labor costs.[13] FAME incorporated economic concepts and financial data into its quantitative model of basketball play. In addition to the complete statistical database for teams and players, FAME included what Guth mysteriously called "an accounting algorithm" that would respond to "trades" by changing team statistics (and win prognostications) when one player was replaced by another from a different team and, finally, a set of "econometrically estimated behavioral equations" that forecasted the likely impact on gate receipts and television revenues of possible trades.

Guth's equations added a crucial component missing from all previous models for quantifying quality basketball play: money. This explains why these equations play such a prominent role in an article ostensibly about Moses Malone's free agency. For money, of course, was what owners were especially concerned about. In the first example Guth demonstrated for Wolff, FAME forecasted that adding Malone to the New Jersey Nets would "improve their 1981–82 44-38 record to 66-16 next season" and "draw 5,695 additional fans per game." Estimating that each fan represents $12.50 in ticket, parking, and concession revenue, Guth predicted that adding Malone would increase the team's revenues by close to $3 million dollars. As Wolff put it, Guth's model "translates those extra wins into extra fans and additional revenue."[14]

As it turns out, New Jersey didn't make Malone an offer. But three days after Wolff's article ran, the Philadelphia 76ers, who had lost to the Los Angeles Lakers in the 1982 NBA Finals, offered Malone $11.8 to 15 million over six years (the final amount would depend on whether his performance triggered bonus clauses).[15] And a week after that, in the September 13 issue of *Sports Illustrated* a sidebar reported FAME's projections for the 76ers upcoming season: their offensive rebound total would jump from 1,031 to 1,368; they would score an additional 1,396 points; and their winning percentage would climb from .707 to .810.[16] Two of these three predictions turned out to be nearly exactly on the mark: the Sixers collected 1,334 offensive rebounds in the 1982–83 campaign, and they won 79.3 percent of their regular season games. Though they only scored thirty-two points more than the previous season, I doubt anybody in Philadelphia was complaining since they also won the NBA championship, with Malone collecting both the regular season and the NBA Finals MVP awards. As Guth later detailed in his NERA report, Philadelphia's ability to do what neither they nor any other team between 1980 and 1988 would do—namely, beat Los Angeles or Boston in the NBA Finals—could be traced back to the enormous boost in offensive rebounding efficiency Malone provided.[17]

My point is not that Guth's model influenced subsequent quantitative models of basketball play. I have found no evidence supporting this. On the contrary, of all the accounts of basketball quantification, only Glockner's even mentions Guth. My point, rather, is that because Guth's approach to quantifying basketball registered broader underlying issues that would shape the future of the NBA, it could also prefigure the turn that counting would take, beginning at precisely this moment of financial crisis for professional basketball. In a future that Guth, ironically and much to his chagrin, could not forecast and so never capitalize upon, the elements of quality basketball play, financial risks, costs, and projected rewards would become part of the calculations run by computers far more powerful than Guth's. These calculations would also become a tool by which owners—the next time they were confronted with an unruly labor force, escalating costs, and declining public interest—could reassert control over basketball play.

#66. Clockwork

As most historians tell it, the NBA benefited already from the arrival in 1979 of two enormously popular and talented, team-oriented college stars—Earvin "Magic" Johnson and Larry Bird, who joined the league's most storied franchises, Los Angeles and Boston. But the league could not put the crisis of the 1970s firmly behind it until the arrival in 1984 of two other figures—rookie superstar Michael Jordan and new commissioner David Stern—who would together spearhead, in deliberate collaboration with manufacturing and media conglomerates, the transformation of the league into a global mega-brand.

Historian Walter LaFeber identifies four factors contributing to what he calls "the globalization of Michael Jordan," which, I would add, set the stage for the subsequent globalization of the NBA as a whole: (1) the rise of the multinational corporation as a new economic entity, (2) the rise of Nike, (3) the emergence of satellite-based telecommunications, (4) Michael Jordan's on-court talent and drive, and his off-court ability to craft a broadly likable persona. Through the interplay of these factors (and other broader cultural shifts in American society), the kindling of Magic Johnson and Larry Bird's LA-Boston rivalry in the 1980s became a blaze of unprecedented popularity and lucre for the league in the 1990s.[18] Moreover, the dominating performance of the U.S. men's team at the 1992 Olympics in Barcelona (the so-called Dream Team—the first American team allowed to feature pros on its roster), captured the imaginations of international fans and inspired a new generation of foreign players to aim for careers in the NBA.

But the icon and motor of all this was Michael Jordan, who appeared to embody in himself and therefore to resolve the competing values invested in basketball over the course of the preceding century: he was individually creative, talented, and assertive but learned to channel this unselfishly so as to enable the prodigious success of his team; he was spectacularly athletic but skilled in basketball fundamentals; and, not least, he was black but "approachable." Jordan's importance can already be seen in the anxious search for the "next Jordan," which began when he first retired in 1993 but continued even after he returned to the game in 1995.

By the time Jordan retired for a second time, in 1998, hailed universally as the Greatest of All Time, the league seemed to be riding high. But coinciding with his final years in the NBA, the league's new cadre of stars, though talented and exciting on the court, were disinterested in fitting their public personas to the model established by Jordan. Raised a generation after Jordan, in the economically devastated and racially polarized climate of American cities during the era of Ronald Reagan, they no longer believed in the underlying narrative that Jordan's commercial success posited: that a black man could succeed and achieve popularity in America if he simply worked hard enough. On the contrary, they openly challenged this narrative and instead adopted a variety of cultural markers that unapologetically asserted an autonomous black experience and ethos.

At the same time, many NBA teams adopted a slow, physical style of defensive play in their attempt to offset and compete with the high-octane offensive power of Jordan's Bulls. This style not only led to a decline in scoring, but the increased physicality naturally led to more on-court scuffles and occasional brawls. And these in turn seemed to confirm the racist narratives that the new so-called hip-hop generation of NBA players was really just gangsters or thugs in basketball uniforms. For many the specter of a return to the crisis conditions of the 1970s loomed large.

All of this reached a fever pitch early in the 2004–5 season when, in the course of a minor shoving match near the end of a game between the Detroit Pistons and Indiana Pacers at the Palace of Auburn Hills in suburban Detroit, a Pistons fan threw a cup of beer at Pacers star Ron Artest, who was at the time peacefully lying on the scorer's table as the official and members of both teams tried to sort out the scuffle. Artest, followed by two Pacers teammates, charged into the stands to confront the fan, with whom they exchanged a few punches. And, though nobody was actually injured, the incident, widely reported in sensational fashion, became the emblem of a league that mainstream white fans and journalists alike viewed, through a racialized lens, as overrun with selfish, violent young black men.

And this only seemed to add off-court cultural insult to the injury that many fans, attached to the Jordan era and their memories of Dream Team-style dominance in international competition, had already experienced when, a few months before, at the 2004 Olympics, the United States team lost an international contest for the first time since pros had been allowed to participate. The narrative seemed complete: a selfish group of violence-prone younger players were destroying the league and the sport (not to mention the country's dominant place in world competition).

By contrast, less athletically gifted international squads seemed to be proving on the court the superiority of unselfish, team-oriented, efficient play. In a February 2004 article in *Esquire* magazine, Chris Jones had praised what he called "the new Black guys": foreign-born players who, having been raised as NBA fans in the wake of the 1992 Olympics and fresh from years of successful international competition, were transforming the NBA. "They play the game with a kind of engineered beauty, economical and drama free, more like the insides of a watch than a racehorse. They play as every part of the whole." By describing their play as clockwork, moreover, Jones, perhaps unwittingly, mobilizes the master metaphor of the scientific revolution, of the Enlightenment, and of industrial era fantasies of a perfectly efficient mechanical process in which each individual part hums along impersonally, content to play its unsung role in the whole. Jones's metaphors, moreover, drawn from engineering and economics, are explicitly anti-aesthetic ("drama free").

I do not claim a simple or direct causal link between Jordan's retirement, the "threatening" rise of a new generation of black stars, and the emergence of international players and teams able to compete successfully against the United States or in the NBA, on the one hand, and the appearance of advanced analytics and, beyond that, of Big Data basketball, on the other. I mean rather to suggest a transformation of the professional basketball landscape in which the collapse of the existing, commercially successful model (let's call it "the Jordan model"), experienced as chaotic and fearsome by those invested in and benefiting from it, together with the appearance of an alternative in the form of international basketball culture, also invited the search for new understandings of how the game worked, including the quantitative efforts of the first wave of basketball analysts. But I also mean to stress something else. The crisis on the court and the cultural crisis off the court were also *financial* crises for the NBA and its owners, who would have been strongly motivated to at least consider quantitative models that seemed to offer a pathway back to a promised land where order, efficiency, and profit were once again the norm.

#67. AI

To get a sense of the connection I'm proposing between the crisis of the Jordan model amid the emergence of the hip-hop generation and the rise of advanced analytics, consider AI. No, not artificial intelligence. The other AI: Allen Iverson, aka The Answer.

Iverson, a six-foot guard, entered the NBA as the first pick in the 1996 draft and played fourteen seasons before retiring in 2010. Iverson led the league in scoring average four times and in steals three times. Twice, Iverson led the league in both categories (the only other player ever to do so was Michael Jordan). He also led the league in minutes played per game seven times. He was elected by fans to start in eleven All-Star Games and won Most Valuable Player in two of them. He was chosen by writers as Rookie of the Year in 1997 and as the NBA Most Valuable Player in 2001, as well as All-NBA First Team three times. He ended his career fourth all-time in minutes played per game, seventh all-time in points per game, and eleventh all-time in steals per game. The traditional box score, in other words, would suggest that Iverson was among the handful of the greatest ever to play.[19]

By the metrics of advanced analytics, however, Iverson rates considerably lower. In fact, in their popular 2006 book *The Wages of Wins*, economists and sports analytics pioneers David Berri, Martin Schmidt, and Stacey Brook determined that "the net value of Iverson during his career is a bit below the average NBA player. We would add," they concluded, "that not only is Iverson not one of the best players in the league, he has generally not been the most productive player on his own team."[20] In basketball, they explained, "wins are solely a function of offensive and defensive efficiency," and Iverson's "efficiency measures are below average."[21] For example, Iverson's true shooting percentage (which accounts for both free throws and the added value of three-point shots, both highly valued by basketball analytics for their contributions to efficiency) is 51.8 percent, a figure that puts Iverson far below the average NBA player.

Berri and his colleagues offer just one example, and it is certainly not that the discourse of basketball analytics cannot accommodate other factors. Recently, analyst Kevin Pelton of ESPN.com rated Iverson forty-sixth all-time in his own rankings of individual players, which combined advanced metrics with subjectively determined factors such as awards. But it is the case that the very logic of analytics, prioritizing what can be measured, as well as efficiency and economic value, serves as a kind of limiting horizon containing whatever other desires might be stirred and values embodied by a given player. Pelton himself put this explicitly: "Analytics is a much bigger part of the game than it was fifteen years ago, even ten years ago. And I think that's kind of contributed to a reassessment of Iverson's ranking all time. I think he would have ranked much higher if we would have done this ten years ago or when he retired."[22]

In an influential review of *Wages of Wins*, Malcolm Gladwell struggled to sustain his own appreciative vision of Allen Iverson driving—"again and again"—to the basket, "twisting and turning and writhing through a thicket of arms and legs of much taller and heavier men." Stirring though this may have been to Gladwell, in the end he retreats from their lure, ceding ground to the unavoidable reality of the numbers: "[A]ll we learn is to appreciate twisting and turning and writhing. We become dance critics, blind to Iverson's dismal shooting percentage and his excessive turnovers, blind to the reality that the Philadelphia 76ers would be better off without him."[23]

Gladwell's description of Iverson's play echoes the appreciative description of the aesthetic values of basketball play that James Naismith offered his audience at the 1913 NCAA convention. But within the culture of moving dots such pleasures are relegated to the realm of illusions that must give way to reality, which is to say, quantitative appraisals of efficiency. In this way, basketball analytics' quantitative assessments of value generate shifts in the criteria used to evaluate players of the past and the playing styles they are seen to embody.

And, in the case of Iverson, at least, this threatens to eclipse more than just an appreciation of the aesthetic value of his play. For Iverson was also widely viewed as the icon of the so-called hip-hop generation in basketball.[24] For NBA executives and franchise owners, these players (and their enthusiastic young followers) presented both the opportunity to tap a potentially lucrative new market of consumers and the threat of collapsing the burgeoning global empire built on the racial crossover appeal of Michael Jordan.[25] For some historians the league's policies during this period amounted to a cynical "assault on blackness" that sought simultaneously to monetize the street credibility of players like Iverson while policing their public persona and private behavior to avoid alienating the league's majority white fan base.[26]

From this vantage point, Iverson's value in basketball history as a cultural and political icon might be rated alongside those of the pioneering black players who first desegregated the game in the early 1950s and the first black superstars who transformed it in the 1960s.[27] And the statistical reassessment of his value as a player begins to remind me of the ways that Luther Gulick and other sober stewards of the game used the scorebook to impose uniform values on the sport and thereby corral the wildness of early basketball players. Thinking about the coincidence of the rise of advanced statistics with the troubles of the post-Jordan era puts one of the most well-known instances of using advanced stats to reassess player performance in a rather different light. But regardless of the specific dynamics at work behind the scenes, it remains the case that by the time Allen Iverson played his last NBA game, on February 20, 2010, the science of moving dots was well on its way to transforming the way basketball would be played, coached, managed, watched, and discussed.

Interlude—Basketball Jesus

#68. God's Own Point Guard

Here is the story, as I remember it, of how I lost my basketball innocence and grimly determined to be the best, purest point guard since God's very own son, Jesus.

Everything was going according to plan. I opened junior year as the starting point guard on our varsity. I had played well in preseason scrimmages and in our regular season opener, where my strong fourth quarter helped our team turn a two-point deficit into a three-point victory. I felt that I'd contributed to the win, I was still playing confidently and freely and my—and our—season was off to a promising start. I eagerly looked forward to practice the following Monday.

On my way from the locker room to the court just before that practice, Coach called me into his office. He explained that some of the seniors felt unhappy that I was starting in place of two of their classmates. Don't worry, though, Coach assured me, just keep doing what you're doing. I have no memory of practice that week, but that Saturday night, I started again. I turned the ball over eight times in our overtime loss. Three days later, in another loss, I turned the ball over seven times. According to Don Lindstrom, in that game we had twenty-nine turnovers as a team. And, according to my father, I had nearly a quarter of them. More specifically, as Mr. Lindstrom noted: "East [our opponent] stole the ball at least 15 times and forced Edgewood into ball-handling mistakes so often the Crusaders got off only eight shots during the first 14 minutes of the second half." During that very stretch I alone had five turnovers.

This was really bad. And it wasn't just the turnovers. I'd had plenty of turnovers sophomore year. But never this many, and, anyway, they hadn't mattered to me or, as far as I could tell, to anybody else. Now, suddenly, they did. They mattered to me and to everybody else. I'd throw the ball away and see Coach clutch his temples or the seniors sneer dismissively. The ball that had once been part of my body suddenly felt shaky in my trembling hands. No longer my animal daemon, it had become a snarling, squirming Chihuahua on speed whenever I dribbled it up court against defenders, who were everywhere and getting faster even as I was getting slower and stupider. What had been the most natural, effortless, thoughtless freedom my teenage being had yet experienced became a kind of excruciating nightmare of racing anxiety and desperate inept striving. By the next game, one of those two seniors had taken my spot in the starting lineup. By the game after that, the other had taken my spot as his backup. And worst of all: I felt relieved. If I wasn't on the court, I couldn't fuck up and cost us games.

My playing time fluctuated a bit as our team struggled to a 6-14 record over the course of the season. But, apart from a couple of games (in both of which I actually played really well), I mostly played around ten minutes a game (out of a possible thirty-two). The only game I played more than fifteen minutes was what would turn out to be the last game of the season—the regional championship game, with a trip to the state tournament on the line. Going into the fourth quarter I had played about nine minutes, mostly in the second quarter. I sat the first couple of minutes of the fourth quarter, while La Crosse Aquinas, on their home court, scored the first eight points of the quarter to build a seven-point lead. With no shot clock to limit their possessions, we'd dug ourselves quite a hole. But over the next six minutes, we stemmed the tide and then rallied so that, with sixteen seconds left, we finally recaptured the lead. We just had to get a stop.

Aquinas worked the ball into its senior forward Bill Skemp who was fouled as he went up for a shot with six seconds to go. He made his first free throw, tying the score, and Coach called our last time-out. Huddling us together, he told the team that make or miss they should get the ball to me and that

I should push it up court as fast as I could, get into the lane if possible, and get off a shot or draw a foul. It should have thrilled me, bringing back the magic (and the Magic) of my sophomore year. But I don't remember being thrilled. The season on the bench had taken its toll. I didn't know who I was as a player, or a person, anymore. Skemp made the free throw. Someone inbounded the ball to me, and I took off. Racing across half court I found myself pulling up for a hanging jump shot—strikingly similar in my memory to the shot captured in the newspaper photo of my nightmare game against East earlier in the year—just inside the free throw line with maybe two seconds left on the clock. It felt good when I let it go. The ball hit the back of the rim, softly bounced to the front, and then fell harmlessly into a sea of outstretched arms, where one of my teammates tried unsuccessfully to tip it in.

We lost 48–47. I had cost us the game and ended the seniors' high school careers and, since none would go on to play in college, their basketball careers. I cried bitterly in the locker room after the game, then some more in the car with our assistant coach (who had been my beloved mentor the year before) on the two-hour drive back to Madison. Of course, he said all the caring and correct things: a game never comes down to a final shot; we'd not have even been playing the game we just lost had I not made my free throws to win the game the night before; I had done exactly what Coach had told me to do. I don't even think I heard him. I did already know all that. But deep, deep beneath that surface, my psyche was rapidly processing the trauma of the game, the trauma of the season—I was riven with interpersonal conflicts and oppressive self-doubt—the trauma of that first conversation with Coach at the start of the year, the trauma of my parents' separation, of my father's violent temper, of what felt like a lifetime of making selfish mistakes that caused arguments in our house.

And what my psyche came up with was this: PASS FIRST.

Meaning: become a pass-first point guard. I was an undersized point guard playing within an offensive system and for a Coach who prized ball control and unerring shot selection above all else. Forget Magic, Yago. This wasn't Showtime and I most definitely was not Magic. It was time to become a playmaker, a floor general. It wouldn't be so bad. Pass-first point guards might not be spectacular or turn out big numbers in the box score (good-bye quantification, my old friend), but with their intelligence and their unerring judgment, and their ball-handling skills, they controlled the complex flowing pattern of player and ball movement on the floor. Nobody yelled at them. Their selflessness put them beyond reproach. Their coaches and teammates loved them. Everybody loved a pass-first point guard.

They were small and in control, and what could be better to the under-sized youngest member of the family than a world run by the smallest. Plus, unlike my father, they controlled games not by dominating others, not by physically threatening them, not by bossing or asserting their will or demands, but rather by giving to others, like my mom. My mom, my psyche figured, was the pass-first point guard of our family, and I loved my mom. It wasn't hard for me, raised Catholic and in Catholic schools, to go further: to see Jesus as God's very own coach on the floor, a divine pass-first point guard. With the twin examples of my mother and Jesus, was there any question that I would compress and shape my savage and destructively selfish scorer's soul, on the court and off, into the very best, most unselfish pass-first point guard that I could?

#69. Mecca: The End

Almost exactly one year to the day since my psyche decided on this makeover of my basketball soul, and just a few days before my team (of which I was now senior co-captain) headed back to La Crosse for the 1983 Wisconsin Independent Schools Athletic Association Class A Region 1 Tournament, a reporter for Madison's *Capital Times* newspaper said this of me, "A point guard, Colas controls the Crusaders offense, which is very crucial this year." Coach Maturi, interviewed for the piece, doubled down: "Yago is the guy who handles it for us. He controls the tempo of the game. Plus, he can shoot the ball much better than people realize. And he handles the ball extremely well." Done. I'd turned myself into God's own point guard.

We were 11-8, which was respectable considering the caliber of our opponents during the year. But Coach had taken much better teams to regionals and, since 1976, had always come up empty in his bid to make the state tournament. And we'd certainly had our ups and downs. Not me though. In the midst of it all, I'd proudly nurtured our team's chemistry: managing

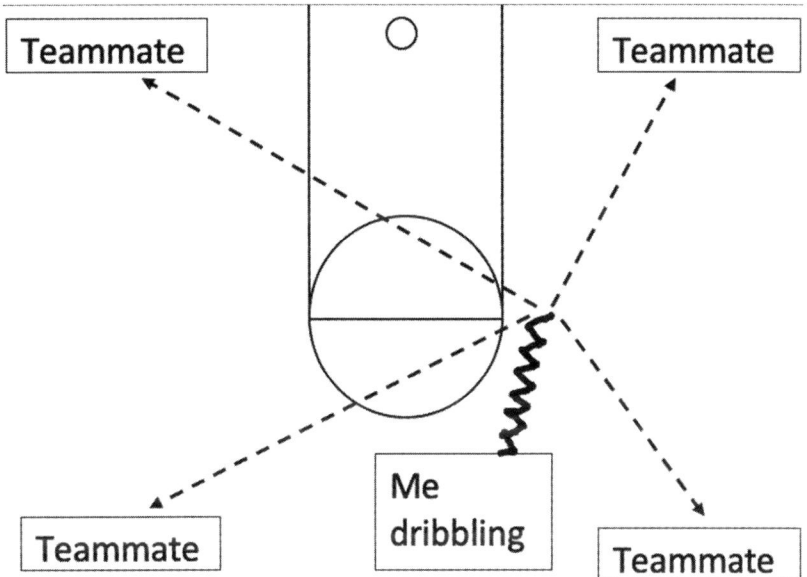

FIG. 7. Diagram of four corners offense.

the temper of our talented but mercurial leading scorer and rebounder; supporting our big but raw sophomore center through the bumps in his development; deftly blending a very, very good and very confident group of juniors into the mix of a team of seniors, my buddies, who after sitting on the bench behind seniors last year were now sitting on the bench behind juniors this year. The petty tensions of a group of adolescent boys were no match for the conciliatory abilities I had forged in the fires of family therapy sessions that were even more terrifyingly conflictual than the family arguments I witnessed at home.

On the court my jobs were: (1) get the ball up the court safely; (2) make sure everyone was where they were supposed to be, doing what they were supposed to do; (3) get the ball to an open scorer; (4) hit the occasional open shot; (5) make free throws; (6) lead our tenacious, hustling defense by example; (7) keep everyone happy. At the end of a game, if we had built a small lead, all these things would come together in a special way. That's when Coach would signal "4" and we would go into our spread, a version of North Carolina's Four Corners, to kill the clock (fig. 7).

"Four" was my basketball heaven, the moment when—after what seemed like a lifetime of deferred gratification and self-sacrifice—the pearly gates swing open and God and Jesus and St. Peter welcome you in and say: "Now. Go forth and get buckets." You see, I was the center of the spread offense. I got to dribble around in the front court, eluding hapless defenders, bouncing passes off my teammates who stood like backstops in each of the four corners of the front court returning my passes and occasionally cutting back door to the basket. The goal was either to get an uncontested layup or to get me fouled. Either was fine with me: a layup for a teammate usually meant an assist for me, and me getting fouled meant points for me. Both meant a win, and the whole thing transformed me into the joyful, confident kid I'd been when I first began dribbling around in our driveway.

That's how I wound up on the line at the end of the Middleton game. And, more dramatically, that's how—just three days after the *Capital Times* confirmed the fullness of my being as a point guard—I wound up shooting fourteen (and making ten) free throws in the final two minutes of the fourth quarter to help seal our victory in a rematch of our regional championship contest against Aquinas and land our team a berth in the state tournament for the first time in almost a decade. As Aquinas' coach put it the next day, "they went up by three or five points and Colas made all those free throws. . . . Once we got down, it was Colas to the line, then Colas back to the line, then Colas again." I had become someone else's nightmare, or as my father might have said, I don't get heart attacks, I give them.

The next week I was lacing up my Converse All-Star Weapons (the "Magic"—not the "Bird"—shoe) in the locker room at MECCA—the aptly named arena where my beloved Bucks played their games. In a few minutes I'd proudly lead my team out for warm-ups prior to our quarterfinal matchup against the heavily (and rightly) favored Oshkosh Lourdes and their six-foot-eight Indiana-bound star, Todd Meier. As Coach had told me privately just prior to the season (mental note: stop having conversations with Coach early in the season): "Let's face it, Yago, your class is a great bunch of guys, but it's only Flint and Mark (two bad-boy transfers to our school who started alongside me senior year) that have made you even respectable as an athletic class."

Lourdes did beat us, but they needed overtime to do it. We all played well, beautifully connected as a team, and I stayed positive, intelligently directed our offense, and controlled the tempo. After the game, Coach told the reporters he was sorry we never had the ball with the score tied or a lead because our spread offense was so good. My father's records show that I had four assists, three steals, one rebound, nine points (4 for 6 from the floor, 1 for 2 from the line), and just two turnovers. It's a good stat line for a pass-first point guard, reflective of a good game, but it doesn't tell the whole story. It doesn't tell you, as Leonard Koppett complained more generally of the prevailing statistics of his time, the when and the how.

It doesn't tell you that when we fell behind 41–35 with 5:33 to go in the game, I found my leading scorer open in the corner to assist on two straight jumpers that brought us within two. It doesn't tell you that I got one of my three steals on their next possession, or that I then hit a jumper of my own from the wing to tie the score 41–41 with two minutes to go. Or that I hit another one to tie it again a minute later. Or that I hit one last one with fourteen seconds to go to send the game into overtime. Half my team's fourth quarter points were on three straight jumpers in the final two minutes: you'd almost think that the heart of a scorer still beat within the chest of that pass-first point guard.

I never forgot that game of course, nor the regional final that got us there, nor Middleton, nor did I ever forget missing the last shot of the season my junior year. But I didn't remember, despite having looked at my father's statistics many, many times over the years, just how often I played most aggressively, freely, and completely—my best—at the end of close games. I didn't realize it because the tally marks my father made on the little yellow sheets didn't specify when things happened or under what circumstances. To find that out, I had to turn from numbers to words: the words, for example, of Don Lindstrom or other writers for the local newspapers.

It's there that I learned—to take the most striking instance—that the day before I missed the last shot of my junior season in the regional final, I had hit two free throws with seconds to go to win our regional semi-final. Nobody knows better than a pass-first point guard that games are not really won or lost on the final shot or even in the final minute. And yet, my scorer's soul swells to life at the discovery that when games were on the line, and my team needed points, I asserted myself and tried, fairly successfully, to find ways to get them.

#70. Never Underestimate an Old Man with a Basketball

A few months after my career ended with Todd Meier's punctuating overtime slam at Mecca, I did something on a basketball court that I'd never been able to do before: I dunked, like Dr. J. Well, actually the only things it had in common with the free-throw line dunk that had so electrified me seven years before was: (1) I didn't dribble on my approach to the hoop, (2) it wasn't in the course of game play, and (3) it was worth no points. But—even though there were no flashbulbs popping or fans roaring, even though, to be honest, I barely got the ball over the rim in my driveway (and the rim, by that time, through years of use, had probably slid down an inch or two)—it was worth everything to me. Somehow that dunk, which I never was able to reproduce, was the culmination of a journey that had begun fourteen years before when I stared up at that same rim from directly under the net feeling that through it I was somehow connected to the sky. On the day of my dunk, well, I *was* connected to the sky.

Now, nearly forty years later, though I still step onto the court, I am no longer connected to the sky. Now, before I even step onto the court, I am tired and sore. Now, my final game and my dunk, far in the past, are as much fantasies I have invented as experiences I remember. Now my games are played on playgrounds and second-rate gymnasiums where I play in pickup games as often as I can. I used to play basketball every day. But now I am not consistent. Sometimes I play four times a week, sometimes I go for months without even picking up the ball. Now, my weight fluctuates wildly over the course of the year, my waistline expanding alarmingly during the winter months and then diminishing when, in a manic recovery of the self-discipline and determination that was once second nature, I embark upon a feverish exercise regime. But even when I do approximate my "playing weight," now I am lucky if I can get my body off the ground high enough to graze the net, whose bottom, hanging eighteen inches below the rim, no longer pulls me magically toward the heavens. Now, between innumerable ankle injuries and muscle atrophy, I have no bounce.

Now when I play, my opponents, for the most part, are young men not much older than I was when I played at Mecca, when I dunked in my driveway (if those things even really happened). These young men are faster, stronger, quicker, and better leapers than I. They are fitter. And, whatever time and life may have already done to their souls, it clearly has not ravaged their bodies as it has mine. Most of them are not only physically better athletes than I am but are also more skilled basketball players than I am now, and maybe than I ever was. And they play an entirely different game than I do. Not only were they all born well after the institution of the three-point line, many can barely remember the league before LeBron James. They are the analytics generation, and even if none of them will ever be optically tracked or even have their performance analyzed by advanced statistical methods, their style of play reflects the changes that the science of moving dots has wrought on basketball.

When we warm up before the game, they all chuck threes. I try, half-heartedly, to join them. Perhaps I imagine that with dedication and effort I could become a three-point shooter (even though I never once played a real game with a three-point line and shots from beyond twenty feet were considered delusional, selfish, and wasteful). Once we start to play, they attack the basket fearlessly, looking for shots at the rim, hoping to draw fouls, or at least collapse the defense before whipping passes out to their adolescent friends perched on the curving wire of the three-point line. In that kind of basketball, I mostly become tentative. Catching the ball beyond the arc, I rarely even look at the rim but instead just try to move it to an open teammate. Faced with the possibility of a drive to the basket, I usually demur, my body rapidly calculating the probability of another ankle injury and deciding it's just not worth it. After all, one of these young guns on their pogo-stick legs will probably swat the attempt into the trees anyway.

I say I mostly become tentative because there is still a small place for me in the game that basketball has now become, a place available exactly because the youngsters so adept at the new game have forgotten it even exists. It is the most universally disparaged and avoided place in basketball today: the mid-range. The mid-range is the area of the court between around eight feet from the basket and the three-point line. Now, I am an excellent mid-range jump shooter, especially if I am unguarded. For this reason I exert the prerogative of age and my confidence as a public speaker to insist that we keep score by "twos and threes," rather than by the prevailing playground convention that awards two points for a shot behind the three-point line, and only one point for a shot inside the arc—a system that further erodes the value of my narrow skill set.

The science of moving dots has taught us that shots from the mid-range are the poorest investments in terms of maximizing offensive efficiency because of the combination of their probability of going in and their value, which is why my teenage opponents never shoot from there. The force of the conventional analytics worldview seems to combine with the narcissism of my young opponents to throw an invisibility cloak around me whenever I drift into the mid-range. I catch the ball, my teenage defender looks at me incredulously and just lays back, awaiting my drive to the rim. I look back at him. Sometimes, emboldened by an infusion of long-lost confidence, I will first defiantly mock his foolishness at leaving me unguarded in the mid-range before rising—well, okay, "rising"—to release the shot. Everything is comfortable in the mid-range. Everything feels good. My body is my own. The ball is once again my friend as it rises happily to its apex and then floats gently down through the net. Through some happy, if perverse, trickle-down effect, the very success of analytics in penetrating the basketball minds of my opponents, has allowed me to extend my pickup career. For now.

9

The Work of Moving Dots

#71. Using Moving Dots

How does the science of moving dots concretely shape decisions; influence tactics, strategy, and play on the court; inform or even create storylines; and color the way we talk about the sport? When I began writing this book, I wanted to devote a chapter to showing readers how basketball analytics worked concretely over the course of the 2018–19 NBA season. I initially imagined that as the season progressed I would track discussions of the NBA on prominent analytics-based websites such as FiveThirtyEight and Nylon Calculus and look for appearances of analytics in the NBA coverage on more mainstream sites like ESPN.com, The Ringer, or The New York Times. I still want to address my initial question and provide a concrete picture of the science of moving dots at work, but I've adopted a different approach to doing so, for reasons that relate to the subject of my book.

First, the quantity of NBA media coverage explicitly addressing or even simply informed by basketball analytics was far greater than I expected or could possibly manage: just between mid-June (when the 2018 NBA Finals ended) and late November (about a month into the season) I found over two thousand items! As the editors of the respected basketball analytics website Nylon Calculus wrote in October 2018: "Sports analytics is a constantly evolving field and keeping up can be a challenge, especially with so much work being divided between the public and private sphere."

Of course this testifies to the pervasiveness of basketball analytics in the culture surrounding the sport. It seems to have become something like an internalized requirement among mainstream sportswriters to support stories and opinions on the NBA with some reference to quantification, especially advanced analytical metrics and, preferably, drawing upon optical tracking data. That's certainly important to note and part of how analytics works in the NBA today, but I already knew that. After all, this rapidly expanding pervasiveness was the premise for this book in the first place.

However, coming face to face with the enormous media footprint of basketball in the summer and fall of 2018 brought a second pertinent issue to the foreground. As with other areas of specialized scientific research, popular accounts and summaries of the science of moving dots tend to oversimplify the work, sometimes sensationally. They thus create inviting targets for critics who wish to caricature and critique the underlying science on the basis of these media oversimplifications. Given my own ambivalent investments, it was important to me to avoid the temptation to indulge in such tendentious, facile, and misleading critiques. I wanted to be balanced, fair, and thorough, and I wanted to be properly informed.

After all, "the world of statistics," Dana Keller assures me on the first page of his book *The Tao of Statistics*, "starts with a question, not with data."[1] It's important for those of us who consume data as seemingly finished, declarative content to bear that in mind and to remember that statistical work may also be moved by the spirit of open-ended adventure driving my own writing here. So, I found myself more interested in understanding the work of basketball analytics from the perspective of those doing it. What questions, issues, and areas of NBA play do the scientists of moving dots themselves currently consider most important?

To find out, I asked a few friends of mine who work in the field (either in the public domain or for NBA franchises) to give me their lists of top questions and issues, I then looked for areas of overlap and created a final list of seven topics. To better understand their interests and efforts, I also asked them to point me to quality sources they found most relevant to defining and approaching these questions and issues. Those sources, even when they predate the current season, form the basis for my reflections on the seven key topics I explore in the rest of this chapter. In exploring these topics, I'm interested not only in understanding the work of the science of moving dots from the point of view of those doing it but also in drawing upon the research I've already shared on the history and rhetorics of counting in basketball to contextualize that work.

#72. Predicting Performance

Just before the 2018–19 NBA season started, the editors and writers at Nylon Calculus came up with a list of "ten questions whose answering will likely guide the next few years of public analytic work." They set three parameters for their questions: (1) they could be worked on in the public sphere, (2) they wouldn't have to be answered with existing datasets alone (In other words, in exploring their questions, authors could imagine or call for new areas of data production.), (3) they would theoretically have an effect on how teams operate on and off the court. On October 1, 2018, Scott LaForest authored the first piece in the series, asking: "How can we predict performance for incoming NBA players?"[2]

It's not surprising that this would be the first question tackled in the series. It is the basic question underlying the multiple tensions structuring *Moneyball*: How to know what the future of a prospect holds? And it is also, in a way, the broadest overarching question of basketball analytics, encompassing many of the other more specific topics and questions I'll address in this chapter. And besides, LaForest points out, "evaluating and selecting the best players is the quickest route to success," especially in the NBA where the smaller number of players per team and their more or less continuous involvement in every play on offense and defense mean that individuals have—for better or for worse—greater impact on team outcomes than in other sports. Moreover, at a deeper level, wishing to predict the future performance of a player in whom a team is about to invest significant financial resources seems an understandable desire in the high-stakes world of NBA competition.

On the other hand (LaForest emphasizes this point twice), "predicting future performance is hard, especially for 19–22-year-old men." But given the stakes, the science of moving dots must continue, undeterred, to look for ways to improve its ability to predict the future performance of prospective players. LaForest first proposes combining machine learning with human intelligence. "An algorithm," he imagines, "can take all the data provided in pre-draft tests and performances to select the top prospects. From there NBA scouts and front office personnel can perform their own due diligence by watching film, scouting games, and interviewing players." He believes that this combination will "improve efficiency"—note the invocation of that rhetoric—and enhance the ability to gain more insights into incoming players. But the suggestion that predictive efforts work best when they combine human intelligence with digital analytic technologies is not in itself original. Even the most aggressive advocate of basketball analytics, Darryl Morey, has emphasized the limitations of quantitative models.[3]

Instead, the originality of LaForest's contribution stems from his specific proposal for how that combination might work best. LaForest writes that for the combination of methods he calls for to work effectively we need "correct data." But what is "correct data," and how should NBA franchises go about creating it? The short version of LaForest's answer is that the league should focus its efforts on finding new ways to measure tactical abilities and psychological qualities to balance its current overreliance on data it collects on physical attributes and technical skills during the annual three-day period of measurement and testing known as the Draft Combine. "By focusing on new ways of quantifying other aspects of the game besides just physical and technical skills," LaForest concludes, "we might be able to make small enough improvement. If we make continuous small improvements over the long run our decisions will eventually improve enough to make a difference in quantifying player selection." LaForest doesn't explain how this data might be gathered (though a subsequent piece in the series, which I'll examine later in this chapter, does address psychological assessment). In that sense the article calls for more extensive quantification of basketball players, without offering concrete details.

But looking at how LaForest arrives at this proposal can shed light on both the tendencies of basketball analytics in the area of performance prediction as well as on its limitations. To define the areas in which he believes the NBA needs to acquire more quantitative data, LaForest draws, rather selectively as I'll show, on a model proposed by sports scientist Fergus Connolly in his nearly five-hundred-page tome called *Game Changer*.

I'll have more to say about *Game Changer* in chapter 11. But for now it's worth pointing out that the book draws upon chaos theory, kinesiology, and ethical philosophy, among many other varied sources, to develop an approach to athletic performance that might better manage—in part by embracing—the complexity and chaotic unpredictability that is present in every moment across multiple scales of team sport competition. It's also worth observing that Connolly makes no secret of his disdain for what he calls "reductionist" models that rely heavily on quantification to evaluate and predict performance. So, it's already somewhat surprising to see Connolly's work pressed into the service of supporting an argument for *more* quantification.

More specifically, I'm surprised to see Connolly's model utilized as the basis for a proposal aimed at helping NBA franchises predict the future performance of prospects. The specific model in question appears in a section of Connolly's book devoted to "The Player." He writes that the tools in this section aim "to help individual athletes: achieve and sustain good health, manage the load of competition and training, encourage adequate rest and recovery, fuel sustainable performance, recognize the warning signs of overtraining and under recovery, avoid harmful, health-damaging lifestyle habits, better understand the main body systems that contribute to health and how to care for them."[4] Notably absent from this list of laudable aims is: improving the ability to predict future performance. That's not surprising when the model is viewed in the proper context, since predicting future performance is not of primary importance *to players*. It is, of course, of great importance to owners and general managers preparing to invest resources in players and perhaps also to gamblers and fans who, likewise, may stake money or emotion on future performance.

Looking still more specifically at the model LaForest borrows in order to aid basketball analysts in identifying untapped data mines, Connolly describes four interdependent factors impacting performance that he calls "coactives": (1) physical, (2) technical, (3) tactical, and (4) psychological. He argues that all four coactives "are present to varying degrees in every event in games and during team preparation" and "must come together in a synchronized manner to allow the player to execute great actions." The model, he hopes, will offer a better way to evaluate and improve game-day performance by better accounting for the "complexity of competition and the athletes themselves in a team context." In this way Connolly proposes it as an improvement on the "reductionist approach" still used by most teams.[5]

And indeed, Connolly's seemingly simple four-category model rapidly becomes more complex, expanding to include multiple subcategories, themselves elaborated in great detail through examples, diagrams, and references to Connolly's usual wide-ranging pool of resources. Even the seemingly straightforward physical coactive requires eight pages in which Connolly describes not only anthropometric measurements of shape, size, and function but twelve additional physical qualities, not to mention also genetic and epigenetic, endocrine, and neural attributes and capacities. Or consider the "psychological coactive" (in which LaForest sees the greatest opportunity for expanding quantification in a way that will positively impact the accuracy of performance prediction). Connolly subdivides this into three "micro coactives": spirituality, emotion, and cognition, each of which is further subdivided.[6] Moreover, Connolly stresses that when it comes to the physical and psychological coactives, approaches that recognize that "body and brain are one" are more effective. In view of the complexity of Connolly's model, LaForest's adaptation, though well-intended and possibly useful, begins to look like an example of the very reductionism Connolly has written his work to counter.

In addition to this reduction of complexity, LaForest's very question presumes a different aim and audience than the model he adapts to address it. LaForest, like most analysts concerned with finding useful models to predict future performance, seems to be thinking about the benefits to NBA franchises who may use such models to avoid making a significant investment of money and resources into players whose future performance will not offer an acceptable return on that investment. Connolly, by con-trast, writes: "We cannot in good conscience look at players as athletic commodities: we must treat them as people whose lives are complex and involve much more than what happens on game day."[7]

I suspect LaForest shares Connolly's sentiment. But the framework established by the intersection of analytics with the business of running NBA franchises seems effectively to exclude it from impacting his proposal to develop quantitative measures of players' "grit, motivation, ability to handle stress or even their sleep habits" so as to "get a better idea of the types of players that can handle stresses of the long NBA season." On the face of it, Connolly's methods also seem aimed at understanding and generating ideas and methods to control and improve athletic performance. But instead of tailoring those efforts to predict and control future outcomes, Connolly does so to improve the overall well-being of athletes, not only as athletes (let alone as commodities) but as human beings. Because he anchors his work in the player as human being, Connolly must immerse himself in the complexity and chaos arising when that human being is faced with the challenges of elite athletic competition. Finally, it is because some of the most important factors impacting that complex process cannot be counted (or we do not yet know how to count them) that Connolly expresses such skepticism toward the quantitative tools of analytics that are by nature limited to what can be counted and, in the process, lead even those who may care about players to miss much of what counts.

#73. Assigning Credit

Ultimately, predicting future performance successfully rests not only on gathering the correct data on an individual player's physical and psychological traits and past playing tendencies but also on correctly understanding how individual performance impacts team play. Otherwise, of course, it would be impossible to know how the predicted future performance of a given individual player is likely to concretely impact a particular team.

Traditionally, to determine individual impact on team success, coaches, the media, and fans would tend to focus on the actions counted in the box score and on the individuals who performed those actions. A player would be credited with points for scoring a basket, perhaps with an assist for making the pass that preceded the successful shot. Such assessments, obviously, ignored most of the actions that were part of the play and, moreover, failed to control for pace of play by scaling box score totals on the basis of possessions. But even more advanced possession-based analytics focused only on the plays that end possessions: made and missed shots, turnovers, offensive and defensive rebounds. In effect, such a focus effectively assumes that the impact of such actions as setting a screen or moving away from the ball to create space for a teammate with the ball is negligible.

In 2014, Harvard University graduate students Dan Cervone and Alexander D'Amour and their professors Kirk Goldsberry and Luke Bornn claimed to have developed a "a coherent, quantitative representation of a whole possession that summarizes each moment of the possession in terms of the number of points the offense is expected to score—a quantity we call *expected possession value*, or EPV."[8] Using the massive data sets generated by the newly installed optical tracking systems, their probabilistic EPV model assigned "a point value to every tactical option available to a player at each moment of a possession."

Their model accounted for the spatial configuration of players on the court as well as quantified representations of those players' abilities to execute their different tactical options such as shooting, passing, or driving. Since the model continuously recalculates EPV in response to the decisions of every player on the floor throughout the possession, it acts—note the business metaphor—"as a stock ticker in providing an instantaneous snapshot of the offense's value" and permits basketball analysts "to learn and evaluate players' actions throughout the entirety of their court time."[9] As an example they provided an analysis of the San Antonio Spurs' final possession, lasting 7.8 seconds, in a 2013 game against the Cleveland Cavaliers. The analysis showed how the value of the Spurs' possession increased from .86 points to 1.36 points when Spurs guard Tony Parker used a Tim Duncan screen to drive into the lane, and then it rose to 1.75 when Parker passed up a contested layup attempt in favor of passing to teammate Kawhi Leonard who was standing unguarded in a corner behind the three-point line. Finally, when Leonard released the shot, the EPV dipped slightly to 1.58. In the interactive graph provided with one account of their research, you can actually watch the dot on the EPV graph rise and fall at the bottom of the screen in response to the moving dots, representing the players of course, sliding around on the court.

In this way, by creating a model for evaluating efficiency that is "more congruent with the flowing nature of the sport" they also opened up the possibility for a more granular distribution of the credit for a successful possession to individuals. In the example above, the traditional box score would have included three points for Leonard (on one made three-point field goal attempt) and one assist for Parker. Early linear weights metrics attempted to convert assists to points. But within the EPV model, every action is measured by the same currency. And, in the example above, Parker would get the largest share of the credit since from the moment he began his drive to the moment Leonard received his pass, the EPV for the possession increased .78 points (from .97 to 1.75). Moreover, he would receive this credit whether or not Leonard made the shot.

From a broader point of view, EPV allows analysts to identify how much value individual players add to possessions as compared to an average player or to compare an array of available tactical choices given a specific set of circumstances. And, as analyst Ben Taylor has noted in his own application of similar methods, these metrics can expose cognitive biases and debunk key myths, especially those surrounding the complex relationship between individual action and team outcome that have dominated basketball culture since the earliest years of the sport's history.[10]

It's clear that the EPV model represents a significant advance in several respects. It better captures both the fluidity of the game and the value of at least some of the actions that create high percentage scoring opportunities for others. In this way, it promises to enhance our appreciation for the abilities of those players whose contributions to the game don't show up in box score totals. On the other hand, it still leaves certain questions unanswered. In the example above, the model would give Parker plus .50 for getting into the lane, but what about the role of Tim Duncan in setting the screen that aided Parker in that endeavor? What about the two other players on the court for the Spurs who stood behind the three-point line opposite Leonard? They didn't touch the ball or set a screen or even move, but as both were reliable three-point shooters, surely their decision to stay put behind the arc helped create space for Parker's drive by forcing the defenders guarding them to hesitate before leaving them to help defend

Parker's drive. How should we quantify the impact of the decisions they made (to move or not to move from one space on the floor to another, for example) during the play? How much is that worth?

But these questions, which surely could be—may have already been—remedied by bigger data sets, more powerful machines, or more creative or sophisticated conceptual tools and statistical methods, still emerge from within the horizon of efficiency. They accept, in other words, the framework of assumptions about what counts that governs basketball counting. And to the extent that they do, even if the science of moving dots succeeds in quantifying for once and for all the alchemical mystery by which myriad, fluid, individually embodied decisions lead to the ball going into the basket, and even if I will be pleased that previously uncounted contributions will be valued, I will still stubbornly hold out for what in a play may count to me but will go uncounted and forgotten forever, either because it does not count or because it cannot be counted.

#74. Optimizing Shots

In the end, from a competitive standpoint, from the standpoint of the science of moving dots, the point of the game is to put the ball in the basket. Of course, long before even the most basic forms of quantification became part of the sport, players and those supervising them knew that making a basket was easier to do under some circumstances than others. A good shot had a high probability of going in and a bad shot, conversely, a low probability. Coaches and players might have a passable rough sense of good and bad shot selection. But the clichéd image of the coach screaming "bad shot" at a player, only to applaud the attempt when it goes in, may say more about just how rough even expert assessments of shot selection were for much of the game's history. Given the importance of getting good shots to overall success and the complexity of the factors determining just what makes a good shot, it's understandable that the science of moving dots has made refining our knowledge of the issue a priority.

For a simple, if potentially misleading, way to understand how basketball analytics approaches shot selection, consider the advanced analytics metric effective field goal percentage. Traditional box score field goal percentage simply divided all field goals made by all field goals attempted. With this a coach might know that Player A makes 60 percent of his field goal attempts while Player B makes only 40 percent of his. If the coach had only this information, he'd probably think that any shot by Player A was a better shot than any shot by Player B. But we know that doesn't make sense. If Player B is standing under the basket and Player A is sixty feet from the basket, we know that Player B's shot will be the better shot. Enter the shot chart, which helps us break down shooting percentage by the location on the court (typically one of eight zones) from where the shot was taken. Consulting a shot chart we might confirm that Player B shoots 85 percent when standing under the basket and Player A shoots only 5 percent when sixty feet from the basket.

But what if we narrow these extreme differences in distance? What if Player B is eight feet from the basket and Player A is twenty-four feet from the basket? Well, if they are in the NBA and they are average players, then Player B's eight-footer will go in about 40 percent of the time and Player A's twenty-four-footer will go in about 36 percent of the time. But don't forget that in the NBA, Player A's twenty-four-footer comes from behind the three-point line and will therefore be worth three points if it goes in. To capture the difference in value of the three-pointer, basketball analytics devised effective field goal percentage. Instead of the simple division of field goals made by field goals attempted, effective field goal percentage divides the sum of two-point field goals made and three-point field goals made times .5 by field goals attempted.

Consider how that changes the assessment of the shot selection options above: if Player B shoots that eight-footer one hundred times, he'll make forty, yielding eighty points for his team, whereas if Player A shoots his twenty-four-footer one hundred times, he'll make thirty-six, yielding 108 points for his team. The scientists of moving dots call those figures "expected shot value." Because the expected shot value of an average NBA three-point attempt is 1.08 points per shot (108 per one hundred shots) and the expected shot value of an average NBA eight-foot attempt is .80 points per shot, the three-pointer is the better shot. That simple and very general calculation is what has led to the dramatic rise in three-point attempts in the NBA since the advent of the science of moving dots.

But basketball analytics isn't only, or even mainly, about shooting more threes, even if that has been the most obviously visible impact of quantification on shot selection. To begin with, basketball analytics has also demonstrated that as much as three pointers are about 33 percent more valuable than eight-footers, shots at the rim are in turn about 33 percent more valuable than three-pointers. But then, these are averages. For any particular player, on any particular team surrounded by a particular set of teammates, against any particular defender and opposing team defense, in any particular game situation, on any particular possession, basketball analytics may well generate a different assessment of the relative quality of a particular set of shot options and therefore a different recommendation regarding which shot is optimal.[11]

Among the factors that the science of moving dots might consider in concrete situations we might find: the distance and angle from the baseline of the potential shooter, whether or not the potential shooter has just caught a pass or is considering shooting off the dribble, whether he is stationary or on the move, how close the nearest defender is (as well as how tall, how good a leaper, and how long he is), how quickly the shooter is able to release the ball on a shot, what the score of the game is and how much time remains in the game, how much time remains on the shot clock for that possession, or where his teammates are and how their projected shot values compare to the potential shooters. Optical tracking technology now provides data sets for each player in each of these scenarios, as well as in combinations of them. Of course, though consideration of these factors will dictate that each team develops its own unique shot selection profile, it's still the case that the overall cumulative effect of the science of moving dots has been an increase in three-point attempts and shots at the rim, an increase in free throw attempts, and a decrease in so-called mid-range shots (from eight feet away out to the three point line).

In his book *Sprawlball*, cartographer and basketball analyst Kirk Goldsberry provides what he calls a "tour of the new era of the NBA" that was ushered in by the combination of the institution of the three-point line in 1979 and the rise of the science of moving dots in the first two decades of the twenty-first century.[12] Goldsberry's tour (to which I shall return in chapter 13), though perhaps oversimplified, shows how the quest to maximize efficiency by optimizing shot selection has wrought a wholesale transformation of the sport that encompasses everything from how individual players develop skills and make specific in-game decisions to how coaches plot tactics and strategies, from how general managers and owners assemble rosters to, ultimately, how the NBA labor market values (or devalues) certain skills and combinations of skills and of course the individual players who possess them.

#75. Rating Defense

Thus far I've only addressed how the science of moving dots has been trying to refine the quantification of basketball offense. But obviously defense is an important part of the sport as well. Offensive possessions in basketball can end in one of four ways: (1) the offense scores, (2) the defense rebounds a missed field goal or free throw, or (3) the offense turns the ball over, or (4) time runs out at the end of a period or game without one of the first three occurring. Leaving aside that last possibility, we are left with two basic possibilities: either the offense scores or else the defense gets the ball back without the offense scoring. The latter outcome is commonly known as a "stop," and it is, of course, the goal of any defensive team. At the individual level, defensive players should be contributing to maximizing their team's chances of getting stops. The question facing the science of moving dots is: How to measure that contribution?

Analysts Stephen Shea and Christopher Baker distinguish between "bottom up metrics" that measure an individual's production built upon records of individual accomplishments (such as a shot made or a rebound) and "top down metrics" that measure an individual's production on the basis of the "production of whole lineups" (such as plus-minus, which tracks the net changes in score when a given player is either on or off the court). Bottom up metrics mislead because of the limited number of types of events tallied. But even when we expand the number of categories of tallied events, bottom up metrics mislead by giving all credit to the player responsible for the end result. Top down metrics can correct for these weaknesses but "suffer from a bias towards players that play on good teams" and do not give enough credit to the end result. Shea and Baker, with the optimism characteristic of the Enlightenment rhetoric of basketball analytics, emphasize the complementary nature of the strengths and weaknesses of the two kinds of metrics. Each indicates a different dimension of the actual value of individual players. As we improve our ability to record and count more of what happens on the basketball floor, bottom up metrics will become more accurate, drawing closer to "actual value," as will top down metrics, as analysts refine the statistical methods by which they "account for and extract the team pull bias."

Traditionally, individual defensive ability was judged on the basis of such box score totals as blocks, steals, and defensive rebounds. Such figures, however, failed to capture both the many other contributions an individual might make to his team's defensive effectiveness and the overall defensive toll that might be taken as a result of an individual focusing on accumulating such statistics. Consider a steal, such as an intercepted pass, an obviously valuable defensive play that not only stops the offensive possession but does so in ways that often lead to a fast break scoring opportunity. But a steal can be the result of many different factors: a defender applying pressure to the passer can force an errant pass that his teammate can easily intercept and take down court for an uncontested basket. The teammate gets credit for the steal and for the basket, while the teammate who arguably made the more important contribution to the play would get no credit at all. Moreover, a player who begins to equate his value with high steals statistics might be tempted to gamble unsuccessfully for steals, leaving himself out of position and his four teammates at a disadvantage. Defense, then, as Shea and Baker acknowledge, shows up the limitations of relying on bottom up metrics.

The advanced possession-based statistical methods pioneered by Dean Oliver in the 1990s and early 2000s, and subsequently further refined by Oliver and others, helped to sharpen the blurry quantitative picture of defense to some degree by utilizing top down metrics. For example, Stephen Shea and Christopher Baker ran traditionally available box score tallies through the mill of advanced possession-based methods and metrics to come up with a new individual defense metric they called "defensive stops gained" (DSG). Their method, they claimed, quantified an individual player's ability to impact his team's ability to make stops by causing turnovers, blocking shots or forcing lower-quality shots, and collecting defensive rebounds, and it did so, moreover, by controlling for the overall quality of the individual's defensive teammates.[13]

However, as Daniel Massop (among others elsewhere) argued in a Nylon Calculus pre-season article asking, "How can we best measure individual impact?": "It is entirely debatable whether or not isolating a player's performance from his team is entirely possible." He points out, for example, that if a player moves from the starting rotation to the bench, his calculated impact is likely to improve, despite nothing about his play changing, simply because he will be spending more of his time on the court matched up against the opponents' own, less-skilled bench players. More importantly, Massop points out, all current individual defensive impact metrics offer only statistical approximations (and sometimes contradictory ones at that) of which individual players are effective defenders. The point, he reminds his readers, is to understand why: What are they doing that makes them effective? Massop imagines that optical tracking data, by vastly expanding our capacity to quantify the myriad events and factors contributing to a defensive stop, has the "great potential" to enhance our bottom up defensive metrics and so to enable us "the 'why' of players being effective defenders."

Be that as it may, it strikes me that perhaps no area of the sport spotlights better the challenges that quantifying efforts face in trying to count everything that counts even by the limited criteria of competitive value, as well as in accounting for the complex relationship between individual and team performance. My point is not that the science of moving dots should necessarily give up its attempts to improve the quantitative representations of individual defensive impact. Rather, I am drawing attention to the ways that this area of basketball analytics suggests the asymptotic shape of progress in the field. In that case, what may be more genuinely illuminating, not to mention healthy from a broader cultural perspective, would be to supplement the ever-hopeful rhetoric supporting these efforts: "We are getting closer and closer to nailing this"—with a stronger emphasis on a rhetoric of impossibility—"but even so we will never actually nail it. And maybe it would be good to think about what we might be losing in the futile pursuit."

#76. Counting Stars

Toward the middle of *Moneyball*, Michael Lewis is explaining how the Oakland A's approached the challenge of replacing Jason Giambi, a star first baseman who had left the team in free agency. Giambi was a singular talent, and even if there were another player like him available on the market, the A's couldn't afford him. From the perspective of baseball analytics, however, that wasn't how the A's viewed the problem. "The important thing is not to recreate the individual. The important thing is to recreate the *aggregate*," manager Billy Beane is quoted as having said. Lewis explains: "He couldn't and wouldn't find another Jason Giambi, but he finds the pieces of Giambi he could at least afford to be without. . . . The A's front office had broken down Giambi into his obvious offensive statistics . . . along with his less obvious one . . . And asked: which can we afford to replace?" "The pieces of Giambi": take a moment to dwell on the implications of that way of speaking. Through the lens of sports analytics, a whole individual is viewed and then broken apart (*analyzed*, from the Greek meaning "to break or cut apart") into an aggregate of parts, each of which is assessed in terms of its productive contributions. In this respect, sports analytics does intellectually almost exactly what capitalism does: treat workers as exchangeable units of productive labor-power. Whether or not this produces the desired results in terms of increases in productivity and efficiency for the franchise, we would be not only callous but foolish not to also consider what it produces in terms of the dehumanization and alienation of athletes.

Thus far my tour of the contemporary work of moving dots has focused on how basketball analysts similarly break down wholes into essential constitutive parts in order to isolate and quantify the skills, tendencies, and actions that contribute to maximizing efficiency at the overall scale of possessions, games, and seasons. In doing so the science of moving dots is working within the grooves of the method articulated by Beane and Lewis. But of course, ultimately, these bits of knowledge must be put together in the large-scale task of constructing a roster of players within the constraints of the collective bargaining agreement and spending limits. And this task remains, inevitably, the task of combining *whole* players, not abstracted statistical pieces. In other words, the analytical work of the science of moving dots also requires a synthetic process of locating those individuals who embody and appear most likely to deliver the statistical pieces that analysts have identified will be necessary for a team to succeed on the court.

Consider the Boston Celtics. In 2017, despite having the best record in the Eastern Conference during the regular season, the Celtics found themselves overmatched in their Eastern Conference Finals series, which the Cleveland Cavaliers won four games to one and by an average margin of victory of twenty points per game. Despite having a group of promising young players and one of the best young coaches in the league, and though they'd lost their best player, Isaiah Thomas, to injury for the final three games of the series, Celtics general manager Danny Ainge appeared to know the team was still at least one move from being able to make it to the NBA Finals and at least two from winning a title. That is why he lured rising Utah Jazz star Gordon Hayward to the team during the first week of free agency. Adding Hayward to his roster prompted two prominent basketball analytics websites to assess the likely outcome of the move and to reflect more generally on the principles of successful roster construction in today's NBA. Would adding Hayward, they asked, make Boston a contender?

Forecasting wizard Nate Silver tackled this question the day after the Hayward signing. Silver uses an individual player metric called Consensus Plus-Minus, or CPM (expressed in net points added or subtracted by the player per one hundred possessions, where the average player adds zero points) to identify the three best players on the thirty-five NBA championship teams going back to 1986. On the basis of that data, he then creates a classification system whereby players whose CPM is +6.0 or higher he calls "Alphas," those with CPM between +3.5 and +6.0 are "Betas," and those with CPMs between +2.0 and +3.5 are called "Gammas." Of course, Alphas, like Jason Giambi, are hard to come by. Championship teams, Silver discovers, usually pair an Alpha with a Beta and a Gamma, but other configurations (such as three Betas) could also make a team a contender. To simplify this further, Silver invents a statistic he calls "star points" whereby a team gets three star points for having an alpha on its roster, two for a beta, and one for a gamma. Calculating the star points for all NBA rosters since 1984–85, Silver projects the championship probability for a team given a certain number of star points. Thus, for example, 216 teams during this period had zero star points and won zero championships, and so Silver calculates the probability of a team with zero star points winning a championship at 0.0 percent (0/216). At the other end of the scale, thirteen teams had eight or more star points and four of them won championships, so Silver concludes that a team with eight or more star points has a 30.8 percent chance (4/13) of winning a title. With the addition of Hayward, the Celtics' roster would have three star points. In the period Silver analyzed, only four of the 143 teams with three star points won titles. Projecting that forward into a probability, he reasons that the Celtics would have only a 2.8 percent chance (4/143) of winning a championship. He concludes that the Celtics "are still a star away from seriously contending for a title—maybe even a superstar away."

A day later, Todd Whitehead of Nylon Calculus refined Silver's approach by asking not only how many stars a team needs to collect but "given a certain level of overall team quality, what is the most effective way to distribute talent within a roster?" To address this question, Whitehead uses a slightly different individual metric than Silver to assess individual player quality (Value Over Replacement Player, or VORP, is calculated differently than CPM but is similarly expressed in points added to a team's margin of victory by a given player above and beyond the zero that would be added by an average player). A team's aggregate VORP will directly correspond to its actual average margin of victory, which has been a reliable predictor of championship success, historically. Whitehead analyzed 375 "good" NBA rosters since 1980 to determine how they distributed their talent and what sort of success they achieved. To quantify talent distribution, Whitehead calculated the "percent-of-team VORP" data for the top twelve players on each roster. That is if a player had a VORP of +2 and his team a VORP of +10, then his percent of VORP would be 20 percent (2/10). He then created a classification system for a roster's talent distribution ranging from "Solo Acts" (exemplified by the 2005–6 Cleveland Cavaliers, for whom LeBron James contributed a whopping 65 percent of the team VORP) to "Team

Efforts" (like the 2013–14 San Antonio Spurs, where seven different players contributed at least 9 percent of the team's VORP). In between these Whitehead arranged "Alpha et al" (one major contributor alongside a few minor contributors), "Dynamic Duos" (two major contributors), "Big 3" (three major contributors), and "Big 4" (four major contributors) roster types.

Whitehead found that "for a given level of overall team quality, an unbalanced roster was more likely to produce a championship than a balanced one." He speculated that in the playoffs—because the number of players getting significant minutes gets smaller—having an Alpha or two is more critical than having a deep bench. Though Whitehead's analysis led him to agree with Silver that merely adding Hayward wouldn't put the Celtics in title contention, it also led him to favor roster imbalance slightly more than Silver. Silver considered that two teams with, say, eight star points accumulated via different configurations of Alphas, Betas, and Gammas to be equally likely to contend for a championship. Team A might get its eight star points from two Alphas and two Gammas, whereas Team B might have three Betas and two Gammas. For Silver the two teams each have a 30 percent chance of winning the title. But Whitehead's analysis suggested that Team A, with its more unbalanced distribution of talent, would have better odds of winning the championship.

Of course such analyses can only provide broad rules of thumb, as both analysts readily acknowledge. As Whitehead says directly "There's no secret formula for winning a championship." Rather, God is in the details of which individual players you have on your roster; what their particular skill sets, strengths, and weaknesses are; and how they work with each other and with their coaching staff. Therefore, basketball analysts must, having assembled a roster of individual players, cycle back to breaking them back down into detailed quantified pieces in order to understand how to capitalize upon the strengths (and mask the weaknesses) of these individuals.

#77. Saving Bodies

Of course, all the technology and methodological sophistication that is brought to bear to maximize the efficiency of individual decision-making and performance on the court has no value if a player is off the court due to injury. That is why the most rapidly growing cutting edge of the science of moving dots entails the development of technologies, methods, practices, and policies to ensure that basketball players "maximize their explosiveness in the core motions specific to the sport while also making sure their bodies move in ways that significantly reduce injury risk."[14] As Senthil Natarajan puts it, "the human body is a machine," so we should be able to "apply mathematical and engineering models to understanding the biomechanics of every action!"[15] The basic aim to use scientific methods and new technologies to improve biomechanical and physiological efficiency in order to aid performance and prevent injury—and even the mechanistic language—is similar to the quest of pioneering physical educators in the late nineteenth century. But of course, the science, the methods, the technologies, and the volume and types of data collected are vastly more sophisticated. The so-called Holy Grail of athlete injury prevention and performance improvement, according to journalist Andy Glockner, would "expertly" combine "in-game tracking data, practice tracking data, and so-called off-site biometric data culled from tracking sleep, monitoring diets, and taking periodic bloodwork to check players' vital levels."[16]

From the perspective of the science of moving dots and of the league and its franchise owners, moving forward on all these fronts in quest of the "Holy Grail" should be a no-brainer, a win-win for every stakeholder in professional basketball. Yes, franchises can better protect their financial investment in players, and coaches may be able to strategize with greater confidence about which players will be available, but fans too can be sure they'll see the best and most exciting stars when they make the significant investment in buying tickets to attend a game in person. And, players will benefit from improved performance, the prospect of longer careers, and, with both of these, bigger paychecks over a longer period of time. As Glockner put it to his audience at the 2016 MIT Sloan Sports Analytics Conference, "I mean, this is keeping players healthy, this is extending careers, this is not having issues after careers. It should be a positive thing," Glockner mused, "right?"[17] And perhaps if the benefits I listed above were the only effects of expanding the scope of basketball analytics to the molecular level, and if the interests of the various stakeholders were always perfectly aligned, it would be viewed as a positive thing by all concerned. But that is not the case.

Consider, as an example, the experience of Golden State Warriors superstar Kevin Durant during the 2019 NBA playoffs. Durant, one of the most dominant players in the NBA over the past several seasons, particularly in the playoffs where he won the NBA Finals Most Valuable Player awards in 2017 and 2018, was having another superlative series in the defending champion Warriors' second-round matchup against the Houston Rockets, the team widely considered to have the best chance of dethroning them. Late in the third quarter of the fifth game, with the series tied at two games apiece, Durant scored his twenty-first and twenty-second points of the game on a jump shot. But then, as he ran back on defense, he suddenly grabbed his right leg and limped off the court. The Warriors went on to win that game and the series without Durant, who was sidelined with what was announced as a "calf injury" for the rest of the Houston series, all four games of the Warriors' next series, and the first four games of the NBA Finals series.

The Warriors won seven of those ten games (including the one in which Durant had originally been injured) but had just dropped two straight against the talented and cohesive Toronto Raptors in the Finals to fall behind, three games to one, with the series headed back to Toronto. Surprisingly, after having first listed him as "questionable" on Friday, June 7 (shortly after Game Four ended in a 105–92 Toronto victory), the Warriors medical staff cleared Durant to play in Monday's Game Five.[18] Durant started the game and his eleven first quarter points helped the Warriors to a six-point lead. But then, about two minutes into the second quarter, as he attempted to maneuver against Toronto defender Serge Ibaka, Durant again clutched his right leg (below the calf) in pain and fell to the floor. Durant did not return and, though Golden State managed to eke out a victory in the game, Toronto won Game Six and the championship three days later. By that time, Durant had already undergone surgery to repair the injury: a ruptured Achilles tendon. The prognosis: Durant, poised to be one of the most prized and highly paid free agents of the off-season, would be likely to miss the entire 2019–20 NBA campaign.

How could this happen? The Warriors have invested as heavily in basketball analytics as any NBA franchise—including in the various rapidly growing areas aimed at injury prevention. According to Coach Steve Kerr, these resources had been marshaled in the rehabilitation of Durant's original injury. When it came to determining Durant's status for Game Five, Kerr said: "When we gathered all the information, our feeling was that the worst thing that could happen was a reinjury of the calf."[19] It was evident from the comments made by all Warriors' officials that they were devastated by Durant's injury, and not only because of the impact on the team: they were clearly moved by compassion for Durant. It seems in this case that the best tools of the science of moving dots and the best intentions of the parties involved were not enough to prevent a catastrophic and probably avoidable injury.

Given publicly available information regarding the situation, and taking public statements at face value, I do not intend to blame individuals involved in the decision to clear Durant. Rather, I aim to draw attention to the power of the *systemic* imperatives that can lead well-qualified and well-intentioned individuals to make poor, harmful decisions. "The roles of team physicians and training staff with respect to player health," sports law expert Michael McCann noted recently, "have long been an area of concern in health law and ethics. While physicians and trainers possess professional duties, including the Hippocratic Oath, to pursue the most ethical and effective care of the patient/client, physicians and trainers who are employed by teams also have employment obligations to those teams."[20] Addressing this ethical concern in her groundbreaking volume *Sport, Technology, and the Body*, Tara Magdalinski carefully points out "This is not to suggest . . . that sports physicians specifically or deliberately operate unethically, but to acknowledge that the athlete's best 'health' interests may not necessarily be the primary or sole concern of their doctor." Or, as McCann puts it, "the team's interest in the player's health could be different from those of the player."[21] It's not hard to imagine that the pressure of these contending interests, as much as any biomechanical forces, snapped Kevin Durant's Achilles tendon.

And these tensions, not to say conflicts, among competing interests are also at the heart of struggles impeding the success of that "Holy Grail"

Glockner talked about. The NBA players union has thus far successfully resisted the implementation of the most intrusive data gathering biometric practices and devices. Players are concerned—like many of us who have much less to lose than they—about how the data gathered about their bodies will be used in contract or trade negotiations, not to mention about privacy: who will own this data? Who will see it? And, even if legal remedies are available in case of leaks or errors where private data has been made public, these cannot undo the damage that might have been done a player in the process. From the fact that players and franchises both obviously share an interest in maintaining the physical health of a player, it does not necessarily—and perhaps it does not, in practice, usually—follow that they share the *same* interest, or that this interest will lead them to the same decisions. As with many issues between labor and management in the NBA, we must not allow the wealth of NBA superstars to blind us to the power differential they face as employees of the league, nor to how this often maps onto racial difference. And as I'll argue in chapter 11, this high-stakes area of the science of moving dots—encompassing big data, biometric technologies, medicine, law, ethics, and politics—could benefit from the extensive work that scholars in critical data studies have been doing in this area, mostly—but not only—beyond the domain of sports, for some time.[22]

#78. Tracking Souls

"The next stop for analytics," wrote Sebastian Pycior, in the third installment of Nylon Calculus's prospective look at emerging trends in the science of moving dots, "is the internal, conscionable space." While none of the meanings of "conscionable" I've been able to track down make any sense in that sentence, I take it that by it Pycior means "psychological." In other words, to use an older and less fashionable idiom, the "subtle knife" that is the science of moving dots is now fearlessly cutting openings into the final frontier of variables impacting player performance: their souls. And, though Pycior acknowledges up front that it's "an extremely tough space to navigate," the enthusiastic optimism with which he surveys the emerging methods and technologies that firms and franchises are using to quantify the psyches of players—whether to brew great "team chemistry," to predict how individuals will respond to the on- and off-court pressures of life in the NBA, or to steer individual player behavior—seems to belie the cautionary note.[23]

While professional sports franchises have long employed personal interviews to gauge the personalities of players—and even some simple forms of intelligence testing to assess their cognitive aptitudes—most of these don't pass scientific muster in terms of methodological rigor and reliability of results. Today, the cutting edge of this cutting edge entails administering tests that are informed by the most advanced psychological theories, themselves based on the statistical analysis of patterns of correlation between personality traits, cognitive aptitudes, and performance outcomes. What companies providing such assessment instruments to franchises promise their clients are more refined, context-sensitive, and objective snapshots of the souls of players. Down the line, Pycior foresees applying predictive analytics to data sets comprised of player social media use to assess and forecast emotional states or using neural networks and machine learning to create predictive models of player behavior. But even if such possibilities still lie in the future, the technologies and methods already in use today seem to offer a more accurate and therefore valuable snapshot of the NBA soul than has been previously available.

With the right information, a franchise may pass on drafting a player who may be highly rated for his skills or athletic ability but may be unlikely to fit in well with that *particular* team's existing roster or coaching staff, or, conversely, they may opt for a less highly prized prospect because on the basis of his psychological profile they have good reason to believe he will exceed general expectations and thrive in the specific environment of that club. For example, the company Athletic Intelligence Measures claims that its "Athletic Intelligence Quotient" test (AIQ) can help teams "find hidden gems that others may overlook" by measuring "the intellectual abilities most used in attaining, enhancing, and applying athletic skills . . . The AIQ identifies an athlete's mental strengths and weaknesses, helps coaches train athletes to reach the highest level of performance, and aids management and player personnel in scouting and roster decisions."[24] The benefits for franchises seem self-evident and echo the now-familiar promise of sports analytics going back to *Moneyball*: exclusive knowledge that provides superiority in risk management and the opportunity to exploit a "market inefficiency."

But even from the point of view of players, the process appears to offer something more nuanced than black and white characterizations of players as "cancers" or "red flags," and therefore has the potential to open more doors to more players with a greater variety of personality types. Putatively universal moral traits (whether virtues or vices) have been mapped onto basketball play in order to control player behavior since the sport's origin. And as the game spread and was played by diverse populations, these blunt psychological pseudo-assessments, sometimes bearing racist assumptions, could often serve to support discrimination against black players especially. So, if new assessments like the Athletics Intelligence Quotient can help to counter the irrational assumptions and racist judgments to which players are subjected, more power to them.

But how does AIQ work? Athletic Intelligence Measures' website explains: "Just as a stopwatch measures speed, the AIQ provides valuable information about an athlete's performance-specific intellectual abilities." That sounds great! Imagine being able to measure "an athlete's performance-specific intellectual abilities" with the same simplicity and precision with which a stopwatch measures speed?[25] But wait: How *does* a stopwatch measure speed? It actually doesn't. A stopwatch measures and displays nothing but the amount of time elapsed between its activation and deactivation. Of course, if we coordinate that activation and deactivation with the beginning and ending of an object (or person's) movement along a path, and we know the distance of that path, then we can use the measurement the stopwatch provides to *calculate average speed* by dividing the distance traversed by the object along its path by the time elapsed between our activation and deactivation of the stopwatch. Galileo provided the equation: v (speed) = d (distance) / t (time).[26]

I learned this myself from my father when I was around eight years old. That's when he used a yardstick to mark out a straight chalk line on the road one house down from ours and another one on the road one house up. The distance between the two fat neon-pink lines was fifty yards. I stood behind one line, my father stood behind the other, one hand raised up above his head, the other clutching a Tag Heuer stopwatch, exactly like the one that mesmerized me every Sunday evening at six p.m. when "60 Minutes" began (and that, having claimed it after his death, now sits on my desk as I write). When his arm came down like a guillotine, I took off, running as fast as I could toward my father, and he activated the stopwatch. As I leaned forward breathlessly pushing through the imaginary tape at the finish line, I could just hear the click of the knurled button as he deactivated the watch. He had not measured my speed. He had obtained the time value "t" that he could use to calculate my average speed.

I have no doubt that the good people at Athletic Intelligence Measures understand this, so I will resist (almost) the snarky impulse to question how intelligent Athletic Intelligence Measures might be given their belief that a stopwatch measures speed. Besides, my point in dwelling on their metaphor and belaboring the actual operation of a stopwatch is not to point out the ignorance of whoever wrote that website copy but rather the arrogance of whoever approved it. To begin with, notice that quantifying how fast something is moving is a pretty complicated perceptual, conceptual, and technological operation—and that was just for average speed. Things move at variable speeds—their speed *changes*, in other words—and quantifying their speed at any given instant along their path is even more complicated. If that is so, how much more complicated can we imagine it must be to quantify a human soul, even if we presume that it will not change?

But the problem runs deeper than just technical complexity. For, it may not just be hard, but misguided. "Adaptability and native creativity on the part of the workforce," poet and corporate consultant David Whyte reminds us, "come through the door only with their passions. Their passions come only with their souls. Their souls love the hidden springs boiling and welling at the center of existence more than they love the company."[27] We might well wonder about the wisdom of wishing for a science that would allow us to bring these hidden springs under predictable control, or simply be grateful for all that currently prevents us from succeeding in doing so.

PART 2 | What Counts

10

Approaching Basketball Experience

#79. Track That Shit!

During the 2018 NBA playoffs, Second Spectrum's optical tracking data revealed that Cleveland Cavaliers star LeBron James was the second-slowest player among all those competing in the league's postseason competition and the slowest in the Cavalier's Eastern Conference Finals series against the Boston Celtics, averaging 3.64 miles per hour: basically a brisk walk or a slow jog.[1]

Whether or not the tracking data accurately registered James's speed, James's postseason effort and performance, especially in the series against Boston, were widely hailed as one of the greatest of all time.[2] Among other things, James—then thirty-one years old and already the NBA's all-time leader in total playoff minutes played and playoff minutes per game—played forty-one minutes per game in the series, including forty-six in Game Six and all forty-eight in the deciding Game Seven. Even analytics-based Five-Thirty-Eight marshaled the numbers to declare James's performance in the series his "greatest masterpiece."[3]

Nevertheless, the story quickly became headline news in every major news outlet. But the story was not the number (in this case 3.64 mph) or the ranking: slowest in series, second slowest in the playoffs. The story was James's verbal *response* to the number. "That's the dumbest shit I've ever heard," James told the reporter who informed him of the data, "that tracking bullshit can kiss my ass. The slowest guy? Get out of here. Tell them to track how tired I am after a game, track that shit. I'm No. 1 in the NBA on how tired I am after the game."

When the NBA announced the installation of tracking cameras just prior to the 2013–14 season, *USA Today* reporter Sean Highkin wrote that the "cameras have the ability to measure speed and distance" so that "debates of quickness between Kyrie Irving and Russell Westbrook will be able to be solved."[4] Strictly speaking, the statement was misleading. The cameras actually only *measure* the distance traveled by players and the time individual players have spent on the floor. With those two values, of course, as I just discussed in chapter 9, it *is* possible to calculate the *average* speed of a player over the course of game play by dividing the total distance traveled by the amount of time spent on the court. And, in fact, it is the result of this calculation that the speed metric on the NBA's statistics website represents.

Now, we may also calculate the speed of any *particular* segment of individual player movement—say a backdoor cut: a sprint back on defense in transition—by dividing the distance traveled by the amount of time. If the time interval is small, we might need to derive it by multiplying the number of frames by the frame rate per second. For example, imagine that LeBron James is set up on the low block away from the ball on offense, when, suddenly, he sprints to the free throw line. The cameras can tell us exactly how far he moved, but let's say for the sake of illustration that he moved twelve feet. We also know that those cameras were capturing the movement at a rate of twenty-five frames per second so that each frame captures .04 seconds of time. If James's cut occupied ten frames, we know that it took him .40 seconds to move twelve feet. The speed of his cut in feet per second would then be twelve feet divided by .4 seconds: around thirty feet per second or about 20.5 miles per hour.

I imagine that Highkin only meant to suggest that the cameras provide the values by which speed could be calculated. But it is nevertheless a bit of a leap to describe this process, which combines digital recording with human observation and calculation, as "the cameras measure speed" (and still a further leap to consider the result of such calculations as an objective measurement of "quickness" capable of resolving debates about the relative quickness of different players). Though seemingly trivial, I think that it is in part by way of such minor, misleading leaps, especially in the mainstream media, that the power of quantifying technologies and of the numbers they generate can be misunderstood, exaggerated, and treated as simple, objective truths by fans.

All this may explain why James was so dismissive of the conclusion that he was the slowest player supplied by that "tracking bullshit." The very nature of the calculations the results of which the NBA portrays as "speed" (but which are in actuality "average speed") seem to ignore the fundamental nature of player movement on the basketball court, which is discontinuous and characterized by many, many movements over short distances at highly variable speeds. Even many reporters commenting on the story noted that James had earlier reported sometimes conserving energy because of his heavy workload.

This brings us to the second part of James's reply. If we may call the first half of the response James's *critique* of this particular method of quantifying basketball, the second half may be read as a *proposal*, perhaps a demand. Generally speaking, the demand is for more comprehensive counting ("track how tired I am after a game"). But implicit in that demand is the assertion that there are things that count that are not counted. Specifically, in this case: fatigue. Of course, sports scientists have many different methods and metrics for quantifying fatigue, as James probably knows firsthand. But, aside from the fact that none of them are used or at least made public by the NBA, I suspect that James was not actually talking about fatigue, but effort, and not only the physical effort that, like fatigue, could be quantified to some degree. I believe that James was talking about some of the psychological factors that drive effort: will, determination, resilience, none of which appear on the NBA's stats page. Perhaps if he would only consent to have his soul tracked, we could verify his claim.

All this is important, to be sure. However, as important as the content of James's critique and demand is what we might call its form. By this I mean to draw attention to the fact, overlooked in accounts of the incident, that a *player* was proposing the alternative metric. In 2010, when he coordinated with friends Chris Bosh and Dwyane Wade to join the Miami Heat, thus forming a "super team" that would capture 2012 and 2013 NBA titles, James outraged the basketball world at least partly because he arrogated to himself powers that had previously been held exclusively by owners and general managers: the power of roster formation.[5] "Track that shit"—though possibly intended merely as an idiomatic reinforcement of his dismissal of tracking data and though certainly less consequential than his 2010 "Decision"—similarly draws attention to power dynamics operating within the league. It is not the players, but the league and its franchises that determine what is to be counted.

But what if they did track that shit? Or better yet, what if basketball analytics embraced the frailty and unpredictability of the body, instead of only extracting its capacity to master circumstances? What if it expanded its understanding of performance to include not only competitive and economic efficiency but also, to use philosopher Richard Shusterman's phrase, "expressive self-fashioning" and the generation of "perceptual appreciation" for spectators?[6] What if it devoted as much attention to the body as end in itself as it does to the body as a means to achieve other ends? And what if instead of viewing the basketball-playing body as the dangerous site of potential error, it were to draw upon it as a somatic storehouse of nonquantitative insight into basketball play? What, in short, if the moving dots designed the system?[7]

What would count? What would they count? What elements of the basketball adventure, I'm led to wonder, might they try to highlight?

#80. The Live Creature

To begin to explore that question, I want to look at basketball play through the lens of what the American philosopher John Dewey called "experience." Dewey wrote many hundreds of pages attempting to define, explicate, and clarify what he meant by "experience," and dozens of philosophers after him have written many thousands of pages scrutinizing Dewey's idea.[8] I find this material fascinating and absorbing in its own right, but much of it leads me away from my book's basic aim: to think about basketball play qualitatively from the perspective of what may not be counted by the science of moving dots. So, to keep Dewey's concept tethered to this concrete purpose, I want to introduce Dewey's notion of experience as he described it in the text that many commentators consider the most mature and concretely developed of Dewey's accounts of the notion: his theory of art, in the book *Art as Experience* (1934).

Though radical in its time, and somewhat controversial among professional philosophers, I imagine that Dewey's argument in *Art as Experience* will resonate with, perhaps even seem obvious to, any basketball fan who has found herself exclaiming "What a beautiful play!" while watching a game. To put it simply, where traditional views of art seek to understand it by analyzing the product: the artwork, Dewey wants to focus on the processes—the *work* of art, we might say—that are sedimented temporarily in that product and then continually released through its circulation, reception, and interpretation. Dewey contends that attempts to understand art have gone wrong because they view art as a specialized object set apart from the rest of human existence. After tracing the historical and conceptual factors leading to this limited view, Dewey attempts then to correct it by starting his own exploration of art from a different premise.

"In order to understand the esthetic in its ultimate and approved forms," he writes, "one must begin with it in the raw; in the events and scenes that hold the attentive eye and ear of man, arousing his interest and affording him enjoyment as he looks and listens." And it is fortunate but not coincidental I think that he furnishes an example from the sporting world: "The sources of art in human experience will be learned," he elaborates, "by him who sees how the tense grace of the ball-player infects the onlooking crowd."[9] Dewey develops his process-centered perspective with a thick description of the existence and experience of what he calls "the live creature," which I read as Dewey's attempt to account for the live creature from "the inside," as it were. Accordingly, I want to use it as a lens, or perhaps point of departure, for an account of the experience of what I am calling the "live basketball player."[10] And I'd like, as you read my summary of Dewey's view, for you to imagine a basketball player in action on the court during a game.

Dewey's description of the live creature begins with what he takes to be the most fundamental fact of its existence: that life unfolds not only *in* an environment but *because of* it. It is possible and may be useful to study the creature as though it existed in isolation. Dewey would not deny this.

His point is that such analysis entails a kind of fictional abstraction from the real conditions of existence. (And further, that those who undertake it often seem then to have forgotten this and as a result mistake this artificially constructed abstraction for the live creature itself.) In real existence though, the live creature is inseparable from—is in fact constituted by—myriad interactions, occurring continuously at many different levels, to effectively create a web of relationships that temporarily arrest and solidify in a relatively stable form we identify as that particular live creature.[11]

But, however stable these forms may appear to be, Dewey wants to emphasize that they are indeed only temporary phases in a web of relational interchanges that is in constant flux. He characterizes this dynamic variation in different ways: as disharmony, adjustment, and harmony of the creature and environment, as gain and loss for the creature seeking to pursue particular aims as well as its more general, fundamental aim to continue existence. What Dewey calls "form" or "order" arise "whenever a stable, even though moving, equilibrium is reached. . . . made out of the relations of harmonious interactions that energies bear to one another." Already here, in the most basic facts of life, Dewey sees "the roots of the aesthetic," for two reasons. First, because "here in germ are balance and harmony attained through rhythm. Equilibrium comes about not mechanically and inertly but out of, and because of tension."[12] But also because this form, order, or equilibrium, developing as it necessarily must out of disruption, conflict, or tension, "bears within itself the germs of consummation akin to the aesthetic."

To this point Dewey has described a live creature as instinctively existing through a ceaselessly varying series of relational interactions punctuated by phases of disharmony and harmony, loss and gain. But he also addresses the specific implications of this condition for human beings for whom the vicissitudes of this condition provoke emotion, both as a sign of break or loss and as a spur to reflection and to purposeful interest in objects as "conditions of realization of harmony," which is incorporated into "objects as their meaning." In this way a *full* experience for the live human creature is integrated. Rather than seeking to avoid moments of resistance and tension, we may consciously cultivate them because of their potentialities, bringing to living consciousness an experience that is unified and total.

And rather than attempting to prolong a state of equilibrium or harmony "beyond its term," we may recognize that it is merely the basis for a new cycle of challenge, adjustment, and growth. In this way, for the live human creature, the relational web constituting existence also involves a temporal dimension. "Only when the past ceases to trouble and anticipations of the future are not perturbing," Dewey writes, "is a being wholly united with his environment and therefore fully alive." Here again, Dewey finds in everyday existence a source of aesthetic experience for "Art celebrates with peculiar intensity the moments in which the past reinforces the present and in which the future is a quickening of what now is."[13]

#81. Basketball Experience

It's helpful, in order to concretize the relevance of Dewey's "experience" to basketball, that he stresses that the "live creature's" manner of existing fully present, simultaneously immersed in, engaged with and aware of the dynamically shifting web of relationships that make not only existence but growth possible *is embodied*. "All senses are equally on the *qui vive*. As you watch, you see motion merging into sense and sense into motion . . . What the live creature retains from the past and what it expects from the future operate as directions in the present. . . . As he watches what stirs about him, he too, is stirred. His observation is both action and preparation and foresight of the future. He is active through his whole being when he looks and listens as when he stalks his quarry or stealthily retreats from a foe. His senses are sentinels of immediate thought and outposts of action, and not, as they so often are with us, mere pathways along which material is gathered to be stored away for a delayed and remote possibility."[14]

"Experience in the degree in which it *is* experience," Dewey continues, "is heightened vitality. . . . It signifies complete interpenetration of self and the world of objects and events [and] affords our sole demonstration of stability that is not stagnation but is rhythmic and developing. Because experience is the fulfillment of an organism in its struggles and achievements in a world of things, it is art in germ. Even in its rudimentary forms, it contains the promise of that delightful perception which is esthetic experience."[15]

I don't think it will take much for an avid basketball fan to imagine particular players in action in Dewey's description. But allow me, using it as a lens, to highlight certain features of *basketball* experience: as relational, dynamic, embodied, and whole in time and space. Live basketball creatures—players and spectators alike—exist in and through a whole, continuously moving world of fluid relationships to others as well as to their own bodies and physical environment. Moreover, basketball experience is marked by rhythms of stability and precariousness, of gain and loss, whose vicissitudes are partly caused by chance or by factors unknown to those undergoing them.

The resulting uncertainty provokes a variety of responses, among them that manifestation of what Dewey called "the quest for certainty" that is basketball analytics. But if we can suspend that impulse, we may find within basketball those intensified experiences that Dewey called "consummatory." In these, a process—say, eating a meal or playing a game—has been brought to fulfillment such that "its close is a consummation and not a cessation."

Finally, Dewey argued, art sensually foregrounds the qualities of consummatory experience to evoke what he called aesthetic experience. In aesthetic experience, we create or enjoy the work or performance for its own sake, and not merely or even primarily for other benefits we may derive from it. Process and product, means and ends, matter and manner, come together to transform experience into art. Similarly, basketball columnist Leonard Koppett once argued that in basketball "the peaks and valleys of spectator delight . . . are reached as easily by awesome maneuver as by the mere fact of scoring."[16] This I call "basketball feeling." And art—whether the medium is basketball or poetry—reveals and feeds the potential for growth and fulfillment in everyday experience.

The processes conducive to basketball feeling entail uncertainty and imaginative, often risky, experimentation. They may often be inefficient and even appear to have failed if the standard for measuring success is victory or profit. Writes one Dewey expert of aesthetic experience: "It does not sacrifice the present to the industrial gospel of efficiency or calculated promises of future yields."[17] If so, then the continued expansion of basketball analytics—whose express purpose is, by contrast, to minimize uncertainty, dispel mystery, and relieve doubt by reaching after fact and reason in order to maximize efficiency and promises of future yields—may undermine basketball's ability to deliver aesthetic experience. As Dewey wrote in the final lines of *Art as Experience*, "Art is a mode of prediction not found in charts and statistics."[18]

#82. Doubts, Mysteries, Uncertainties

There's nothing wrong with, for example, Scott LaForest's question about how to improve performance prediction. It really just instantiates the question that drives all predictive analytics: What will happen in the future? And it's more than understandable to raise that question. In my view, it's an unavoidable part of being human. As I said in discussing the situation of the live basketball player, wanting to know is a natural response to the uncertainty and flux of basketball experience. The issue is not, then, whether or not we should want to know what's going to happen. We *will* want to know what's going to happen. The issue I'm interested in instead is how we relate to that desire and to the radical uncertainty—the radical unknowing—to which it testifies. The question is: What do we do with our desire to know? Doubling down on the instruments of knowledge—such as measurement and quantification—is one possible response. But Dewey—notwithstanding his deep respect for and steadfast advocacy for the scientific method as the best means for discovering facts—suggested in *Art as Experience* that a different response is possible.

To get to that response, though, Dewey first critically reviews the conditions that lead us to miss the alternative response or to resist it if we do see it. To do so, he offers a capsule account of the history of "contempt for the body, fear of the senses, and the opposition of flesh to spirit," noting that in modern society it manifests itself as the hierarchical compartmentalization of occupations through which practical activity is separated from insight, "imagination from executive doing, significant purpose from work, and emotion from thought and doing."[19] Within that framework, we reduce the body and senses to mere isolated instruments devoid of interrelationship or intrinsic meaning and whose only value resides in furnishing a painful or pleasurable point of departure for the valued work of thinking and doing. In this world, social "prestige goes to those who use their minds without participation of the body and who act vicariously through control of the bodies and labor of others."[20]

This social arrangement and the cultural attitudes it crystalizes runs counter to—and indeed entails a fragmentation of—the experience of the live creature. "Sense," Dewey writes, canvassing the many connotations of the word, should signify a "meaning so directly embodied in experience as to be its own illuminated meaning." This, he asserts, "is the only signification that expresses the function of sense organs when they are carried to full realization." In such fully realized moments of experience, not only sense, but emotion and intellect are fully and cooperatively engaged so that the isolation and opposition of any one to the other appears as a kind of violence. Given that, for Dewey, "experience" is really just another word for "living," it makes sense that he lands on the bold statement that "oppositions of mind and body, soul and matter, spirit and flesh all have their origin, fundamentally, in fear of what life may bring forth": fear, in other words, of the future, which is necessarily uncertain and unknowable.[21]

As an alternative to this fear, to the degradation of the body, sense, and emotion in favor of the intellect and reason, and to the hierarchical social structures that both flow from and reinforce this basic fearful stance, Dewey turns to art. Art, because it is in Dewey's view essentially linked to the unified processes of lived experience, offers a different—less fear-driven—way to respond to the flux and uncertainty that "life may bring forth." "Art," writes Dewey (and I want you to think "basketball play") "is proof that man uses the materials and energies of nature with intent to expand his own life, and that he does so in accord with the structure of his organism—brain, sense-organs, and muscular system. Art is the living and concrete proof that man is capable of restoring consciously, and thus on the plane of meaning, the union of sense, need, impulse and action characteristic of the live creature."[22]

In emphasizing this point Dewey also explicitly criticizes as stunted and sterile any use of reason that proceeds by first pretending to set aside as inferior and irrelevant our sensual, emotional or intuitive, and poetic or artistic capacities. "'Reason,'" Dewey writes, "at its height cannot attain complete grasp and a self-contained assurance. It must fall back upon imagination—upon the embodiment of ideas in emotionally charged sense."[23] Dewey was consistent throughout his career in emphasizing two points about reason and scientific thinking: (1) they constitute the indispensable best tools we have for discovering facts, (2) facts are not the only discoveries that matter.

Dewey drives his point home by drawing upon the words of an artist, the nineteenth-century English poet John Keats, and, in particular, upon a letter, famous among literary scholars, that Keats wrote to his brothers in 1817 in which he describes a "quality" that "went to form" great writers "and which Shakespeare possessed so enormously." The quality, which Keats called "negative capability" is the capacity "of being in uncertainties, mysteries, doubts, without any irritable reaching after fact and reason." Given that, in Dewey's words, we live in a "world of surmise, of mystery, of uncertainties," "'reasoning' must fail man." "Ultimately," Dewey contended, "there are but two philosophies. One of them accepts life and experience in all its uncertainty, mystery, doubt, and half-knowledge and turns that experience upon itself to deepen and intensify its own qualities—to imagination and art. That is the philosophy of Shakespeare and Keats."[24] And according to one expert, it was the philosophy of Dewey, which may be why Dewey concludes *Art as Experience* by affirming the cognitive and moral value of art. "Art," he writes, elaborating the alternative to "charts and statistics," "insinuates possibilities of human relations not to be found in rule and precept, admonition and administration."[25]

11

The Ethics of Understanding Basketball

#83. Starlings, or, Chaos and Complexity

Imagine this is a metaphorical evocation of basketball play: "A flight of screaming birds, a school of herring tearing through the water like a silken sheet, a cloud of chirping crickets, a booming whirlwind of mosquitos." French philosopher Michel Serres offers these images of what he calls "the multiple." Serres argues that philosophy has never been very comfortable with such entities, whose defining features are dynamically changing relations among elements that are themselves, upon closer inspection, composed of dynamically changing relations among elements and so on to the very bottom; except that there is, it turns out, no bottom. Philosophy, he claims, is "fascinated by the unit": "that herd must be singular in its totality and it must also be made up of a given number of sheep or buffalo. We want a principle, a system, an integration, and we want elements, atoms, numbers" and, he could have added, quanta.[1] Serres's "flight of screaming birds" appears also as an image in the poet and corporate consultant David Whyte's book *The Heart Aroused*, where—now transformed into a flock of starlings depicted in a 1799 letter from Keats's contemporary, the poet Samuel Taylor Coleridge—it stands for and motivates his reflections not on the multiple, per se, but rather on complexity and chaos.[2] For me, the image suggests also the complex, fluid dynamics of the basketball experience.

While Serres and Whyte begin with poetic imagery, both authors inform their reflections with insights from the overlapping, interdisciplinary scientific fields known as "chaos theory" and "complex systems theory." These study, describe, and model the features of nonlinear dynamical systems—from a swinging pendulum to an ecosystem—whose behavior does not conform to the predictions of linear equations. Researchers have identified a number of peculiar features characteristics of such systems. First, they are highly sensitive to initial conditions, meaning that changing just one miniscule and seemingly trivial variable from the outset can result in massively different behaviors—this is commonly known as "the butterfly effect," as in a butterfly flapping its wings in Toledo can cause a hurricane in the Caribbean. This sensitivity arises because of another peculiarity of such systems: dynamic feedback that can amplify the effects of small-scale variations. As the behavior of these systems unfolds, they tend to produce both unsuspected richness and variety of behavior, sometimes referred to as turbulence. At the same time, seemingly paradoxically, from this apparently chaotic behavior ordered structures and patterns emerge spontaneously out of the interplay of the elements comprising the system.[3]

That basketball play is, strictly speaking, nonlinear will be no surprise to anyone familiar with the history of basketball analytics, or indeed, anyone who has ever watched a basketball game. Throughout the history of attempts to quantify the sport, analysts have emphasized this feature in contrast to baseball, where events unfold in a discrete, linear sequence. Indeed, they frequently emphasize the difference to highlight the difficulties of quantifying basketball play. But this does not mean that the complexity of basketball experience paralyzes the science of moving dots. For it also has been the subject of some advanced research by scientists creating models of basketball play using theories of complex systems. While this research certainly has disclosed statistical patterns (that are in turn supposed to represent behavioral patterns) in basketball's past, it does not have, nor does it claim to have, predictive power.[4]

In his popular book *Game Changer*, sport scientist and consultant Fergus Connolly applies the theory of nonlinear dynamic system to sport and makes this the premise of what might be called a detailed "user's manual" for elite athletes and those who work with them. Reviewing the basic features of such systems, Connolly deduces what he calls the "macro principle of unpredictability": "that because we can expect to (possibly) know only the initial conditions, we cannot predict outcomes. I say 'possibly' because in many cases we don't have all the information about even the initial conditions (despite what the prophets of the Big Data movement might tell you)." More generally, Connolly sums up the daunting complexity of sport: "we should stop trying to quantify and measure every aspect of sports in the hope that it will allow us to better manage the outcome. It won't, because there are too many variables interacting with each other, and these variables change from game to game."[5] And, I would add, from moment to moment.

This may explain why Connolly's book actually begins not with this theoretical exposition but with a "thick" narrative description of NFL quarterback "Tom Brady's 2.3 seconds of chaos" from the instant just preceding the snap of the football during a Super Bowl game to the instant his teammate, a Patriots receiver, catches his pass for a touchdown. Simply noting that the description takes up four double-columned pages of the oversized book gives a sense of how *much* detail Connolly provides. But of course, the number alone does not do justice to the quality and richness of the detail, which ranges from the sounds in the stadium, to the sometimes minute movements of the players, to Brady's breathing and the biochemical events occurring in different parts of Brady's body as he drops back and sets to throw. Though it is a narrative, and densely technical, it also manages to be highly poetic.

It may be obvious that I am making a claim for the unique abilities of language—of words rather than numbers—to convey the sort of complexity characterizing basketball experience. But Connolly's description is also illuminating in that the focus is on the player, on his subjective experience of objective conditions within his body and in his environment, and on the decision he makes in the course of interacting with it. Indeed, throughout the book, as I pointed out in chapter 9, Connolly is at pains not only to account for the rich nonquantifiable complexity of athletic experience, but to put the athlete—the live creature, Dewey might say—at the center of that experience.

The implications for basketball in the era of the science of moving dots might be drawn out by returning to David Whyte's reflections on starlings.

Whyte first observes that the collective pattern of behavior exhibited by the flock is not the result of some predetermined plan but rather the spontaneous effect of each individual starling following a specific set of behavioral imperatives in its own way. The phenomenon of complex patterns arising from relatively simple individual behaviors is known in complex systems theory as the principle of self-organizing emergent properties. But then Whyte makes the metaphorical—which is to say, essentially, *poetic*—leap to a modern corporation and the individual employees that comprise it.

Describing the challenges faced by corporate managers and executives as they confront the enormously complex, rapidly changing network of interlocking systems within which they must make decisions, Whyte first encourages them to lay down the burden of "imperial command, from the top down." Not only is it unnecessary, it is doomed to fail because "we have less wisdom than the emergent intelligence of many individuals given enough information and the ability to ask." "Stop," he exhorts executives, "treating people as if they are herbivorous animals about to stampede out of control unless you are constantly riding the herd." And instead, let the behavior of the organization "emerge from the bottom up." Everything is to be gained, he argues, by acting "as if each person were an individual human being who has made a conscious choice to work with you and all the others."[6]

Taking his words back into the basketball world, the image comes to my mind of running Rajiv Maheswaran's TED Talk in reverse, so that the flattened, moving dots spring back to life not only as basketball players but as the multi-dimensional human beings they actually are, endowed with exceptionally developed embodied intelligence and highly refined capacities for cooperative adaptation. It strikes me that any approach to understanding the chaotic complexity of basketball experience that does not incorporate the perspective, technical knowledge, intuitive wisdom, and voices of the moving dots themselves is doomed to miss and, more dangerously, to miss what—and the very fact *that*—it has missed.

#84. Raw Data is an Oxymoron

This issue of how the science of moving dots seeks to grasp the complexity of basketball experience can also be approached from the perspective of critical data studies, which is why I borrowed, for the title of this adventure, from Lisa Gitelman's pioneering critical data studies anthology. The provocative title, as she and Virginia Jackson put it in their introduction to the volume, is meant not so much as an argument but rather as "a friendly reminder and a prompt" to bear in mind that the data "are always cooked."[7] She does not mean, of course, that they are rigged deliberately to mislead, but rather that they are always generated and that this process of making data *presupposes* interpretation and imagination. The strange sound of the verbs I might use to describe what Gitelman is talking about—making data, producing data, fabricating data—suggests to me how naturally we approach data as though it were raw, appearing directly as a pristine gift from nature. Indeed, the very word "data," which became part of the English lexicon during the Scientific Revolution, was borrowed from the Latin word meaning "gift," or given. And yet the work of critical data scholars offers a convincing case for the value of understanding data as a product, not to mention a commodity. "There is much more to conceptualizing data," writes Rob Kitchin, "than science and business generally acknowledge."[8] Though I cannot pursue all the interesting avenues opened by this view, I nevertheless want briefly to introduce it to the conversation about basketball analytics because of the implications it has for, first, how we assess the knowledge claims that the science of moving dots makes, and second, how we might address the ethical implications of the rapid quantification of the sport.

The claim that data is always cooked rests on the premise that data is the *result* of a series of operations whereby human beings (or their technological proxies such as instruments, sensors, cameras, etc.) select from the flux of the world certain elements to observe, record, organize, and analyze. The decision about what to select and what instruments and methods to use, in turn, are necessarily framed by presuppositions made by the investigators (some of which are unconscious), by the socially and culturally agreed upon norms of the investigative community within which their results are to be shared and refuted or validated, and by the economic and political structures and agendas supporting the practice. "While many analysts may accept data at face-value, and treat them as if they are neutral, objective, and pre-analytic in nature, data are in fact framed technically, economically, ethically, temporally, spatially and philosophically. Data do not exist independently of the ideas, instruments, practices, contexts and knowledges used to generate, process and analyze them."[9] All this "cooking" precedes and shapes the gathering of so-called raw data.

Then, on this foundation of constraining intellectual presuppositions and material imperatives, data production itself entails an abstraction from the dense, material complexity of the world so that the results are necessarily reductive representations of the world from which data have been taken or, to put this slightly differently: fabricated "constructions about the world." From this standpoint, data appears less as a gift given by nature and more like a theft, something we have taken away from nature. This has implications for the status of the knowledge claims made on the basis of the data. Let me be clear: I do not mean to claim that the constructed, reductive nature of data renders it false or useless to the task of understanding the world better. I mean something more subtle and complex.

I mean, first, that we may be better off approaching data the way we approach art or any other human artifact that purports to say something about the world from a specific, limited perspective and social context, with specific limitations, and in the service of particular interests or aims: that is, understanding that it will deliver some insights and perpetuate some blind spots, enable certain practical actions in the world and disable others. This is an inevitable consequence of the fact that all data (whether a statistical report or a painting) is the result of a dynamic, engaged human interaction with the stuff of the world. Artists and humanists know this and sometimes even attempt to bake an explicit reflection upon that condition into the final product, as I have with my autobiographical interludes and coda. But science has to some degree advanced, and it certainly has gained cultural authority as a privileged source of truth and knowledge by imagining that it operates at an objective remove from the world it would know. And this leads me to my second meaning.

John Dewey, in a metaphor particularly apt in the sporting context, called this presumption of objective remove the "spectator" theory of knowledge in which "knowing is viewing from outside." "But," argued Dewey, "if it be true that the self or subject of experience is part and parcel of the course of events, it follows that the self *becomes* a knower ... In virtue of a distinctive way of partaking in the course of events. The significant distinction is no longer between the knower *and* the world; it is between different ways of being in an of the movement of things."[10] To the degree that science and business disavow their participation in the movement of things and the constructed nature of data and of the knowledge claims based on it, they actually veer further from knowledge and truth.

I recognize that—at least in the domain of basketball analytics—such disavowals appear most frequently in media presentations of basketball data and do not necessarily reflect the views of analysts themselves. For example, Nate Silver's book *The Signal and the Noise* is an eloquent extended warning against just these errors. However, his popular website, FiveThirtyEight, is not always so carefully explicit, often relegating disclaimers and methods to fine print—perhaps a tacit acknowledgement that most readers visiting the site are interested not in uncertainty but rather in certainty.[11]

Yet this very circumstance suggests that analysts like Silver may need to emulate artists and humanists in emphasizing the biased, partial, and limited nature of the knowledge they offer, as a way of helping to forestall misleading characterizations of their work. It is not, in other words, a matter of criticizing (or defending) the privately held views with which data scientists approach their work. It is about calling them to involve themselves in a public context in which they explicitly distance themselves from misleading accounts of their work that attribute to it objectivity or "Truth," and to instead avow and emphasize how their insights are both enabled and limited by their particular way of partaking in the course of basketball events.

#85. The Care of the Quantified Self

Now, the claim of critical data studies goes further than pointing out that data are socially constructed abstractions from reality with limited—if often publicly overstated or overestimated—epistemological value. As Kitchin notes: "Data are not merely an abstraction and representative, they are constitutive, and their generation, analysis and interpretation have consequences," and those consequences include ethical and social or political dimensions. It's hard to put this more clearly than Kitchin does here: "data are key inputs into systems that paradoxically are implemented in the name of making societies more secure, safe, competitive, productive, efficient, transparent, and accountable, yet do so through processes that monitor, discipline, repress, persuade, coerce, and exploit people. There is a fine balance then between using data in emancipatory and empowering ways and using data for one's own ends and to the detriment of others, or in ways contrary to the wishes of those the data represents." And, he adds, addressing an ambiguity especially pertinent in the case of the science of moving dots, "Often seemingly opposing outcomes are bound together so that people can be both liberated and coerced simultaneously—they gain personal benefit at the same time as they become enmeshed in a system that seeks to gain from their participation."[12]

In the same year that SportVU cameras appeared in every NBA arena, scholar Mark Andrejevic warned of a "reconfiguration of the relationship between forms of knowledge and power" in what he had earlier called "the digital enclosure" and identified two particular areas of concern: the "increasing asymmetry between those who are able to capture, store, access, and process the tremendous amounts of data produced by the proliferation of digital interactive sensors of all kinds; and second, ways of understanding and using information that are uniquely available to those with access to the database."[13] Though there is as yet little academic research into these issues as they bear out in sport, communications and sport expert Andrew Baerg, building on the work of Andrejevic and others, has shed at least some theoretical light on, as he puts it, "how athletes might respond to Big Data monitoring" of the sort employed by the science of moving dots through its use of optical tracking systems and various biometric technologies and testing.

Baerg points out that the most of the "proprietary statistics generated by Big Data algorithms" as well as "the algorithms that generate the numbers are not accessible to athletes." It may be that some athletes have the economic resources to access proprietary algorithms *and* the intellectual capital to know what to do with them, but many do not. Given this, Baerg asks, "Is it possible for athletes to overcome this expression of the digital divide and possess some control over the conditions of their surveillance?

Or is subjecting oneself to corporately controlled surveillance a necessary condition for participation in 21st-century professional sport? What is an athlete to do?"[14] Baerg explores two possible responses: emphasizing privacy to a greater degree and moving to becoming what is called "a quantified self."

The drive to secure greater privacy faces two main hurdles. First, some of the data generated by the science of moving dots are simply more granular versions of what anyone watching a game could see for themselves: How many dribbles did a player take before shooting a jump shot? How many times did another player rotate over to help prevent a drive on defense? What is a player's vertical leap? It would be difficult to argue that such information is private when it represents something that the public can already see—even if they cannot calculate it with the same precision—for themselves.

Health data, whether gathered on or off the court, would seem to be another matter, since gathering it—whether on sleep, diet, or genetics—by definition involves accessing behaviors or conditions that were previously hidden, especially when this information is correlated with on-court metrics. Nevertheless, according to Baerg, "privacy arguments opposing Big Data, the correlations it allows, and the unforeseen claims that can be made from these correlations end up being met by a presumed interest in the athlete's well-being." Moreover, athletes may be persuaded that the promised increases in career longevity and productivity are worth the trade-off in privacy. And the claim that athletes should have access to all the data and algorithms possessed by their franchises (or their corporate partners) could well run up, ironically, against the corporations' right to privacy![15]

In view of the hurdles facing athletes wishing to resist the science of moving dots on the grounds of privacy, Baerg also explores another possible response for NBA players: participating in what is known as "the Quantified Self" (QS) movement, essentially a rejection of Big Data's claims in favor of learning to generate one's own forms of analytics. "Where Big Data aspires," according to Baerg, "to a potentially limitless sample size, the QS movement emphasizes an n of 1. The QS movement is much more interested in idiosyncrasy than algorithmically generated patterns." This interest "extends to the types of measuring media used to collect and aggregate data. Authority is not tacitly conferred on technologies that automatically generate allegedly objective quantitative data." Instead, "one collects data one chooses to collect, in the manner one chooses to collect it, and inputs these data manually as a way to develop a deeper sense of the context in which data are produced." For proponents of QS, its "bottom-up form of analytics" permits them to "step outside of a corporate and scientific institutional hegemony when it comes to their data" and has the potential, for example with respect to health data, to challenge the technological or "market definition of health" implicitly favored by employers.

What might this look like? As Baerg documents, some NBA players have already begun to invest, to varying degrees, in generating their own data, for example by hiring their own personal data analysts. Moreover, in some cases their agents have contracted the services of private data analysis experts to generate quantitative pictures of their clients' performance and value that may be used to counter management perspectives in contract negotiations. Of course, many players lack the resources to undertake such initiatives. And, even for those who do, the disruptive potential of participating in QS will be constrained by the inherently asymmetrical power relations between labor (the players) and the owners of the means of production (franchise owners) within a capitalist economy. After all, the QS movement still operates on the same playing field as the science of moving dots (even if it uses a different playbook, so to speak), and within that field, owners have much greater resources and, ultimately, the power to simply ignore the information presented by players or their negotiating agents.[16]

#86. Toward a Basketball Deep Ecology

Returning to John Dewey, we may find a third path not considered by Baerg. According to one commentator, "the most pressing problem of modernity, in Dewey's view, is to humanize techno-industrial civilization, 'making it and its technology a servant of human life.'"[17] Dewey, to be clear, was by no means averse to science and technology, per se. On the contrary, he saw in the methods of the natural and biological sciences a model for how all inquiry, formal or informal, and in any domain, should be conducted. But, believing that the knowledge thus acquired should serve "the enrichment of immediate experience through the control over action that it exercises,"

Dewey always broadened the perspective, investigating the full natural, cultural, moral, social, and political context in which science and technology were operating.

Such an investigation, Dewey insisted, should be conducted publicly and collectively, so as to be sure that the interests of the politically or economically privileged minority would be checked by others, especially by those subject to the effects of science and technology. Only in this way did Dewey think we could take adequate stock of whether science and technology were fulfilling their purpose of making our lives more significant. Dewey's aim, which inspired mine in this book, is not to resist or reject scientific inquiry or technological advancement but rather to humanize, diversify, and democratize these processes. Or, as Dewey expert Steven Fesmire puts it, "to reclaim and affirm technology on behalf of more fulfilling lives."[18]

To do so, Dewey argued, requires us to insist that our technology serve more than "the pursuit of mechanical efficiency." Efficiency, of course, whether in basketball or in any domain of life, can only be measured in relation to a predetermined goal or purpose such as making as many points as possible in as few possessions as possible. While having a goal or purpose in mind is indispensable to any process of inquiry (whether in science, the humanities, or even the arts), the emphasis on efficiency tends to fix that goal and endow it with a transcendent authority and meaning. That, in turn, has the effect of gradually causing us to lose sight of other purposes or values, especially those that appear at first glance as at odds with the pursuit of efficiency—in much the same way that hurtling along a highway in haste to reach our destination as quickly as possible might cause us to miss other potentially rewarding byways, sights, or experiences. The first and most precious among the casualties is the forward-looking, open-ended processual nature of scientific inquiry itself. But, sadly, these are the very qualities that allow inquiry to remain open to the full range of undiscovered possibilities dwelling in the situation and therefore capable of responding to the full range of human needs and desires.

Dewey's views on these matters, ultimately, are predicated on his views of experience, which is to say, existence or life, as a constantly shifting fabric of relationships. We may, at any given moment, necessarily focus on the "being" or "identity" or "thing" that appears to us to crystallize in relatively stable form for some period of time—a sensation of pain, a human life, a gust of wind. But if we lose sight of the fact that this seemingly stable being is an effect of our perception and reflection, we risk losing contact with the fluid, complex nature of reality and, with that, the ability to adapt and respond to as well as to grow within reality. In this, Dewey anticipated the view of the theories of complex systems that I described above.

Pulling together the various strands of thought I've described in this chapter—chaos and complex systems theory, critical data studies, and Dewey's reflections on science and technology—I find myself inspired to imagine something like an ecological approach to basketball experience and to the role that the science of moving dots might play in that approach. "'The essence of deep ecology,'" in the words of Arne Naess, the movement's founder, "'is to ask deeper questions' . . . about the foundations of our modern, scientific, industrial, growth-oriented, materialistic worldview and way of life."[19] Rather than taking that paradigm as given and then asking what humans can do to preserve an environment we view ourselves as separate from, above, and in charge of, we begin from a premise—very similar to Dewey's—that we only *are* with and in virtue an environment that is constantly changing and from which we cannot be extricated.

Asking deeper questions of basketball culture might begin by asserting the premise that *quality* of basketball experience cannot be captured by measurements of efficiency and its associated metrics, just as the measure of the health of a natural environment cannot be measured solely by the value of the raw materials extracted from it. Then, in order to get a better understanding of basketball experience, we would have to emphasize relational networks rather than merely focusing solely on isolated individual parts and attend to dynamic processes rather than to those elements that hold still long enough to be measured or counted. In order to develop such an ecological approach, we would need, additionally, to expand and diversify the voices and interests taken into account in decision-making processes and to democratize the distribution of power among those voices and interests. Doing so, of course, would likely broaden, deepen, and augment the range of values to be considered when approaching the sport.

All of this, I'm afraid, sounds idealistic, and probably vague and messy. NBA basketball, after all, some will insist, is a business, a capitalist enterprise whose ultimate purpose is to generate profits for business owners. Everything else—entertainment of spectators, enjoyment or fulfillment of players, care for the well-being of all involved in the sport, employment of others in the industry—can only be viewed as secondary and subordinate to that driving purpose and so as either a means to achieving it or a beneficial side effect of having done so. To which I reply, sure, that's true, but is that the best that we can do? More pointedly, is the best we can do with the marvel of human complexity that is basketball play to reduce it to a business and to sacrifice everything else to maximizing the efficiency of its operation as such? I cannot accept that.

As Steven Fesmire puts it: "Quality of life is sometimes eroded by pursuit of mechanical efficiency, and there are generally more effective, inclusive, and enduring means to secure consummations than fixating on new and ever-more-efficient devices."[20] For Dewey, these more "effective, inclusive, and enduring means" could be found by emphasizing the aesthetic experiences of everyday life and by encouraging the intensification of such experiences through art. And it may just be that approaching basketball experience aesthetically offers an important means to view the sport ecologically and so to press the dazzling methods and insights of the science of moving dots into the service of cultivating a broader, more diverse, and therefore healthier range of values.

Interlude—Basketball Supernatural

#87. Supernatural

One of the most important books I took from my father's collection when he died was a Spanish translation, published in 1865, of *An Introduction to the Study of Experimental Medicine* by French physiologist Claude Bernard (1813–78). According to the inscription in my father's handwriting, he bought and read it in 1948, his third year of medical school, just a few months before he read *Methodology of the Sciences*.

When I hold it close to my face and breathe in, I can smell my father: paper and pipe tobacco.

As he was dying, and knew he was dying, my father shared a great deal with me directly in our nightly FaceTime conversations. But there was much he wanted to convey to me that he was too tired, or addled by medication, or overloaded with the toxins of cancer—or that was too large, inchoate, and fundamental—to express.

At those moments, he would sometimes tell me something that I should read: seemingly invoking an author as intermediary or an angelic intercessor who would communicate on his behalf, to impart some elemental wisdom, or to sink an essential piece of himself into me. One of these I am now holding. Bernard was one of my father's heroes. I don't remember now exactly why this was, but I have the strong impression that Bernard had articulated something fundamental about what it meant to my father to pursue a scientific career.

Indeed, as I open it, the book is filled with the marginal marks of my father's approval. I can feel his excitement upon encountering, as his fingers turned these very pages mine now turn, the words of a kindred spirit who was also a giant pioneering trailblazer along the path my father was just beginning to tread. The signs are everywhere: long passages my father underlined, bracketed on both sides, and marked with exclamation points, sometimes two.

I imagine my father in khakis and a pith helmet, proudly following close behind as Bernard hacks a trail through the tangled brush of ignorance littering the field of medicine.

But I'm not reading the book very carefully, or really at all, just skimming it for signs of my father's interest. *Pace* Crispín, it takes a lot of effort for me to read Spanish, especially nineteenth century scientific Spanish translated from nineteenth century scientific French. Papá would be disappointed, I'm sure, but also, he'd probably chuckle (proudly self-aware of his magnanimous indulgence) at my lack of self-discipline. And perhaps he'd be gratified that my attention is on him, rather than Claude Bernard.

Anyway, I'm just flipping pages when the steady mileposts of nonverbal graphic approval are interrupted. My father's own words, his thoughts, now appear in the margin. He is adding his voice to Bernard's, echoing his hero. Or no, wait, he's not echoing. I look more closely to decipher the tiny cursive Spanish inscribed in fading pencil.

He is talking back to Bernard!

Bernard entitled this section of his book "Doubt in Experimental Reasoning."

"The experimenter's stumbling block," Bernard writes, "consists in thinking that he knows what he does not know, and taking for absolute, truths that are only relative. Hence, the unique and fundamental rule of scientific investigation is reduced to 'doubt.'"[1]

Now my father begins to underline:

Experimental reasoning is precisely the reverse of scholastic reasoning. Scholasticism must always have a fixed and indubitable starting point; and, unable to find it either in external things or in reason, it takes it from some irrational source, such as a revelation, a tradition, or a conventional or arbitrary authority.[2]

There! Right there. Up on the upper left-hand margin of page ninety-four, comes my father's voice, quietly pointing out: "It may also be a genuine authority."

On the next page he gets a bit sassier. When Bernard continues his dismissal of "Scholastics or systematizers" who "never question their starting point, to which they seek to refer everything" and "who have a proud and intolerant mind and do not accept contradiction," my father replies, unconvinced, "On this there would be much to discuss."[3]

I hear this with a vaguely menacing undertone, as though he were telling me, after I crept into the house five minutes past my curfew on a Friday night in high school, "We will discuss this in the morning." Oh shit.

Lastly, my father, feeling himself, ventures a direct contradiction. Bernard asserts that the Scholastic's reasoning is sterile "since by his absolute principle, he puts himself outside of nature, in which everything is relative." My father disputes him: "It is that the very point lies outside of nature. In the supernatural realm, it produces fertile insights."[4] I swell with pride! My nineteen-year-old father is a fucking baller—he's all "Hold up! Slow your roll there Bernard! You're not the boss of my mind!"

But I also feel shocked: What the fuck was he thinking? Not for challenging Bernard—that's awesome—but for challenging him *on this point*, for defending Scholasticism: the embodiment of prescientific, pre-Enlightenment, medieval dogmatism.

(For those who might not know: Have you ever heard reference to counting how many angels can dance on the point of a needle? People use that phrase to characterize an argument that is technical, specialized, and delusional to the point of becoming practically irrelevant. Well, that phrase first emerged as a way to describe Scholasticism.)

I mean my father is a scientist. He *is* science. He *is* the Enlightenment.

Guided by science, we observe carefully with our senses. We measure what is tangible. We have empirical evidence. We record meticulously. We are logical in drawing conclusions.

When Bernard challenges Scholasticism for using irrational authority as a starting point for reasoning, he's thinking of religious faith, or existing doctrine. I'm surprised to find my father hinting that these may be "genuine" authorities, just as I am surprised to hear him warn Bernard that they're gonna have to discuss further whether Scholastics accept contradiction. But none of this compares to my father's bold assertion that Scholasticism "produces fertile insights" about "*the supernatural.*" The supernatural? Fertile insights like how many angels can dance on the point of a needle? What's next, a defense of alchemy?

But then, as when we played chess, my father was always infinity moves ahead of me. Maybe all he was doing with these marginal disputations was internalizing and practicing Bernard's very lesson—to doubt, to question authority—by applying them to the categorical assertions of his hero, Bernard himself. And if so, what could be more courageous than to do so by defending medieval thought (remember Michael Lewis?) against its arrogant dismissal by modern science?

#88. Wilt, My Basketball Satan

While as a boy I was drawn viscerally to identify with perimeter players because they were (relatively speaking) small, like me; the Big Men were in a separate category altogether, and Wilt Chamberlain was the biggest and the baddest of the Big Men. Neither loved nor hated, nor unnoticed, I felt for the Big Men a vertigo-like combination of attraction and terror. They were like dinosaurs to me, absurdly large, another species with a whole different way of moving than anyone else on the court. And like dinosaurs, I was fascinated with them but also frightened by them. I don't think my mind really knew yet how to assimilate their difference. But it was more than just their size that was inassimilable to me.

Rationally, I could comprehend their function on the court as shot blockers, rebounders, and inside scorers, but emotionally and aesthetically I couldn't really understand or connect to their style and their values. What did it mean—what could it mean?—to be so huge, to take up so much space, to live so close to the rim? What would it be like to be unable to handle the ball and to be okay with just receiving passes? Wouldn't you feel selfish? Wouldn't you feel anxious depending on others like that? What if they didn't pass to you? What if you fumbled the ball away?

But also, wouldn't there be a lot of pressure on you—just someone else doing all the work and you get the pass? You better put it in the hole every time or else everyone would surely hate you. I'd rather be the one passing. Then, when the big-for-nothin' doofus misses the bunny, I can seethe inside and sublimate my anger by telling him not to worry about it, that I understand he's trying his best. Just like Jesus. Just like my mom.

Enter my very own snake in the garden. For, despite my steady self-fashioning along the lines of God's own point guard and his proxy, my mother, no player excited me more than Wilt Chamberlain, the Big Dipper. And I was never more excited to see a Bucks game than I was to see that one I described earlier, when Wilt's Lakers came to play in Madison, my very own city, on March 1, 1972. I knew about Wilt's one-hundred-point game (and that it had happened exactly ten years minus one day from when I would be seeing him), of course. I knew about his fifty-points-per-game, twenty-six-rebounds-per-game season in 1961–62. I knew about all his individual records. I knew about his rivalry with Bill Russell of the Celtics, about how Wilt struggled to gain recognition as a winner and thereby to belie the perception that he was a selfish individualist who never learned to accommodate his massive talent with a successful team framework.

Wilt was unreal to me as a person, like JFK or Michael Jackson. Even seeing him *in* person, from just a few yards away as I did that night, my mind struggled to assimilate his reality. With even the greatest of the other players I saw live during those years, I was able to enjoy the way their mythical greatness was incarnated before my eyes, rendering them human and accessible: I might never walk its full length, but there was a single basketball court linking me to Walt Frazier. Not so with Wilt. He played on a different court entirely. He played in a universe of his own. With Wilt, my juvenile intellectual and emotional gears creaked a bit and stalled. He was, undeniably, there, a living individual, walking and talking before my eyes. But somehow, I couldn't quite accept it. He was truly, as they say, larger than life, more than real. My young mind and heart were thrilled and blown by the dimensions of his presence.

Also, my dad hated Wilt. I'd always thought it was because Wilt endorsed Nixon in the 1972 presidential campaign, but when I recently asked my dad about it, shortly before he passed away, he didn't remember that at all. He remembered preferring Russell to Chamberlain in the context of their rivalry because of the usual thing: Russell was able to more intelligently integrate his own astonishing abilities with those of his teammates. In my dad's words, "Chamberlain was blessed (or cursed) with a powerful physical presence which he used to neglect team play."

Now, this is a much more muted and reasonable expression of his aversion than what I recall, which makes sense since my dad had mellowed considerably. Also, I am no longer a small six-year-old boy. But at the time, my dad's preferences and desires seemed enormous to me: they were the most important desires in a household in which everyone's desires seemed more important than mine. So if he hated Wilt Chamberlain, it was as though, when I looked through the eyes of my father's desires at Wilt on the television screen, the big man slowly morphed into a scowling, bullying, roaring demon. Even his jersey number, 13, looked menacing and vaguely evil to me.

Except it wasn't quite that simple because already at that age I was finding secret ways to rebel, and one of them was by secretly loving the player my dad obviously hated. Sure. But that doesn't quite explain it either because, in many ways, though he disliked him, my dad *was* the Chamberlain of our family: our offense revolved entirely around him. He was unapologetically self-assertive to say the least, he was a dominating presence, and he wasn't a great team player, at least that's how it looked to me. On Christmas Eve, when we opened our presents, we opened them in descending order of age beginning with my father and ending with me, which in my child's mind meant from biggest to smallest, Wilt Chamberlain to Tiny Archibald. So maybe in disliking Chamberlain on the grounds that he wasn't a team player, my dad was unconsciously expressing a dislike for himself and a wish to be more like Russell.

That sort of analysis is tricky business and I don't really believe I know what the situation *really* was or what my dad was *really* thinking. What I do feel certain of, though, is that—justly or not, and certainly unconsciously—I identified Wilt and my father, and I believe now that in my secret love of Wilt I found a way to express not only a secret love and admiration for my father but also a secret desire to be like him. Which is to say, to be the opposite of a point guard, to be the guy who could take sixty shots a game and not feel bad because he knew that he could make thirty-six of them, knew that he could score one hundred points. What would that be like? It must feel awesome to be Wilt! The center of everyone's attention, all the energy of the game directed toward you, and it doesn't make you feel bad, like you've done something wrong or are hurting someone else, it just feels natural and right because it *is* natural and right because you are bigger and stronger than everyone else and, well, you cannot be stopped. You should do whatever you want because you can do whatever you want. If it was wrong, someone, something should stop you, should *be able* to stop you.

To this day, to the degree that I understand success in life, I articulate it in terms of basketball, perhaps as something like "know when to take your shot, and know when to give it up" and a series of other corollary metaphors related to defense and rebounding. The elements of that vocabulary and the mythological figures that would stand for some basic forces were forged back in those days I am recalling. I spent much of my life (spend some of it still today) veering madly between my outward worship of the abstract, unselfish point-guard ideal and my shameful, secret fascination with the scoring machine, the player who, as they say in basketball parlance, has no conscience. Point guard or scorer? Walt or Wilt? Mom or Dad? Christ or Satan? These were the extreme dichotomies that shaped my growing up, and learning to blur them or elude them altogether might be one way that I would describe what it means to me, in my life, to become an adult.

#89. David and Goliath

On November 12, 1972, Father Henry McMurrough, Monsignor of St. Paul's University Catholic Center, after giving me my First Holy Communion, gave me an inscribed copy of *The Children's Bible*. The book came with an LP. You could listen to the stories as you followed along in the book—a beep indicating when you should turn the page if you couldn't read, which, obviously, I could, excellently. I listened to this record—well—religiously. I loved the stories and I loved Father Mac, as our family called him. He was six feet three inches tall, which, importantly, made him the tallest person in our house when he'd come for dinner, and he had hairy arms. I wished he was there every night because everyone was happy around him. And also, because he would *both* get down on the floor in the basement and play with me and my little kid toys *and* go out to the driveway and play two-on-two with me against my two brothers. But as much as my love for Father Mac attached me to that book, what I remember most vividly are the images. The ones that most riveted me were, in reverse order: (3) the finger writing on the wall in the story of Daniel, (2) an eyeless Samson bringing the house down and, (1) a before-and-after sequence that first shows unbeatable Goliath flexing as he taunts the cowering Israelites and then in mid-fall as he is laid low by David.

Looking at those pictures today, I am struck by how complicated and confusing they were for me. On the face of it, yeah, I wanted to be David. After all, as Wilt Chamberlain himself once said, "Nobody roots for Goliath." I was the youngest and the smallest, and David seemed to have figured out a way to get around those disadvantages—also, I actually had a little slingshot of my own. But on the other hand, I was drawn to Goliath, much as I was drawn to Wilt Chamberlain when I saw him play in Madison later that winter. I felt sorry for Goliath. It seemed unfair that David won just because God was on his side. And even though the whole point of the story is that Goliath is *not* invincible, I kind of didn't care: I still wanted to be three cubits tall and to have gigantic muscles and to strike terror into everyone's hearts just by shaking my fist. Maybe I was also intuitively playing the odds: David may have killed Goliath, but in the simulations run by my imagination, as in the world I actually lived in, Goliath won far more often than not. So, it wasn't so obvious to me who I should try to become. But today, as I stare at the images again, the feelings seem clearer: I'm for Goliath.

Malcolm Gladwell, with whom I do not normally find myself in agreement as you have seen, wrote a whole book about the metaphor of David and Goliath and how, in his view, the proper lessons of the story have been overlooked. Gladwell argues that it is only from a superficial and ignorant perspective that David *appears* to be the underdog. It turns out that Goliath, who "many medical experts now believe" suffered from acromegaly, which not only accounted for his enormous size but also dimmed his vision and slowed his reflexes, "had as much chance against David," who was evidently an expert in the deadly martial tactic of slinging, "as any Bronze Age warrior with a sword would have had against an opponent armed with a .45 automatic pistol." Goliath was actually the underdog!

But if that is so, Gladwell points out, it is only because David was astute enough to understand that the giant's strength could be turned into a weakness, so long as he didn't try to beat him at his own game. I like Gladwell's account because it makes space for a more mature version of my young heart's ambivalence. I'm no longer a little boy and so I need not be torn between identifying with a seemingly doomed shepherd boy who wins because he is favored by an omnipotent being or identifying with the biggest dude I can imagine, even if he happened to lose this one time. Instead, I can identify with them both for making the best of what they had: two flawed human beings turning disadvantage to advantage. Pitted against each other, one of them had to lose. But there's nothing fateful about who it would be. Goliath turned an illness into a strength that served him very, very well until he unexpectedly encountered an opponent who also understood how to turn a disadvantage into a strength, not to mention how to turn an opponent's strength into their disadvantage. In this sense, both of them also understood that one way to beat the odds is to exploit whatever it is that the oddsmakers have not accounted for; understood, in other words, that what counts, sometimes, is exactly that which has not been counted, let alone incorporated into predictive algorithms.

12

———

Feeling Basketball

#90. Somaesthetics

According to philosopher Richard Shusterman, himself one of the world's foremost experts on Dewey's aesthetic theory, humanists in the West have ignored the body because it expresses the fundamental ambiguity of our human condition—"between power and frailty, worthiness and shame, dignity and brutishness, knowledge and ignorance." Secretly desiring "to transcend mortality, weakness, and error and to live like gods," Western humanistic thinkers have privileged the mind, understood as the disembodied locus of permanence, truth, and virtue. From that perspective, the perishable, inconstant, impertinent body will at best be treated instrumentally: it becomes the unfortunately indispensable tool, the material substrate, whose value lies in the degree to which it facilitates the pursuit of our quasi-divine ends, which ultimately include, perhaps, shedding the limits of our human embodiment altogether.[1]

Basketball analytics reinforces this longstanding devaluation of the body. In its quest to understand basketball bodies in order to improve basketball performance, the science of moving dots manifests both a profound underlying dissatisfaction with these bodies' limitations and a relentless utilitarian drive to transcend them by perfecting the body as an instrument for making both baskets and dollars. The title of one journalist's investigation of the phenomenon—Andy Glockner's *Chasing Perfection*—succinctly summarizes these investments as does, for that matter, Maheswaran's triumphant visual flattening of the bodies of players into digitized two-dimensional dots.

Indeed, the very term "efficiency"—the alchemical gold of basketball analytics—expresses this instrumental and mechanistic view of the basketball body. In the fever dreams of the science of moving dots, the basketball player becomes a machine for manufacturing, from as few inputs as possible, a maximum output of points and profits. This dehumanizing tendency leads me to see in basketball analytics the ethically alarming specter of what philosopher Michael Atkinson describes as a "Fordist, assembly-line athlete production world."[2]

To some, the scenario thus evoked might seem hyperbolic, but it may be plausible as a description of one possible outcome of current tendencies. Consider the prediction of a "brain trust of futurists and experts" assembled to analyze trends shaping the future of sports that, within the next twenty years, "the line between artificial body parts and natural ones will gradually blur as medical scientists converge on how to rebuild humans—first for injury recovery, then for life extension, and eventually for enhancement."[3] Atkinson traces these potentially dehumanizing tendencies to "the record-setting, goal-achieving, personal-best logics of most mainstream sports cultures," which, as I've shown in the case of basketball, are closely tied to the financial interests of owners. As a result, athletes' bodies are "quantitatively assessed through a continuum of performance metrics and ideas" and mapped against idealized standards so as to diagnose and resolve kinesiological inefficiencies. But what the market, quantitative metrics, and transformative technologies see as problems to be solved, Atkinson sees as the wellspring for such vital dimensions of competitive athletics as "doubt, drive, joy, effort, pain, uncertainty, bonding, effort, suffering, chance, spirituality and divinity."[4]

Of course, all of what Atkinson seeks to foreground slips from view in the face of, or at least becomes subservient to, winning athletic and economic competition. As I've shown, the imperative to count and keep score in basketball predates the rise of the science of moving dots by a century. James Naismith, after all, stipulated in the last of the original thirteen rules that "the side making the most goals . . . shall be declared the winner" and he even (in rule 11) charged the referee "to keep account of the goals."[5] Naismith clearly believed that competition and counting were vital parts of the game he invented. But it's useful to recall that Naismith's understanding of the nature and purpose of competition was rather different than the prevailing—and seemingly natural—contemporary view that prizes winning above all else as an end in itself. In fact the currently predominant view is a relatively recent transformation—effected in part by the combined impact of commercialization and the mass media—of a much older view of competition grounded in classical sporting traditions. In this older view, which was held by Naismith, competition (Latin: *com+petere*, or "striving together") binds opponents together in the shared effort to achieve physical and moral excellence.[6] The drive to win, certainly, may be an important spur to that effort, but it is a means, not an end in itself.

But when winning becomes, in Vince Lombardi's famous slogan, "the only thing," then quantification—keeping score to begin with—becomes essential. How, after all, are you supposed to know who won if you don't keep score? And given the obvious ways in which the final score abstracts and distills from the qualitative phenomena comprising the contest itself, it's easy to see how the "vital dimensions of athletics" that Atkinson enumerates fade from view, becoming wispy ghosts that are only invited onto the stage in postgame narrative explanations of why the score came out the way it did. "Scoring," philosopher Stephen Connor writes, "always involves a gap between the quality of the game as it is played, and the quantitative register into which it is translated by the score. . . . The two orders, of quality and quantity, are in essence incommensurable, meaning that there is no common measure available to translate one into other."[7] Connor may be right when he adds that "without the rational, there would be no way of apprehending the real, except as a vague and indefinite sense of forms and forces." But this does not mean that quantification is the *only* rational discourse available for apprehending the real.

#91. Grace

In fact, James Naismith himself—in that 1913 address to the NCAA that I described in chapter 6—once provided a superb example of a nonquantitative, rational discourse that nonetheless apprehended the qualitative, real complexity of basketball, pointedly contrasting it with the poverty of the score. "The main interest in basket ball," Naismith wrote:

> lies in watching the kaleidoscopic changes which take place. Every moment of a game is full of thrills, when expert players handle the ball. The instantaneous action of the reflexes, when a ball is caught, in deciding where it shall go, demands a great amount of coordination. There is not time to think out a play, but reflex judgment must control, and the action must be performed with lightning rapidity. No prettier sight can be found in athletic achievement than in a game where the ball, without any preconceived plan, passes from man to man in a series of brilliant movements and lands in the goal, or is cleverly intercepted when a goal seems inevitable. We watch such a game with an increasing admiration for the wonderful capacity of the human frame for accomplishing the seemingly impossible. No amount of rough work, even if it should result in a goal for our side, can compare with such a spectacle. It is indeed a narrow mind that puts goals before grace, scores before skill.[8]

Naismith describes basketball play as a fluid, complex phenomenon ("kaleidoscopic changes," "lightning rapidity") in which the reflex actions of bodies in motion generate peaks of both affective ("full of thrills") and cognitive ("increasing admiration") intensity in spectators.

We are accustomed to associating aesthetics exclusively with objects formally considered works of art. We imagine it to be concerned with defining the intangible qualities distinguishing such works, offering subjective adjudications of matters of "taste," and perhaps also safeguarding the cultural privilege of the middle class. But, aesthetics "was born," as Terry Eagleton reminds us, as an eighteenth century "discourse of the body"—a way of rationally approaching the complex material qualities of the real *without* taking it apart.[9] Even more recently, Dewey, as I showed in chapter 10, sought to ground his aesthetic philosophy in the experience of the "live creature" adapting continuously, much like Naismith's basketball players, to its changing environment.[10] With this notion of aesthetics in mind, we can see in Naismith's description a compelling account of the aesthetic delights available in basketball play, at least if one does not put "scores before skill" or "goals before grace."

"Grace," in fact, occupies a special place in Hans Gumbrecht's recent attempt to forge a vocabulary for praising the athletic beauty in the unfolding movements of "bodies that adapt themselves to multiple forms and functions."[11] Gumbrecht sees grace as "a function of how distant a body and its movements appear to be from consciousness, subjectivity, and their expression."[12] He is, in other words, describing what Naismith called "reflex actions" and "reflex judgments" performed under such time constraints that "there is not time to think out a play." Gumbrecht and Naismith, I think, highlight the exhibition in basketball play of what we might call "successful embodiment," where by "embodiment" I mean to signal the inextricability of bodies and selves.[13] This is play as "flow" or "being in the zone." In awkwardness, injury, illness and, of course, death, we may experience embodiment as an inconvenient or even agonizing demonstration of our limitations. In basketball, as Gumbrecht and Naismith help us to appreciate, we can see embodiment as a thrilling and inspiring condition for excellence and beauty.

Mechanical repetition in practice—perhaps aided by scientific understandings of the human body—may be the indispensable material condition for the cultivation of grace (or what trainers might call "muscle memory") in athletes. But the fascination grace exerts on spectators arises precisely because it is exhibited *unpredictably* in order to overcome seemingly insurmountable obstacles. This incalculability or, as Naismith put it, lack of "any preconceived plan," is what makes it possible that there is "no prettier sight in athletic achievement" than basketball. As Leonard Koppett put it, "any knowledgeable crowd will cheer louder for a fancy pass, behind the back, or through the legs, that doesn't lead to a score than it will for a routine basket."[14] Koppett used the term "style"—obviously an aesthetic term—to describe what that "knowledgeable crowd" was responding to. But in the context of his account we can see that its importance lies in part in the surprise it engenders. To say that style surprises is to say that it deviates from what is expected where what is expected is understood—crucially in the present context—as the most efficient way to score points.

But if that is so, then the surprise of style delights also because it *embraces*—rather than attempts to minimize—risk. Perhaps even the most sophisticated concepts and technologies will never eliminate "chance" and "risk" completely from athletic competition, but this should not lead us to underestimate their potential to shrink the range of valuable physical and affective experiences that chance and risk generate. According to Gumbrecht, "the chance to win and the risk of losing,"—whether at the level of a season, a game, or a possession—"produce narrative, epic, and drama" along with the whole range of affective experiences that such forms convey and provoke.[15] Given a context framed by physical limitations, chance, and risk, competitive sports like basketball offer athletes and spectators alike the rich aesthetic and ethical experience of "our embodied existence and the extent of its capabilities."[16]

#92.Fan-tastic!

"NBA action," says American movie star Michael Douglas with a big smile from his courtside seat at a Lakers game in 1988, "it's *faaaann*tastic!" The moment was part of a series of short promotional spots that the NBA paid to run on television from 1980 through 1992. Though the details of the format varied somewhat, the basic formula involved showing a montage of clips of professional basketball play, in-game fan reactions, cheerleaders, dancers, and mascots. Most of the ads featured a musical soundtrack that would be interrupted by the exclamations of broadcasters before concluding with either a narrator or a celebrity spectator, like Douglas, providing the tag line: "NBA action: it's *faaann*tastic!"

The conventional view on this campaign is that it formed part of the constellation of good fortune, good business—including media—decisions and very good basketball players (like Magic Johnson, Larry Bird, and Michael Jordan, among others) that rescued the NBA from the brink of collapsing in the late '70s and instead ushered in a golden age of pro basketball that led to massive popularity, revenues, and global expansion under the watchful guidance of commissioner David Stern. From that point of view, the slogan is obviously a catchy play on words—made more memorable by the well-known celebrities repeating it—designed to attract exactly what the NBA was lacking: fans.

But I think there's more to be made of the word "fantastic" and the campaign's visuals than just that. To begin with, the single word "*fantastic*" conjoins the observer (the *fan*) with the observed "NBA action" (which is "fantastic") into a single relational space. This relation between observer and observed is what is "*fantastic*," and since it is the modifying predicate for "NBA action," the ad tells us, in effect, that "NBA action" *is* exactly this relation between the two: a relation activated by the dynamic, interactional act of *watching*. *That* is what is "*fantastic*."

We know of course that fantastic just means "extraordinarily good or attractive." That seems simple enough. But when I look at the synonyms for it, two things occur that I find interesting. First, I see in all of them, to varying degrees, the signal that what is fantastic has not only exceeded the norm but has exceeded reality altogether. Thus, we go from "excellent," "outstanding," and "first-rate" to "marvelous" and "out of this world." Already the definition itself used an adverb—"extraordinarily"—that nudges the fantastic beyond ordinary reality. All that is before we get to the second definition: "imaginative or fanciful, remote from reality." But, second, other synonyms seem to move us away from what *is* fantastic to what happens *to us* in its presence: "dazzling" or "breathtaking." Others—like "sensational" or "marvelous" or, indeed, "wonderful"—blur the line between what is fantastic and what we feel when it erupts into our lives. This, second meaning is older and connects us to the word's roots in the Greek term for "imagine" or "have visions." Now, though the words sound similar "fan" (shortened from "fanatic") and "fantastic" actually have different roots. Fanatic comes from the Latin word for temple (*fanam*) so that a *fanaticus* was one inspired by the Gods. But for literary theorist Tzvetan Todorov, the fantastic as a genre of literature portrays the uncertainty experienced by a person (reader or character) "who knows only the laws of nature," when confronted "by an event which cannot be explained by the laws of this familiar world"— perhaps by the appearance of a god.[17]

Or a god on the hardwood. Which might be what NBA great Larry Bird was feeling when, in 1986, after Michael Jordan dropped sixty-three points in Boston on Bird's Celtics, he remarked that his opponent was "God disguised as Michael Jordan." Nobody had ever scored that many points in an NBA playoff game and Bird explained that he thought nobody ever would do that against his team, who would, after all, go on to win the championship that season. It was a singular event, unreal, but, damn, part of what's unreal about it is that it's real. But it wasn't only the number of points, it was the way he scored them: "This way. That way. Horizontally. Vertically. Diagonally," gushed columnist Bob Ryan in the next day's *Boston Globe*, "in ways never conceived of" by all the past greats of basketball history. Ryan also imagined the other end of that fantastic relationship when he described the effect on observers and rivals of the dawn of the "Age of Jordan": "As long as Mr. Jordan is known to be present in this hemisphere, no rival lead is safe, no palm is dry, no throat swallows easily and no stomach is settled. A man who scores 63 points out of the flow is a man to fear, respect and idolize."[18]

Jordan's performance was, well, *fan*tastic! But the NBA's promotional campaign doesn't only express this with its slogan. It also portrays this relationship by the structure of the montage, which shows both players playing and fans watching them play (and sometimes players watching other players and even praising what they see). There are the astounding, surprising, wondrous feats of the players: the highflying, powerful but gracefully coordinated dunks; the clever, deceptive, geometrically impossible no-look passes; the imaginatively improvised improbable shots; and the passionate wonder of the fans—bodies raised out of seats by the same invisible current that yanked Robb and me to our feet when we watched Dr. J.'s free-throw line dunk—ecstatic to be surprised and emotionally overwhelmed by the singularity of what they are watching.

But as a last, perhaps obvious, but nevertheless crucial step, it draws *us* into the relational network as we view the montage: we watch too and by watching enter the relational zone of the *fan*tastic. At the same time, we are tantalized by the promise that we could enter that zone anytime by tuning in to or attending an NBA game. It's true that the very nature of a highlight montage, which entails the proliferation of singular events, seems to undercut the very singularity of performance that makes NBA action fantastic. But if this does not turn us away by making the appearance of the gods a routine, mundane event, it could be because we never know when it will happen; the campaign only promises that if we keep watching the gods will show up.

In the European Middle Ages, I learned from historian Caroline Walker Bynum, the term "wonder" referred to a non-appropriative affective and cognitive response to something irreducibly singular that eluded human categories of knowledge and analysis.[19]

I'm tempted, I admit, to simplify things and say, as Einstein did, that "the process of scientific discovery is, in effect, a continual flight from wonder."[20] After all, the "Enlightenment's program," German philosophers Theodor Adorno and Max Horkheimer told us, "was the disenchantment of the world. It wanted to dispel myths, to overthrow fantasy with knowledge."[21] And we've already seen that David Hand sees quantification as valuably taking the mystery out of things, and that baseball's pioneers of Sabermetrics saw themselves as scientific warriors vanquishing the fanciful notions of medieval thinking.

But I don't think it's actually that simple, and so I don't want merely to counter that proposition by turning my back on science (or quantification) per se. Though some fans and even NBA insiders dismiss analytics by adopting an anti-intellectual rhetoric, I believe that is a dangerous position, particularly so in an age when the findings of scientists on such urgent public matters as global warming are questioned in the very same terms in the highest levels of our government. But equally dangerous is a blind acceptance of every practice, method, or discourse that promises progress by adopting the banner of "objectivity" and "science."

We need another option. Isabelle Stengers, an influential Belgian historian and philosopher well known for laying low the claims of science to be the "thinking brain of humanity," nevertheless appears to promise such an option when she writes that "silencing the power of wonder is not to be identified with a scientific attitude" but instead with "science as it has been mobilized in defense of public order."[22] What does she mean by this distinction between "a scientific attitude" and "science as it has been mobilized in defense of public order"? And what does it have to do with the relationship between "*fantastic*" NBA action and basketball analytics?

Stengers recalls an imaginary conversation between two giants of the French Enlightenment: Denis Diderot and Jean-Baptiste d'Alembert. Stengers describes d'Alembert as a mathematician and a mechanist who helped produce the "definitive set of functions, self-contained equations" that came to be called "rational mechanics" and who promoted "a closed definition of rational science" and ignored—as a matter of arbitrary opinion—whatever exceeded that definition. In this imaginary conversation, authored by Diderot, the two are arguing about feeling, thought, and the nature of life and, in particular about the "original generation of animals": Which came first, in other words, the chicken, or the egg? In the midst of this, Diderot poses what has become a famous, very simple question: "Do you see this egg? With this you can overthrow all the schools of theology, all the churches of the earth. What is this egg?" According to Stengers, Diderot wasn't just talking about the theology of a creator God but also about "that other temple, the academic science of his time" which refused "the challenge of the egg, in the name of its own restricted definitions."

Now, Diderot himself considered "the mathematical science of matter and motion" to be "the epitome of human reason." But here, according to Stengers, he is asking d'Alembert to *"give to the egg the power to challenge* his well-defined categories." This is where Stengers introduces wonder into her argument by calling what Diderot brought to bear against d'Alembert "the power of wonder." But she is quick to clarify that she does not mean by wonder a mysticism that demands "d'Alembert bow down before the egg." Diderot was just challenging d'Alembert, she says, "not to explain it away with his conception of matter," "to have him accept being affected, troubled, surprised, but also being forced to think and question his own knowledge" so that he could renounce "any claim that would imply a privileged link between [our] knowledge and general overbearing adjectives like 'rational,' 'objective' and 'scientific.'"

In this conversation, in other words, Diderot and d'Alembert embody, respectively, the distinction between "a scientific attitude" and "science as it has been mobilized in defense of public order." Stengers traces it back to "the end of the Enlightenment in France, when scientists officially accepted this role." But what was the threat to public order? It was a population defined as "gullible, ready to follow any quack or swindler" so that, Stengers concludes, "Modern science as a blind destroyer of traditional practices" began "when scientists accepted the role of guardians of an infantile public."[23]

I admit it's going too far to say that basketball analysts have set themselves up in "a temple" as "guardians of an infantile" NBA culture. But it's not going too far by much. As we have already seen, there are more than just faint, distorted echoes of d'Alembert's priestly certainty in the rhetoric of many working in basketball analytics. In fact, the science of sports analytics has recently expanded from vague characterizations of the prejudices of intuitive scouts and blind spots of emotional fans to including more rigorous scientific accounts of the cognitive biases gripping unscientific observers and leading them to fallacious conclusions.[24]

Still, if all this were just a question of rhetoric and attitude, it probably wouldn't occasion Stenger's painstaking analysis, or my own. But Stengers' concerns, mobilized through Diderot, pertain not only to attitudes and rhetorics but especially to the institutionalized connections between scientific practices and the economic operations of capitalism. And from that point of view, when the sports analytics market grows exponentially more crowded with the devices, methods, and promises of an ever-expanding number of startups—estimated at close to $800 million today and expected to grow to $15 billion over the next half decade and when the firm Second Spectrum has a $275 million contract with the NBA—Stenger's concerns for the fate of wonder, mobilized in the service of a "scientific attitude" and against the institutionalization of science for profit, hits closer to home.

And that's it right there. When all is said and done, when the clamor inside me grows quiet, I feel sure of this one thing: the measure of any technology of the basketball body should be the degree to which it contributes to our capacity to experience wonder.

13

Counting What Counts in Basketball

#94. Dubs

"That," to paraphrase from *The Matrix*, Agent Smith's cool declaration as he pins Neo to a subway rail as a train rushes out of the tunnel at him, "is the image of inevitability." My figure (fig. 8) shows the odds each team had of winning an NBA championship on a monthly basis from just before the start of the 2015–16 season to just after the end of the 2018–19 season. I have found this image to be one of the most compelling ways to convey my experience of the dominance of the Golden State Warriors over the rest of the NBA in the past four seasons, a span during which, in the average week, their odds of winning the title were 46 percent. Out of the countless thousands of simulations run by FiveThirtyEight's predictive algorithms during that span, the Warriors won almost one out of every two. And we don't even have the numbers for the 2014–15 season, during which the Warriors romped to sixty-seven wins and their first championship of this era. The next season they broke the record for most wins in a regular season, winning seventy-three games and losing only nine. And, in April of this past season, the Warriors broke the record—their own, by the way—for the most wins in a five-season span and then won five more games (of their final six). As the picture shows, the Dubs—as they are known: Dubs for W's, as in Warriors, as in Wins—have towered over the rest of the league during the period.

During the stretch, in the flood of media articles extolling their effectiveness and beauty, the only doubts really just served to highlight their

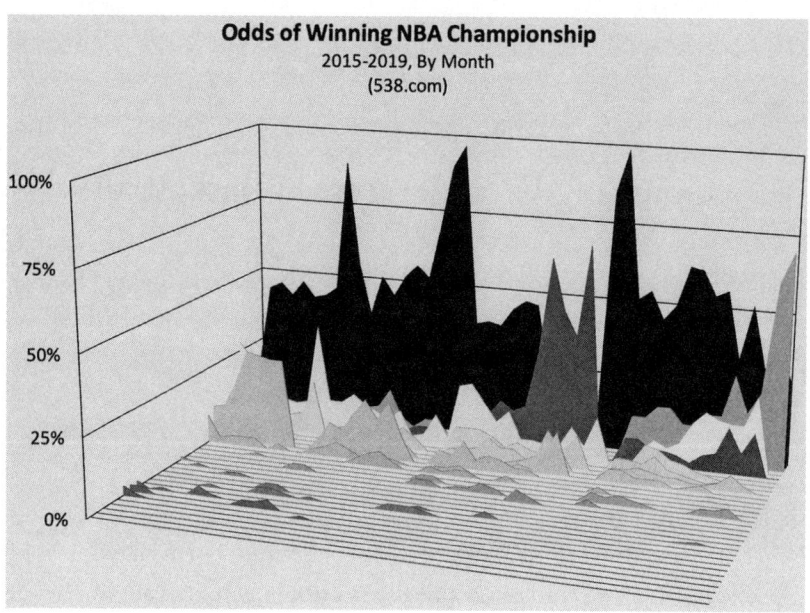

FIG. 8. Odds of winning an NBA championship.

dominance: Had the Warriors broken basketball? Were they the most dominant team of all-time? Would boredom with how easy it was or injury to one of their superstars derail them? Of course, Neo found his mojo and sprang up off the tracks, so it wasn't really the image—or in Neo's case, the sound—of inevitability for him as it turns out. And, as the figure shows, and any fan knows, the Warriors' titles weren't inevitable either. More on that in just a moment. But for now, just look at that ominous Warrior mountain range. If you're toiling in the foothills or flatlands below, or especially if you're a fan of those doing so, it sure must feel like inevitability.

How did they do it? The answer, in a word, is efficiency. According to the database at Basketball-Reference.com, Warriors teams from 2014–15 through 2018–19 posted three of the seven highest efficiency margins in NBA history. Over the same five seasons, of the 150 team efficiency margins (thirty teams over five seasons), the Warriors had three of the top four, four of the top ten, and five of the top twelve. Only one other franchise occupied even two of those twelve slots. This is not necessarily surprising since efficiency is highly correlated with team success. Drilling deeper into this by looking at the so-called Four Factors that correlate with efficiency, we find that the Warriors posted the top four season effective field goal percentage marks among all teams over that period and led the league in this category in each of the five seasons in question. But this also won't surprise anyone who has seen the Warriors play. Their point guard, Steph Curry, is widely considered the greatest shooter in NBA history, his backcourt partner Klay Thompson has been among league leaders in three-point shooting, forward Kevin Durant, acquired before the 2017 season, is not only a superb three-point shooter, but one of the most efficient mid-range shooters in the sport, and the rest of the Warriors tend to limit themselves to shots they can make.[1]

But if the Warriors' efficiency clearly stems from the superlative talent of its core group of players, it also owes a great deal to the ability of Coach Steve Kerr to utilize and blend their abilities and that, in turn, depends a great deal on the fact that the Warriors have used analytics extensively, not only to assemble a roster that will mesh, but to inform decisions about how to use the players they have. Golden State was, for example, one of the franchises to try out the league's optical tracking system back in 2009. And they use the data and advanced metrics the system makes possible—such as the expected point value model's data I described in chapter 9—to select players and, especially, to determine rotations and even to develop plays designed to get individual players spatially on the court in situations where the science of moving dots predicts they will be most efficient. In 2016 the franchise earned the "Best Analytics Organization" at the annual Sloan Sports Analytics Conference.[2] The Dubs' management team was featured in a *New York Times* magazine article that emphasized the broader circumstances making this possible: a location in the tech-heavy Silicon Valley that draws individuals who have the experience and expertise to make use of cutting-edge technology, especially related to data production and analysis.[3] That extends to players such as Andre Iguodala and Durant who are themselves investors in various tech firms in the Bay Area.[4] In this sense the Warriors' on-court dominance is both directly and indirectly supported by broader trends in American society that emphasize the development of technology, data analytics, and economically-centered performance metrics to maximize efficiency and profit. If only symbolically (but not, I think, only symbolically), the branding of their home arena by the software company Oracle speaks to these connections.

Golden State is undeniably efficient and effective. Yet a growing number of fans, even some initially stirred to wonder by their play, understandably find their games to lack dramatic or emotional interest: for there can be little "consummatory"—let alone aesthetic—experience when there is little uncertainty concerning outcome, and there is little of that when the Warriors take the floor. For all the fluid precision one witnesses as the Dubs circulate through their offensive sets, effortlessly zipping the ball around the court to break down bewildered defenses and find ridiculously open shots, and for all the flair and joy some of their plays show in the process, there remains something repetitive and predictable about a Warriors' possession, a War-riors' game, and even a Warriors' season. Here as well the name of their home arena—Oracle—speaks to the mix of forecasting and fate that has seemed to many to attend the Warriors' success over the past several years.

Support for the position came from an unexpected quarter when Todd Whitehead of the basketball analytics site Nylon Calculus used the meth-ods and metrics of the science of moving dots to show ways in which the Warriors' have indeed eliminated much of the unpredictability inherent in basketball, though he remained hopeful that this would be a temporary condition and pointed out that excitement could remain high where the Warriors were not directly involved.[5] I'm interested here and in the rest of this chapter in ways that quantification and the methods of basketball analytics can be used, as Whitehead did in that example, to amplify other voices and perspectives, to spotlight some of the negative effects of the single-minded pursuit of efficiency, and to showcase instead some of the other things that count in basketball.

#95. Improbability

The first and perhaps best-known interruption of the Warriors' otherwise untroubled dominance of the NBA can help illustrate, first, how improbable such an interruption was, second, how that very improbable interruption was dependent on other things that count in the sport, and even how quantification and analytics technologies and methods can help shine a light on these alternative values.

In 2016 the defending champion Warriors won an NBA record seventy-three regular season games, recording the fifth highest efficiency margin in league history. In their best-of-seven Finals series against the Cavaliers, they held a three games to one lead, a deficit from which no NBA team had ever recovered to win a Finals series. And, given Golden State's significant lead in efficiency over the first four games, a repeat championship appeared inevitable. In fact, after the fourth game, FiveThirtyEight used its complex algorithms and tens of thousands of game simulations to give Golden State a 95 percent chance of winning the title. Even after the Cavaliers unexpectedly won the next two games, the Warriors were still given a 65 percent chance of winning the seventh and final game. Let's go back to that game.

With the score tied and just under two minutes remaining in the seventh and deciding game, the Warriors' Andre Iguodala snatched a defensive rebound. At that moment, according to basketball analytics, the probability that the Warriors would win the game and so the title, climbed to 57.6 percent. A few seconds later, having passed the ball and streaked up court, Iguodala received a return pass in stride just steps from the basket. The science of moving dots calculated that he had a 65 percent chance of making his shot and that when he did, the Warriors win probability for the game—and therefore the championship—would jump to close to 70 percent.

But it didn't.

Because instead, this happened: LeBron James raced the length of the court catching up to Iguodala just in time to leap—while carefully avoiding a foul—and slap his layup attempt harmlessly against the backboard. With the block, the Warriors' win probability plummeted to 47 percent; when Cleveland grabbed the resulting rebound, it dropped still further to 42 percent. And, indeed, the Cavaliers, you may know, went on to win the game and the title.

Watching the play live, I felt—well—wonder; a wonder that lifted me out of my seat and drew a shout from my throat; a wonder that was a direct function of the improbability surrounding the event. And so, in my description, I've tried to repurpose the quantifying tools of basketball analytics for the alternative somaesthetic aim of highlighting and sharing that wonder with you.

Similarly, in a segment of the ESPN series "Sports Science," we learned exactly how rapidly LeBron James—slow, tired LeBron James, in the forty-seventh minute of his ninety-seventh game of the season no less—had to accelerate, how fast he had to run, how high he had to jump, how perfectly he had to time his takeoff, and how narrow was the window of opportunity he had to execute the wonderful block that defied the odds. ESPN marshaled the science of moving dots (in this case optical tracking data, knowledge of physics and mathematics, and digitally enhanced video) not to maximize efficiency but rather to frame and thereby intensify our sense of wonder at the astonishing capacity of LeBron's basketball body, to accomplish, as basketball's inventor put it, "the seemingly impossible."

#96. How to Build the Best

Just after the start of the 2018 season, Todd Whitehead, whose dazzling data visualizations for Nylon Calculus have earned him the respect of many in the world of the science of moving dots, used his talents to disrupt business as usual yet again, this time with respect to one of the most frequent and contentious topics of discussion in the basketball culture: Who are the greatest NBA players of all time? To grasp the originality and interest in this context of Whitehead's experiment, we should look at some of the ways this question has been approached in the past.

For example, if you'd asked that question in April of 1950, the answer would have consisted of ten names. That's because in April of 1950 "all-time"—in reference to the National Basketball Association—comprised exactly one season of play. The ten players chosen by a panel of sportswriters to fill out the All-NBA First and Second teams that season were, effectively, the ten best NBA players of all time. Since then, the same method has been used annually to name the season's best players to All-NBA teams (an NBA third team was added in 1989). You might, then, start by considering which players have been named to those teams most frequently. Just taking the top ten names on that list wouldn't give you a bad start in a discussion of the greatest NBA players of all-time. It would be headed by four players—Kareem

Abdul-Jabbar, Kobe Bryant, Tim Duncan, and LeBron James, each of whom has been named fifteen times. Karl Malone and Shaquille O'Neal have each been named fourteen times, and Bob Cousy, Dirk Nowitzki, Hakeem Olajuwon, and Dolph Schayes, each twelve times.

But while this might not be a bad start, few would consider this a very reliable indicator overall. To begin with it favors players who have had long careers and thus more opportunities to make the selection. But also, because players are effectively only compared with other players from the same season, it favors players who played in seasons when the overall pool of talent in the league was shallower. We might find a better list by consulting one of the innumerable lists one can find of the top "X" NBA players of all time. For example, in 1996 the NBA itself conducted a poll of experts, including players, coaches, executives, and journalists, to come up with its own list of the top fifty players since the league's founding. Of course, that list ignores players—such as LeBron James or Kobe Bryant, to name just two—whose careers unfolded after 1996.

Typically arguments over the question wind up turning on the relative weight to give individual statistical accomplishments (such as points per game) and team accomplishments of which an individual was a part (such as NBA championships), as well as awards a player was given by peers or expert panels (such as MVP awards or All-NBA selections). Typically, the criteria for selection in these lists are not explicitly defined. Even when we know something about what the criteria were, they frequently shift or are combined in arbitrary ways, and, moreover, we get little in the way of evidence or explanation supporting the claim that this criterion or configuration of criteria should be used. Moreover, to the degree that such lists rely exclusively on unadjusted box score data, they fail to account for contextual factors that impact a player's performance.

This is where the science of moving dots comes in. In 2016 ESPN's resident basketball analytics expert Kevin Pelton devised a method "to rate every player in the NBA history on a relatively level playing field." The quantitative basis upon which Pelton elaborated his more complex method is a metric called Win Shares, developed by Neil Paine, that "attempts to divvy up credit for team success to individuals on the team."[6] In a nutshell, the formula looks to adjust individual performance in the statistical categories tallied in the box score in relation to both team performance and league averages. As I described in chapter 9, basketball analytics has been looking for ways to quantify individual contributions to both offense and defense, but these nascent efforts have not yet impacted single-number player metrics like Win Shares. Pelton used an adjusted version of Paine's Win Shares combined with a quantified index of awards given to players by contemporaries based on a subjective-factors metric to come up with his own statistic called "Championships Added," which estimates how individuals contributed to their team's chances of winning a championship.[7]

Pelton's method, and others based on the statistical methods and insights of basketball analytics, has the clear virtue of making its method transparent and providing a clear and rational explanation for having chosen it. And, in his case, at least, Pelton also attempts to make clear the ways in which his methods were biased and what the impact of that bias might be, concretely, on the ranking it generated; as he did in acknowledging the surprisingly low ranking for Allen Iverson that I noted in chapter 8. Its disadvantage, from my perspective, is in the weight it gives to winning and, in particular, to winning championships. And I don't mean only that some superb players, for reasons that could hardly be attributed to their individual talent, effort, or performance, simply were not in a position to win or in some cases even contend for championships. I mean also to point out that Pelton's method *decides* that what counts most is winning titles and therefore what should be counted are those things that analysis of historical data have shown to be correlated with winning titles.

But what if that's not what matters to you? What if "greatness" in an NBA player means something different to you as a fan? This is where Whitehead's contribution stands out. For Whitehead built an interactive algorithm that allows fans to give greater or lesser weight to a variety of possible criteria. Fans are invited to input their opinions "on the relative value of seven player traits: "Superiority, Longevity, Efficiency, Team Success, Peak Form, Buckets, and #Rangzzzz" (meaning championships). The relative importance you give to these traits helps to define your personal ranking formula by assigning weights to a series of related stats. For example, move the superiority slider up to "important" and your rankings will become more heavily influenced by the number of All-NBA team selections and MVPs that each player earned during his career."[8] You can then adjust the results further using multipliers that allow you to discount players from certain eras, positions, or teams.

I like Whitehead's "personal G.O.A.T. factory" as he calls it in part because it puts (some of) the power of the algorithm back in the hands of fans (or players if they were to use it). But it's also a valuable contribution to addressing some of my concerns about the science of moving dots because it does not pretend to be objective. On the contrary, as Whitehead states, it is a "project that's meant to encourage us to confront our own value systems and to recognize the validity of ranking criteria distinct from our own." Not only does this erode some of the cultural authority that tends to accompany algorithmic rankings based on quantitative data, but it explicitly invites reflection on that authority and discussion of the fact that every ranking system is based on a system of values that are, ultimately, subjective.

I only wish that Whitehead had included a slider for "style" or for "cool"—perhaps based on the number of SLAM or GQ magazine covers a player had appeared on. Or how about one for "wokeness" based on the number of times a player has voiced progressive political opinions in the media or through local political activism? The point is not, of course, that these should be your values, nor that there could be some objective measure of them. It is rather that in Whitehead's device, I see a hopeful sign that within the science of moving dots some analysts are pressing their skills, expertise, and platform in the service of a greater range of values and voices.

#97. Wildness

Basketball analyst Kirk Goldsberry opens his recent book *Sprawlball* by asserting that "the convergence of computing, spatially referenced game data, and our culture's increasingly manic urges for quantification and efficiency," along with "a new generation of players, coaches, and executives who grew up with three-pointers and Michael Lewis books," has transformed "the entire aesthetic of basketball."[9] This transformation is characterized, he writes later, "by three interrelated trends: positional versatility, perimeter shooting, and isolation play."[10]

These are the elements that the combination of the science of moving dots and the quest for efficiency have determined, within the competition for efficient point production in basketball, are valuable, and that the league's decision makers therefore value in the basketball labor market through salary premiums. These premiums function as incentives that in turn further entrench the pervasiveness of these elements at the expense of other game elements and styles of play. Goldsberry's problem with this, therefore, does not lie with any of these elements, per se, but rather with the "homogenous aesthetic" that results: "A monocultural ditch of catch-and-shoot jump shots," which he finds dull and predictable. He misses he says, "the dynamism and athleticism required to score inside the arc" and "Jordan's fadeaways, Hakeem's dream shakes, and Abdul-Jabbar's skyhooks."[11]

Goldsberry's book is a visually arresting documentation, via the stories centered on key, representative players—among them some of the NBA's most bankable stars like Steph Curry, James Harden, and LeBron James— the development of whose styles of play reflects the imperatives and effects of the "moneyball aesthetic." He makes an argument I find convincing and consonant with my own in this book, that whatever the intentions of individual decision makers—be they players, general managers, coaches, owners, NBA executives, or analysts—the broader market forces within which the NBA is caught make the transformation he is talking about likely to continue; unless, that is, the league makes a conscious effort to change course. As Goldsberry points out, there is precedent for this. Factors such as "aesthetics, tactical diversity, and entertainment" have prompted previous rule changes over the course of NBA history from the implementation of the shot clock, to speed play, to widening the lane to curtail the dominance of big players, to the three-point shot itself.

As I say, I find myself agreeing with Goldsberry's argument and diagnosis and sympathetic to his preference for a more diverse game. So, I am not particularly interested in countering it so much as riffing of it, in particular off of two key rhetorical axes—metaphors, really, at least in a sense—that seem to structure Goldsberry's view. The very title of his book—*Sprawlball*—not only sums up the spread of basketball play to ever-greater distances from the hoop but reflects Goldsberry's training as a geographer. In this way, space, urban space in particular, seems to offer the overarching conceptual lens and rhetorical metaphor driving Goldsberry's view and argument. It is as though Goldsberry sees the basketball court as a city. Within that city, he might say, people used to live in many different areas and conditions. But now a rapidly expanding mass migration has left the urban core (near the hoops) and its immediately adjacent residential neighborhoods (the midrange) vacant in favor of a suburban landscape (beyond the three-point line) of strip malls, fast food and fast casual restaurants, and big box stores. This spatial perspective spurs, in turn, the second of Goldsberry's conceptual and rhetorical investments: diversity. Where, in the old days, the variety of spaces and conditions "inhabited" by basketball residents required a corresponding variety of techniques, tactics, and styles (ways of living as it were), the new sprawling suburban game has spawned a homogenization of techniques, tactics, and styles.

I certainly can appreciate the value of diversity and variety on aesthetic grounds. I too worry about elements of game play that used to count for something but are increasingly discounted, metaphorically and literally, within the science of moving dots. And so, I'm tempted to try to lend force to Goldsberry's argument by bringing to bear an additional perspective that is, I believe, implied by his urbanist spatial paradigm, but that he never makes explicit. I am talking about thinking about what the systems theorists I referenced in chapter 11 call "requisite variety" and, in particular, of the form this takes in ecology's deep concerns with biodiversity. Framed in this way, the stakes of the transformations Goldsberry documents can be shown to be perhaps higher than simply the passing of one aesthetic paradigm in favor of another. If that is all there is to it, then who is to say that what Goldsberry and I prefer is actually better and worth preserving over the styles that have replaced it and which, if the soaring value of NBA franchises is any indication, many consumers prefer? But thinking in terms of requisite variety raises the possibility that life itself is at stake—at least the life of basketball. The question is: What to do about it?

I'm going to turn to an unexpected place for the image of a solution, so please bear with me. In the beautiful concluding essay, entitled "Margins," of his 1977 work about the transformation of American agriculture along lines similar to what Goldsberry describes in *Sprawlball*, farmer and poet Wendell Berry describes a curious agricultural practice he discovered among farmers in Peru. Rather than gridding their entire fields from fencerow to fencerow, these farmers leave wild areas at the margins. In these wild, uncultivated margins between their fields, there among the weeds, every year, something new grows, something that withstands the pests or droughts that have destroyed the known and the given. "The hedgerows are marginal areas," Berry writes, "little thoroughfares of wilderness closely crisscrossing the farmland, and in them agriculture is constantly renewing itself in direct response to what threatens it. This network of wilderness threading through the fields serves the Andean farmer as a college of agriculture and wilderness station. . . . Set thus in the light of a truly healthy agriculture, our land-grant college complex may be seen less as a symbol of our agricultural success than as a symptom of our failure."[12]

Berry is talking about experimentation of course, which aligns perfectly with Goldsberry exhortation that the NBA's executives recover some of the experimental passion for tinkering and trial and error that characterized the league throughout much of its history. One might assume that Peruvian farmers could not afford to leave areas of their plots uncultivated for the sake of experimentation, but it turns out, it seems, that they cannot afford *not* to do so. But Berry's juxtaposition of the Peruvian farmers' methods of experimentation with that of "the land-grant college complex" helps illuminate that experimentation can take many forms. It's clear in the context of his essay that the experimentation that takes place in the land-grant college complex is too tightly wedded to large-scale capitalist agriculture and therefore too responsive to its imperatives to maximize efficiency and profit. This in turn requires minimizing risk and that, as we know from the history of counting in basketball, means using all available technologies and intellectual methods to quantify risk in relation to potential return on investment.

With this in mind, the question for Goldsberry and others working *within* the league and from the perspective of the science of moving dots is whether they can, like the farmers of Peru, discipline themselves and leave room for something wild, something with no evident value but whose apparent value may only emerge with time and a change in circumstances: something incalculable, unpredictable, improbable, impossible. After all, isn't that the spirit of uncertainty from which the experiment that was basketball first occurred? Isn't that the force of wild adventure that is present in every dribble, every shot? What if that wildness is what counts most in basketball?

Coda

#98. Hang Gliding, or, My Stinking Soul

Sometimes I wonder about the attraction those images of wild experimentation hold for me. I tend to think of myself as a very cautious—let's say calculating—person. I like to have a pretty good idea of how something is likely to turn out before I try it. Perhaps there's something dishonest, or at least disingenuous, about my calling for *others* to stop trying to count everything, to just accept that risk and vulnerability are an inescapable part of our existence, in basketball and elsewhere, and instead to just embrace that risk, dive headlong into the dark waters of experimentation even though we don't know what lies beneath the surface. Easy for me to say: it's not my money. And besides, if I don't really do that, what business do I have arrogantly calling others to do so? But maybe, in that case, that overstated exhortation to adventure is a call to myself, to some inner part of me that would like to shed the paralyzing burden of the fear of the unknown that holds me back so often, in so many areas of my life. There must be in me some of the wildness, some desire for or at least minute, visceral inclination toward adventure.

Let me tell you a story. More than twenty years ago I was accompanying a group of retired University of Michigan alumni, mostly in their sixties and seventies but some in their eighties, on a guided tour of South America. In exchange for giving them a few cultural enrichment lectures during the two-week trip, all my expenses were paid. It was a pretty sweet gig. My only concern, really, was that I—then in my early thirties—wouldn't conform in style or substance to their expectations, shaped in the '40s, '50s, and '60s, of what a respectable Michigan professor would be. I worried they wouldn't like me. And that is why when at the Houston airport I met our tour coordinator, a young guy about my age named Doug, I latched onto him. He seemed easygoing and friendly. I was back on the playground on the first day of kindergarten and Doug would be my friend and protector. He seemed to respond warmly, and we hit it off immediately. So much so, in fact, that in that very first conversation, he volunteered that he had a hookup with a guy in Rio who would take us hang gliding! "Awesome!" I lied, ignoring the knot in my stomach. Afraid of heights, few things could be less appealing to me than hurling myself off a mountain. But, apparently, one of those few things was humiliating myself by admitting it to my new buddy.

Anyway, Rio was a few stops and more than a week away, I calculated, and there would be plenty of time to get out of it. As the first week of the trip passed I grew more comfortable with the routines. I liked the alumni and they liked me. Doug and I hung out after hours, swapping life stories. And the few times that he brought up hang gliding, say as we enjoyed a meal with a few of the oldsters, I just smiled as broadly as I could and said I was super stoked and couldn't wait. When we finally got to Rio it was too late in the day to go, Doug told me. I feigned resigned understanding, and Doug and I instead spent the afternoon playing pick-up soccer with local kids on the beach and sipping caipirinhas at the bar in the hotel pool. On the morning of the second day, I was having breakfast with some of the older ladies, when Doug joined us. Crestfallen, he informed me that he'd talked to his guy and the wind wasn't right today. Realizing that tomorrow was our last day there and that I was almost in the clear, I decided to play up my disappointment. "Damn! I've been looking forward to this for a week and now we have only one more chance! What if the wind doesn't turn?" "I know," Doug said, sadly, "I know. We'll just have to hope for the best." Indeed, I thought to myself.

Day three began much like day two, with me at breakfast with an eighty-three-year-old widow from Detroit named, incredibly, Betty Page. Betty was a pretty sassy old broad, smart and funny and with a remarkably adaptable manner and a willingness to push herself physically on some of our excursions that had impressed me. She was my favorite, and she, in turn, had a big soft spot for me. Betty and I had just sat down with our buffet breakfasts when Doug bounded breathlessly up to our table. "It's on! The guys will be here in half an hour to take us up the mountain! Only thing is it's going to be seventy-five dollars and they only take cash." "Oh, shit," I said, "I don't have it. I still have to buy gifts for people back home. That sucks! But I'll still ride up with you and watch you go." Doug, of course, was chill about it. But then Betty piped up. "Oh Yago! You've been talking about hang gliding this whole trip. They've told us that we aren't allowed to tip you, but your lectures have been so enjoyable and informative and you've been so friendly and caring that I would like to pay for this." "No, no, Betty," I protested, "I couldn't possibly accept that." But I was no match for Betty, nor for the cosmic forces that, acting through her, were pushing me off that cliff.

And so, I found myself in the back of a jeep pulling into a gravel parking lot in the Tijuca National Park, high above the city. To my left I saw a "ramp": mere planks of weathered wood painted green, suspended somehow from the site of the mountain. A small group milled about the area, some unpacking gear from their jeeps, some chatting as they stood on the ramp, gesturing casually toward the abyss. My guide, DeHilton, explained to me that first we had to learn to take off. This entailed harnessing ourselves to the hang glider and then running together in the parking lot, practicing synchronizing our steps so that our knees wouldn't bump causing one or both of us to trip and plummet over the edge of the ramp. The second key, he explained, was that at takeoff you keep running with your legs, even after you're off the ramp. Like Wile E. Coyote, I thought, whose momentum carried him over the edge of a cliff. I imagined the moment he realizes he's in midair, and first his legs, then the rest of his body, are yanked down by gravity into the canyon below, ending in the soft pop of a cloud of dust. But DeHilton was a good teacher, patient and clear in his explanations, and with the chill vibe I always associated with surfers. It didn't take long before he was satisfied that I had it down. We removed ourselves from the glider to wait while other individuals and pairs took their turns. I paced around the parking lot. I joked nervously with Doug. I accepted from a nearby stranger the offer of a hit off the joint he was smoking.

Then DeHilton called out to me. It was time to put the glider back on and take our place in line. As we stood near the back edge of the ramp, only a couple of parties in front of us waiting for the signal to go, DeHilton put his hand on my shoulder. "Yago," he said, impossibly calmly, "you seem very tense." I looked at him, uncomprehending. I don't think I said anything, but I remember that I was thinking that my relationships back home were in good order, that everyone knew that I loved them. He began to massage my shoulder. "Don't worry," he reassured me, "everything will be fine. There's only one thing you can do to mess this up."

Hold up. Hold. Up. Isn't that something I should've known before? Another glider soared off the ramp so that only one remained before us. DeHilton continued. "See this bar here?" He gestured to a long horizontal steering bar directly in front me at chin level. "Don't grab this bar." He explained that's what he used to steer the glider and that if I grabbed it, the glider would plummet. I can handle that, I thought. But then he added, "But when we take off you are going to want to grab the bar."

So, he's basically telling me that there is only one thing I can do that will doom this flight and send us both to our deaths and I will have an irresistible impulse to do that thing. My heart, already racing, pounded even faster. I was nauseous. I shouldn't have smoked that joint. I couldn't feel anything. The ramp started to spin slowly around me. As if underwater, the sound of DeHilton's voice reached me: "So what you do, when you want to grab the bar, is grab the loop on my vest instead. In fact," he concluded, "just do that no matter what. As soon as we take off, grab this loop. Do it now. Try it." I did.

Seconds later, it was our turn. I saw the windsock fluttering limply and then suddenly stiffening. The spotter's voice called out: "Go!" We sprang into action, our steps synchronized; I was counting them like we practiced: One. Two. Three. Four. Five. Six. Seven. Eight. Nine. We took the last step off the platform; I remembered to keep running my legs; I remembered to grab the loop. For a moment we descended, and then, I heard a sound unlike anything I heard before or since: a soft, but impossibly deep and persistent, whoosh, like an exhalation; but it was more than sound, it was tangible, a rising, expanding pillow of air buoying us up. It was the breath of God.

DeHilton and I looked at each other. We both smiled as we rose, soaring in spiraling circles with hawks, drifting over the mountainside, the neighborhoods, the high rises of downtown, out over the ocean, accompanied always by that profound, profoundly reassuring, whispering breath. An infinite amount of time later, DeHilton guided our descent toward the beach, reminding me of the protocol for landing (touch down and let yourself run along with the momentum of the glider). Moments later, we were there, on the beach, on the earth. I felt exhilarated beyond anything I have ever felt in my life. I felt proud, courageous, invincible. And I knew, before I was even asked, the answer to the inevitable question: "No. I will never do anything like this again."

I have told this story countless times, to students, friends, and colleagues. I tell it because I think it imparts an important lesson about fear: first, often the initial impulse you have in the face of fear is the thing most likely to materialize your fear, and second, that you can't simply suppress that impulse, you have to find a constructive way to channel it. But I also tell it because it presents me in a charmingly self-deprecating light, like an extended humble-brag. And in that way it protects me against the uncertainty and fear I am experiencing in that particular conversation or relationship. I tell it so that people will like me and find me funny, wise, admirable, unconventional, and vulnerable. That is, I keep myself invulnerable. The story is true, just as I have told it, but the way I use it makes the telling of it a lie.

Oops. I did it again.

There must be in me some of the wildness, some desire for, or at least a minute, visceral inclination toward adventure and the vulnerability it brings, right? And yet its voice seems so faint, its force so feeble compared to the countervailing grip of the fearful, fearsome voices that warn me ceaselessly of all that could go wrong, that insist that I measure carefully before I cut, if I cut at all. The moral of the autobiographical interludes I have woven into this book has been that numbers, introduced to me as an indispensable tool to guide my growth and protect me from danger, became, under the circumstances of my life, a berating taskmaster, constantly reminding me of how far I was from where I should be. Locked in this ambivalent embrace with quantification, numbers cipher my own fear of adventure, my desperate need for reassurance that I am good enough, my constant awareness that I am not and, moreover, my certainty that any step I take will only make that last fact obvious to everyone I have fooled. Numbers, in short, have reflected back to me my stinking—incorrigibly, irredeemably stinking—soul.

I am writing this, the last section of this book, in a moment where, unexpectedly, I have been forced to embark on an adventure. The details are not all mine to share, but suffice it to say that I am fifty-four years old, suddenly unemployed, with few prospects, and facing a deep personal crisis as a result of having hurt the person who has loved me best, and whom I have loved most—if not very well, in this world. Numbers, of course, did not do this to me. Numbers had nothing to do with this. I did this to myself. But I did it to myself as a result of the personal psychodynamics for which the uses of numbers I have described in this book—obsessively, but narrowly measuring value and calculating risk in the futile pursuit of perfection— serve as a symbol. Facing a new situation that I experienced as deeply risky, with deepening, clamoring doubts about my own value, I grabbed the bar and, in doing so, I brought my very worst nightmares to life. Now they are with me all the time, taunting and mocking me, as I find myself, like in a dream, not dead from the fall but somehow right back on the back edge of a ramp jutting out into space, waiting for the signal to run, and to keep running out into thin air, uncertain whether the breath of God will come to lift me again or not.

There must be in me some of the wildness, some desire for, or at a least a minute, visceral inclination toward adventure—along with the capacity to abide uncertainty and trust in my own judgment, or at least resilience, that adventure requires. Right? Or will I spend the rest of my life stupidly believing the stats that say I can't do it, stupidly waiting for the odds to change—my hands welded to the bar that I will, with the inevitable efficiency of a Steph Curry three-pointer, pull, time and again, dooming me to another self-inflicted catastrophe?

#99. When Counting Counts

The truth is: I was always a fearful child. When I'd ride bikes with the other kids in our hilly neighborhood, and they raced down steep hills at break-neck speed, I always lagged behind, cautiously pumping my brakes so as not to get out of control. Jumping from boulders or climbing playground structures filled me with anxiety, and I did my best to avoid situations where the pressure to do so would be too great. I was always afraid of falling and getting hurt. But the threat of physical injury wasn't my only fear. There used to be a clock in my bedroom shaped like a black cat with a white stomach. Its tail wagged and eyes blinked with the passing of the seconds. At some point I became unaccountably terrified of it and it had to be removed to the hallway. When *Jaws* came out, I slept on the floor next to my parents' bed for days, never mind that I hadn't seen the ocean since I was two and the closest one was 1,500 miles away.

Long before that, for no reason that I can recall, at bedtime I would curl my too-small body into my mother's side of my parents' enormous king-size bed. My mother would say goodnight, and I would insist she say, so that I could repeat, line by line, a Spanish prayer:

Angel de la guardia, dulce compañia,
No me dejes solo, ni de noche, ni de dia
Porqué soy muy chiquitico, y me perdería

Guardian angel, sweet companion,
Don't leave me alone, neither at night, nor during the day,
Because I am very, very small, and I would get lost.

Later, after I'd fallen asleep, my father would come up, wake me, and then scoop me up in his arms and, in a brisk trot, carry me to my room, where he would "spike" me into my own bed—really a pretty careful, gentle plunk—and shout "Touchdown!" Those are memories of comfort.

Though I was desperate to wear a real football uniform and joined a team so as to get one, it only took one look at an oncoming blocker for me to recalculate the importance of the uniform relative to the dread that the prospect of contact caused me. I quit. My father and I did, however, watch football together on Sundays, and we even placed friendly wagers on the games each week, probably beginning around the time I was eight. He had a system for making predictions. And so did I. I don't know what his was, but in my case, I would calculate the average of Team A's points scored per game and Team B's points allowed per game to set my prediction for Team A's points and then do the inverse to get my prediction for Team B's points. I didn't think to make adjustments for injuries or home-field advantage. Or to weight more recent performance more heavily, or to consider the strengths of their respective schedules, or even their performance against the same opponents. I did, however, occasionally feel within me an irresistible impulse to adjust the prediction when it meant that a team I liked—whether because of a player or the look of their uniforms—was going to lose.

I don't know how I came out in those weekly wagers, but I know I loved watching the games with my father, loved making the calculations, and was proud of my system and my ability to make the calculations on my own, with paper and pencil. I loved explaining my system to my father and noticing the quiet approval and even quieter pride soften his features. Perhaps he was seeing that our weekly discussions of Martin Gardner's mathematical games and puzzles, which we'd play with together every Saturday after he got back from the public library with the latest issue of *Scientific American*, were paying off. My father certainly loved me a lot. He used to call me "*la alegria de mi vejez*" (the joy of my old age) and "*el hijo en que tengo mis complacencias*" (the son with whom I am well pleased—the words that in the Bible descend from the heavens, the voice of God, when Jesus is baptized by John the Baptist).

Recalling my pervasive fears and his love causes me to think about the prominent role that numbers and measuring and calculating played in our relationship. I've said I felt tyrannized and judged by—even as I internalized and inherited—his mania for measurement. But now another perspective appears. My father was tortured by his own fears, I know: of things getting out of control, of losing what was precious to him. I think of what I have learned in the course of writing this book about the history of counting, and measurement, and calculation. We only try to quantify the things that matter to us, we only count what counts. But sometimes we discount other things that count just because they cannot be counted. And because the things that count that we *can* count are so precious to us, attending to what cannot be counted appears a risky luxury.

Now I think that, whatever else was motivating him, in teaching me how to quantify, my father was, first of all, passing on to me—like a king passing a great sword to his child—the best tool he had for managing his own fears, perhaps hoping to equip me with something that would attenuate my own, very evident, terrors. But even more so, in quantifying me and teaching me how to quantify myself, I think he was conveying to me—in a medium in which he felt most safe—how precious I was to him, how much I counted, how much he loved me. The point, in other words, all along, was not that numbers wouldn't save me—Lord knows numbers have not saved me from myself—but that love would.

And so, it occurs to me that, whatever else is driving the expansion of the science of moving dots, whatever else may be motivating individual basketball analysts, somewhere within the impulse to quantify basketball is the feeling that basketball is precious, that basketball counts: that, as my father loved me, basketball analysts love basketball. But "love," writes another unlikely authority, the late Jesuit priest Anthony DeMello in a book bequeathed to me not by my father but rather by my mother, "can only exist in freedom. The true lover seeks the good of his beloved which requires especially the liberation of the lover from the beloved."[1] If so, if that is how the science of moving dots can love basketball, then that strikes me as a very powerful shared common ground upon which to have real conversations, perhaps sometimes even arguments, about the sport we all love, about what we love in it, about how to set it free from our love, and so about counting and about what counts in basketball.

NOTES

INTRODUCTION

1. National Basketball Association, "Official Scorer's Report."
2. National Basketball Association, "Leonard 18' Pullup Jump Shot."
3. Coy and Morse, *Hoop Genius*; Webb, *Basketball Man*, 66; Weyand, *Cavalcade of Basketball*, 6; Rains and Carpenter, *James Naismith*, 46.
4. Hacking, *Emergence of Probability*, 36.
5. Thelia, *Bounce*.
6. Colás, *Ball Don't Lie!*; Applin, "Muscular Christianity"; Horger, "Play by the Rules"; McLaughlin, *Give and Go*; George, *Elevating the Game*.
7. Sutton-Smith, *Ambiguity of Play*, 215.
8. Sutton-Smith, *Ambiguity of Play*, 52–54; Spariosu, *Dionysus Reborn*, 15–17; Caillois, *Man, Play and Games*, 99–128 and 145–60.
9. Spariosu, *Dionysus Reborn*; Caillois, *Man, Play and Games*.
10. Bernstein, *Against the Gods*, 22.
11. Huizinga, *Homo Ludens*, 30–31 and 71–75; Spariosu, *Dionysus Reborn*, 12–14.
12. Huizinga, *Homo Ludens*, 30–31 and 46–75; Caillois, *Man, Play and Games*, 14–15; Spariosu, *Dionysus Reborn*, 12–13; Crowther, *Sport in Ancient Times*, 46; Kyle, *Sport and Spectacle*, 55–58, 73–88; Kyle, "Greek Athletic Competitions," 21–35; and Hawhee, *Bodily Arts*.
13. Sutton-Smith, *Ambiguity of Play*, 91–92 and 96–102.
14. Tarver, *I in Team*; Cohan, *We Average Unbeautiful Watchers*.
15. Andrews and Carrington, *A Companion to Sport*, 13 and 407–10.
16. Sutton-Smith, *Ambiguity of Play*, 36–44.
17. Cavallo, *Muscles and Morals*; Putney, *Muscular Christianity*.
18. Horger, "Play by the Rules."

19. Sutton-Smith, *Ambiguity of Play*, 129–32; Spariosu, *Dionysus Reborn*, 53–68; see also Huizinga, *Homo Ludens*, 105–72 and Ackerman, *Deep Play*, 126–27.

20. Schiller, "Aesthetic Education of Man," 298.

21. Ackerman, *Deep Play*, 136–42.

22. Suits, "Elements of Sport," 55.

23. Hyland, *Philosophy of Sport*, 115–17.

24. Elcombe, "Philosophers Can't Jump," 207–11; Colás, "Getting Free."

25. Sutton-Smith, *Ambiguity of Play*,173; Feezell, "Pluralist Conception of Play," in *Philosophy of Play*.

26. Csikszentmihalyi, *Flow*, 72–77.

27. Csikszentmihalyi, *Flow*, 62–67; Ackerman, *Deep Play*, 24; Sutton-Smith, *Ambiguity of Play*, 185.

28. Cooper, *Playing in the Zone*, 31–38; Feezell, *Sport, Play, and Ethical Reflection*; Csikszentmihalyi, *Flow*, 96–99.

29. Sutton-Smith, *Ambiguity of Play*, 11, 201–4, 213. See also Kieran Egan's remarks on ironic understanding in *Educated Mind*, 155–62.

30. Pullman, *Amber Spyglass*, 182.

31. Pullman, *Amber Spyglass*, 183. For more on the ideas about truth and knowledge embodied in the alethiometer see Colás, "Telling True Stories." And for an eloquent set of reflections on the cultural history of oracles, past and present, see Wood.

32. Ironically, this formulation came to me via the work of one of the premier chroniclers of and participants in the basketball analytics movement, my friend Seth Partnow, who headlined a 2015 essay on the use of analytics for defensive analysis "Not everything that can be counted counts." I modified it, I thought, originally. But it turns out that sociologist William Bruce Cameron used the same phrase to caution against over-reliance on quantitative methods in his discipline in the 1963 book *Informal Sociology*, 13.

INTRODUCTORY INTERLUDE—RECORDS

1. Challaye, *Metodología de las ciencias*. 35.

1. THE SCIENCE OF MOVING DOTS

1. Maheswaran, "Basketball's Wildest Moves."

2. Second Spectrum, "Second Spectrum Home."

3. Heitner, "$250 Million Data Deal"; Washburn, "Sunday Basketball Notes."

4. Brief, "SportVU Analytics"; Detrick, "Closing the WNBA's Analytics Gap."

5. Guttman, *From Ritual to Record*.

6. Heeren and Palmer, *Basic Ball*; Lahman, "History by the Numbers."

7. Koppett, *Essence of the Game*, 219.

8. Koppett, *Essence of the Game*, 223.

9. Baumer and Zimbalist, *Sabermetric Revolution*, 21–22.

10. Manley, *Basketball Heaven*, 4.

11. Oliver, *Basketball on Paper*, 82–83.

12. Oliver, "New Measurement Techniques."

13. Oliver, "New Measurement Techniques."

14. Oliver, *Basketball on Paper*, 23–25.

15. Oliver, *Basketball on Paper*, 25.

16. Berri, Schmidt, and Brook, *Wages of Wins*, 99–100.

17. Oliver, "Roboscout and the Four Factors."; Oliver, *Basketball on Paper*, 63; Kubatko et al., "Starting Point," 12–13.

18. Kubatko et al., "Starting Point."

19. Oliver, "Yahoo! Groups." See also Oliver's 1996 summary of his methods and findings to date: Oliver, "Fundamentals for Analyzing Basketball."

20. Berri, "Calculate Wins Produced"; Basketball-Reference, "NBA Win Shares."

21. Berri, Schmidt, and Brook, *Wages of Wins*.

22. See, for example, Ballard, "Measure of Success."

23. Alamar, "A First Step"; Alamar, *Sports Analytics*; Albert and Koning, eds., *Statistical Thinking in Sports*; Severini, *Analytic Methods in Sports*; Miller, *Sports Analytics and Data Science*; Martin, *Sports Performance Measurement*; Nibali, "Data Game."

24. Baumer and Zimbalist, *Sabermetric Revolution*, 85–94; Shea and Baker, *Basketball Analytics*, 2–4.

25. Reimer, "First Sports Analytics Degree"; Fisher, "Colleges Offer Analytics Track."

26. NBA, "NBA Partners with Stats LLC."

27. Loeffelholz, Bednar, and Bauer, "Predicting NBA Games"; Teramoto and Cross, "Performance Factors."

28. MIT Sloan Sports, "XY Panel"; Goldsberry, "CourtVision"; Goldsberry and Weiss, "Dwight Effect"; Chang et al., "Quantifying Shot Quality," Maheswaran, *Three Dimensions of Rebounding*; Partnow, "Splitting the Basketball Atom."

29. Cervone et al., "POINTWISE" and for a more accessible popular account see Goldsberry, "DataBall."

30. Kreiswirth, "ESPN *The Magazine*'s Analytics of the NBA."

31. Fusionetics, "Athlete Management System,"

32. P3, "Applied Sports Science" and P3, "Professional Athletes."

33. Glockner, *Chasing Perfection*, 118–19; Nibali, "Data Game," 54–56.

34. Goldsberry, *Sprawlball*; Clinchy, "The 3-Point Shot?," Restifo, "Nylon Calculus 101," Ross, "Welcome to Smarter Basketball."

35. Badenhausen and Ozanian, "NBA Team Values 2019."

36. Maese, "NBA Embraces Advanced Analytics."

37. Partnow, "Splitting the Basketball Atom."
38. Badenhausen and Ozanian, "NBA Team Values 2019."
39. Glockner, *Chasing Perfection*, see especially the chapter entitled "Faster, Stronger, More Explosive," 105–26. See also for more details on the technologies and measures utilized in sports science today Martin, *Sports Performance Measurement and Analytics*; Nibali, "Data Game."

INTERLUDE—RULERS

1. Lindstrom, "Colas, Edgewood Slip Past Middleton."
2. Kula, *Measures and Men*.
3. Hand, *Measurement Theory and Practice*, 12.
4. Hand, *Measurement Theory and Practice*, 4.
5. Crosby, *Measure of Reality*, 11.
6. Crosby, *Measure of Reality*, 11–12.

2. THE CULTURE OF MOVING DOTS

1. Cindy Boren, "Charles Barkley Really, REALLY, Hates Analytics," *Washington Post*, February 11, 2015.
2. Burke, *Rhetoric of Motives*, 40.
3. Koppett, *Essence of the Game*.
4. Watts, "'Voice' and 'Voicelessness.'"
5. Merry, *Seductions of Quantification*, 36.
6. Kramnick, "Introduction," xi–xii; see also Hobsbawm, *Age of Revolution*, 20–21.
7. Putnam, "Beyond the Fact/Value Dichotomy," 135–41; *Collapse of the Fact Value Dichotomy*.
8. Lewis, *Moneyball*, xiv; but see also an elegant neo-Enlightenment apology for baseball analytics in Thorn and Palmer, *Hidden Game of Baseball*, 3–4.
9. Gary Washburn, "Just a Numbers Game"; Maheswaran, "Basketball's Wildest Moves."
10. Shea and Baker, *Basketball Analytics*, vii.
11. Berri, Schmidt, and Brook, *Wages of Wins*, 2.
12. Taylor, *Thinking Basketball*, 9.
13. Bellotti, *Basketball's Hidden Game*, 2.
14. Oliver, *Basketball on Paper*, 81.
15. Hand, *Measurement Theory and Practice*, 4.
16. Thomson, "Electrical Units of Measurement," 73.
17. Porter, *Trust in Numbers*.
18. Daston and Galison, *Objectivity*, 4, 381.
19. Kwa, *Styles of Knowing*, 196, 220.
20. Shea and Baker, *Basketball Analytics*, 2.

21. Fried and Mumcu, *Sport Analytics*, 17.
22. Severini, *Analytic Methods in Sports*, 1.
23. Shea and Baker, *Basketball Analytics*, 27.
24. Shea and Baker, *Basketball Analytics*, 35–62.
25. Glockner, *Chasing Perfection*, 121, 126.
26. Glockner, *Chasing Perfection*, 7.
27. Alexander, *Mantra of Efficiency*, 169.
28. Alexander, *Mantra of Efficiency*, 12, 169–70.
29. Catapult Sports, *Why Athlete Analytics?*
30. Hacking, *Taming of Chance*.
31. Alamar, *Sports Analytics*, 50.
32. On quantification and sports betting, see Winston, *Mathletics*; Gould, *Mathematics in Games, Sports, and Gambling*. On the historical connection between gambling and probability theory see Hacking, *Emergence of Probability*; Daston, *Classical Probability*; Gigerenzer et al., *Empire of Chance*. And, on the likely effects of the removal of the federal ban on sports betting, see Windhorst, "New Jersey Gambling Case."
33. Miller, *Sports Analytics and Data Science*, v.
34. Alamar, *Sports Analytics*.
35. Oliver, *Basketball on Paper*, 3.
36. Winston, *Mathletics*.
37. Nibali, "Data Game."
38. Kurz, "Adam Smith on Markets"; Davenport and Harris, *Competing on Analytics*, 37–44.
39. Ballard, "Measure of Success."
40. Wharton, "NBA's Adam Silver."
41. Knaflic, *Storytelling with Data*, 2.
42. Goldsberry, "Department of Defense"; Levy, "Offensive Style Changes."
43. Tufte, *Quantitative Information*.
44. Cairo, *Truthful Art*.
45. Yau, *Visualize This*, 2, 342.
46. Halpern, *Beautiful Data*, 15.
47. Halpern, *Beautiful Data*, 1.
48. See Ballard, "Measure of Success"; Lewis, "No-Stats All-Star"; Heeren and Palmer, *Basic Ball*; Shea and Baker, *Basketball Analytics*; Glockner, *Chasing Perfection*.

INTERLUDE—NUMBERS

1. Lakoff and Núñez, *Where Mathematics Comes From*, 15; Dehaene, *Number Sense*, 39, 42; Weise, *Numbers, Language, and the Mind*, 102.

2. Dantzig, *Number*, 7.

3. Dantzig, *Number*, 7.

4. Dantzig, *Number*, 8.

5. Dantzig, *Number*, 9.

6. Dantzig, *Number*, 10.

7. Hand, *Measurement Theory and Practice*, 7.

8. Cohen, *A Calculating People*.

9. Weiss, *Sport*, 165–66.

10. Ken Burns, "First Inning: Our Game."

3. COUNTING, AMERICA'S GAME

1. In their book, *Sabermetric Revolution*, sports economists Baumer and Zimbalist do a thorough job of documenting the impact of *Moneyball* (book and movie), of correcting the instances of "artistic license" taken in both, and of documenting the spread of analytics in baseball and beyond. See especially, chapters 1 and 2.

2. Lewis, *Moneyball*, xiv.

3. Henry, "Bill James."

4. Lewis, *Moneyball*, 18.

5. Ifrah, *Universal History of Numbers*.

6. Lewis, *Moneyball*, 18, 37.

7. Novak, *Joy of Sports*, 59.

8. Lewis, "No-Stats All-Star."

9. Nationalpastime.com, "This Day in Baseball History."

10. Schwarz, *Numbers Game*, 4.

11. Thorn, *Baseball in the Garden of Eden*, 120–21.

12. Voigt, *American Baseball*, 91.

13. Lewis, *Moneyball*, 70–71.

14. Lewis, *Moneyball*, 71.

15. Chadwick, "Model Base Ball Player."

16. Tygiel, *Past Time*, 19.

17. Hobsbawm, *Age of Revolution*, 284.

18. Porter, *Rise of Statistical Thinking*, 22–23.

19. Cohen, *A Calculating People*, 225.

20. Schwarz, *Numbers Game*, 6.

21. Schiff, *"Father of Baseball,"* 71.

22. Quoted in Schiff, *"Father of Baseball,"* 84.

INTERLUDE—THERMOMETERS

1. Hankins, *Science and the Enlightenment*, 16.

1. Gerber, *Innovators and Institutions*, 339.
2. McKenzie, *Exercise in Education and Medicine*, 268–69.
3. Hitchcock, *Need of Anthropometry*, 3.
4. Hitchcock, *Need of Anthropometry*, 6.
5. Kroll, *Perspectives in Physical Education*, 46, see also Park, "Physiologists, Physicians, and Physical Educators"
6. Hitchcock, "President Hitchock's Address."
7. Hobsbawm, *Age of Revolution*, 284.
8. Quetelet, *A Treatise on Man*, 99, 100.
9. Hitchcock, "President Hitchock's Address," 9.
10. Park, "Physiologists, Physicians, and Physical Educators," 151; also Park, "Athletes and Their Training," 88.
11. Quoted in Hoberman, *Mortal Engines*, 71.
12. Engle Merry, *Seductions of Quantification*, 36.
13. See Hoberman, *Mortal Engines*; Berryman and Park, *Sport and Exercise Science*; Park, *Gender, Sport, Science*; and Gould, *Mismeasure of Man*.
14. Park, "Physiologists, Physicians, and Physical Educators," 149.
15. Quoted in Hoberman, *Mortal Engines*, 68.
16. Shapin, *Scientific Revolution*, 30–46; Principe, *Scientific Revolution*, 87–90; Magdalinski, *Sport, Technology, and the Body*, 33–36; Shilling, *Body in Culture, Technology, and Society*.
17. Martin, *Sports Performance Measurement and Analytics*, 1, emphasis added.
18. For example, Flowers, "Russell Westbrook."
19. Meylan, "Marks for Physical Efficiency," 109.
20. Meylan, "Marks for Physical Efficiency," 109.
21. Magdalinksi, *Sport, Technology, and the Body*, 5; see also Overman, *Protestant Ethic*, 175–92 and Holowchak and Reid, *Aretism*, 97–106.
22. Shogan, *Making of High-Performance Athletes*, 15, 101.
23. Hitchcock, "President Hitchock's Address," 8.
24. Hitchcock, "President Hitchock's Address," 8.
25. Gulick, "Physical Education: A New Profession," 64.
26. Gulick, "Physical Health, Education, Recreation," 57.
27. Dorgan, *Luther Halsey Gulick*; Gerber, *Innovators and Institutions*, 348–56; Lee, *History of Physical Education*, 198–201.
28. Cavallo, *Muscles and Morals*, 4 and Sutton-Smith, *Ambiguity of Play*, 36–44.
29. Cavallo, *Muscles and Morals*, 5.
30. Cavallo, *Muscles and Morals*, 9 and 88–124; see also D. J. Mrozek, *Sport and American Mentality*, especially 28–102.

31. Gulick, *Efficient Life*, 52, emphasis added.

32. Gulick, *Efficient Life*, 184, emphasis added.

33. Gulick, *Philosophy of Play*, 119, 261.

34. Gulick, *Philosophy of Play*, 193.

5. COUNTING FOR CHARACTER

1. Naismith, *Basketball*, 56, emphasis added.

2. Naismith, "James Naismith Handwritten Manuscript."

3. Naismith, "Basket Ball" (1914), 339–40.

4. Naismith, *Rules for Basket Ball*, 3.

5. Naismith, *Basketball*, 57, emphasis added.

6. Naismith, "Basket Ball" (1892), 146.

7. Naismith, "Basket Ball" (1892), 147.

8. Naismith, "Basket Ball" (1892), 147.

9. Gulick, "Physical Health, Education, Recreation," 56–58.

10. Gulick, "Our Platform." See also Applin, "Muscular Christianity," 22–30.

11. Rains and Carpenter, *James Naismith*, 57.

12. Applin, "Muscular Christianity," 35.

13. Association Notes, "Clippings ('Basket Ball Fever')," 232.

14. See, for example, Naismith, "Basketball Letter," which included a little poem touting the skills of the Springfield Faculty team and taunting their opponents.

15. Applin, "Muscular Christianity," 39, 42.

16. Naismith, *Rules for Basket Ball 1893*, 16; see also, published two months later, Naismith and Gulick, *Basket Ball*.

17. "Personals and News," 199.

18. L. W. Allen, "Basket Ball at Hartford," 58, emphasis added.

19. Halsted, "Basket Ball," 76.

20. "Is Basket-Ball a Danger."

21. Peterson, *Cages to Jump Shots*.

22. Gulick, "Basket Ball"; "Ethics of Basketball"; "How to Use Basket Ball."

23. McCurdy, Naismith, and Cornelius, "Report of Athletic League Committee," 128–29.

24. Naismith, "How to Start Basket Ball"; Reach, "Basket Ball as an In-Door Game"; Berenson, "Basket Ball for Women."

25. Naismith and Gulick, *Basket Ball*, 16.

26. W. E. Allen, "Forward," 45–46.

27. Applin, "Muscular Christianity," 52–53.

28. "Official Basket Ball Rules, 1895," 139–40.

29. "Basket Ball League, 1894–1895," unpublished notebook, Springfield College Archive.

30. International Committee of Young Men's Christian Associations, *Basket Ball Rules*.

31. Gulick, "Editorial," 13.

32. Gulick, "How to Score Basket Ball" (1898), 107.

33. Gulick, "How to Score Basket Ball" (1903), 154.

34. Spalding and Bros., "Complete Basket Ball Outfit," (advertisement).

35. Hepbron, "Official Rules, Season 1903–1904," emphasis added.

36. Griffith-Clark Physical Education Service Co., *Fundamentals of Basketball*.

INTERLUDE—ONE ON ONE

1. Hickey, *Air Guitar*, 155.

6. COUNTING FOR COMPETITION

1. Naismith, "Basket Ball" (1913), 70.

2. Naismith, "Basket Ball" (1913), 71.

3. Naismith, "Basket Ball" (1913), 70.

4. Naismith, "Basket Ball" (1913), 71.

5. Naismith, "Basket Ball" (1913), 71.

6. Naismith, "Basket Ball" (1913), 71.

7. Morgan, "Eastern Intercollegiate League," 194.

8. Morgan, "Eastern Intercollegiate League," 195.

9. Morgan, "Eastern Intercollegiate League," 197.

10. Morgan, "Eastern Intercollegiate League," 203.

11. Messer, *How to Play Basket Ball*, 100; Angell, *Basket Ball for Coach*, 87.

12. Wardlaw and Morrison, *Basket Ball*, 209.

13. Wardlaw and Morrison, *Basket Ball*, 209.

14. Wardlaw and Morrison, *Basket Ball*, 209–10.

15. Morgan, "Eastern Intercollegiate League 1921–1922."

16. Holman, *Scientific Basketball*; Meanwell, *Science of Basket Ball*; Forrest Allen, *My Basket-Ball Bible*.

17. Carow, "Standardized Scheme for Scoring."

18. See, for similar quantifying efforts published in the 1930s, Hines, "An Efficiency Rating Chart"; Dill, "Useful Plan for Scoring"; May, "Self-Analysis Charts"; Gibble, "Individual Basketball Rating Chart"; Hashagen, "Scoring Charts"; Gibble, "Hitting Averages in Basketball"; DesCombes, "Self-Rating Chart for Basketball"; Voltmer and Watts, "Rating Scale of Player Performance." Bliss, "Squad and Team Progress," and Trythall, "Diagnostic Basketball."

INTERLUDE—MEASURING STICKS

1. Erving, *Dr. J: The Autobiography*, 292–93.

7. COUNTING FOR COMMERCE IN COLLEGE

1. F. C. Allen, "Address by the President."
2. Naismith, "Is Basketball Injurious."
3. Cummings, "Effect of Basketball Practice"; Hammett, "Basket Ball Affects College Men."
4. Noble, "Acquisition of Skill"; Brace, "Testing Basketball Technique."
5. Messersmith and Corey, "Distance Traversed"; Fay and Messersmith, "Distances Traversed"; Fay and Messersmith, "Effect of Rule Changes"; Messersmith and Bucher, "Distance Traversed by Big Ten"; Messersmith, Laurence, and Randels, "Study of Distances Traversed"; Messersmith, "Study of the Distance Traveled."
6. The trend is captured in two textbooks from the second half of the 1940s: Clarke, *Application of Measurement to Health* and Bovard, Cozens, and Hagman, *Tests and Measurements*. Individual studies include Brace, "Testing Basketball Technique" and *Measuring Motor Ability*; Griffith, "Experiments in Basketball"; Friermood, "Basketball Progress Tests"; Young and Moser, "Short Battery of Tests"; Case, "Analysis of the Effects"; Kimball, "Comparative Study"; Moser, "Basketball Skill Tests"; Carlson, "Methods in Teaching Basketball"; Schwartz, "Knowledge and Achievement Tests"; Cross, "Comparison of the Whole Method"; Glassow, Colvin, and Schwarz, "Studies in Measuring Basketball"; Dyer, Schurig, and Apgar, "Basketball Motor Ability Test."
7. Dimick, "Formulation of a Basketball Scoring Method," 2.
8. Dimick, "Formulation of a Basketball Scoring Method," 51.
9. Dimick, "Formulation of a Basketball Scoring Method," 5 and 58.
10. Daley, "NYU Five Downs Notre Dame"; O'Riley, "17,623 See Stanford Stop LIU."
11. Applin, "Muscular Christianity," 171.
12. Elbel and Allen, "Evaluating Team and Individual Performance," 538.
13. Elbel and Allen, "Evaluating Team and Individual Performance," 555.
14. Dean, *Progressive Basketball*.
15. Dean, *Progressive Basketball*, 14.
16. Hobson, *Scientific Basketball*, viii.
17. Effrat, "Columbia Defeats Fordham."

8. COUNTING FOR COMMERCE IN THE NBA

1. McDermott, "'He Don't Know.'"
2. Pluto, *Loose Balls*; FreeDarko Collective, *Undisputed Guide to Pro Basketball*, 83.
3. "Ruling Favors Haywood"; Criblez, *Tall Tales and Short Shorts*, 40–43.
4. Eskenazi, "Schoolboy Accepts $3-Million."

5. FreeDarko Collective, *Undisputed Guide to Pro Basketball*, 105–6; Criblez, *Tall Tales and Short Shorts*, 79–80.

6. Koppett, "Basketball Merger Crumbles."

7. Montgomery, "Spirits Get Stars."

8. Goldaper, "NBA Sets Price Tags."

9. Deford, "Bounding into Prominence."

10. Wolff, "Searching for a Promised Land."

11. Glockner, *Chasing Perfection*, 10–11.

12. Guth, "Basketball by the Numbers."

13. Schneider-Mayerson, "'Too Black.'"

14. Wolff, "Searching for a Promised Land."

15. Goldaper, "Malone Contract."

16. Creamer, "Moses and the Promised Land."

17. Guth, "Basketball by the Numbers."

18. LaFeber, *Michael Jordan*. For an analysis of these broader cultural shifts see Andrews, *Michael Jordan, Inc.* and Colás, *Ball Don't Lie!*

19. Basketball-Reference, "Allen Iverson Stats."

20. Berri, Schmidt, and Brook, *Wages of Wins*, 156.

21. Berri, Schmidt, and Brook, *Wages of Wins*, 156, 112.

22. Arnovitz and Pelton, "Allen Iverson's All-Time #NBArank."

23. Gladwell, "Game Theory."

24. Boyd, *Young, Black, Rich, and Famous*, 151–60.

25. Lane, *Under the Boards*, 36 and Leonard, *After Artest*.

26. George, *Elevating the Game*.

27. George, *Elevating the Game*.

9. THE WORK OF MOVING DOTS

1. Keller, *Tao of Statistics*, 1.

2. LaForest, "Nylon Questions."

3. Lewis, *Undoing Project*, 22–51.

4. Connolly, *Game Changer*.

5. Connolly, *Game Changer*.

6. Connolly, *Game Changer*.

7. Connolly, *Game Changer*.

8. Cervone et al., "POINTWISE," 1.

9. Cervone et al., "POINTWISE," 4.

10. Taylor, *Thinking Basketball*; Taylor, "Measuring Creation."

11. See for some examples of the analytics literature on shot selection, Restifo, "Nylon Calculus 101"; Shea, "Analytics and Shot Selection"; Baker, "Expected Points Model";

Maheswaran, "Advanced Tracking Data"; Shea, "Visualizing Player Shot Selection"; Levy, "Continuing Evolution" and "Shot Selection"; Kitnaw, "Player Types."

12. Goldsberry, *Sprawlball*. Goldsberry also addresses what he terms the "aesthetic" effects of these changes. I'll examine this aspect of his work in chapter 13.

13. Shea and Baker, *Basketball Analytics*, 51–54.

14. Glockner, *Chasing Perfection*, 106.

15. Natarajan, "Nylon Questions."

16. Glockner, *Chasing Perfection*, 118.

17. Glockner, *Biometrics*.

18. NBA, "Kevin Durant to Play."

19. Shiller, "Kerr Explains."

20. McCann, "Kevin Durant's Achilles Injury."

21. Magdalinski, *Sport, Technology, and the Body*, 80. McCann, "Kevin Durant's Achilles Injury."

22. Baerg, "Big Data, Sport, and the Digital Divide."

23. Pycior, "Nylon Questions."

24. Athletic Intelligence Measures, LLC, "Athletic Intelligence Measures."

25. Athletic Intelligence Measures, LLC, "Athletic Intelligence Measures."

26. Hewitt, *Conceptual Physics*, 41.

27. Whyte, *Heart Aroused*, 7.

10. APPROACHING BASKETBALL EXPERIENCE

1. Lloyd, "Final Thoughts."

2. Winfield, "LeBron James."

3. Paine, "Eastern Conference Crown."

4. Highkin, "NBA's New Tracking Stats."

5. Colás, *Ball Don't Lie!*

6. Shusterman, *Thinking Through the Body*, 27.

7. Richard Shusterman (about whom more below) describes projects in human-computer interaction that have sought to incorporate a user perspective into the design process, *Thinking Through the Body*, 12. See also Hook, *Designing with the Body*.

8. For an accessible introduction to Dewey's thought, including extensive discussion of his use of the term "experience," see Fesmire, *Dewey*.

9. Dewey, *Art as Experience*, 10–11.

10. See for a Deweyian approach to sport Elcombe, "Sport, Aesthetic Experience, and Art."

11. Dewey, *Art as Experience*, 18–25. Dewey's view of life as a systemic, complex process prefigures biological theories of life built upon complex systems theories that I will discuss further in chapter 11. See, for an accessible overview, Capra, *Web of Life*.

12. Dewey, *Art as Experience*, 20.
13. Dewey, *Art as Experience*, 24.
14. Dewey, *Art as Experience*, 24.
15. Dewey, *Art as Experience*, 25.
16. Koppett, *Essence of the Game*, 20.
17. Fesmire, *Dewey*, 214.
18. Dewey, *Art as Experience*, 352.
19. Dewey, *Art as Experience*, 20, 26.
20. Dewey, *Art as Experience*, 27.
21. Dewey, *Art as Experience*, 28.
22. Dewey, *Art as Experience*, 31.
23. Dewey, *Art as Experience*, 40.
24. Keats quoted in Dewey, *Art as Experience*, 34, 41.
25. Alexander, *Human Eros*, 390 and Dewey, *Art as Experience*, 352.

11. THE ETHICS OF UNDERSTANDING

1. Serres, *Genesis*, 2–3.
2. Whyte, *Heart Aroused*, 219.
3. For broad, accessible overviews of the field, see Gleick, *Chaos* and Capra, *Web of Life*. Somewhat narrow, yet still systematic accounts accessible to non-specialists include Holland, *Complexity* and Smith, *Chaos*.
4. For a general example see McGarry et al., "Sport Competition" and for one focusing on basketball specifically see García-Rubio et al., "Rating-Time Coordination."
5. Connolly, *Game Changer*, 21–22.
6. Whyte, *Heart Aroused*, 274.
7. Gitelman and Jackson, "Introduction," 2.
8. Kitchin, *Data Revolution*, 21.
9. Kitchin, *Data Revolution*, 2.
10. Dewey, "Recovery of Philosophy," 42.
11. Silver, *Signal and the Noise*.
12. Kitchin, *Data Revolution*, 165. Nor are these only the concerns of scholars. The same views have been expressed in some recent books by those with inside experience in the workings of, especially, big data analytics. See O'Neill, *Weapons of Math Destruction*; Muller, *Tyranny of Metrics*. And even a small but influential minority of sports writers has raised these issues, most notably Tom Haberstroh. See Torre and Haberstroh, "Increasingly Invasive Tests."
13. Andrejevic, "Surveillance in the Digital Enclosure," 297 and *Infoglut*, 17.
14. Baerg, "Digital Divide," 7.
15. Baerg, "Digital Divide," 8–11.

16. Baerg, "Digital Divide," 11–15 and, for more details on the situation in the NBA, see Torre and Haberstroh.

17. Fesmire, *Dewey*, 152 and Dewey, *Individualism, Old and New*, 108.

18. Fesmire, *Dewey*, 210.

19. Naess, quoted in Capra, *Web of life*, 7–8.

20. Fesmire, *Dewey*, 212–13.

INTERLUDE—BASKETBALL SUPERNATURAL

1. Bernard, *Medicina experimental*, 93.

2. Bernard, *Medicina experimental*, 94.

3. Bernard, *Medicina experimental*, 95.

4. Bernard, *Medicina experimental*, 95.

12. FEELING BASKETBALL

1. Shusterman, *Thinking Through the Body*, 35.

2. Atkinson, "Essence of Being," 363.

3. McHugh, Bronson, and Watters, "Future of the Athlete."

4. Atkinson, "Essence of Being," 364.

5. Naismith, *Basketball*, 55.

6. Rains and Carpenter, *James Naismith*, 80; Boxill, "Competition," 343.

7. Connor, *Philosophy of Sport*, 151–53.

8. Naismith, "Basket Ball," (1914), 346.

9. Eagleton, *Ideology of the Aesthetic*, 13.

10. Dewey, *Art as Experience*.

11. Gumbrecht, *Praise of Athletic Beauty*, 68.

12. Gumbrecht, *Praise of Athletic Beauty*, 168.

13. Woodward, *Embodied Sporting Practices*.

14. Koppett, *Essence of the Game*, 20.

15. Gumbrecht, *Praise of Athletic Beauty*, 77.

16. Mumford, *Watching Sport*, 140.

17. Todorov, *Fantastic*, 25.

18. Ryan, "The Show Is Michael Jordan's."

19. Bynum, "Wonder."

20. Quoted in Rothenberg, *Flight from Wonder*, 179.

21. Horkheimer and Adorno, *Dialectic of Enlightenment*, 1.

22. Stengers, "Diderot's Egg," 7, 11.

23. Stengers, "Diderot's Egg," 11–12.

24. Lewis, *Undoing Project*, 15–51; Taylor, *Thinking Basketball*.

13. COUNTING WHAT COUNTS

1. See, for example, Goldsberry, "Golden State Warriors."
2. NBA, "'Best Analytics Organization'"; Beardsley, "Winning with Data Science."
3. Schoenfeld, "Venture Capitalists."
4. Booton, "Andre Iguodala"; Bradley, "Warriors' Stephen Curry"; Lemire, "Kevin Durant Discusses Tech."
5. Whitehead, "Ruin the NBA?"
6. Basketball-Reference, "NBA Win Shares."
7. Pelton, "My All-Time Rankings."
8. Whitehead, "NBA Top 50."
9. Goldsberry, *Sprawlball*, 2.
10. Goldsberry, *Sprawlball*, 199.
11. Goldsberry, *Sprawlball*, 201.
12. Berry, *Unsettling of America*, 178.

CODA

1. De Mello, *Way to Love*, 36.

BIBLIOGRAPHY

Ackerman, Diane. *Deep Play*. New York: Vintage Books, 1999.

A. G. Spalding and Brothers. "Complete Basket Ball Outfit." In *Spalding's Official Basket Ball Guide*, 168–69. New York: American Sports Publishing, 1903.

Alamar, Benjamin. "A First Step." *Journal of Quantitative Analysis in Sports* 1, no. 1 (April 2005).

Alamar, Benjamin C. *Sports Analytics: A Guide for Coaches, Managers, and Other Decision Makers*. New York: Columbia University Press, 2013.

Albert, Jim, and Ruud H. Koning, eds. *Statistical Thinking in Sports*. New York: Chapman and Hall/CRC, 2008.

Alexander, Jennifer Karns. *The Mantra of Efficiency: From the Waterwheel to Social Control*. Baltimore: Johns Hopkins University Press, 2008.

Alexander, Thomas M. *The Human Eros: Eco-Ontology and the Aesthetics of Existence*. New York: Fordham University Press, 2013.

———. *John Dewey's Theory of Art, Experience, and Nature: The Horizons of Feeling*. Albany: State University of New York Press, 1987.

Allen, Forrest C. "Address by the President." *The Athletic Journal* 9, no. 10 (June 1929): 15.

———. *My Basket-Ball Bible*. Kansas City: Smith-Grieves, 1924. https://babel.hathitrust .org/cgi/pt?id=mdp.39015015214847;view=2up;seq=2.

Allen, L. W. "Basket Ball at Hartford, Conn." *Physical Education* 3, no. 4 (June 1894): 58.

Allen, W. E. "Forward." *Physical Education* 4, no. 3 (May 1895): 45–46.

Anderson, Harry. "Afternoon Session." In *Proceedings of the American Association for the Advancement of Physical Education*. Brooklyn: Rome Brothers, 1886.

Andrejevic, Mark. *Infoglut: How Too Much Information Is Changing the Way We Think and Know*. New York: Routledge, 2013.

———. "Surveillance in the Digital Enclosure." *The Communication Review* 10, no. 4 (2007): 295–317. https://doi.org/10.1080/10714420701715365.

Andrews, David L., ed. *Michael Jordan, Inc.: Corporate Sport, Media Culture, and Late Modern America.* Albany: State University of New York Press, 2001.

Andrews, David L., and Ben Carrington, eds. *A Companion to Sport.* Oxford: Wiley-Blackwell, 2013.

Angell, E. D. *Basket Ball for Coach, Player, and Spectator.* New York: Thos. E. Wilson, 1921.

Applin, Albert G. "From Muscular Christianity to the Market Place: The History of Boys' and Men's Basketball in the United States, 1891–1957." PhD diss., University of Massachusetts, 1982.

Arnovitz, Kevin, and Kevin Pelton. "Allen Iverson's All-Time #NBArank." ESPN.com, January 27, 2016. http://espn.go.com/blog/truehoop/post/_/id/74002.

Association Notes, Providence, RI. "Clippings ('Basket Ball Fever')." *Physical Education* 2 (March 1893): 15.

Athletic Intelligence Measures, LLC. "The AIQ Will Help You Find Hidden Gems That Others May Overlook." Athletic Intelligence Measures, 2019. http://athleticintel .com/aiq/.

Atkinson, Michael. "Heidegger, Parkour, Post-Sport, and the Essence of Being." In *A Companion to Sport,* edited by David L. Andrews and Ben Carrington, 359–74. West Sussex, UK: Blackwell, 2013.

Badenhausen, Kurt, and Mike Ozanian. "NBA Team Values 2019: Knicks on Top at $4 Billion." Forbes, February 6, 2019. https://www.forbes.com/sites/kurtbadenhausen /2019/02/06/nba-team-values-2019-knicks-on-top-at-4-billion/.

Baerg, Andrew. "Big Data, Sport, and the Digital Divide: Theorizing How Athletes Might Respond to Big Data Monitoring." *Journal of Sport and Social Issues* (2016): 1–18.

Baker, Chris. "How an NBA Team Can Use an Expected Points Model." *Basketball Analytics* (blog). March 16, 2016. https://www.basketballanalyticsbook.com /2016/03/16/how-an-NBA-team-can-use-an-expected-points-model/. No longer valid.

Ballard, Chris. "Measure of Success." *Sports Illustrated,* October 24, 2005.

Basketball-Reference. "Allen Iverson Stats." Basketball-Reference.com. Accessed July 16, 2019. https://www.basketball-reference.com/players/i/iversal01.html.

———. "NBA Win Shares." Basketball-Reference.com, n.d. https://www.basketball -reference.com/about/ws.html.

Baumer, Andrew, and Andrew Zimbalist. *The Sabermetric Revolution: Assessing the Growth of Analytics in Baseball.* Philadelphia: University of Pennsylvania Press, 2013.

Beardsley, Bove. "Winning with Data Science, Golden State Warriors Style." *Dataconomy* (blog). July 4, 2017. https://dataconomy.com/2017/07/golden-state-warriors -data-science/.

Bellotti, Robert. *Basketball's Hidden Game: Points Created, Boxscore Defense, and Other Revelations*. New Brunswick NJ: Night Work Publishing, 1988.

Berenson, Senda. "Basket Ball for Women." *Physical Education* 3, no. 7 (September 1894): 106–9.

Bernard, Claude. *An Introduction to the Study of Experimental Medicine*. Translated by Henry Copley Greene. Henry Schuman, 1949.

Bernard, Claudio. *Introducción al estudio de la medicina experimental*. Buenos Aires: Emecé, 1865.

Bernstein, Peter L. *Against the Gods: The Remarkable Story of Risk*. New York: John Wiley and Sons, 1996.

Berri, Dave. "How to Calculate Wins Produced—The Wages of Wins Journal." *The Wages of Wins Journal* (blog). 2011. http://wagesofwins.com/how-to-calculate -wins-produced/.

Berri, David J., Martin B. Schmidt, and Stacey L. Brook. *The Wages of Wins: Taking Measure of the Many Myths in Modern Sport*. Stanford: Stanford University Press, 2006.

Berry, Wendell. *The Unsettling of America: Culture and Agriculture*. San Francisco: Sierra Club Books, 1977.

Berryman, Jack W., and Roberta J. Park, eds. *Sport and Exercise Science: Essays in the History of Sports Medicine*. Champaign: University of Illinois Press, 1992.

Bliss, James G. "Measuring Individual Squad and Team Progress." In *Basketball: A Text-Book for Coaches, Players, Recreation Leaders, Students and Teachers of Physical Education*, 179–97. Philadelphia: Lea and Febiger, 1929.

Booton, Jen. "Golden State Warriors' Andre Iguodala on Wearables, Tech Investing, Golf." SportTechie, August 11, 2017. https://www.sporttechie.com/warriors-andre -iguodala-talks-wearables-and-tech-investing/.

Bovard, John F., Frederick W. Cozens, and E. Patricia Hagman. *Tests and Measurements in Physical Education*. Philadelphia: W. B. Saunders, 1949.

Boxill, Jan. "Competition." In *The Bloomsbury Companion to the Philosophy of Sport*, edited by Cesar R. Torres, 343–44. New York: Bloomsbury, 2015.

Boyd, Todd. *Young, Black, Rich, and Famous: The Rise of the NBA, the Hip Hop Invasion, and the Transformation of American Culture*. Lincoln: University of Nebraska Press, 2008.

Bradley, Logan "Golden State Warriors' Stephen Curry Shows Kids Importance of Coding." SportTechie, December 21, 2017. https://www.sporttechie.com/golden -state-warriors-stephen-curry-code-org-kids-importance-coding/.

Brace, David Kingsley. *Measuring Motor Ability: A Scale of Motor Ability Tests*. New York: A. S. Barnes, 1930. https://babel.hathitrust.org/cgi/pt?id=mdp.39015020830660 ;view=2up;seq=1.

———. "Testing Basketball Technique." *American Physical Education Review* 29 (April 1924): 159–65.

Brief, Sam. "SportVU Analytics Taking Hold in College Hoops." *Sports Brief* (blog). April 15, 2015. https://thesportsbrief.net/2015/04/15/sportvu-analytics-taking -hold-in-college-hoops/. No longer valid.

Burke, Kenneth. *A Rhetoric of Motives.* Berkeley: University of California Press, 1969.

Burns, Ken. "First Inning: Our Game." *Baseball.* PBS, September 18, 1994. http://www .pbs.org/kenburns/baseball/about/credits1.html.

Bynum, Caroline Walker. "Wonder." *American Historical Review* 102, no. 1 (February 1997): 1–26.

Caillois, Roger. *Man, Play and Games.* Translated by Meyer Barash. Urbana: University of Illinois Press, 2001.

Cairo, Alberto. *The Truthful Art: Data, Charts, and Maps for Communication.* New Riders, 2016.

Cameron, William Bruce. *Informal Sociology: A Casual Introduction to Sociological Thinking.* New York: Random House, 1963.

Capra, Fritjof. *The Web of Life: A New Scientific Understanding of Living Systems.* New York: Anchor, 1996.

Carlson, H. C. "Methods in Teaching Basketball Skills." *Journal of Health and Physical Education* 6, no. 9 (November 1935): 37–43. https://doi.org/10.1080/23267240 .1935.10625735.

Carow, J. W. "Standardized Scheme for Scoring in Basket Ball." *American Physical Education Review* 32, no. 8 (October 1927): 616–25. https://doi.org/10.1080/23267224 .1927.10651887.

Case, Everett N. "An Analysis of the Effects of Various Factors on the Accuracy of Shooting Free Throws in Basketball." Master's thesis, University of Southern California, 1934.

Catapult Sports. *Why Athlete Analytics?,* 2013. https://www.youtube.com/watch?v= iF3kpaMGV6w.

Cavallo, Dominick. *Muscles and Morals: Organized Playgrounds and Urban Reform, 1880–1920.* Philadelphia: University of Pennsylvania Press, 1981.

Cervone, Dan, Alexander D'Amour, Luke Bornn, and Kirk Goldsberry. "POINTWISE: Predicting Points and Valuing Decisions in Real Time with NBA Optical Tracking Data." Cambridge MA, 2014.

Challaye, Félicien. *Metodología de las ciencias.* Translated by Emilio Huidobro and Edith Tech de Huidobro. Barcelona: Editorial Labor, 1935.

Chang, Yu-Han, Rajiv Maheswaran, Jeff Su, Sheldon Kwok, Tal Levy, Adam Wexler, and Kevin Squire. "Quantifying Shot Quality in the NBA." 2014. http://www.sloans-portsconference.com/wp-content/uploads/2014/02/2014-SSAC-Quantifying -Shot-Quality-in-the-NBA.pdf.

Clarke, H. Harrison. *The Application of Measurement to Health and Physical Education.* New York: Prentice-Hall, 1945.

Clinchy, Evans. "How Important Is the 3-Point Shot in Today's NBA?" *Nylon Calculus* (blog). February 13, 2015. http://nyloncalculus.com/2015/02/13/important-three -point-shot-todays-nba/.

Cohan, Noah. *We Average Unbeautiful Watchers: Fan Narratives and the Reading of American Sports.* Lincoln: University of Nebraska Press, 2019.

Cohen, Patricia Cline. *A Calculating People: The Spread of Numeracy in Early America.* Chicago: University of Chicago Press, 1982.

Colás, Santiago. "Telling True Stories, or the Immanent Ethics of Material Spirit (and Spiritual Matter) in Philip Pullman's His Dark Materials." *Discourse* 27, no. 1 (Winter 2005): 34–66.

Colás, Yago. *Ball Don't Lie! Myth, Genealogy, and Invention in the Culture of Basketball.* Philadelphia: Temple University Press, 2016.

———. "Getting Free: The Arts and Politics of Basketball Modernity." *Journal of Sport and Social Issues* 39, no. 4 (2015): 267–86.

Connolly, Fergus. *Game Changer: The Art of Sports Science.* Las Vegas: Victory Belt, 2017.

Connor, Steven. *A Philosophy of Sport.* New York: Reaktion, 2011.

Cooper, Andrew. *Playing in the Zone: Exploring the Spiritual Dimension of Sports.* Boston: Shambhala, 1998.

Coy, John, and Joe Morse. *Hoop Genius: How a Desperate Teacher and a Rowdy Gym Class Invented Basketball.* Minneapolis: Carolrhoda Books, 2013.

Creamer, Robert. "Moses and the Promised Land." *Sports Illustrated*, September 13, 1982.

Criblez, Adam J. *Tall Tales and Short Shorts: Dr. J, Pistol Pete, and the Birth of the Modern NBA.* Lanham MD: Rowman and Littlefield, 2017.

Crosby, Alfred W. *The Measure of Reality: Quantification in Western Society, 1250–1600.* New York: Cambridge University Press, 1997.

Cross, Thomas J. "A Comparison of the Whole Method, the Minor Game Method, and the Whole Part Method of Teaching Basketball to Ninth-Grade Boys." *Research Quarterly. American Physical Education Association* 8, no. 4 (December 1, 1937): 49–54. https://doi.org/10.1080/23267402.1937.10761849.

Crowther, Nigel B. *Sport in Ancient Times.* Westport CT: Praeger, 2007.

Csikszentmihalyi, Mihaly. *Flow: The Psychology of Optimal Experience.* New York: Harper and Row, 1990.

Cummings, Robert A. "A Study of the Effect of Basketball Practice on Motor Reaction, Attention and Suggestion, and Suggestibility." *Psychological Review* 21 (January 1914): 356–69.

Dantzig, Tobias. *Number: The Language of Science.* Edited by Joseph Mazur. New York: Plume, 2007.

Daston, Lorraine. *Classical Probability in the Enlightenment.* Princeton: Princeton University Press, 1988.

Daston, Lorraine, and Peter Galison. *Objectivity*. New York: Zone Books, 2010.

Davenport, Thomas H., and Jeanne G. Harris. *Competing on Analytics: The New Science of Winning*. Updated, with a new introduction. Boston: Harvard Business Review Press, 2017.

Dean, Everett. *Progressive Basketball*. New York: Prentice-Hall, 1942.

Deford, Frank. "Bounding into Prominence." *Sports Illustrated*, February 19, 1979.

Dehaene, Stanislas. *The Number Sense: How the Mind Creates Mathematics*. New York: Oxford University Press, 2011.

De Mello, Anthony. *The Way to Love: The Last Meditations of Anthony de Mello*. New York: Image Books, 1995.

DesCombes, Don. "The Use of a Self-Rating Chart for Basketball." *Athletic Journal* 20, no. 4 (December 1939): 11.

Detrick, Ben. "Closing Basketball's Gender Data Gap." *New Yorker*, June 4, 2015. http://www.newyorker.com/news/sporting-scene/closing-basketballs-gender-data-gap.

Dewey, John. *Art as Experience*. Edited by Jo Ann Boydston. Vol. 10: 1934. The Later Works, 1925–1953. Carbondale: Southern Illinois University Press, 2008.

———. *Experience and Nature*. Edited by Jo Ann Boydston. Vol. 1: 1925. The Later Works, 1925–1953. Carbondale: Southern Illinois University Press, 2008.

———. *Individualism, Old and New*. Edited by Jo Ann Boydston. Vol. 5: 1929–1930. The Later Works, 1925–1953. Carbondale: Southern Illinois University Press, 2008.

———. "The Need for a Recovery of Philosophy." In *The Middle Works, 1899–1924*, edited by Jo Ann Boydston, 3–48. Collected Works of John Dewey. Carbondale: Southern Illinois University Press, 2008.

Dill, W. A. "Useful Plan for Scoring Basketball." *Athletic Journal* 16, no. 6 (February 1936): 31.

Dimick, Harold A. "Formulation of a Basketball Scoring Method That Will Measure General Offensive Efficiency." Master's thesis, University of Southern California, 1938.

Dorgan, Ethel Josephine. *Luther Halsey Gulick, 1865–1918*. New York: Bureau of Publications, Teachers College, Columbia University, 1934.

Dyer, Joanna T., Jennie C. Schurig, and Sara L. Apgar. "A Basketball Motor Ability Test for College Women and Secondary School Girls." *Research Quarterly. American Association for Health, Physical Education, and Recreation* 10, no. 3 (October 1, 1939): 128–47. https://doi.org/10.1080/10671188.1939.10622502.

Eagleton, Terry. *The Ideology of the Aesthetic*. Malden MA: Blackwell, 1990.

Egan, Kieran. *The Educated Mind: How Cognitive Tools Shape Our Understanding*. Chicago: University of Chicago Press, 1997.

Elbel, E. R., and Forrest C. Allen. "Evaluating Team and Individual Performance in Basketball." *Research Quarterly. American Association for Health, Physical Education, and*

Recreation 12, no. 3 (October 1, 1941): 538–55. https://doi.org/10.1080/10671188.1941.10624668.

Elcombe, Tim L. "Philosophers Can't Jump: Reflections on Living Time and Space in Basketball." In *Basketball and Philosophy*, edited by Jerry Walls and Gregory Bassham, 207–19. Lexington: University Press of Kentucky, 2008.

———. "Sport, Aesthetic Experience, and Art as the Ideal Embodied Metaphor." *Journal of the Philosophy of Sport* 39, no. 2 (2012): 201–17.

Erving, Julius. *Dr. J: The Autobiography*. New York: Harper, 2013.

Fay, Paul J., and Lloyd L. Messersmith. "Distances Traversed by College and High School Basketball Players and Effect of Rule Changes Upon Distance Traversed in College Games." *Athletic Journal* 18, no. 9 (May 1938): 37.

———. "The Effect of Rule Changes upon the Distance Traversed by Basketball Players." *Research Quarterly. American Association for Health and Physical Education* 9, no. 2 (May 1, 1938): 136–37. https://doi.org/10.1080/23267429.1938.10625086.

Feezell, Randolph. "A Pluralist Conception of Play." In *The Philosophy of Play*, edited by Emily Ryall, Wendy Russell, and Malcolm MacLean, 11–31. New York: Routledge, 2013.

———. *Sport, Play, and Ethical Reflection*. Urbana: University of Illinois Press, 2012.

Fesmire, Steven. *Dewey*. New York: Routledge, 2015.

Fisher, Eric. "Colleges Offer Analytics Track." Sports Business Daily, June 5, 2017. https://www.sportsbusinessdaily.com/Journal/Issues/2017/06/05/In-Depth/Data-side.aspx.

Flowers, Andrew. "Russell Westbrook Is the Greatest Triple-Double Machine in Recorded History." *FiveThirtyEight* (blog). April 11, 2016. https://fivethirtyeight.com/features/russell-westbrook-is-the-greatest-triple-double-machine-in-recorded-history/.

FreeDarko Collective. *FreeDarko Presents the Undisputed Guide to Pro Basketball History*. New York: Bloomsbury, 2010.

Fried, Gil, and Ceyda Mumcu, eds. *Sport Analytics: A Data-Driven Approach to Sport Business and Management*. New York: Routledge, 2017.

Friermood, H. T. "Basketball Progress Tests Adaptable to Class Use." *Journal of Health and Physical Education* 5, no. 1 (January 1934): 45–47. https://doi.org/10.1080/23267240.1934.10620662.

Fusionetics. "Athlete Management System." *Fusionetics* (blog). Accessed May 12, 2018. http://www.fusionetics.com/solutions/sports/athlete-management-system/. No longer valid.

Gallagher, Shaun, Lauren Reinerman-Jones, Bruce Janz, Patricia Bockelman, and Jorg Trempler. *A Neurophenomenology of Awe and Wonder: Toward a Non-Reductionist Cognitive Science*. New York: Palgrave Macmillan, 2015.

García-Rubio, Javier, Miguel Ángel Gómez, María Cañadas, and J. Sergio Ibáñez. "Offensive Rating-Time Coordination Dynamics in Basketball. Complex Systems Theory Applied to Basketball." *International Journal of Performance Analysis in Sport* 15, no. 2 (August 1, 2015): 513–26. https://doi.org/10.1080/24748668.2015.11868810.

George, Nelson. *Elevating the Game: Black Men and Basketball*. Lincoln: University of Nebraska Press, 1999.

Gerber, Ellen W. *Innovators and Institutions in Physical Education*. Philadelphia: Lea and Febiger, 1971.

Gibble, Alfred T. "Hitting Averages in Basketball." *Athletic Journal* 20, no. 3 (November 1939): 46.

———. "An Individual Basketball Rating Chart." *Athletic Journal* 19, no. 2 (October 1938): 26.

Gigerenzer, Gerd, Zeno Swijtink, Theodore Porter, Lorraine Daston, John Beatty, and Lorenz Krüger. *The Empire of Chance: How Probability Changed Science and Everyday Life*. New York: Cambridge University Press, 1989.

Gitelman, Lisa, and Virginia Jackson. "Introduction." In *Raw Data Is an Oxymoron*, 1–14. Cambridge MA: MIT Press, 2013.

Gladwell, Malcolm. "Game Theory." *New Yorker*, May 29, 2006. http://www.newyorker.com/magazine/2006/05/29/game-theory-2.

Glassow, Ruth B., Valarie Colvin, and Marguerite M. Schwarz. "Studies in Measuring Basketball Playing Ability of College Women." *Research Quarterly. American Association for Health and Physical Education* 9, no. 4 (December 1, 1938): 60–68. https://doi.org/10.1080/23267429.1938.11802465.

Gleick, James. *Chaos: Making a New Science*. New York: Viking, 1987.

Glockner, Andy. *Biometrics: The Next (and Biggest) Analytics Frontier (Sport Science Track)*, 2016. http://www.sloansportsconference.com/content/biometrics-the-next-and-biggest-analytics-frontier/.

———. *Chasing Perfection: A Behind-the-Scenes Look at the High-Stakes Game of Creating an NBA Champion*. Philadelphia: DaCapo, 2016.

Goldsberry, Kirk. "CourtVision: New Visual and Spatial Analytics for the NBA," 2012.

———. "DataBall." *Grantland* (blog). February 6, 2014. http://grantland.com/features/expected-value-possession-NBA-analytics/.

———. "Department of Defense." *Grantland* (blog). February 24, 2015. http://grantland.com/features/department-of-defense/.

———. "How the Golden State Warriors Are Breaking the NBA." *FiveThirtyEight* (blog). November 24, 2015. https://fivethirtyeight.com/features/how-the-golden-state-warriors-are-breaking-the-NBA/.

———. *Sprawlball: A Visual Tour of the New Era of the NBA*. New York: Houghton Mifflin Harcourt, 2019.

Goldsberry, Kirk, and Eric Weiss. "The Dwight Effect: A New Ensemble of Interior Defense Analytics for the NBA." Boston MA, 2013.

Gould, Ronald J. *Mathematics in Games, Sports, and Gambling.* New York: CRC Press, 2010.

Gould, Stephen Jay. *The Mismeasure of Man.* New York: Norton, 1996.

Griffith, Coleman R. "Experiments in Basketball." *Athletic Journal* 10 (June 1930): 9–12.

Griffith-Clark Physical Education Service Co. *Fundamentals of Basketball: Arranged in Text Book Form.* Champaign: Griffith-Clark Physical Education Service, 1900.

Gulick, Luther. "Basket Ball." *Physical Education* 4, no. 9 (November 1895): 120.

———. "Editorial." In *Spalding Official Basket Ball Guide,* edited by Luther Gulick, 5–15. New York: American Sports Publishing, 1898.

———. *The Efficient Life.* New York: Doubleday, 1913.

———. "Ethics of Basketball." In *Official Basket Ball Rules,* edited by Luther Gulick, 5–10. New York: American Sports Publishing, 1896.

———. "How to Score Basket Ball." In *Spalding's Official Basket Ball Guide 1898–1899,* edited by Luther Gulick, 100–101. New York: American Sports Publishing, 1898.

———. "How to Score Basket Ball." In *Spalding's Official Basket Ball Guide,* edited by George C. Hepbron, 154–55. New York: American Sports Publishing, 1903.

———. "How to Use Basket Ball." In *Spalding's Official Basket Ball Guide,* 31–33. New York: American Sports Publishing, 1896.

———. "Our Platform." *Physical Education* 1, no. 1 (March 1892): 2–6.

———. *A Philosophy of Play.* New York: Charles Scribner and Sons, 1920.

———. "Physical Education: A New Profession." In *Proceedings of the American Association for the Advancement of Physical Education.* Ithaca: Andrus and Church, 1890.

———. "Physical Health, Education, Recreation." *Triangle* 1, no. 4 (May 15, 1891): 56–58.

Gumbrecht, Hans Ulrich. *In Praise of Athletic Beauty.* Cambridge MA: Belknap Press, 2006.

Guth, Louis A. "Basketball by the Numbers: Free Agents, Computers, and the NBA." N/E/R/A Topics. White Plains NY: National Economic Research Associates, 1984.

Guttman, Allen. *From Ritual to Record: The Nature of Modern Sports.* New York: Columbia University Press, 2004.

Hacking, Ian. *The Emergence of Probability: A Philosophical Study of Early Ideas about Probability Induction and Statistical Inference.* New York: Cambridge University Press, 2006.

———. *The Taming of Chance.* Cambridge, UK: Cambridge University Press, 1990.

Halpern, Orit. *Beautiful Data: A History of Vision and Reason since 1945.* Durham NC: Duke University Press, 2014.

Halsted, A. T. "Basket Ball." *Physical Education* 3, no. 5 (July 1894): 76.

Hammett, C. E. "How Basket Ball Affects College Men." *American Physical Education Review* 23, no. 5 (May 1918): 309–16.

Hand, David J. *Measurement Theory and Practice: The World through Quantification.* London: Arnold, 2004.

Hankins, Thomas L. *Science and the Enlightenment.* Cambridge, UK: Cambridge University Press, 1985.

Hashagen, Kenneth A. "Scoring Charts." *Athletic Journal* 19, no. 4 (December 1938): 20.

Hawhee, Debra. *Bodily Arts: Rhetoric and Athletics in Ancient Greece.* Austin: University of Texas Press, 2004.

Heeren, Dave, and Pete Palmer. *Basic Ball: New Approaches for Determining the Greatest Baseball, Football, and Basketball Players of All-Time.* Haworth NJ: St. Johann Press, 2011.

Heitner, Darren. "The NBA's Six Year, $250 Million Data Deal." *Forbes*, September 22, 2016. https://www.forbes.com/sites/darrenheitner/2016/09/22/the-nbas-six-year-250-million-data-deal/#27c7f80c481d.

Henry, John. "Bill James." Time.com. May 8, 2006. http://content.time.com/time/specials/packages/article/0,28804,1975813_1975844_1976446,00.html.

Hepbron, George T., ed. "Official Rules, Season 1903–1904." In *Spalding's Official Basket Ball Guide*, 68–90. New York: American Sports Publishing, 1903.

Hewitt, Paul. *Conceptual Physics.* 12th ed. Glenview IL: Pearson Education, 2015.

Hickey, Dave. "The Heresy of Zone Defense." In *Air Guitar: Essays on Art and Democracy*, by Dave Hickey, 155–62. Los Angeles: Art Issues Press, 1997.

Hines, Clarence. "An Efficiency Rating Chart for Basketball Players." *Athletic Journal* 16, no. 3 (November 1935): 24.

Hitchcock, Edward. *The Need of Anthropometry.* Brooklyn: Rome Brothers, 1887.

———. "President Hitchock's Address." In *Proceedings of the American Association for the Advancement of Physical Education.* Brooklyn: Rome Brothers, 1887.

Hoberman, John. *Mortal Engines: The Science of Performance and the Dehumanization of Sport.* Caldwell NJ: Blackburn Press, 1992.

Hobsbawm, Eric. *The Age of Revolution, 1789–1848.* New York: Vintage, 1996.

Hobson, Howard. *Scientific Basketball.* New York: Prentice-Hall, 1949.

Holland, John. *Complexity: A Very Short Introduction.* New York: Oxford University Press, 2014.

Holman, Nat. *Scientific Basketball.* New York: Incra Publishing, 1922.

Holowchak, M. Andrew, and Heather L. Reid. *Aretism: An Ancient Sports Philosophy for the Modern Sports World.* New York: Lexington Books, 2011.

Hook, Kia. *Designing with the Body: Somaesthetic Interaction Design.* Cambridge MA: MIT Press, 2018.

Horger, Marc T. "Play by the Rules: The Creation of Basketball and the Progressive Era, 1891–1917." Ohio State University, 2001.

Horkheimer, Max, and Theodor W. Adorno. *The Dialectic of Enlightenment: Philosophical Fragments*. Edited by Gunzelin Schmid Noerr. Translated by Edmund Jephcott. Stanford: Stanford University Press, 2002.

Huizinga, Johan. *Homo Ludens: A Study of the Play-Element in Culture*. New York: Roy Publishers, 1950.

Hyland, Drew A. *Philosophy of Sport*. St. Paul MN: Paragon House, 1990.

Ifrah, Georges. *The Universal History of Numbers: From Prehistory to the Invention of the Computer*. Translated by David Bellos, E. F. Harding, Sophie Wood, and Ian Monk. New York: John Wiley and Sons, 2000.

International Committee of Young Men's Christian Associations. *Basket Ball Rules and Score Blanks 1895*. New York: International Committee of Young Men's Christian Associations, 1894.

"Is Basket-Ball a Danger: The Subject Fully Discussed." *Young Men's Era*, August 16, 1894.

Keller, Dana K. *The Tao of Statistics: A Path to Understanding (With No Math)*. Thousand Oaks: Sage, 2006.

Kimball, Edward. "Comparative Study of the Whole and Part Methods of Teaching Basketball Fundamentals." Master's thesis, University of Southern California, 1934.

Kitchin, Rob. *The Data Revolution: Big Data, Open Data, Data Infrastructures, and Their Consequences*. New York: Sage, 2014.

Kitnaw, Natnael. "Player Types by Shot Selection." *Nylon Calculus* (blog). August 8, 2018. https://fansided.com/2018/08/08/nylon-calculus-player-type-shot-selection/.

Knaflic, Cole Nussbaumer. *Storytelling with Data: A Data Visualization Guide for Business Professionals*. Hoboken NJ: John Wiley and Sons, 2015.

Koppett, Leonard. *The Essence of the Game Is Deception: Thinking about Basketball*. Boston: Little, Brown, 1973.

Kramnick, Isaac. "Introduction." In *The Portable Enlightenment Reader*, edited by Isaac Kramnick, ix–xxviii. New York: Penguin, 1995.

Kreiswirth, Carrie. "ESPN *The Magazine*'s Analytics of the NBA Body Issue, on Newsstands Friday." ESPN MediaZone. February 16, 2016. http://espnmediazone.com/us/press-releases/2016/02/espn-the-magazines-analytics-of-the-NBA-body-issue-on-newsstands-friday/.

Kroll, Walter P. *Perspectives in Physical Education*. New York: Academic Press, 1971.

Kubatko, Justin, Dean Oliver, Kevin Pelton, and Dan T. Rosenbaum. "A Starting Point for Analyzing Basketball Statistics." *Journal of Quantitative Analysis in Sports* 3, no. 3 (July 2007): Article 1.

Kula, Witold. *Measures and Men*. Princeton: Princeton University Press, 2014.

Kurz, Heinz D. "Adam Smith on Markets, Competition, and Violations of Natural Liberty." *Cambridge Journal of Economics* 40, no. 2 (2016): 615–38.

Kwa, Chunglin. *Styles of Knowing: A New History of Science from Ancient Times to the Present.* Translated by David McKay. Pittsburgh: University of Pittsburgh Press, 2011.

Kyle, Donald G. "Greek Athletic Competitions: The Ancient Olympics and More." In *A Companion to Sport and Spectacle in Greek and Roman Antiquity,* edited by Paul Christesen and Donald G. Kyle, 21–35. Malden MA: John Wiley and Sons, 2014.

———. *Sport and Spectacle in the Ancient World.* Oxford: Blackwell, 2007.

LaFeber, Walter. *Michael Jordan and the New Global Capitalism,* exp. ed. New York: Norton, 2002.

LaForest, Scott. "Nylon Questions: How Can We Predict Performance for Incoming NBA Players?" *Nylon Calculus* (blog). October 1, 2018. https://fansided.com/2018/10/01/nylon-calculus-predict-performance-incoming-NBA-players/.

Lahman, Sean. "History By the Numbers." In *Total Basketball: The Ultimate Basketball Encyclopedia,* 753. Toronto: Sport Media Publishing, 2003.

Lakoff, George, and Rafael Núñez. *Where Mathematics Comes From: How the Embodied Mind Brings Mathematics into Being.* New York: Basic Books, 2000.

Lane, Jeffrey. *Under the Boards: The Cultural Revolution in Basketball.* Lincoln: University of Nebraska Press, 2007.

Lee, Mabel. *A History of Physical Education and Sports in the U.S.A.* New York: John Wiley and Sons, 1983.

Lemire, Joe. "Kevin Durant Discusses Tech in Upcoming Episode of 'The Boardroom.'" SportTechie. March 14, 2019. https://www.sporttechie.com/exclusive-kevin-durant-steve-nash-espn-boardroom/.

Leonard, David J. *After Artest: The NBA and the Assault on Blackness.* Albany: SUNY Press, 2012.

Levy, Ian. "The Continuing Evolution of NBA Shot Selection." *Nylon Calculus* (blog). March 16, 2018. https://fansided.com/2018/03/16/nylon-calculus-continuing-evolution-NBA-shot-selection/.

———. "Offensive Style Changes for the 2017–18 Season." *Nylon Calculus* (blog). March 7, 2018. https://fansided.com/2018/03/07/nylon-calculus-offensive-style-changes-2017-18-season/.

———. "Why Is Shot Selection so Important?" *Nylon Calculus* (blog). May 8, 2018. https://fansided.com/2018/05/08/nylon-calculus-shot-selection-important/.

Lewis, Michael. *Moneyball: The Art of Winning an Unfair Game.* New York: Norton, 2003.

———. "The No-Stats All-Star." *New York Times Magazine,* February 13, 2009. http://www.nytimes.com/2009/02/15/magazine/15Battier-t.html.

———. *The Undoing Project: A Friendship That Changed Our Minds.* New York: Norton, 2017.

Lindstrom, Don. "Colas, Edgewood Slip Past Middleton." *Wisconsin State Journal,* February 9, 1983, sec. Sports.

Lloyd, Jason. "Final Thoughts: On LeBron James and the Speed Required To . . ." The Athletic. Accessed May 22, 2018. https://theathletic.com/363766/2018/05/22/final-thoughts-on-lebron-james-and-the-speed-required-to-tie-this-series/.

Loeffelholz, Bernard, Earl Bednar, and Kenneth W. Bauer. "Predicting NBA Games Using Neural Networks." *Journal of Quantitative Analysis in Sports* 5, no. 1 (January 2009).

Magdalinski, Tara. *Sport, Technology, and the Body: The Nature of Performance.* New York: Routledge, 2009.

Maheswaran, Mahesh. "The Three Dimensions of Rebounding | MIT Sloan Sports Analytics Conference." February 28, 2014. http://www.sloansportsconference.com/?p=13011.

Maheswaran, Rajiv. *The Math behind Basketball's Wildest Moves.* Accessed June 28, 2019. https://www.ted.com/talks/rajiv_maheswaran_the_math_behind_basketball_s_wildest_moves.

———. "What Advanced Tracking Data Reveals about Shooters." ESPN.com. May 16, 2016. http://www.espn.com/NBA/playoffs/2016/story/_/id/15530589.

Manley, Martin. *Basketball Heaven.* Topeka KS: FACTS Publishing, 1988.

Martin, Lorena. *Sports Performance Measurement and Analytics: The Science of Assessing Performance, Predicting Future Outcomes, Interpreting Statistical Models, and Evaluating the Market Value of Athletes.* Old Tappan NJ: Pearson Education, 2016.

May, C. R. "Self-Analysis Charts for High School Basketball Players." *Athletic Journal* 17, no. 7 (March 1937): 24.

McCann, Michael. "Kevin Durant's Achilles Injury and the Potential Legal Implications." SI.com. June 17, 2019. https://www.si.com/NBA/2019/06/17/kevin-durant-achilles-injury-warriors-thunder-bob-myers-steve-kerr.

McCurdy, J. H., James Naismith, and Thomas Cornelius. "Report of Athletic League Committee." *Physical Education* 3, no. 8 (October 1894): 128–29.

McGarry, Tim, David I. Anderson, Stephen A. Wallace, Mike D. Hughes, and Ian M. Franks. "Sport Competition as a Dynamical Self-Organizing System." *Journal of Sports Sciences* 20, no. 10 (2000): 771–81.

McHugh, Josh, Po Bronson, and Ethan Watters. "The Future of the Athlete." September 2015. http://futureof.org/sports/the-athlete/.

McKenzie, R. Tait. *Exercise in Education and Medicine.* 2nd ed. Philadelphia: W. B. Saunders, 1915.

McLaughlin, Thomas. *Give and Go: Basketball as a Cultural Practice.* Albany: SUNY Press, 2008.

Meanwell, Walter E. *The Science of Basket Ball for Men.* Madison: Democrat Printing, 1924.

Merry, Sally Engle. *The Seductions of Quantification: Measuring Human Rights, Gender Violence, and Sex Trafficking.* Chicago: University of Chicago Press, 2016.

Messer, Guerdon N. *How to Play Basket Ball: A Thesis on the Technique of the Game.* New York: American Sports Publishing, 1910.

Messersmith, Lloyd L. "A Study of the Distance Traveled by Basketball Players." *Research Quarterly. American Association for Health, Physical Education, and Recreation* 15, no. 1 (March 1, 1944): 29–37. https://doi.org/10.1080/10671188.1944.10624811.

Messersmith, Lloyd L., and Clum C. Bucher. "The Distance Traversed by Big Ten Basketball Players." *Research Quarterly. American Association for Health, Physical Education, and Recreation* 10, no. 3 (October 1, 1939): 61–62. https://doi.org/10.1080/10671188.1939.10622495.

Messersmith, Lloyd L., and Stephen M. Corey. "The Distance Traversed by a Basketball Player." *Research Quarterly. American Physical Education Association* 2, no. 2 (May 1, 1931): 57–60.

Messersmith, Lloyd, Jane Laurence, and Karl Randels. "A Study of Distances Traversed by College Men and Women in Playing the Game of Basketball." *Research Quarterly. American Association for Health, Physical Education, and Recreation* 11, no. 3 (October 1, 1940): 30–31. https://doi.org/10.1080/10671188.1940.10627262.

Meylan, G. L. "Marks for Physical Efficiency." *American Physical Education Review* 10, no. 2 (1905): 106–12. https://doi.org/10.1080/23267224.1905.10649949.

Miller, Thomas W. *Sports Analytics and Data Science: Winning the Game with Methods and Models.* Old Tappan NJ: Pearson Education, 2016.

MIT Sloan Sports Analytics Conference. "XY Panel: The Revolution in Visual Tracking." Sportvision. March 2, 2013. http://www.sloansportsconference.com/?p=10069.

Morgan, Ralph. "The Eastern Intercollegiate League." In *Spalding's Official Basket Ball Guide 1915–1916*, edited by William H. Ball, George C. Hepbron, and Oswald Tower, 191–207. New York: American Sports Publishing, 1915.

———. "The Eastern Intercollegiate League 1921–1922 and All Eastern Intercollegiate League Teams." In *Spalding's Official Basketball Guide 1922–1923*, 43–53. New York: American Sports Publishing, 1922.

Moser, Helen A. "The Use of Basketball Skill Tests for Girls and Women." *Journal of Health and Physical Education* 6, no. 3 (March 1935): 53–55.

Mrozek, D. J. *Sport and American Mentality, 1880–1910.* Knoxville: University of Tennessee Press, 1983.

Muller, Jerry Z. *The Tyranny of Metrics.* Princeton: Princeton University Press, 2018.

Mumford, Stephen. *Watching Sport: Aesthetics, Ethics, and Emotion.* New York: Routledge, 2012.

Naismith, James. "Basket Ball." *Triangle* 1, no. 10 (January 15, 1892): 144–47.

———. "Basket Ball." In *Eighth Annual Convention of the National Collegiate Athletic Association*, 63–75. 1913.

———. "Basket Ball." *American Physical Education Review* (1914): 339–51.

———. *Basketball: Its Origin and Development.* Lincoln: University of Nebraska Press, 1996.

———. "Basketball Letter from Dr. James Naismith," 1894. Springfield College Digital Collections. http://cdm15370.contentdm.oclc.org/cdm/ref/collection/p15370coll2/id/351.

———. "How to Start Basket Ball." *Physical Education* 2, no. 11 (January 1894): 179–80.

———. "Is Basketball Injurious." *Athletic Journal* 8, no. 2 (October 1927): 18–19.

———. "James Naismith Handwritten Manuscript Detailing First | Lot #19007." Heritage Auctions. February 1892. https://sports.ha.com/itm/basketball-collectibles/others/james-naismith-handwritten-manuscript-detailing-first-basketball-game-basketball-s-equivalent-of-the-book-of-genesis-is/a/706-19007.s.

———. *Official Scorebook for the Basketball League at Springfield College, 1894–1895.* Springfield, 1895.

———. *Rules for Basket Ball.* Springfield MA: Springfield Printing and Binding, 1892.

———. *Rules for Basket Ball 1893.* Springfield MA: Triangle Publishing, 1893.

Naismith, James, and Luther Gulick. *Basket Ball.* Springfield MA: American Sports Publishing, 1894.

Natarajan, Senthil. "Nylon Questions: How Can an Analytic Approach Be Applied to Rest and Injury Prevention?" *Nylon Calculus* (blog). October 3, 2018. https://fansided.com/2018/10/03/nylon-questions-analytic-approach-rest-injury-prevention/.

National Basketball Association. "Leonard 18' Pullup Jump Shot (2 PTS) (Siakam 1 AST)." NBA Stats. December 21, 2018. https://stats.NBA.com/events/?GameEventID=10&GameID=0021800470&Season=2018-19&flag=1&title=Leonard%2018%27%20Pullup%20Jump%20Shot%20(2%20PTS)%20(Siakam%201%20AST).

———. "Official Scorer's Report: Final Box." NBA.com, December 21, 2018.

Nationalpastime.com "This Day in Baseball History—October 22nd," Touching Base with History. October 22, 2014. http://www.nationalpastime.com/site/index.php?fact_day=22&fact_month=10.

NBA. "NBA Partners with Stats LLC for Tracking Technology." NBA.com, September 5, 2013. http://www.NBA.com/2013/news/09/05/NBA-stats-llc-player-tracking-technology/. No longer valid.

———. "Warriors Earn 'Best Analytics Organization' Award at 2016 MIT Sloan Sports Analytics Conference." Golden State Warriors. March 20, 2016. http://www.NBA.com/warriors/news/warriors-earn-best-analytics-organization-award-2016-mit-sloan-sports-analytics-conference.

NBA, From NBA Twitter and media. "Kevin Durant to Play in Game 5 vs. Raptors." NBA.com. Accessed June 25, 2019. http://www.NBA.com/article/2019/06/10/durant-game-time-decision-game-5-finals.

Nibali, Maria. "The Data Game: Analyzing Our Way to Better Sport Performance." In *Sport Analytics: A Data-Driven Approach to Sport Business and Management*, edited by Gil Fried and Ceyda Mumcu. New York: Routledge, 2017.

Noble, Stewart Grayson. "The Acquisition of Skill in the Throwing of Basketball Goals." *American Physical Education Review* 28 (March 1923): 139–40.

Novak, Michael. *The Joy of Sports: End Zones, Bases, Baskets, Balls, and the Consecration of the American Spirit.* rev. ed. Lanham MD: Madison Books, 1994.

"Official Basket Ball Rules, 1895." *Physical Education* 3, no. 9 (November 1894): 138–41.

Oliver, Dean. *Basketball on Paper: Rules and Tools for Performance Analysis.* Dulles: Brassey's, 2004.

———. "The Fundamentals for Analyzing Basketball." Journal of Basketball Studies, March 17, 1996. http://www.rawbw.com/~deano/articles/basics.html.

———. "New Measurement Techniques and a Binomial Model of the Game of Basketball." *Journal of Basketball Studies* (blog). 1991. http://www.rawbw.com/~deano/articles/bbalpyth.html.

———. "Roboscout and the Four Factors of Basketball Success." *Journal of Basketball Studies* (blog). June 1, 2004. http://www.rawbw.com/~deano/articles/20040601_roboscout.htm.

———. "Yahoo! Groups." APBR_Analysis, February 10, 2001. https://groups.yahoo.com/neo/groups/apbr_analysis/conversations/topics/1.

O'Neil, Cathy. *Weapons of Math Destruction: How Big Data Increases Inequality and Threatens Democracy.* New York: Crown, 2016.

Overman, Steven J. *The Protestant Ethic and the Spirit of Sport: How Calvinism and Capitalism Shaped America's Games.* Macon GA: Mercer University Press, 2011.

P3. "Applied Sports Science." P3, January 4, 2012. http://www.p3.md/applied-sports-science/.

———. "Professional Athletes." P3, January 4, 2012. http://www.p3.md/services/professional-athlete/.

Paine, Neil. "This Eastern Conference Crown Is Truly LeBron's Masterpiece." *FiveThirtyEight* (blog). May 28, 2018. https://fivethirtyeight.com/features/this-eastern-conference-crown-is-truly-lebrons-masterpiece/.

Park, Roberta J. "Athletes and Their Training in Britain and America, 1800–1914." In *Sport and Exercise Science: Essays in the History of Sports Medicine*, edited by Jack W. Berryman and Roberta J. Park, 57–107. Champaign: University of Illinois Press, 1992.

———. *Gender, Sport, Science: Selected Writings of Roberta J. Park.* Edited by J. A. Mangan and Patricia Vertinsky. New York: Routledge, 2009.

———. "Physiologists, Physicians, and Physical Educators: Nineteenth-Century Biology and Exercise, Hygienic and Educative." In *Sport and Exercise Science: Essays in the History of Sport Medicine,* edited by Jack W. Berryman and Roberta J. Park, 137–81. Urbana: University of Illinois Press, 1992.

Partnow, Seth. "Not Everything That Can Be Counted Counts. A Quick Note On Meaning and Misleading Stats." *Nylon Calculus* (blog). March 18, 2015. http://nyloncalculus.com/2015/03/18/not-everything-that-can-be-counted-counts-a-quick-note-on-meaning-and-misleading-stats/.

———. "Splitting the Basketball Atom." *Nylon Calculus* (blog). July 14, 2014. http://nyloncalculus.com/2014/07/14/splitting-basketball-analytics-atom/.

Pelton, Kevin. "How I Made My All-Time Rankings." ESPN.com. January 29, 2016. https://www.espn.com/NBA/insider/story/_/id/14671128.

"Personals and News." *Physical Education* 2, no. 12 (February 1894): 199.

Peterson, Robert C. *Cages to Jump Shots: Pro Basketball's Early Years.* Lincoln: University of Nebraska Press, 2002.

Pluto, Terry. *Loose Balls: The Short, Wild Life of the American Basketball Association.* New York: Simon and Schuster, 1990.

Porter, Theodore M. *The Rise of Statistical Thinking, 1820–1900.* Princeton: Princeton University Press, 1986.

———. *Trust in Numbers: The Pursuit of Objectivity in Science and Public Life.* Princeton: Princeton University Press, 1995.

Principe, Lawrence M. *The Scientific Revolution: A Very Short Introduction.* Oxford: Oxford University Press, 2011.

Pullman, Philip. *The Amber Spyglass.* Book III. New York: Knopf, 2000.

Putnam, Hilary. "Beyond the Fact/Value Dichotomy." In *Realism with a Human Face,* edited by James Conant, 135–41. Cambridge MA: Harvard University Press, 1990.

———. *The Collapse of the Fact Value Dichotomy and Other Essays.* Cambridge MA: Harvard University Press, 2002.

Putney, Clifford. *Muscular Christianity: Manhood and Sports in Protestant America, 1880–1920.* Cambridge MA: Harvard University Press, 2001.

Pycior, Sebastian. "Nylon Questions: How Can an Analytic Approach Be Applied to Player Psychology?" *Nylon Calculus* (blog). October 2, 2018. https://fansided.com/2018/10/02/nylon-questions-analytic-approach-applied-player-psychology/.

Quetelet, Adolphe. *A Treatise on Man and the Development of His Faculties.* Edinburgh: William and Robert Chabers, 1842.

Rains, Rob, and Helen Carpenter. *James Naismith: The Man Who Invented Basketball.* Philadelphia: Temple University Press, 2009.

Reach, Robert. "Basket Ball as an In-Door Game for Winter Amusement and Exercise." *Physical Education* 2, no. 2 (April 1893): 21–22.

Reimer, Alex. "Syracuse University Will Launch First Sports Analytics Degree in the U.S." *Forbes*, May 11, 2016. http://www.forbes.com/sites/alexreimer/2016/05/11/syracuse-university-will-launch-first-sports-analytics-degree-in-the-u-s/.

Restifo, Nick. "Nylon Calculus 101: Expected Value and Shot Selection." *Nylon Calculus* (blog). August 17, 2015. http://nyloncalculus.com/2015/08/17/nylon-calculus-101-expected-value-and-shot-selection/. No longer valid.

Ross, Terrance F. "Welcome to Smarter Basketball." *Atlantic*, June 25, 2015. http://www.theatlantic.com/entertainment/archive/2015/06/NBA-data-analytics/396776/.

Rothenberg, Albert. *Flight from Wonder: An Investigation of Scientific Creativity*. New York: Oxford University Press, 2015.

Sargent, Dudley. "Anthropometric Measurements." In *Proceedings of the American Association for the Advancement of Physical Education*. Brooklyn: Rome Brothers, 1886.

Schiff, Andrew J. *"The Father of Baseball": A Biography of Henry Chadwick*. Jefferson NC: Garland, 2008.

Schiller, Friedrich. "On the Aesthetic Education of Man." In *The Bloomsbury Anthology of Aesthetics*, edited by Joseph Tanke and Colin McQuillan, 286–99. New York: Bloomsbury, 2012.

Schneider-Mayerson, Matthew. "'Too Black': Race in the 'Dark Ages' of the National Basketball Association." *International Journal of Sport and Society* 1, no. 1 (2010): 223–33.

Schwartz, Helen. "Knowledge and Achievement Tests in Girls' Basketball on the Senior High School Level." *Research Quarterly. American Physical Education Association* 8, no. 1 (March 1, 1937): 143–56. https://doi.org/10.1080/23267402.1937.10761809.

Schwarz, Alan. *The Numbers Game: Baseball's Lifelong Fascination with Statistics*. New York: Thomas Dunne Books, 2004.

Second Spectrum. "Second Spectrum Home." Second Spectrum, 2015. http://www.secondspectrum.com/.

Serres, Michel. *Genesis*. Translated by Genevieve James and James Nielson. Ann Arbor: University of Michigan Press, 1995.

Severini, Thomas A. *Analytic Methods in Sports: Using Mathematics and Statistics to Understand Data from Baseball, Football, Basketball, and Other Sports*. New York: CRC Press, 2015.

Shapin, Steven. *The Scientific Revolution*. Chicago: University of Chicago Press, 1996.

Shea, Stephen. "Analytics and Shot Selection." ShotTracker. 2016. https://shottracker.com/articles/analytics-shot-selection.

———. "Visualizing Player Shot Selection and Efficiency." *Basketball Analytics* (blog). February 16, 2017. http://www.basketballanalyticsbook.com/2017/02/16/visualizing-player-shot-selection-and-efficiency/.

Shea, Stephen, and Christopher E. Baker. *Basketball Analytics: Objective and Efficient Strategies for Understanding How Teams Win*. St. Louis MO: Advanced Metrics, 2013.

Shiller, Drew. "Kerr Explains How Dubs Never Thought KD Could Tear Achilles." NBCS Bay Area, June 12, 2019. https://www.nbcsports.com/bayarea/warriors/steve-kerr -says-warriors-never-thought-kevin-durant-could-tear-achilles.

Shilling, Chris. *The Body in Culture, Technology, and Society*. Thousand Oaks CA: Sage, 2005.

Shogan, Debra. *The Making of High-Performance Athletes: Discipline, Diversity, and Ethics*. Toronto: University of Toronto Press, 1999.

Shusterman, Richard. *Thinking through the Body: Essays in Somaesthetics*. New York: Cambridge University Press, 2012.

Silver, Nate. *The Signal and the Noise: Why So Many Predictions Fail—But Some Don't*. New York: Penguin, 2015.

Smith, Leonard. *Chaos: A Very Short Introduction*. New York: Oxford University Press, 2007.

Spariosu, Mihai I. *Dionysus Reborn: Play and the Aesthetic Dimension in Modern Philosophical and Scientific Discourse*. Ithaca NY: Cornell University Press, 1989.

Stengers, Isabelle. "Diderot's Egg: Divorcing Materialism from Eliminativism." *Radical Philosophy* 144 (August 2007): 7–15.

Suits, Bernard. "The Elements of Sport." In *The Philosophy of Sport: A Collection of Original Essays*, edited by Robert G. Osterhoudt, 48–64. Springfield IL: Thomas, 1973.

Sutton-Smith, Brian. *The Ambiguity of Play*. Cambridge MA: Harvard University Press, 1997.

Tarver, Erin C. *The I in Team: Sports Fandom and the Reproduction of Identity*. Chicago: University of Chicago Press, 2017.

Taylor, Ben. "Measuring Creation with the Box Score." *Nylon Calculus* (blog). August 11, 2017. https://fansided.com/2017/08/11/nylon-calculus-measuring-creation -box-score/.

———. *Thinking Basketball*. Self-published, 2016.

Teramoto, Masaru, and Chad Cross. "Relative Importance of Performance Factors in Winning NBA Games in Regular Season versus Playoffs." *Journal of Quantitative Analysis in Sports* 6, no. 3 (May 2010).

Thelia, Jerome. *Bounce: How the Ball Taught the World to Play*. Documentary. Bounce Group, 2015.

Thomson, William. "Electrical Units of Measurement." In *Popular Lectures and Addresses*. Vol. 1:73–136. London: MacMillan, 1889.

Thorn, John. *Baseball in the Garden of Eden: The Secret History of the Early Game*. New York: Simon and Schuster, 2011.

Thorn, John, and Pete Palmer. *The Hidden Game of Baseball: A Revolutionary Approach to Baseball and Its Statistics*. rev. ed. New York: Doubleday, 1985.

Todorov, Tzvetan. *The Fantastic: A Structural Approach to a Literary Genre*. Translated by Richard Howard. Ithaca NY: Cornell University Press, 1975.

Torre, Pablo S., and Tom Haberstroh. "Advanced, Increasingly Invasive Tests Being Used to Monitor NBA Players." ESPN.com. October 2, 2014. http://www.espn.com/NBA/story/_/id/11629773.

Trythall, Donald L. "Diagnostic Basketball." *Athletic Journal* 11, no. 5 (January 1931): 22–23.

Tufte, Edward R. *The Visual Display of Quantitative Information*. 2nd ed. Cheshire CT: Graphics Press, 2001.

Tygiel, Jules. *Past Time: Baseball as History*. New York: Oxford, 2000.

Voigt, David Quentin. *American Baseball: From Gentleman's Sport to the Commissioner System*. Norman: University of Oklahoma Press, 1966.

Voltmer, E. F., and Ted Watts. "A Rating Scale of Player Performance in Basketball." *Journal of Health and Physical Education* 11, no. 2 (February 1940): 94–97. https://doi.org/10.1080/23267240.1940.10619554.

Wardlaw, Charles Digby, and Whitelaw Reid Morrison. *Basket Ball: A Handbook for Coaches and Players*. New York: C. Scribner's Sons, 1921.

Washburn, Gary. "For Second Spectrum, Basketball Is Just a Numbers Game." BostonGlobe.com, August 22, 2015. https://www.bostonglobe.com/sports/2015/08/22/analytics-emerging-coaching-tool/s48TbOisEr35kjyLeAlzFP/story.html.

Watts, Eric King. "'Voice' and 'Voicelessness' in Rhetorical Studies." *Quarterly Journal of Speech* 87, no. 2 (May 2001): 179–96.

Webb, Bernice Larson. *The Basketball Man: James Naismith*. rev. ed. Lawrence KS: Kappelman's Historic Collections, 1994.

Weise, Heike. *Numbers, Language, and the Mind*. Cambridge, UK: Cambridge University Press, 2003.

Weiss, Paul. *Sport: A Philosophic Inquiry*. Carbondale: Southern Illinois University Press, 1969.

Weyand, Alexander M. *The Cavalcade of Basketball*. New York: Macmillan, 1960.

Wharton University of Pennsylvania. "The NBA's Adam Silver: How Analytics Is Transforming Basketball." Knowledge@Wharton. June 1, 2017. http://knowledge.wharton.upenn.edu/article/NBAs-adam-silver-analytics-transforming-basketball/.

Whitehead, Todd. "Did the Warriors Really Ruin the NBA?" *Nylon Calculus* (blog). July 26, 2018. https://fansided.com/2018/07/26/nylon-calculus-warriors-postseason-excitement-index/.

———. "My Personal NBA Top 50: How to Build the Best." *Nylon Calculus* (blog). November 12, 2018. https://fansided.com/2018/11/12/personal-NBA-top-50/.

"Why Athlete Analytics?" YouTube. 2013. https://www.youtube.com/watch?v=iF3kpaMGV6w.

Whyte, David. *The Heart Aroused: Poetry and the Preservation of the Soul in Corporate America*. New York: Doubleday, 1996.

Windhorst, Brian. "NBA and MLB Are Preparing to Profit from Supreme Court Ruling on New Jersey Gambling Case." ESPN.com. May 14, 2018. http://www.espn.com/NBA/story/_/id/22847790/NBA-mlb-preparing-profit-supreme-court-ruling-new-jersey-gambling-case.

Winfield, Kristian. "LeBron James Is Having One of the Greatest NBA Playoffs Ever. What Was His Best Performance?" SBNation.com. May 26, 2018. https://www.sbnation.com/2018/5/26/17397526/lebron-james-highlights-NBA-playoffs-2018-games-ranked.

Winston, Wayne L. *Mathletics: How Gamblers, Managers, and Sports Enthusiasts Use Mathematics in Baseball, Basketball, and Football*. Princeton: Princeton University Press, 2009.

Wolff, Alexander. "Searching for a Promised Land." *Sports Illustrated*, August 29, 1982.

Wood, Michael. *The Road to Delphi: The Life and Afterlife of Oracles*. New York: Picador, 2003.

Woodward, Kath. *Embodied Sporting Practices: Regulating and Regulatory Bodies*. New York: Palgrave Macmillan, 2009.

Yau, Nathan. *Visualize This: The FlowingData Guide to Design, Visualization, and Statistics*. Indianapolis IN: Wiley, 2011.

Young, Genevieve, and Helen Moser. "A Short Battery of Tests to Measure Playing Ability in Women's Basketball." *Research Quarterly. American Physical Education Association* 5, no. 2 (May 1, 1934): 3–23. https://doi.org/10.1080/23267402.1934.10761606.

INDEX

Page locators in italics refer to illustrations.

basketball (*cont.*)

aesthetics of, 7–9, 12–13, 142–43, 189, 232–33, 235–36, 252, 262–63, 265–67, 281; affective responses to, 189, 252, 266, 267–69, 270–72, 276, 278, 295; coaches, 140–44, 147–51, 162–70; complexity of, 205–6, 240–43, 265–66; creativity in, 10, 13, 106; defense in, 31, 33, 36, 38, 166–67, 213–16; ecological approach to, 249–51, 283–85; economics of, 63, 126, 165, 168, 171, 176–85, 206–7, 220, 252, 263, 282; and efficiency, 35, 59–62, 119, 185–88, 250–52, 263, 282; ethical issues in, 225, 231–32, 242, 246–49, 263, 267; and fandom, 12, 125–28, 171, 252, 267–69, 278; invention of, 118–23; labor issues in, 177–82, 263; as moral instrument, 7–9, 119, 120–23, 127, 142–43; offense in, 32–33, 35–36, 39, 145, 163–64, 166–67, 182, 188, 208, 213, 280; and play, 9–13; purposes of, 7–9, 118–23; and risk, 4–5, 63, 267, 284; role of competition in, 11, 63–65, 123–25, 140–53, 188, 263–64, 267; and social issues, 7–9, 122–23, 129, 186–87, 189–90; teamwork in, 121, 123, 132, 142–43, 145, 147; and uncertainty, 4–5, 237–39, 266–67, 276, 285. *See also* basketball analytics; basketball statistics; NBA (National Basketball Association)

basketball analytics: authority of, 16, 37, 56–57, 66–68; and competition, 17, 56, 57, 60, 63–65, 188–89, 203, 217–19, 263–64, 280; credibility of, 37, 54, 56–57, 66, 68, 190; and digital technology, 3, 15, 37–41, 51, 66; economic aspects of, 17, 36, 40, 52, 61, 63–65, 188, 203, 216, 236, 263, 272, 276;

and efficiency, 35–36, 39, 56, 57, 59–61, 63, 65, 188–89, 204, 210, 216, 220, 232, 236–37, 263, 280; ethical aspects of, 17, 244, 246–52, 263, 298n32; impacts of, 3, 30, 40–41, 263, 281–85; and objectivity, 52, 56, 57, 58–60, 63, 67–68, 71, 244, 246; and prediction, 11; and quantification, 3, 31–32; rhetorical justifications for, 15, 50–72, 204, 214, 215, 272; and risk, 5, 11, 51–52, 57, 62–64, 65, 220, 236; and statistical methods, 3, 30, 33–37, 39, 59, 60, 210, 214, 280. *See also* basketball statistics

basketball statistics: assists, 32–33, 39, 150, 167, 207, 209; blocks, 31, 44, 58, 69, 176–77, 183, 214; box score and, 30–32, 44, 77, 79, 87–88, 102, 125, 140, 144–45, 150, 166–67, 182, 188, 193, 207, 209, 211, 214, 279–80; counting stats, 31; defensive rebounds, 182, 208, 214–15; derived stats, 31; effective field goal percentage, 36, 211, 275; expected possession value, 39, 208–9; field goal attempts, 40, 147, 211; field goals made, 31, 44, 130, 164, 176–77, 211; fouls, 1–2, 30–31, 120–21, 125, 129–30, 134, 145, 148–50, 166, 199; Four Factors, 36, 185, 275; free throw attempts, 212; free throw rate, 36; free throws made, 31, 44, 176; pace, 35–36, 73, 207, 254; points, 31, 33, 125, 131, 143–45, 148, 163–64, 166, 207–9; possessions, 33–35, 39–40, 60, 63, 65, 164, 182–83, 208–9, 212–14, 216–17, 250; rebounds, 31, 36, 38, 132, 164, 169, 176–77, 182, 213–15; scorekeeping and, 9, 30, 33, 129–31, 143–44, 146–47, 149–51, 163, 165, 166, 168–69, 190; shot charts in, 147, 149, 211; turnovers, 31,

muscular Christianity, 12, 61, 102, 107

mystery, 210, 236–37, 239, 270

record keeping (*cont.*)
    See also basketball statistics: box
    score and; basketball statistics:
    scorekeeping and
risk, 4, 6–7, 10, 10–11, 51–52, 57, 63–65,
    225, 267, 284, 287, 292

Sabermetrics. *See* baseball analytics;
    Moneyball
science, 15–17, 36–37, 53–61, 65, 66–68,
    79, 83–89, 101–3, 105–8, 119, 147–49,
    220, 226, 244–46, 249–52, 270–72;
    and scientific basketball play, 122–25,
    128–30, 132, 142–44, 169–70; and
    scientific method, 15, 53, 55, 60, 67,
    79–80, 84, 97, 164, 169–70, 220, 237,
    239; and scientific revolution, 15, 103,
    187, 244
Second Spectrum, 29–30, 38, 41, 152, 161,
    229, 272
Shea, Stephen, 38, 58–60, 213–14
spectators. *See* basketball: and fandom
sports analytics, 83–84, 91, 104, 207–8,
    216, 237, 246, 248–49, 272, 275. *See
    also* baseball analytics; basketball
    analytics
SportVU, 37–38, 41, 247
statistics, 11, 35–36, 58–60, 63, 77–78, 90,
    101, 141, 190, 202, 214, 237–39, 245,
    247; concept of average in, 100–101,
    103, 209, 211–12, 280. *See also* baseball
    analytics; basketball analytics;
    basketball statistics; quantification
steals. *See* basketball statistics
stops. *See* basketball statistics
superstition, 53, 55, 58, 84, 97

surprise, 47, 79, 84, 99, 129, 241, 266, 275

technology: critiques of, 15–16, 231,
    247–48, 249–51, 263, 272, 284; and
    efficiency, 61, 219–20, 263, 284; in
    Enlightenment rhetoric, 51, 53, 56, 65
truth, 18, 58, 60, 67–68, 84–86, 245–46
turnovers. *See* basketball statistics

uncertainty, 3–5, 7, 63, 236–39, 246, 263,
    268, 276, 285, 291–92

value, 16–18, 54, 56, 57, 210, 251–52, 277,
    280–81; aesthetic, 142–44, 189–90,
    239, 281–85; competitive, 36, 59–64,
    83, 92, 142–44, 152, 164, 165, 179, 181–
    85, 188–89; economic, 32, 59–64, 92,
    165, 177, 179, 181–85, 213, 249, 250–52,
    281–85; ethical, 90, 105–6, 108, 125,
    128–29, 142–44, 239; social, 128–29,
    189–90

wearables. *See* biometrics; the body
Whitehead, Todd, 218–19, 276, 278–81
wildness, 19, 97, 124, 190, 281, 284–85,
    287, 291–92
winning. *See* basketball: role of compe-
    tition in; basketball analytics: and
    competition
wonder, xvii, 4, 6, 22, 46, 81–82, 89, 116,
    136, 145, 170, 181, 226, 232, 269–72,
    276–78, 287. *See also* basketball:
    affective responses to; emotion

YMCA (Young Men's Christian
    Association), 106, 121–28, 140